D1559897

Profiling Shakespeare

The title of this collection, *Profiling Shakespeare*, is meant strongly in its double sense. These essays show the outline of a Shakespeare rather different from the man sought by biographers from his time to our own. They also show the effects, the ephemera, the clues and cues, welcome and unwelcome, out of which Shakespeare's admirers and dedicated scholars have pieced together a vision of the playwright, whether as sage, psychologist, lover, theatrical entrepreneur, or moral authority. This collection brings together classic pieces, hard-to-find chapters, and two new essays. Here, Garber has produced a book at once serious and highly readable, ranging broadly across time periods (early modern to postmodern) and touching upon both high and popular culture.

Marjorie Garber is William R. Kenan, Jr., Professor of English and American Literature and Language and chair of the Department of Visual and Environmental Studies at Harvard University. Her recent book, *Shakespeare After All* (Pantheon, 2004), was chosen as one of Newsweek's ten best non-fiction books of the year and was awarded the 2005 Christian Gauss Book Award from Phi Beta Kappa.

PR
2899
G33
2008
Web

Profiling Shakespeare

Marjorie Garber

Routledge
Taylor & Francis Group

NEW YORK AND LONDON

First published 2008
by Routledge
270 Madison Ave, New York, NY 10016

Simultaneously published in the UK
by Routledge
2 Park Square, Milton Park, Abingdon, Oxon OX14 4RN

Routledge is an imprint of the Taylor & Francis Group, an informa business

© 2008 Taylor & Francis

Typeset in Berkeley by Swales & Willis Ltd, Exeter, Devon
Printed and bound in the United States of America on acid-free paper
by Sheridan Books, Inc.

All rights reserved. No part of this book may be reprinted or reproduced
or utilized in any form or by any electronic, mechanical, or other means,
now known or hereafter invented, including photocopying and recording,
or in any information storage or retrieval system, without permission in
writing from the publishers.

Trademark Notice: Product or corporate names may be trademarks or
registered trademarks, and are used only for identification and explanation
without intent to infringe.

Library of Congress Cataloging in Publication Data
Garber, Marjorie B.
Profiling Shakespeare / Marjorie Garber.
p. cm.
Includes bibliographical references and index.
ISBN13: 978–0–415–96445–6 (hbk)
ISBN10: 0–415–96445–8 (hbk)
ISBN13: 978–0–415–96446–3 (pbk)
ISBN10: 0–415–96446–6 (pbk)
1. Shakespeare, William, 1564-1616. I. Title.
PR2899.G33 2008
822.3'3–dc22
2007037786

ISBN10: 0–415–96445–8 (hbk)
ISBN10: 0–415–96446–6 (pbk)
ISBN10: 0–203–93098–3 (ebk)

ISBN13: 978–0–415–96445–6 (hbk)
ISBN13: 978–0–415–96446–3 (pbk)
ISBN13: 978–0–203–93098–4 (ebk)

For Winthrop A. Burr,
with gratitude

Contents

Acknowledgments

Most of the essays in this book have been previously published, either in collections of my own work or in journals and occasional volumes. A few small alterations have been made, but otherwise the essays appear in their original form. I am grateful to Sara Bartel, Sol Kim Bentley, Marcie Bianco, Emily Filler, William Germano, Eliza Hornig, Annette Lemieux, Larry Switzky, and Beth Vesel for their support at various stages of the book's development, and for their assistance in bringing it to fruition.

"Shakespeare's Ghost Writers," "Hamlet: Giving Up the Ghost," and "Macbeth: The Male Medusa" were all originally published in *Shakespeare's Ghost Writers* (New York: Methuen, 1987). "Shakespeare as Fetish" was first published in *Shakespeare Quarterly* 41.2 (1990), "Character Assassination" in *Media Spectacles* (Eds. Marjorie Garber, Jann Matlock, and Rebecca L. Walkowitz. New York and London: Routledge, 1993), and "Out of Joint" was in *The Body in Parts: Fantasies of Corporeality in Early Modern Europe* (Eds. David Hillman and Carla Mazzio. New York: Routledge, 1997). "Character Assassination," "Shakespeare as Fetish," "Roman Numerals," and "Second-Best Bed" were all published in *Symptoms of Culture* (New York: Routledge, 1998). "Shakespeare's Dogs" was published in *Shakespeare and the Twentieth Century: The Selected Proceedings of the International Shakespeare Association World Congress, Los Angeles, 1996* (Eds. Jonathan Bate, Jill L. Levenson and Dieter Mehl. Newark: U of Delaware P; London: Associated University Presses, 1998). "Shakespeare's Faces" (as "Looking the Part") was published in *Shakespeare's Face* (Nolen, Stephanie, et al. Toronto: Alfred A. Knopf Canada, 2002). "Shakespeare's Laundry List" (as "Historical Correctness") was included in *Quotation Marks* (New York: Routledge, 2003) and in *A Manifesto for Literary Studies* (Seattle: Walter Chapin Simpson Center for the Humanities: Distributed in the U.S.A. by the University of Washington Press, 2003).

"MacGuffin Shakespeare" and "Fatal Cleopatra," were also in *Quotation Marks*. "What Did Shakespeare Invent?" was presented as a lecture at the Shakespeare Association of America meeting in New Orleans, February 2004.

A Note on the Text

Unless otherwise noted, references in the text to Shakespeare's plays are from the following *Arden Shakespeare* editions: *Antony and Cleopatra*, ed. John Wilders (London: Arden Shakespeare, 2002); *As You Like It*, ed. Agnes Latham (London: Methuen & Co. Ltd, 2000); *The Comedy of Errors*, ed. R. A. Foakes (Walton-on-Thames: Methuen & Co. Ltd, 1962); *Coriolanus*, ed. Philip Brockbank (London: Methuen & Co. Ltd, 2001); *Cymbeline*, ed. J. M. Nosworthy (Walton-on-Thames: Thomas Nelson & Sons Ltd, 1998); *Hamlet*, ed. Harold Jenkins (London: Methuen & Co. Ltd, 1982); *Julius Caesar*, ed. David Daniell (London: Arden Shakespeare, 2000); *King Henry IV, Part 1*, ed. David Scott Kastan (London: Arden Shakespeare, 2002); *King Henry IV, Part 2*, ed. A. R. Humphreys (Walton-on-Thames: Thomas Nelson & Sons Ltd, 1999); *King Henry V*, ed. T. W. Craik (London: Routledge, 2005); *King Henry VI, Part 2*, ed. Ronald Knowles (London: Thomas Nelson and Sons Ltd, 2001); *King Henry VIII*, ed. R. A. Foakes (Walton-on-Thames: Thomas Nelson & Sons Ltd, 1997); *King John*, ed. E. A. J. Honigmann (Walton-on-Thames: Thomas Nelson & Sons Ltd, 1998); *King Lear*, ed. R. A. Foakes (Walton-on-Thames: Thomas Nelson and Sons Ltd, 1997); *King Richard II*, ed. Charles R. Forker (London: Arden Shakespeare, 2002); *King Richard III*, ed. Antony Hammond (London: Methuen & Co. Ltd, 2006); *Love's Labour's Lost*, ed. H. R. Woudhuysen (London: Arden Shakespeare, 2001); *Macbeth*, ed. Kenneth Muir (Walton-on-Thames: Thomas Nelson & Sons Ltd, 1997); *Measure for Measure*, ed. J. W. Lever (Walton-on-Thames: Thomas Nelson & Sons Ltd, 1998); *The Merchant of Venice*, ed. John Russell Brown (London: Arden Shakespeare, 2003); *The Merry Wives of Windsor*, ed. Giorgio Melchiori (Walton-on-Thames: Thomas Nelson and Sons Ltd, 2000); *A Midsummer Night's Dream*, ed. Harold F. Brooks (Walton-on-Thames: Thomas Nelson & Sons Ltd, 1997); *Much Ado About*

Nothing, ed. A. R. Humphreys (Walton-on-Thames: Thomas Nelson & Sons, 1998); *Othello*, ed. E. A. J. Honigmann (London: Arden Shakespeare, 2006); *Pericles*, ed. F. D. Hoeniger (London: Arden Shakespeare, 2000); "The Phoenix and the Turtle," *The Poems*, ed. F. T. Prince (Walton-on-Thames: Thomas Nelson and Sons Ltd, 1998); *Romeo and Juliet*, ed. Brian Gibbons (Walton-on-Thames: Thomas Nelson & Sons Ltd, 1997); *The Tempest*, eds. Virginia Mason Vaughan and Alden T. Vaughan (London: Arden Shakespeare, 2000); *Titus Andronicus*, ed. Jonathan Bate (London: Arden Shakespeare, 2003); *Troilus and Cressida*, ed. David Bevington (Walton-on-Thames: Thomas Nelson and Sons Ltd, 1998); *Twelfth Night*, eds. J. M. Lothian and T. W. Craik (London: Arden Shakespeare, 2005); *Two Gentlemen of Verona*, ed. Clifford Leech (Walton-on-Thames: Thomas Nelson and Sons Ltd, 1969); *Two Noble Kinsmen*, ed. Lois Potter (Walton-on-Thames: Thomas Nelson and Sons Ltd, 1997); *The Winter's Tale,* ed. J. H. P. Pafford (London: Arden Shakespeare, 2001).

Shakespeare's Profile

The title of this collection, *Profiling Shakespeare*, is meant to incorporate the varying meanings of "profiling" in use today, from the drawing or silhouette to the record of a person's psychological and behavioral traits. The outline of a face or head; the biographical sketch of a public figure; the personality disclosed through responses to a social science questionnaire; the description of the probable characteristics of an unknown perpetrator, developed by investigators to help identify suspects. Each kind of profile will play some part in this book.

These essays show the outline of a Shakespeare rather different from the man sought so earnestly and eagerly by biographers from his time to our own. And they also show the effects, the ephemera, the clues and cues, welcome and unwelcome, out of which Shakespeare's admirers, fans and dedicated scholars have pieced together a vision of the playwright—whether as sage, pundit, lover, philosopher, psychologist, or successful businessman.

My method here might be described as the obverse of biographical investigation: in each of these essays I follow the traces, inadvertencies, odd emphases and significant repetitions that have characterized the quest for Shakespeare, from the "authorship controversy" to the "second-best bed" he bequeathed to his wife in his will. Although many of these pieces have appeared before, the impact of seeing them all together is revealing: what is produced is, in fact, just what the title promises: a "profile" of Shakespeare, in the sense used by contemporary social science and law enforcement as well as the more traditional aesthetic and biographical sense.

Profiling Shakespeare contains essays on "Shakespeare's Faces" (the over- and under-interpretation of portraits of Shakespeare to make them match the viewer's fantasies and fears), on "Character Assassination" (the quotation and unwitting misquotation of Shakespeare in public affairs), on the "Second-Best Bed," on "Shakespeare's Dogs," and on "McGuffin Shakespeare" (the critical practice, here described in a term borrowed from Alfred Hitchcock, of pursuing phantom clues and phrases that have entered the texts through the imaginative emendations of editors). Like the discussion of portraits, the essays on "Shakespeare's Ghost Writers" and "Shakespeare's Laundry List" analyze the quest to find the man behind the plays, and read that age-old quest as a cultural symptom of transference, idealization, longing for stability and authority, and a variety of other needs and wishes. "*Bartlett*'s Familiar Shakespeare" pursues this theme by looking at the way the authorizing phrase "Shakespeare says" has become a mantra in venues from journalism to Congress to motivational speaking, and discusses both the desire for, and the impossibility of possessing, a knowledge of Shakespeare's true opinions.

"Shakespeare as Fetish" describes the phenomenon of Shakespearean celebrity in three disparate but telling instances; "Fatal Cleopatra" looks at the doomed quest for "character" behind the magniloquent language of the plays. Two other essays, "Out of Joint" and "Roman Numerals," look at the cultural transition of terms and practices: "Roman Numerals" begins with a discussion of the way act, scene, and line numbers in editions of Shakespeare achieved their aura of canonicity because of the effect of a numeral system that no longer had practical value and had thus become iconic. "Out of Joint" discusses the surprising omnipresence and importance of such connections and disconnections—from knees and elbows to syntax, skeletons and dismemberment—on language, puppets, and plays. As with "Hamlet: Giving Up the Ghost," this essay engages with contemporary literary theory to assess the ways in which Shakespeare creates the language, and the critical scenario, by which critics are then able to recognize and hail him.

In the introduction to a previous collection of essays, *Symptoms of Culture*, I describe my critical practice in a way that has remained constant over time: "to read culture as if it were structured like a dream, a network of representations that encodes wishes and fears, projections and identifications, all of whose elements are overdetermined and contingent." Another collection, *Quotation Marks*, stresses the attention to the word as a signifying detail: my essays often "take as their starting points, and frequently as their points of return, a word or phrase that is uttered in quotation marks—or perhaps one should write, 'in quotation marks.'" Nowhere is this truer, or more indicative of cultural desire, than in the case of Shakespeare. Indeed, as I wrote then, " 'Shakespeare' these days is a metaphor as well as a man, a belief system and a literary standard as well as a set of works: the word 'Shakespearean' is likely to appear as an adjective describing cataclysmic political events, or sports contests, or massive outpourings of grief, without any but the most general reference to the playwright or his plays." This is as much the case now as it was then: over the period of a few weeks the phrase "Shakespearean proportions" appeared in journalistic descriptions of the war in Iraq, the final season of the television series *The Sopranos*, and the denouement of a professional hockey game, to cite just three instances out of many. This "Shakespeare effect," the conviction that Shakespeare is not of an age but for *our* time, has always fascinated me as a reader, a critic, and a "Shakespearean," and informs the core quest of this book.

At a time when many Shakespeare scholars are turning to biography for answers about the man Emerson said "wrote the text of modern life," *Profiling Shakespeare* points in a different direction—toward the traces, hints, clues, and "evidence" ("real" and "forged," persuasive and risible) that have led us on this high-stakes, high culture scavenger hunt to "know" Shakespeare. Returning to themes I set forth in *Shakespeare's Ghost Writers*, several pieces of which are reprinted in this volume, I suggest that Shakespeare is indeed an "effect" in modern and postmodern culture. Yet Shakespeare is no less real, and no less fantasied, for being made of these *disjecta membra*. In fact the Shakespeare who emerges from these pages is the Shakespeare we write and cite, as well as the Shakespeare we act and read.

Shakespeare's Ghost Writers

—Shakespeare? he said. I seem to know the name.

James Joyce, *Ulysses*

I

Who is the author of Shakespeare's plays? To many scholars and admirers of Shakespeare, this question has the rhetorical status of the question "Who is buried in Grant's tomb?" It is greeted by orthodox Stratfordians with umbrage, derision, and contemptuous dismissal of so intense an order as to inevitably raise another question: what is at stake here? Why, in other words, has the doubt about Shakespeare's authorship persisted so tenaciously, and why has it been so equally tenaciously dismissed?

The issue, as participants in the controversy see it, is whether the author of the plays is in fact the man who lived in Stratford, received with his father a grant of arms making him a propertied gentleman, prospered and bought New Place, one of the finest houses in Stratford, married Anne Hathaway, and bequeathed her his second best bed. No one denies that a man named William Shakespeare lived in Stratford; what is vigorously objected to in some quarters is that it was this same man who wrote the plays. It is argued that the very paucity of literary biographical material suggests that the authorship is in doubt, or, indeed, is itself a fiction, designed to obscure the "real" author, who by virtue of rank, gender, or other disabling characteristics could not with safety have claimed the plays for his (or her) own. Here, very briefly, is the case against Shakespeare as Shakespeare:

1. We know relatively little about the life, despite a significant collection of legal or business documents. Surely the greatest poet of his time would have left a more vivid record, including the comments of his contemporaries. No one in his home town seems to have thought of him as a celebrated author. Most of the encomia for "Shakespeare" were written after the death of the Stratford man, and some, like Jonson's famous poem affixed to the Folio, praise "Shakespeare" but may not identify him with the prosperous citizen of rural Warwickshire.

2. The plays show a significant knowledge of the law, more than could have been acquired in a casual way. Francis Bacon was a lawyer; Bacon wrote the plays.

3. The plays are clearly written by someone at home with the court and the aristocracy, and could not have been written by a plebeian. Edward de Vere, seventeenth Earl of Oxford, was a nobleman; Oxford wrote the plays. (If this belief held general sway, Stanley Wells would now be presiding over the publication of "*The Oxford Oxford*.")

4. The plays show a significant degree of classical learning, and also a certain witty detachment about university education. The Shakespeare of Stratford may have picked up his small Latin and less Greek at the Stratford grammar school, but we have no records proving that Shakespeare attended the school, and several rival claimants (Marlowe, Bacon, Oxford, the Countess of Pembroke, Queen Elizabeth) had demonstrably more rigorous training in both language and the classics.

5. Finally, it is pointed out that there are extant only six signatures of Shakespeare, all of which are so crabbed and illegible as to suggest illiteracy or illness. Three of the signatures appear on his will and three others on business documents, none of them in a literary connection. One scene from *Sir Thomas More*, a play in six distinct manuscript hands, is said to be by Shakespeare: these 147 lines, ascribed to "Hand D," have been subjected to much scrutiny, and have given rise to elaborate conjecture about Shakespeare's process of composition. Yet even G. Blakemore Evans, who goes so far as to include the lines in *The Riverside Shakespeare*, and who describes them as "affording us a unique view of what Shakespeare's 'foul papers' may have looked like,"[1] admits that the evidence for the attribution, which was in fact not suggested until 1871, is inconclusive.

Against these latter two arguments, orthodox Stratfordians respond in a number of ways: first, by touting the excellence of the Stratford grammar school (according to James G. McManaway in the official Folger library pamphlet on the controversy, its headmaster made as much money as his counterpart at Eton, and a person with equivalent training today would, in his words, be "a Ph.D. at Harvard"[2]); second, by insisting that Shakespeare's father would "never deny his first-born son the privileges of schooling to which his . . . position entitled him";[3] and third, by asserting that the nonsurvival of Shakespeare's literary hand "has no bearing on the subject of authorship."[4] Manuscripts that went to the print shop prior to 1700 were universally discarded once the plays were set in type, and other English Renaissance authors (e.g., Spenser, Ralegh, and Webster) left similarly scanty paper trails. Yet no one quarrels about Spenser's authorship, or Ralegh's, or Webster's, or Milton's.

This, of course, is precisely the point. Why is it different for Shakespeare? Why is so much apparently invested in finding the "real" ghost writer, or in resisting and marginalizing all attempts to prove any authorship other than that of "the poacher from Stratford" (to cite the title of a recent book on the Shakespeare authorship)? "Without possibility of question," maintains the Folger ghost-buster, "the actor at the Globe and the gentleman from Stratford were the same man."[5] Then why does the question persist? *That* is the question, or at least it is the question that I would like to address. I would like, in other words, to take the authorship controversy seriously, not, as is usually done, in order to round up and choose among the usual suspects, but rather in order to explore the significance of the debate itself, to consider the ongoing existence of the polemic between pro-Stratford-lifers and pro-choice advocates as an exemplary literary event in its own right.

One of the difficulties involved in taking the authorship question seriously has been that proponents of rival claims seem to have an uncanny propensity to appear a bit loony—literally. One of the most articulate defenders of the Earl of Oxford authorship is one John Thomas *Looney*. (An "unfortunate name," commented *Life* magazine in an article on the authorship question—but, his defenders say, "an honorable one on the Isle of Man, where it is pronounced "Loney."[6] It was Looney, appropriately enough, who won Freud to the Oxford camp.) Nor is Mr. Looney the only contender for unfortunateness of name: a zealous Shakespearean cryptographer, who proves by numerological analysis that the real author could be either Bacon or Daniel Defoe, is George M. *Battey* ("no more fortunately named than Mr. Looney," comments an orthodox chronicler of the controversy, and, "quite properly, no more deterred by it"[7]). Batty or loony, the ghost seekers' name is legion, and they have left an impressive legacy of monuments to human interpretative ingenuity.

It was not until the mid-nineteenth century that the full energies of the authorship controversy declared themselves, on both sides of the Atlantic, with the 1857 publication of Delia Bacon's 675-page *The Philosophy of the Plays of Shakespeare Unfolded*, arguing the case for Francis Bacon (no relation) and of William Henry Smith's *Bacon and Shakespeare*, shortly followed by the first impassioned defense, *William Shakespeare Not an Impostor*, by George Henry Townsend.[8]

Out of these diverse beginnings has grown a thriving industry, which to this day shows no signs of abating. Some sense of its magnitude can be gleaned from the fact that when, in 1947, Professor Joseph Galland compiled his bibliography of the controversy, entitled *Digesta Anti-Shakespeareana*, no one could afford to publish the 1500-page manuscript.[9] And that was forty years ago. The flood of publications has continued, culminating in the recent and highly acclaimed version of the Oxford case, *The Mysterious William Shakespeare: The Myth and the Reality*, by Charlton Ogburn, Jr.

What, then, can be said about this strange and massive fact of literary history? It is significant that the Shakespeare authorship controversy presents itself at exactly the moment Michel Foucault describes as appropriate for appropriation: the moment when the "author-function" becomes, in the late eighteenth and early nineteenth centuries, an item of property, part of a "system of ownership" in which strict copyright rules define the relation between text and author in a new way. It is not until there is such a thing as property that violations of property can occur; it is not surprising that the claims for rival authorship arise at the moment at which, in Foucault's words, "the transgressive properties always intrinsic to the act of writing became the forceful imperative of literature."[10] It may well be, therefore, that an analysis of the Shakespeare case will shed light on the general question raised by Foucault: "What is an author?"

Instances of the appropriative, even mercantile nature of the controversy abound. Described by one observer as a kind of "middle-class affair,[11] the debate has largely been waged by lawyers and medical men, followed by members of the clergy and retired army officers. Not surprisingly, it became a popular forensic topic and inevitably the subject of litigation. In 1892–93, the Boston monthly magazine *The Arena* sponsored a symposium which took testimony for fifteen months. Among the pro-Baconian plaintiffs was Ignatius Donnelly, a Minnesota Congressman who had written a book called *The Great Cryptogram*, in which he attempted at great length to apply a cipher invented by Bacon. Donnelly had come across the cipher in his son's copy of a children's magazine entitled *Every Boy's Book*. By means of Bacon's "Bi-literal cipher," a secret "infolded" message could be placed within an innocent "infolding" text. The twenty-five-member jury in the case, which included prominent Shakespearean scholars and actors, found for the man from Stratford. A different verdict, however, was forthcoming in the 1916 courtroom battle on the tercentenary of Shakespeare's death. Two convinced Baconians, the cryptographer Elizabeth Wells Gallup and her financial backer Colonel Fabyan, were sued by a motion picture manufacturer, William N. Selig, who hoped to profit from the tercentenary by filming some of the plays, and felt that the slur on the Stratfordian authorship would lessen the value of his product. In this case the judge, finding that "Francis Bacon is the author," awarded Colonel Fabyan $5000 in damages. Although the verdict was later vacated, the case made legal history.

Since both of these cases involved claims for a secret cipher, this may be the moment to say something about the role of codes and ciphers in the anti-Stratfordian cause. The purported discovery of a latent message encrypted in the manifest text provides the grounds for a startling number of cases for alternative authorship. The proliferation of ciphers can be seen as another transgressive correlative to the conception of literature as property. Here, the property violation happens not *to* the text but *within* the text. While copyright laws attempt to demarcate the bounds of literary property, cryptographers set out to uncover ghostlier demarcations, to show that the text itself is haunted by signs of rival ownership. Such codes, ciphers, anagrams, and acrostics can be as fanciful as Mrs. C. F. Ashmead Windle's assertion that proof of the existence of a cipher was to be found in *Othello*: the island of Cyprus clearly was meant to be read by those in the know as "cipher us."[12] Or they can be as complex as Dr. Orville Ward Owen's wheel, a remarkable contraption the size of two large movie reels, across which some 1000 pages of Renaissance literary texts could be wound and stretched for the better application of the cipher. Strictly speaking, Owen was not the inventor of the wheel—he credits that achievement to Bacon himself, in Bacon's "Letter to the Decipherer," which Owen found "infolded" in the text of the so-called Shakespeare plays. The letter to the decipherer, which is in code, contains instructions for cracking the code—useful, of course, only to one who has already done so. Owen's commitment to the truth of his method ultimately compelled him to believe that Bacon was the author not only of the works of Shakespeare, Greene, Marlowe, and so on, but also of a posthumous translation of one of his own Latin works, heretofore credited to his literary secretary and executor, Dr. Rawley. During the writing of his book on *Sir Francis Bacon's Cipher Story*, Dr. Owen received periodic visitations from Bacon's ghost, thus becoming perhaps the first to pursue his research under the aegis of the ghost of a ghost writer. Convinced that tangible proof of Baconian authorship was to be found in a set of iron boxes, he obtained financial backing from the ever-optimistic Colonel Fabyan, and began excavations for them in the bed of the River Wye.

The search for buried treasure indeed often accompanies the unearthing of encrypted messages here, just as it does in Poe's *Gold Bug*. Delia Bacon is notorious for having waited, shovel in hand, in Shakespeare's tomb, suddenly assailed by doubts about what she was digging for. On that occasion, the ghost of Shakespeare (whoever he was) declined to unfold himself.

But if, on the one hand, the isolated Looneys and Batteys always seem to be out there with their shovels, on the other hand examination reveals a significant degree of institutional as well as financial investment in the question. As recently as 1974, the most articulate contemporary spokesman for the Oxford case, Charlton Ogburn, Jr., created a scandal by publishing an article urging his views in *Harvard Magazine*, the alumni bulletin of his alma mater. The outcry was intense and prolonged. Harvard Professors Gwynne Evans and Harry Levin published a scathing reply in a subsequent number of the magazine, and letters deploring the threat to *veritas* continued to pour in for months. ("I'm amazed, shocked, and disgusted that THE magazine of the world's greatest university should actually publish more of the stale old spinach on the Oxford lunacy"; "I am certain that Professor Kittredge is turning over in his grave"; "Charlton Ogburn is a fool and a snob," and much more in the same vein.[13]) Reviving the notion of legal recourse to proof, Ogburn called for a trial to settle the issue. Philip S. Weld, a prominent newspaperman and former president and publisher of *Harvard Magazine*, offered to defray the costs of litigation, including "box lunches and sherry for the opposing players," and proposed that "If no one at Harvard wishes to argue the case for the Stratfordian, perhaps you could engage someone from the Yale English Department."[14]

In fact, a survey of the available literature on the "Shakespeare question" produces an uncanny number of references, often seemingly superfluous, to Harvard as an institution. The rhetorical role assigned to Harvard in the authorship controversy is not adventitious. The University itself becomes in effect a Ghost Underwriter, guaranteeing the legitimacy of whatever side invokes its name as a sign of power and authority. This is one reason why the outcry over Ogburn's article in *Harvard Magazine* became so heated, moving one letter writer to characterize the published defense of the Stratford man by the Harvard professors as "paranoid, shrill, and even hysterical."[15] Something else is being defended—or attacked—here. What is the ghost that walks?

At this point it might be useful to hazard a few conjectures about the kinds of investment that motivate the controversy on both sides:

1. *Institutional investments.* Anti-Stratfordians accuse the "orthodox" of economic and egocentric commitment to such establishments as the Shakespeare Birthplace and the thriving tourist industry in Stratford, England; the Folger Shakespeare Library in Washington, with its handsome building, theater, and gift shop; and publishing projects like *The Riverside Shakespeare*, from which considerable financial benefit—as well as professional advancement—can be reaped. But there is institutionalization on the other side as well. Both Baconians and Oxfordians have established organizations to further their causes. The Bacon Society was founded in England in 1885; the Bacon Society of America in 1922;

the Shakespeare Fellowship, later the Shakespeare Authorship Society, promoting the claims for Oxford, was formed in London in 1922; and its American counterpart, the Shakespeare Fellowship, in 1939. The *Shakespeare-Oxford Society Newsletter* and the *Shakespeare Authorship Review* are going concerns.

2. *Professional investments*. Related to such institutions is what might be called the guild mentality of the academic community. Professors who regularly lecture and publish on the plays of Shakespeare do not as a rule write books extolling rival claimants for authorship. A Shakespearean's identity seems to hinge on the identity of Shakespeare. This produces a schism that can be read in a number of ways: either as representatives of sanity protecting scholarly seriousness against the Looneys and Batteys, or as guardians of the ivy tower protecting their jobs and reputations against true intellectual openness and the subversive ideas of outsiders.

3. *"Psychological" investments*. For some combatants, "Shakespeare" represents a juggernaut, a monument to be toppled. Thus he is fragmented, marginalized into a committee (the group authorship theory) or even a conspiracy. As the author of *An Impartial Study of the Shakespeare Title* puts it, "No one man in the Sixteenth Century, or in any century before or since, leaving out the God-man, our Savior, could use as many words as are found in the plays."[16] A related phenomenon follows the pattern of Freud's family romance, which involves the desire to subvert the father, or to replace a known parent figure with an unknown, greater one, in this case a member of the nobility instead of a country fellow from Stratford. S. Schoenbaum persuasively suggests this as one reason for Freud's own belief in the Oxford candidacy.[17]

4. *"Territorial" investments*. By far the greatest number of contributions, on both sides of the question, have come from Americans; in an 1884 bibliography containing 255 titles, almost two-thirds were written by Americans. In 1895 the Danish critic Georg Brandes fulminated against the "troop of half-educated people" who believed that Shakespeare did not write the plays, and bemoaned the fate of the profession. "Literary criticism," which "must be handled carefully and only by those who have a vocation for it," had clearly fallen into the hands of "raw Americans and fanatical women."[18] Delia Bacon, often credited with beginning the whole controversy, was, of course, both. But while she was ultimately confined to a mental hospital, she had succeeded in attracting to her defense—though not necessarily to her point of view—such distinguished allies as Hawthorne and Emerson. Nor can we ignore the redoubtable Maria Bauer, who in the late 1930s received permission to excavate in Williamsburg, Virginia, for the proof of Bacon's authorship, and who, in her book *Foundations Unearthed*, exhorted her fellow Americans: "Cast your vote for [Bacon as] the great Founder, the empire-builder

of your Nation and your Culture" by digging up the treasure trove in the "Bruton Vault."[19] This was the democratization of authorship with a vengeance.

Writers as different as John Greenleaf Whittier and Mark Twain, too, professed doubts about the Stratford man. Twain, who himself wrote under a pseudonym, and who had felt impelled to correct exaggerated reports of his own death, wrote an essay entitled "Is Shakespeare Dead?" in which he faults the Stratfordians for conjecturing a life story out of little or no evidence. Twain then goes on to declare himself a "Brontosaurian," theorizing an immense body from a few ambiguous bones. "The Brontosaurian doesn't really know which of them did it, but is quite composedly and contentedly sure that Shakespeare *didn't*, and strongly suspects that Bacon *did*."[20] As Emerson wrote to his brother about the forthcoming publication of *Representative Men*: "Who dare print, being unlearned, an account of Plato . . . or, being uninspired, of Shakespeare? Yet there is no telling what we rowdy Americans, whose name is Dare, may do!"[21]

"We rowdy Americans" have had a variety of motivations for interest in the authorship question. First, there is what might be called an impulse to reverse colonization, a desire to recapture "Shakespeare" and make him new (and in some odd way "American") by discovering his true identity, something at which the British had failed. Second, and in some sense moving in the opposite direction, there is an ambivalent fascination with aristocracy, as something both admired and despised. Thus the great democrat, Walt Whitman, declares himself "firm against Shakespeare —I mean the Avon man, the actor."[22] Those "amazing works," the English history plays, could, he asserted, have only had for their "true author" "one of the 'wolfish earls' so plentiful in the plays themselves, or some born descendant and knower."[23] Charlie Chaplin, born in England but achieving success in America as the common man's hero, declared in his autobiography: "I'm not concerned with who wrote the works of Shakespeare . . . but I hardly think it was the Stratford boy. Whoever wrote them had an aristocratic attitude." Authorship of the autobiography is on the title page attributed to *Sir* Charles Spencer Chaplin.[24]

A third American motivation might loosely be described as mythic or "Unitarian"—the desire to believe in Shakespeare as a kind of God, transcending ordinary biography and fact. Thus, taking a gently ironic view of the efforts of "the Shakespeare Society" to find salient facts about the poet, Emerson asserts, "Shakespeare is the only biographer of Shakespeare; and even he can tell nothing, except to the Shakespeare in us."[25] "He was," writes Emerson, "the farthest reach of subtlety compatible with an individual self—the subtlest of authors, and only just within the possibility of authorship."

But attachments to Shakespeare have not always remained on this side idolatory, as the pious reference to the vocabulary of the God-man (a Holy Ghost-writer?) attests. Another American, Henry James, confessing himself to be "sort of 'haunted' by the conviction that the divine William is the biggest and most successful fraud ever practiced on a patient world,"[26] fictionalized the skepticism as well as the fascination provoked by such bardolatry in a late short story entitled "The Birthplace." The story is often described as being about the tourist industry at Shakespeare's birthplace in Stratford. But the proper names never, in fact, appear. The poet is referred to throughout as "Him" with a capital "H," and his writings, similarly capitalized, as a "Set" of the "Works." Far from casting doubt on the story's referent, however, James's typical indirection is here the perfect vehicle for his subject: no direct naming could have represented as well the paradoxes of the authorship controversy.

As the story opens, Mr. and Mrs. Morris Gedge have just been hired as docents of the Birthplace. The Birthplace Trust appears in the story as the "Body," the indwelling poet as the "Spirit," the process of exhibition is known as the "Show," and the "Show" includes the telling of certain "Facts" about which Gedge becomes increasingly dubious. He suggests to his wife a modification of discourse which amounts to an imposition of Jamesian style:

> "Couldn't you adopt . . . a slightly more discreet method? What we can say is that things have been *said*; that's all *we* have to do with. 'And is this really'—when they jam their umbrellas into the floor—'the very *spot* where He was born?' 'So it has, from a long time back, been described as being.' Couldn't one meet Them, to be decent a little, in some such way as that?"[27]

In search of enlightenment, Gedge haunts the "Holy of Holies of the Birthplace," the "Chamber of Birth," scene of the Primal Scene, which should contain the Fact of Facts—the fact that He was born there—or indeed, born at all. "He *had* to take it as the place where the spirit would most walk and where He would therefore be most to be met, with possibilities of recognition and reciprocity.[28] But the ghost never appears. Like Gertrude in *Hamlet*, Gedge sees nothing at all. In a proto-New-Critical or proto-Foucauldian move, he finally confides to a pair of visiting Americans that the author does not exist. "Practically, . . . there *is* no author; that is for us to deal with. There are all the immortal people—*in* the work; but there's nobody else."[29]

The rest of Gedge's career is instructive for academics, for he first makes the mistake of openly displaying his doubts—"giving the Show away," as the representative of the Body says when he arrives to reprove him. But once reminded of his jeopardy, Gedge turns completely around, and, freed of the burden of an indwelling author, himself becomes one, gaining such fame as a raconteur that the Body doubles his stipend.

The crucial point here is the independence—both in terms of entrepreneurship and of artistic freedom—conferred upon the Morris Gedges of the world by the absence of the author—by the hole at the center of things. In a similar spirit Mark Twain alleged rather gleefully about Shakespeare that *"he hadn't any history to record. There is no way of getting around that deadly fact."*[30] Emerson, we can recall, likewise rejoiced in the picture of a Shakespeare "only just within the possibility of authorship," and in his *Journals* he raises the question once more: "Is it not strange," he asks, "that the transcendent men, Homer, Plato, Shakespeare, confessedly unrivalled, should have questions of identity and of genuineness raised respecting their writings?"[31] This is in part what *makes* them transcendent.

In fact, poets and writers who address the "Shakespeare Question" in the nineteenth and twentieth centuries tend to embrace the question *as* a question, preferring its openness to the closure mandated by any answer. This is as true in England as it is in America. Dickens remarks—in a letter much cited by anti-Stratfordians—that "It is a great comfort, to my way of thinking, that so little is known concerning the poet. The life of Shakespeare is a fine mystery and I tremble every day lest something should turn up."[32] With this splendid reversal of Mr. Micawber, Dickens aligns himself with the Gedge camp.

Moreover, the most famous statements about Shakespeare as a creative artist—the ones we all grew up on—make very similar kinds of assertions. Coleridge characterizes him as "our myriad-minded Shakespeare."[33] Keats evolved his celebrated concept of "Negative Capability" to describe the quality "which Shakespeare possessed so enormously . . . that is, when a man is capable of being in uncertainties, mysteries, doubts, without any irritable reaching after fact and reason,"[34] and wrote that "Shakespeare led a life of Allegory; his works are the comments on it."[35] Dryden, in a phrase equally familiar, calls Shakespeare "the man who of all modern, and perhaps ancient, poets had the largest and most comprehensive soul."[36] The suggestion in all of these cases is of a kind of transcendent ventriloquism. It is as though Shakespeare *is* beyond authorship, beyond even the "plurality of egos" that Foucault locates in all discourse that supports the "author-function."[37] Matthew Arnold's sonnet on Shakespeare marks out the issue clearly:

> Others abide our question. Thou art free.
> We ask and ask—Thou smilest and art still,
> Out-topping knowledge.[38]

The "foiled searching of mortality" fails to disclose the answer: "Thou, who didst the stars and sunbeams know, / Self-schooled, self-scanned, self-honored, self-secure, / Didst tread on earth unguessed at—Better so!" (8–11). Better so indeed. We have described the investment in various answers, but a great deal seems invested in *not* finding the answer. It begins to become obvious that Shakespeare is the towering figure he is for us not despite but rather *because of* the authorship controversy. He is *defined* by that controversy, as, equally, he defines *it*, making Foucault's use of him as an example almost tautologous. "Shakespeare" is present as an absence—which is to say, as a ghost. Shakespeare as an author is the person who, were he more completely known, would not be the Shakespeare we know.

Formulations like "What is an author?" and "the death of the author," which have engaged the imagination of contemporary theorists, draw much of their power and fascination from "the kinship between writing and death"[39]—a little less than kin and more than kind. Freed from the trammels of a knowable "authorial intention," the author paradoxically gains power rather than losing it, assuming a different kind of authority that renders him in effect his own ghost. It begins to become clear that to speak about "ghost writing" is not merely to play upon words. As Foucault writes,

> we find the link between writing and death manifested in the total effacement of the individual characteristics of the writer . . . If we wish to know the writer in our day, it will be through the singularity of his absence and in his link to death, which has transformed him into a victim of his own writing."[40]

If you want to know the author—*in* the text, as well as *of* or *behind* the text—look to see who's dead.

Consider, for example, the tradition that has grown up about Shakespeare as an actor in his own plays. Nicholas Rowe, in the *Life* printed with his 1709 edition of the *Works*, writes that "tho' I have inquir'ed I could never meet with any further account of him this way, than that the top of his performance was the ghost in his own *Hamlet*."[41] Rowe's edition was published ninety-three years after Shakespeare's death—his information is hearsay, rumor, or better, but it is not an eyewitness account. It therefore belongs properly with the affect of the Shakespeare story rather than with its irreducible facts. A less reliable account reports that Will Shakespeare's younger brother, having been asked about the parts played by his celebrated sibling, described seeing him "act a part in one of his own comedies, wherein being to personate a decrepit old man, he wore a long beard, and appeared so weak and drooping and unable to walk, that he was forced to be supported and carried by another person to a table, at which he was seated among some company, who were eating, and one of them sung a song."[42] This part has been identified as that of Old Adam in *As You Like It*, who enters the scene in question (2.7) borne on Orlando's shoulders, like Anchises borne on the shoulders of his son Aeneas.

Both of these traditional accounts are suggestive. Each casts Shakespeare as a father figure advising his son, and placed at a disadvantage by age (or death) so that he requires the son to enact his will. Old Adam, in whom appears "the constant service of the antique world" (2.3.57) personates the dead Sir Rowland and his lost ways of civility. It is he who warns Orlando about treachery in the Duke's court, and encourages him to seek safety in Arden. We may see this as appropriate to a play-wright's role, giving his protagonist motive for action, so that the casting acts as a kind of metadramatic shadow or reflection of the relationship between author, actor, and plot. But the role of ghost writer here is doubled. Each of these figures achieves his own erasure, first presenting or representing the imperative of the father, then dis-appearing from the play.

II

We would search the "public" in vain for the first reader: i.e., the first author of a work. And the "sociology of literature" is blind to the war and the ruses perpetuated by the author who reads and by the first reader who dictates, for at stake here is the origin of the work itself. The *sociality* of writing as *drama* requires an entirely different discipline.
Jacques Derrida, "Freud and the Scene of Writing"

Let us return, then, to our original question. Who is the author of Shakespeare's plays? Is it possible that, in this already over-determined controversy, there is at least one more determining factor? Is there something in the nature of these plays that some-how provokes, as it responds to, the authorship controversy? Are there, in other words, explicit scenes of ghost writing in the plays themselves? It has long been noted that Shakespeare's plays are full of questions of authority, legitimacy, usurpation, authorship and interpretation. Indeed, drama as a genre not only permits but also encodes the dissemination of authority. This is in part what authorizes such formu-lations as "negative capability" and "myriad-mindedness." But can the more *particular* details of the authorship controversy as we have just documented it somehow be seen to be anticipated and overdetermined by the plays? Can the "Shakespeare Question" be situated within the text itself? Is the authorship controversy in part a textual effect?

There are in fact an uncanny number of ways in which the plays can be seen to stage the controversy. Such scenes of encoded authorship encompass everything from ghosts that write and writers who function as ghosts, to handwriting analyses, signa-ture controversies, the deciphering of codes, the digging of graves, the silencing of madwomen, the staging of plays that get away from their authors, and the thematizing of myriad other forms of doubt and discontinuity within authorial identity and control. Before I come to mention some specific instances in which ghost writing takes place in Shakespeare's plays, however, it may be useful to set these remarks into a theoretical framework, and to give some idea of how I will be using the concept of a *ghost* here and in the chapters that follow.

In *Beyond the Pleasure Principle* (1920), Freud discusses the ways in which the compulsion to repeat results from "the power of the repressed"—the ways, that is, in which that which has been repressed, because of its repression, keeps breaking through. Transference neurosis, the repetition of repressed memory as present experience, results from the retention of unconscious ideas, their refusal to become conscious and accessible to the patient and the analyst. The patient "is obliged to *repeat* the repressed material as a contemporary experience instead of . . . *remembering* it as something belonging to the past."[43] We might make use of a theoretical metaphor here, and describe such repetition as restaging or replaying. Freud himself explicitly refers to the unconscious as "another theater," and compares the reenactment involved in repetition, with its apparently paradoxical yield of pleasure even in unpleasurable experience, to the experience of drama—and, specifically, tragedy:

> the artistic play and artistic imagination carried out by adults, which, unlike children's, are aimed at an audience, do not spare the spectators (for instance, in tragedy) the most painful experiences and can yet be felt by them as highly enjoyable. This is convincing proof that, even under the dominance of the pleasure principle, there are ways and means enough of making what is in itself unpleasurable into a subject to be recollected and worked over in the mind.[44]

A tragedy is like an unpleasurable memory – or, rather, it is like the displacement of that repressed memory into the "working through" that is "artistic imagination" but also theatrical performance. This compulsion to repeat, this "perpetual recurrence of the same thing"[45] that strikes us as uncanniness in life and as structure in art, is one of the functions performed in Shakespeare's plays by the figure of the ghost.

Another useful analogue for the concept of a *ghost* as I am using it here can be found in what Jacques Derrida has called the "logic of the supplement."[46] The word "supplément," in French, means both a *substitute* and an *addition*. These terms, normally thought of as mutually exclusive, come together in the supplement in such a way that the binary logic of identity and noncontradiction is replaced by a different kind of logic. Barbara Johnson glosses that other logic as follows. In this chart, all statements are to be taken as equivalent to the statement, "A is a supplement to B."

1. A is added to B.
2. A substitutes for B.

3. A is a superfluous addition to B.
4. A makes up for the absence of B.
5. A usurps the place of B.
6. A makes up for B's deficiencies.
7. A corrupts the purity of B.
8. A is necessary so that B can be restored.
9. A is an accident alienating B from itself.
10. A is that without which B would be lost.
11. A is that through which B is lost.
12. A is a danger to B.
13. A is a remedy to B.
14. A's fallacious charm seduces one away from B.
15. A can never satisfy the desire for B.
16. A protects against direct encounter with B.[47]

The ghosts in Shakespeare's plays function as supplements in many, perhaps all, of these ways. The reader can test this out by selecting a ghost (or a character performing a ghost-function) and filling in the blanks. But if A stands for the ghost, who or what is B? If A is the Ghost of Old Hamlet, for example, is B the living Old Hamlet, Hamlet, Claudius, Ophelia, Horatio, Denmark, *Hamlet*, Shakespeare, the England—or the court—of Queen Elizabeth, a modern theatrical audience? Yes. Such is the promiscuous supplementarity of ghosts. Such, too, is the source of their power, and their danger.

A ghost is an embodiment of the disembodied, a re-membering of the dismembered, an articulation of the disarticulated and inarticulate. "Were I the ghost that walked," says Paulina to Leontes in *The Winter's Tale*, discussing his "dead" wife Hermione,

> I'd bid you mark
> Her eye, and tell me for what dull part in't
> You chose her: then I'd shriek, that even your ears
> Should rift to hear me; and the words that follow'd
> Should be 'Remember mine.' (5.1.63–7)

We might notice the similarity of this scenario to *Hamlet*, where the ghost of the dead spouse does walk and cries "Remember me," the import of his words entering like daggers into his wife's ears when Hamlet, like Paulina, transmits the message.[48] In both of these dramatic cases, the appearance of the ghost comes at the time when the living spouse has effected, or is about to effect, a repetition and a substitution, through remarriage.

The effect of uncanniness produced by the appearance of a ghost is related simultaneously to its manifestation as a sign of potential proliferation or plurality and to its acknowledgement of the loss of the original—indeed, to the loss of the certainty of the concept of origin. The representation of the fear of loss through multiplication is familiar from the interpretation of dreams and myths, as for example in Freud's essay on "Medusa's Head" (1922), where the proliferation of swarming snakes compensates for and covers over the fear of castration, or in the "The Uncanny" (1919), where he writes that "this invention of doubling as a preservation against extinction has its counterpart in the language of dreams, which is fond of representing castration by a doubling or multiplication of the genital symbol."[49] The dual question—of plurality and the lost original—is directly relevant to the phenomenology of ghosts. And it is equally relevant to the phenomenology of the work of art. It is here, in the overlapping status of the ghost and the art object, or the ghost and the text, that the further significance of Shakespeare as a ghost writer—as a writer of ghosts, and as their ghostly written—manifests itself.

This peculiar characteristic of ghostliness—that the ghost is a copy, somehow both nominally identical to and numinously different from a vanished or unavailable original—has special ramifications for art forms which, like Elizabethan and Jacobean drama, are regarded by their contemporary cultures as marginal, popular, or contestatory. Consider the status of such analogous art forms as translation, photography, and film, forms that depend upon the production of "original copies." In two important essays, "The Task of the Translator" and "The Work of Art in the Age of Mechanical Reproduction," the cultural critic Walter Benjamin returns again and again to these two themes: multiplication and "the original."[50] For translation and mechanical reproduction are, precisely, means by which the original and its primacy are put in question. And thus they are ways of making—of calling up—ghosts. The two essays are uncannily concerned with the same issues, and the language in which Benjamin conducts his argument is itself suggestively ghostly—e.g., "A translation issues from the original—not so much from its life as from its afterlife,"[51] or "Even the most perfect reproduction of a work of art is lacking in one element: its presence in time and space, its unique existence at the place where it happens to be."[52] "The technique of reproduction," writes Benjamin, "detaches the reproduced object from the domain of tradition. By making many reproductions it substitutes a plurality of copies for a unique existence. And in permitting the reproduction to meet the beholder or listener in his own particular situation, it reactivates the object produced."[53] In fact, if we substitute the word *ghost* for *translation* or *reproduction* in any of these statements ("in permitting the *ghost* to meet the beholder or listener in his own particular situation . . .") we can see how cognate the conditions of ghostliness and reproduction or nonoriginality really are. It may be objected that in the last passage quoted above, Benjamin refers to "a plurality of copies," where in Shakespeare's plays the ghosts of Hamlet's father and Banquo and Julius Caesar are not multiply replicated, but are themselves possessed of "a unique existence." This is certainly the case; but the "unique existence" each possesses is, I would contend, importantly different from the nonghostly existence of those characters as we encounter them (Banquo, Caesar) or hear about them (Old Hamlet) in the plays. I will have more to say about this gap between the ghost and its living "original" in the chapters that follow. For the present, though, I want to suggest that the idea of a "plurality of copies" does play an important role in the ghostly uncanniness of Shakespeare's plays, as for example in the phenomenon of many men marching in the king's coats (*King Henry IV, Part 1* 5.3.25; also *King Richard III* 5.4.11–12: "I think there be six Richmonds in the field; / Five I have slain today instead of him"); in the disturbing capacity of ghosts to move about (*Hamlet* 1.5.164: "*Hic et ubique?* Then we'll shift our ground"); and in the profoundly uncanny sensation of doubleness experienced in and produced by the "twin" plays, *The Comedy of Errors* and *Twelfth Night*. In *The Comedy of Errors* the mechanism of textual effect is at work, as the concept of a ghostly double is transferred from that of the twin sons to their father:

Adriana:	I see two husbands, or mine eyes deceive me.
Duke:	One of these men is genius to the other:
	And so of these, which is the natural man,
	And which the spirit? Who deciphers them?
S. Dromio:	I sir, am Dromio, command him away.
E. Dromio:	I sir, am Dromio, pray let me stay.
S. Antipholus:	Egeon art thou not? or else his ghost? (5.1.331–7)

Perhaps the most instructive parallel suggested by Benjamin's essay on mechanical reproduction is that of photography, and of the photographic negative, which is described as a shadow or reverse of a work that has no "original":

> To an ever greater degree the work of art reproduced becomes the work of art designed for reproducibility. From a photographic negative, for example, one can make any number of prints; to ask for the "authentic" print makes no sense.[54]

In this connection it is interesting to recall that one of the familiar terms used in modern parlance to describe a faint, false, sometimes secondary photographic image is *ghost*—and that a *ghost* is also, in printing, a variation or unevenness in color intensity on a surface intended to be solidly tinted, a phenomenon often observed in the printing of newspapers. The photographic negative is in fact very like a ghost; it reifies

the concept of an absent presence, existing positively as a negative image. In a negative
we see light as dark and dark as light; we see, in effect, what is not there.

> *Hamlet*: Do you see nothing there?
> *Queen*:   Nothing at all, yet all that is I see.
> *Hamlet*: Nor did you nothing hear?
> *Queen*:   No, nothing but ourselves.
> *Hamlet*: Why, look you there, look how it steals away!
>   My father, in his habit as he lived!
>   Look where he goes, even now, out at the portal!
>   *Exit Ghost.* (3.4.132–8)

The analogy between a ghost and a photograph is made by Robert Lowell in a
poem suggestively titled "Epilogue":

> We are poor passing facts,
> warned by that to give
> each figure in the photograph
> his living name.[55]

Without the label of the "living name," inscribed on the back of the photograph or
beneath it in the album, such figures will become anonymous, dislocated from the
context in which they are identifiable and identified. So writing fixes, pins down. This
is ghost writing too, writing that calls up ghosts from the past, from the passing.

In 1927 Abel Gance, who made the great film, *Napoléon*, predicted that
"Shakespeare, Rembrandt, Beethoven will make films."[56] The study of films made
of, or from, Shakespeare's plays has by this time, of course, become a recognized
subspeciality of Shakespeare studies, so that in that sense we can say Gance's
prediction has come true. "Shakespeare"—Shakespeare's works—has made films.
But in another sense, his words describe what Shakespeare had already achieved,
in furnishing his plays with ghost writers, with writing ghosts and ghosts who
demand to be written. Gance's exultant claim for some Shakespeare of the future
writes history backward, and describes not "Shakespeare" but Shakespeare, whoever
he was.

The appearance of ghosts within the plays is almost always juxtaposed to a scene
of writing. Hamlet takes dictation from the Ghost of his father: "My tables, meet it
is I set it down / That one may smile, and smile, and be a villain!" (1.5.107–8) Old
Hamlet's script is a revenge tragedy, perhaps the Ur-*Hamlet*. Hamlet will alter the
script, will himself sign and seal what he will describe as a "play" on the voyage to
England. But in this first encounter with the Ghost we see a further rewriting of
authority as well.

> I'll wipe away all trivial fond records,
> All saws of books, all forms, all pressures past
> That youth and observation copied there,
> And thy commandment all alone shall live
> Within the book and volume of my brain. (1.5.99–103)

"Thy commandment" (to revenge) replaces all the saws and pressures, or seals, of the past. In this post-Mosaic transmission of the law from father to son one kind of erasure (or "wiping away") is already taking place. The Ghost himself is under erasure—"'tis here, 'tis here, 'tis gone"—visible and invisible, potent and impotent. But *all* ghosts are under erasure; that is their status.[57] What Hamlet writes down in *his* tables is the doubled plot of the Mousetrap play, for to smile and smile and be a villain is not only a description of Claudius, but also of Hamlet, just as Hamlet glosses the figure of "one Lucianus, nephew to the King" in the Mousetrap as both a sign of his knowledge of Claudius' guilt in the past, and a threat of his own revenge in the future. The integration of the Ghost into the composite figure of "Hamlet the Dane" begins with this scene of writing, as Hamlet writes himself into the story and writes the Ghost out, revising the revenge imperative (and the imperative of the revenge play).

The ghost of Julius Caesar is appropriated as a ghost writer by Mark Antony in the funeral oration. It is clear from the moment of the assassination that the conspirators have killed the wrong Caesar, the man of flesh and blood and not the feared and admired monarch. They have, so to speak, killed the wrong author-function, the one associated with the proper name and not with the works. Brutus's despairing cry, "O Julius Caesar, thou art mighty yet. / Thy spirit walks abroad and turns our swords / In our own proper entrails" (5.3.94–6) records his sense of Caesar as uncanny omnipresence, and conflates his two sightings of the Ghost with the self-destructive actions of the conspirators. Antony will himself become a "seizer" of opportunity, in the public reading of Caesar's will, "under Caesar's seal" (3.2.233), that leaves his money and pleasure-grounds to the people. In effect he makes Caesar, the dead and living Caesar of the author-function, his own ghost writer, the more effaced, the more powerful.

Brutus, who actually sees great Caesar's ghost, participates in a crucial scene of writing and authorial appropriation, an appropriation that occurs, significantly, *before* the assassination itself, as Brutus walks at night in his orchard. A letter is thrown in at his window, and, as he reads it, he writes it:

> "Brutus, thou sleep'st; awake, and see thyself.
> Shall Rome, etc. Speak, strike, redress."
> "Brutus, thou sleep'st; awake."

> Such instigations have been often dropped
> Where I have took them up.
> "Shall Rome, etc." Thus must I piece it out:
> Shall Rome stand under one man's awe? What Rome?
> My ancestors did from the streets of Rome
> The Tarquin drive, when he was called a king.
> "Speak, strike, redress." Am I entreated
> To speak and strike? O Rome, I make thee promise,
> If the redress will follow, thou receivest
> Thy full petition at the hand of Brutus! (2.1.46–58)

Brutus supplies this anonymous document with what is in fact a dead (i.e., inanimate) author—"Rome." "Rome" enjoins him to join the conspiracy. "Shall Rome, etc."— like many of the Shakespeare ciphers—gives the interpreter considerable latitude to inscribe his own message ("thy full petition at the *hand* of Brutus"). The hand that rewrites here is of course also the hand that kills. The anonymity of the communication itself encodes authority—the importunings of a mere individual, like Cassius, are suspect because they are tied to a flawed human persona, and to personal motives. Receiving the letter, Brutus elects to ignore the possibility of a merely human agent, and to regard it instead as an uncanny answer to his own latent thought, about himself and his love-relationship to Rome. Here Brutus becomes his own ghost writer, and gives to the author he creates the pseudonym of "Rome."

Another kind of ghostly self-erasure can be seen in the famous "deposition scene" in *King Richard II* (4.1). There Richard, denying any possibility of a split between persona and role, the king's two bodies (or the proper name of the author and his works, to use Foucault's partition), sees himself as erased, tranformed into a shadow or ghost of himself, when he is deposed by Bolingbroke:

> I have no name, no title—
> No, not that name was given me at the font—
> But 'tis usurped . . .
> O that I were a mockery king of snow,
> Standing before the sun of Bolingbroke,
> To melt myself away in water-drops! (4.1.255–62)

A "deposition" is both a forced removal from office and a piece of testimony taken down for use in the witness's absence (as well as the term describing the lowering of Christ's body from the cross—Richard's view of the event). Richard here deposes at his own deposition, figuring himself as a snowman whose whiteness and impermanence is tragically vulnerable to the kingly sun. He is already a voice from the past, and the disembodied voice, the ghost of Richard II, will haunt the rest of the tetralogy with increasing power.

Bolingbroke had faulted the "skipping king" Richard for his availability to the people. He himself, by being seldom seen, will be more wondered at, more the stuff of legend, reverence, and fantasy. Like Arnold's vision of a Shakespeare "unguessed-at—Better so!"—this strategy locates power in absence: absence of personality, absence of fact, absence of peculiarity. But the question is also one of suitability, of fitting the role. Richard is the lineal king, the king by Divine Write, by Holy Writ. But Bolingbroke, like Bacon, fits the part, with his winning manners and his "fair discourse" (2.3.6). It is striking that one of his complaints against Richard is that the king has erased his name and coat of arms from the windows of the family estate, "leaving me no sign / Save men's opinions and my living blood / To show the world I am a gentleman" (3.1.25–7).

As with a "deposition," so with a "will"—the dead hand is a living voice replacing the original author, and open to interpretation. Thus, in *The Merchant of Venice*, Portia complains that in the mandatory casket choice "the will of a living daughter [is] curb'd by the will of a dead father" (1.2.23–5). Shakespeare—if it is he—puns on his own name as an absent presence enforcing desire and authority (or failing to enforce them) throughout the *Sonnets*, and, as we have seen, Mark Antony makes of the "will" of the murdered Caesar read aloud to the plebeians a document that encodes his own "will," his own authority over the original conspirators.

But if ghosts are often writers, so too are writers often ghosts. The question of Shakespeare's signature, especially as it appears (three times) on his *will*, can also be situated within the text. A signature, as Derrida has shown, is a sign that must be iterated to be recognizable, a sign of the simultaneous presence and absence of a "living hand," which stands for its signator in that person's absence. "By definition, a written signature implies the actual or empirical nonpresence of the signer."[58] A signature, then, is very like a ghost, as will become explicitly the case when Hamlet on shipboard takes his father's signet, providentially carried in his purse, and signs the name of "Hamlet" to the letter he has forged in the careful calligraphy of a professional scribe. ("I once did hold it, as our statists do, a baseness to write fair . . . but, sir, now / It did me yeoman's service" (5.2.33–6). The "changeling" letter that sends Rosencrantz and Guildenstern to their deaths is signed by Hamlet—but by which Hamlet? It is the underwritten script of the Ghost's imperative superscribed by the son's educated hand.

III

As the current affected the brachial plexus of the nerves, he suddenly cried
aloud, "Oh! The hand, the hand!" and attempted to seize the missing member.
The phantom I had conjured up swiftly disappeared, but no spirit could have
more amazed the man, so real did it seem.

S. Weir Mitchell, *Injuries of Nerves*

Again the plays are thematizing the authorship controversy: the question of the
identification of signatures and handwriting (could Shakespeare write? could his
parents? could his daughters? why have we no literary remains in his hand, or—if
any—just the *Thomas More* fragment?) is a question configured in the plays not only
in Hamlet and Old Hamlet, but in Edmund's forged letter purporting to come from
his brother Edgar. "You know the character to be your brother's?" asks Gloucester,
using the Renaissance term for handwriting, for letter of the alphabet, and also for
cipher or code. "It is his hand, my lord; but I hope his heart is not in the contents"
(*King Lear* 1.2.62; 67–8). The character, of course, is Edmund's, the letter a forgery
of *his* jealousy and not of Edgar's. Likewise, Maria's forged letter to Malvolio in *Twelfth
Night* is made possible by an uncanny resemblance between her handwriting and
Olivia's. Indeed, the phenomenon of life imitating art has never been more amply
demonstrated than in the proliferation of questers after the Shakespeare cipher. Their
great model and predecessor, the most ingenious cryptographer of them all, is
Malvolio, who opens Maria's forged letter to discover not only ciphers and codes but
an anagram as well: "Why, this is evident to any formal capacity. There is no obstruc-
tion in this. And the end: what should that alphabetical position portend? If I could
make that resemble something in me! Softly! 'M.O.A.I.'— . . . 'M.'—Malvolio! 'M'!
Why . . . that begins my name! . . . 'M'—But then there is no consonancy in the
sequel; that suffers under probation: 'A' should follow, but 'O' does . . . 'M.O.A.I.'
This simulation is not as the former: and yet, to crush this a little, it would bow
to me, for every one of these letters are in my name" (2.5.117–41). Mrs. Windle,
Dr. Owen, and Ignatius Donnelly are pale shadows of this strong precursor.

In these forgeries the text itself becomes a ghost writer: the scriptwriting capacity
takes on a power of its own, supplementing the plot and radically altering it. And
once more, as in the plays, so in the authorized biography. Critics search in vain
for the "speech of some dozen or sixteen lines" (2.2.535) that Hamlet inserts in
"The Murder of Gonzago" as an indicator of his secret knowledge. In just the same
way, editors have scrutinized the manuscript of *Sir Thomas More* for undoubted
proof of Shakespeare's authorship, and have fixed at last on the 147 lines written by
"Hand D."

The spectral presence of the "hand" haunts the editorial tradition in another way as well, in connection with a particularly compelling example of authorial fragmentation. In *Titus Andronicus* Lavinia, who enters the stage with "*her hands cut off and her tongue cut out, and ravished*" (2.4. stage direction), is assigned the task of writing *without* hands. Urged by his brother Marcus to moderate his language of grief and despair, "teach her not to lay / Such violent hands upon her tender life," Titus (who has himself been tricked into cutting off one of his own hands) retorts angrily: "What violent hands can she lay upon her life?":

> Ah, wherefore dost thou urge the name of hands . . .
> O handle not the theme, to talk of hands,
> Lest we remember still that we have none.
> Fie, fie, how franticly I square my talk,
> As if we should forget we have no hands,
> If Marcus did not name the word of hands. (3.2.25–33)

In the next scene (4.1) Lavinia begins to rifle through her nephew Lucius's books with her stumps, turning the leaves of Ovid's *Metamorphoses*, to point to the "tragic tale of Philomel . . . of Tereus' treason and his rape" (47–8) as the narrative of her own experience. But her audience is puzzled. "Give signs, sweet girl," implores Titus (61), and Marcus devises a better plan. As so often in this play, the stage direction says it all: "*He writes his name with his staff, and guides it with feet and mouth*":

> This sandy plot is plain. Guide, if thou canst,
> This after me. I have writ my name
> Without the help of any hand at all. (69–71)

Lavinia's inscription on the "sandy plot" indicates the truth of her condition, identifying her rapists as the sons of Tamora. "There is enough written upon this earth / To . . . arm the minds of infants to exclaims" (84–6). *In-fans*, unable to speak, disarmed by her mutilation, Lavinia signs her deposition with a missing hand, a hand that is both "bloody and invisible."

Given this no-holds-barred approach to the act of writing in the play, it is unsettling to notice how often phrases like "on the one hand . . . and on the other" appear in criticism of the play. T. S. Eliot calls it "a play in which it is incredible that Shakespeare had any hand at all," M. C. Bradbrook observes that in the play "Shakespeare was trying his hand at the high style," and E. M. W. Tillyard points out admiringly that "the author holds everything in his head"—all textual effects of the play's embarrassing power.[59] J. C. Maxwell, the Arden editor of *Titus Andronicus*, writes of the authorship question that "in the palmy days of disintegration of the

Shakespeare canon, almost all practising dramatists of 1585–95 were called in to take a hand in *Titus*"[60]; three times he mentions "Peele's hand" (twice on p. xxv, and again on p. xxvi), and he comments about Kyd that "there is nothing in the writing to suggest that he had any hand in it" (xxvii). Twice in the introduction he uses the formulation "on the one hand . . . and on the other" (xxxiv; xxxviii), and in the textual apparatus of the play he is fond of the technical designation "headless line" to denote a line of verse with only nine metrical feet. Thus the footnote to 2.3.115 reads, "best read as a headless line," and 5.2.62 is described as "an effectively solemn headless line" while Titus's multiply overdetermined request, "Speak, Lavinia, what accursed hand / Hath made thee handless in thy father's sight" (3.1.66) is likewise described as "a headless line." Nor is Maxwell wholly unaware of these anatomical excrescences. In a note to Act 5 scene 2, when Tamora comes to Titus's study and finds him writing "in bloody lines," lamenting his loss of eloquence ("how can I grace my talk, / Wanting a hand to give it action?"), the Arden editor cites B. L. Joseph, *Elizabethan Acting*, who quotes in turn from John Bulwer's *Chironomia* (1644):

> "The moving and significant extension of the *Hand* is knowne to be so absolutely pertinent to speech, that we together with a speech expect the due motion of the *Hand* to explaine, direct, enforce, apply, apparrell, & to beautifie the words men utter, which would prove naked, unless the cloathing *Hands* doe neatly move to adorne and hide their nakednesse, with their comely and ministeriall parts of speech."[61]

Here body parts and parts of speech seem inextricably intertwined. Titus asks Tamora on this occasion, "Is not thy coming for my other hand?" (5.2.27), and she later comments to herself, "I'll find some cunning practice out of hand / To scatter and disperse the giddy Goths" (77–8). At the close of the play Marcus urges that "the poor remainder of Andronici . . . hand in hand all headlong hurl ourselves" (5.3.131). It is tempting to add to this proliferating textual effect by pointing out that the style of *Titus Andronicus*, characterized by distortion of scale and perspective, has much in common with the late sixteenth-century expressive style known as Mannerism—a style that traces its etymology to the word "hand" (ME *menere* from Norman French, from OF *maniere*, from Vulgar Latin *manuaria*, "way of handling," manner, from *manuarius*, of the hand, from *manus*, the hand).

Literal ghosts, portentous Senecan stalkers from the revenge tradition, tend in Shakespeare's plays to be male and paternal. But as the example of Lavinia suggests, there is another whole group of ghost writers in his plays who are similarly under erasure, and these ghost writers are women—women marginalized by their gender, by their putative or real madness, or by their violation. The story of Delia Bacon—overprotected by her brother, misled by a theology student into thinking he would marry her, gaining authority as a seer and prophetess from her rejection, and with it the license to go abroad and speak dangerous things, dying mad—this is the story of Ophelia. "Her speech is nothing," says a Gentleman to Horatio and the Queen,

> Yet the unshaped use of it doth move
> The hearers to collection. They aim at it,
> And botch the words up fit to their own thoughts,
> Which, as her winks and nods and gestures yield them,
> Indeed would make one think there might be thought,
> Though nothing sure, yet much unhappily. (*Hamlet* 4.5.8–13)

To this statement, itself a foreclosure of judgment ("her speech is nothing"), Horatio adds an even more political warning? "'Twere good she were spoken with, for she may strew / Dangerous conjectures in ill-breeding minds" (14–15). The "unshaped use" of Ophelia's speech—rather like the "questionable shape" in which the Ghost appears to Hamlet (1.4.43)—is an invitation to fill in the blank. Traditionally dressed in white, Ophelia is marked as "virginal and vacant," as Elaine Showalter points out,[62] her white dress in contrast to Hamlet's suits of solemn black. If his costume is explicitly described (indeed, self-described) as an "inky cloak" (1.2.77), she is the blank page, the tabula rasa. But the white dress is also the sign, and the shroud, of a ghost. And just as Horatio's word "strew," in the passage we have just noticed, predicts Ophelia's flower-giving, so Laertes's description of the scene as "a document in madness: thoughts and remembrance fitted" (176–7) identifies the documentary evidence, the displacement of the written and the writable, that Ophelia's subject position compels. The flower-giving scene and its "document" closely resemble Lavinia's tracing on the "sandy plot." Both incidents present women writing as ghosts. Both suggest that women's writing is ghost writing.

Similarly marginalized, similarly erased, moving through the events of her play like a ghost, Cassandra is dismissed by her brothers as "our mad sister" (*Troilus and Cressida* 2.2.98), but the design toward which she moves, the story she tells, is the story of the Trojan War. Cassandra's authority is such that she speaks the truth and is not believed—and this is also the case with Ophelia and indeed with Lady Macbeth. Lady Macbeth's sleepwalking places her physically in exactly the condition of present absence, marginal stance, and legible erasure we have come to expect of such ghosts. Indeed, perhaps the most threatening female authority of all in the plays is also the most effaced—Sycorax, Caliban's mother, predecessor magician to Prospero, whose name is evoked as the justification for his authority and authorship on the island—and who never appears in the play. Like Claribel, who would be the next heir to Naples but is half a world away in Tunis, Sycorax exists beyond the play's margins, and only Miranda remains as another figure of female self-erasure in the present, eagerly accepting her father's tutelage in the Elizabethan World Picture.

Thus, again and again, the plays themselves can be seen to dramatize questions raised in the authorship controversy: who wrote this? did someone else have a hand in it? is the apparent author the real author? is the official version to be trusted? or are there suppressed stories, hidden messages, other signatures?

As will become clear in the chapters that follow, the plays not only thematize these issues, they also theorize them, offering a critique of the concept of authorship and, in particular, of the possibility of origin. Authorship itself will be seen as a belated and disputable matter. When Troilus cites the fidelity of his love for Cressida as "truth's authentic author" (*Troilus and Cressida* 3.2.176) for lovers "in the real world to come" (168), or when Brutus and Cassius view themselves as heroic regicides in the eyes of "ages hence" (*Julius Caesar* 3.1.111) they are not, as they think, standing at the beginning of the story, but somewhere in the middle. The histories of which they imagine themselves authors are already in process. Neither Troilus nor Cassius is "author of himself," and the texts they so confidently envisage are inflected, ironically, toward tragedy.

If it is a wise father that knows his own child, so it is a wise character who knows he is in search of an author. The undecidability of paternity, articulated again and again in the plays by putative fathers like Lear, Leontes, Leonato, and Prospero, is analogous to, and evocative of, the undecidability of authorship. Thus a play like *Pericles*, long thought to be the product of dual authorship, enacts its own family romance by dwelling insistently on the incest riddle with which it begins:

> He's father, son, and husband mild;
> I mother, wife, and yet his child:
> How they may be, *and yet in two*,
> As you will live, resolve it you. (1.1.69–72)

And even this incest riddle, later rearticulated in the mystery of Marina's parentage (5.1.90ff.) is qualified by Gower's narrative prologue: "I tell you what mine authors say" (1.Chorus.20). The origin is always deferred. The search for an author, like any other quest for parentage, reveals more about the searcher than about the sought, for what is demanded is a revisitation of the primal scene.

Hamlet: Giving Up the Ghost

But the calling back of the dead, or the desirability of calling them back, was a ticklish matter, after all. At bottom, and boldly confessed, the desire does not exist; it is a misapprehension precisely as impossible as the thing itself, as we should soon see if nature once let it happen. What we call mourning for our dead is perhaps not so much grief at not being able to call them back as it is grief at not being able to want to do so.

Thomas Mann, *The Magic Mountain*

The phantom which returns to haunt bears witness to the existence of the dead buried within the other.

Nicholas Abraham, "Notes on the Phantom"

For here the day unravels what the night has woven.

Walter Benjamin, "The Image of Proust"

A murder done in Vienna

In the fall of 1897 Sigmund Freud's mind was running on *Hamlet*. A letter he wrote to Wilhelm Fliess in October contained the first exposition of the Oedipus complex, later to be elaborated in *The Interpretation of Dreams* (1900) but here already fully articulated, both as it presents itself in Sophocles and, in a more repressed and hysterical fashion, in *Hamlet*:

Everyone in the audience was once a budding Oedipus in fantasy, and each recoils in horror from the dream fulfillment here transplanted into reality, with the full quantity of repression which separates his infantile state from his present one.

Fleetingly the thought passed through my head that the same thing might be at the bottom of *Hamlet* as well. I am not thinking of Shakespeare's conscious intentions, but believe, rather, that a real event stimulated the poet to his representation, in that his unconscious understood the unconscious of his hero. How does Hamlet the hysteric justify his words, "Thus conscience does make cowards of us all?" How does he explain his irresolution in avenging his father by the murder of his uncle—the same man who sends his courtiers to their death without a scruple and who is positively precipitate in murdering Laertes? How better than through the torment roused in him by the obscure memory that he himself had contemplated the same deed against his father out of passion for his mother, and—"use every man after his desert, and who should 'scape whipping?" His conscience is his unconscious sense of guilt. And is not his sexual alienation in his conversation with Ophelia typically hysterical? And his rejection of the instinct that seeks to beget children? And, finally, his transferral of the deed from his own father to Ophelia's? And does he not in the end, in the same marvellous way as my hysterical patients do, bring down punishment on himself by suffering the same fate as his father of being poisoned by the same rival?[1]

Less than a month before, Freud had written to Fliess the famous letter in which he reveals his "great secret"—that he has abandoned the seduction theory: "I no longer believe in my *neurotica*."[2] Persuaded by the surprising frequency with which such seductions by fathers of children seemed to occur in his patients, and by the fact that the unconscious contains no "indications of reality," he had determined that such acts were plausibly to be considered as fantasies rather than as personal history: "surely such widespread perversions against children are not very probable"; "in all the cases, the *father*, not excluding my own, had to be accused of being perverse."[3]

Reversing himself on so crucial a point, and in effect dismantling the theory he had counted on to bring him wealth and fame, Freud addresses himself, in the letter to Fliess, to his own emotions. He had expected to be "depressed, confused, exhausted,"[4] but he feels just the opposite. "It is strange, too, that no feeling of shame appeared."[5] In fact, he feels impelled to take a journey, and now proposes to visit his friend in Berlin. "If during this lazy period I were to go to the Northwest Station on Saturday evening I could be with you by noon on Sunday,"[6] or, if this does not suit their schedules, "do the same conditions obtain if I go straight to the Northwest Station on Friday evening?"[7]

The proposal for a visit is treated as a digression, from which Freud now recalls himself:

Now to continue my letter. I vary Hamlet's saying, "To be in readiness": to be cheerful is everything! I could indeed feel quite discontent. The expectation of eternal fame was so beautiful, as was that of certain wealth, complete independence, travels, and lifting the children above the severe worries that robbed me of my youth. Everything depended on whether or not hysteria would come out right. Now I can once again remain quiet and modest, go on worrying and saving.[8]

Yet this apparent digression, this detour via the Northwest Station, in fact takes him directly back to the subject: *Hamlet*, and the way in which "a real event" might make the unconscious understand the intentions of the hero. For in this passage Freud twice proposes a journey to the Northwest Station, a locus that suggests what is literally a new train of thought. It is Hamlet, of course, who announces that he is "but mad north-north-west" (2.2.374), feigning madness for a purpose. Freud's slip into the Northwest Station will likewise confirm that he is not "depressed, confused, exhausted; afflicted with shame," or "discontent," as he might be, but actually in control of his daydreams of fortune and independence, however he appears to the outside world. His letter to Fliess concludes with the hope that he will soon hear "How all of you are and whatever else is happening between heaven and earth."[9] "There are more things in heaven and earth, Horatio, / Than are dreamt of in your philosophy" (1.5.174–5), says Hamlet to his confidant, conceiving the plan to "put an antic disposition on" (180), to present himself as mad north-north-west. Fliess is an appropriate Horatio figure, idolized as a man of superior learning. But we may even hear a faint reminder of another passage from Shakespeare's play here, Hamlet's half-sardonic, half-serious self-accusation to Rosencrantz and Guildenstern: "I am very proud, revengeful, ambitious . . . What should such fellows as I do crawling between earth and heaven?" (3.1.124–9).

Freud's projected journey to the Northwest Station has about it something of the same quality as the Italian walk he describes in his essay on "The Uncanny" in which time after time he arrived at the same place, "recognizable by some particular landmark"[10]—a "factor of involuntary repetition which surrounds with an uncanny atmosphere what would otherwise be innocent enough, and forces upon us the idea of something fateful and inescapable where otherwise we should have spoken of 'chance' only."[11] The recognizable landmark here is both the railway terminus and *Hamlet*. When he came to write up his ideas about Hamlet for *The Interpretation of Dreams* (1900), Freud himself made the same connection, bringing the quotation to the surface:

> The prince in the play, who had to disguise himself as a madman, was behaving just as dreams do in reality; so that we can say of dreams what Hamlet says of himself, concealing the true circumstances under a cloak of wit and unintelligibility: "I am but mad north-north-west."[12]

Hamlet is a play not only informed *with* the uncanny but also informed *about* it. The Ghost is only the most explicit marker of uncanniness, the ultimate articulation of "uncertainty whether something is dead or alive."[13] In *Hamlet*, as we shall see, Shakespeare instates the uncanny as sharply as he does the Oedipus complex—or, to put the matter more precisely, Freud's concept of uncanniness finds as explicit an expression in the play as does his concept of the complicated sexual rivalry between father and son.

The essay on "The Uncanny," as we have already several times noted, goes out of its way to deny the status of Shakespearean ghosts *per se* as instances of this phenomenon. We have seen that *Hamlet* is the subtext for some of Freud's own self-analysis. It is also a powerful subtext for the essay on "The Uncanny," despite (or because of?) the explicit disavowals of the relevance of Shakespeare's ghosts. Thus the central literary work that provides Freud with his chief enabling example of uncanniness, Hoffmann's story "The Sand-Man," is described in terms that closely resemble the plot of *Hamlet*:

> In the story from Nathaniel's childhood, the figures of his father and Coppelius represent the two opposites into which the father-image is split by the ambivalence of the child's feeling: whereas the one threatens to blind him, that is, to castrate him, the other, the loving father, intercedes for his sight. That part of the complex which is most strongly expressed, the death-wish against the father, finds expression in the death of the good father, and Coppelius is made answerable for it.[14]

This division of the father into loving and threatening figures, one castrating and the other protecting, is accompanied by the presence of an apparently desirable young woman who turns out to be a mechanical creation of the bad father (Coppola / Coppelius) working in collusion with *her* supposed father, Professor Spalanzani: "But Olympia was an automaton whose works Spalanzani had made, and whose eyes Coppola, the Sand-Man, had put in."[15] This would be an unfairly reductive description of Ophelia, to be sure, but there are striking similarities in the structures of the two situations. In both the young woman is used as a bait or lure for a transaction involving the young man, the threatening father, and the "Professor," his colleague or accomplice. As a consequence of these events (the death of his father, the threats of the Sand-Man, the discovery of the girl-doll's true nature, the betrayal of the old men in league against him) the young student goes mad and kills himself.

Thus in not talking about *Hamlet* Freud is in a sense talking about *Hamlet*, and Hamlet's relationships with Claudius, Polonius, Ophelia, and the Ghost. Indeed the passage on the *non*applicability of the Shakespearean ghosts to the kind of uncertainty Freud calls "the uncanny" is introduced at precisely this point in his explication of "The Sand-Man," as a way of turning from the apparent but unimportant uncanniness of Olympia's status ("uncertainty whether an object is living or inanimate"[16]) to the centrality of the castration complex as figured in the Sand-Man's threat to put out Nathaniel's eyes.

Two kinds of things cause a sensation of uncanniness: beliefs that have been surmounted, and repressed complexes.

An uncanny experience occurs either when repressed infantile complexes have been revived by some impression, or when the primitive beliefs we have surmounted seem once more to be confirmed . . . these two classes of uncanny experience are not always sharply distinguishable. When we consider that primitive beliefs are most intimately connected with infantile complexes, and are, in fact, based upon them, we shall not be greatly astonished to find the distinction often rather a hazy one.[17]

The distinction between what has been repressed and what has been surmounted cannot be transposed onto the uncanny in fiction without profound modification; for the realm of phantasy depends for its very existence on the fact that its content is not submitted to the reality-testing faculty.[18]

Here we have returned to the distinction that Freud makes in his letter to Fliess rejecting the seduction theory, between what happened "in reality" and what happened in fantasy. In *Hamlet*, as I will want to suggest, such distinctions, insofar as they can be made, are presented in the guise of encapsulated artifacts, or what are often called "insets": the play within the play, the story of Old Hamlet's death ("sleeping within my orchard"—a dream? and if so, whose?), Ophelia's disturbingly knowledgeable ballads with their disconcerting sexual references, so ambiguously (and ambivalently) applicable to her father, brother, and lover.

But at the center of the question of uncanniness lies not only the castration complex but also the compulsion to repeat. "Whatever reminds us of this inner *repetition-compulsion* is perceived as uncanny."[19] Repetition, and the repetition compulsion, are figured throughout *Hamlet*: in the double play, dumbshow and dialogue, their double existence never satisfactorily explained despite the ingenuity of critics; in the Queen's two marriages, the twin husbands ("Look here upon this picture, and on this, / The counterfeit presentment of two brothers" [3.4.53–4]); in the double murder of fathers, Hamlet's father killed by Claudius, Laertes' father killed by Hamlet.

Every critical observation on doubling in the play, from the psychoanalytic ("the decomposing of the original villain into at least three father figures, the ghost, Polonius, and Claudius"; "The splitting of the hero into a number of brother figures: Fortinbras, Horatio, Laertes, and Rosencrantz-and-Guildenstern")[20] to the rhetorical ("the most pregnant and interesting of [the play's] linguistic doublings is undoubtedly hendiadys")[21] is an implicit commentary on the compulsion to repeat.

Moreover, *Hamlet* is a play that enacts the repetition compulsion even as it describes it. (1) The ghost of old Hamlet appears to young Hamlet and urges him to revenge; (2) the ghost of young Hamlet, "pale as his shirt," "with a look so piteous in purport / As if he had been loosed out of hell / To speak of horrors" (2.1.81–4) appears to Ophelia in her closet and, in dumbshow, raising a sigh both "piteous and profound" (94), returns from whence he has come; (3) the ghost of Ophelia, mad, appears before her brother Laertes and incites him to revenge for the death of their father Polonius.

What, indeed, is revenge but the dramatization and acculturation of the repetition compulsion?

The anamorphic ghost

The agent of repetition here, clearly, is the ghost. And what is a ghost? It is a memory trace. It is the sign of something missing, something omitted, something undone. It is itself at once a question, and the sign of putting things in question. Thus Barnardo, one of the officers on guard duty, suggests that "this portentous figure / Comes armed through our watch so like the King / That was and is the question of these wars" (*Hamlet* 1.1.112–14). Onstage, as in the plot of a tale or story, a ghost is the concretization of a missing presence, the sign of what is there by not being there. "'Tis here!" "'Tis here!" "'Tis gone!" cry the sentries (1.1.145–7).

Horatio's learned disquisition, reminding his onstage hearers and his offstage audience simultaneously of events in classical Rome and in Shakespeare's recent play *Julius Caesar*, offers an historical (and stage-historical) context for the ghost:

> In the most high and palmy state of Rome,
> A little ere the mightiest Julius fell,
> The graves stood tenantless and the sheeted dead
> Did squeak and gibber in the Roman streets. (1.1.116–19)

Horatio associates the appearance of a ghost with the death of Julius Caesar. Jacques Lacan associates it with the castration complex, the "veiled phallus":

> The hole in the real that results from loss, sets the signifier in motion. This hole provides the place for the projection of the missing signifier, which is essential to the structure of the Other. This is the signifier whose absence leaves the Other incapable of responding to your question, the signifier that can be purchased only with your own flesh and blood, the signifier that is essentially the veiled phallus . . . swarms of images, from which the phenomena of mourning rise, assume the place of the phallus: not only the phenomena in which each individual instance of madness manifests itself, but also those which attest to one or another of the most remarkable collective madnesses of the community of men, one example of which is brought to the fore in *Hamlet*, i.e., the ghost, that image which can catch the soul of one and all unawares when someone's departure from this life has not been accompanied by the rites that it calls for.[22]

What does it mean to say that the ghost takes the place of the missing signifier, the veiled phallus? The ghost—itself traditionally often veiled, sheeted, or shadowy in form—is a cultural marker of absence, a reminder of loss. Thus the very plot of *Hamlet* replicates the impossibility of the protagonist's quest: "the very source of what makes Hamlet's arm waver at every moment, is the narcissistic connection that Freud tells us about in his text on the decline of the Oedipus complex: one cannot strike the phallus, because the phallus, even the real phallus, is a *ghost*."[23]

Thus, not only is the ghost the veiled phallus, but the phallus is also a ghost. Lacan takes as his point of departure Freud's essay on "The Passing of the Oedipus Complex" (1925), which explores the dilemma of the child caught between his desires and his fear of castration. When the inevitable conflict arises between the child's narcissistic investment in his own body and the "libidinal cathexis of the parent-objects," writes Freud,

> the object-cathexes are given up and replaced by identification. The authority of the father or of the parents is introjected into the ego and there forms the kernel of the super-ego, which takes its severity from the father, perpetuates his prohibition against incest, and so insures the ego against a recurrence of the libinal object-cathexis.[24]

We might think that Freud's "super-ego" and Lacan's "Name-of-the-Father" would both be names for the Ghost in *Hamlet*. Yet this Lacan seems explicitly to deny when, writing on the subject of certainty in "The Unconscious and Repetition," he remarks on "the weight of the sins of the father, borne by the ghost in the myth of Hamlet, which Freud couples with the myth of Oedipus."

> The father, the Name-of-the-Father, sustains the structure of desire with the structure of the law—but the inheritance of the father is that which Kierkegaard designates for us, namely, his sin.
>
> Where does Hamlet's ghost come from, if not from the place from which he denounces his brother for surprising him and cutting him off in the full flower of his sins? And far from providing Hamlet with the prohibitions of the Law that would allow his desire to survive, this too ideal father is constantly being doubted.[25]

The Ghost is incompletely a representative of the Law, because both he and the tale he tells allow the son to doubt. He puts in question his own being as well as his message. Is he a spirit of health or goblin damn'd? Is this the real Law? Is this the truth? As long as the Law of the father is doubted or put in question, it cannot be (or is not) internalized, not assimilated into the symbolic, and therefore blocks rather than facilitates Hamlet's own passage into the symbolic, where he will find his desire. The finding of desire is the recognition of lack, the acceptance of castration. But the doubt Hamlet experiences gives him the idea that there is something left. "It is here," says Lacan, "that Freud lays all his stress—doubt is the support of his certainty."

He goes on to explain why: "this is precisely the sign," he says, "that there is something to preserve. Doubt, then, is a sign of *resistance*."[26]

To put the matter in a slightly different way: the Name-of-the-Father is the dead father. *This* father—the Ghost—isn't dead enough. The injunction to "Remember me" suggests that he is not quite dead. Hamlet must renounce him, must internalize the Law by forgetting, not by remembering. This is the only way he can be put in touch with his own desires, and with the symbolic.

But Hamlet is the poet of doubt. Polonius reads aloud to the King and Queen Hamlet's love poem to Ophelia, a paean to negation:

> Doubt thou the stars are fire,
> Doubt that the sun doth move,
> Doubt truth to be a liar,
> But never doubt I love. (2.2.115–18)

The meaning of "doubt" is itself in doubt as the phrase is repeated, shifting from something like "dispute" or "challenge" to "suspect" or "fear." The litany of doubt here is an invitation to put things in question, at the same time that it puts in question the whole procedure of putting something in question. When we consider, additionally, the very dubious "truth" value of the statement that "the stars are fire" and "the sun doth move"—both presumptions put in question by Renaissance science—we find that a verse that purports to assert certainty and closure in fact undermines that certainty in every gesture.

We should distinguish here between repression and foreclosure in the child's experience of the symbolic order. Repression (*Verdrängung*) submerges or covers over unconscious thoughts that foreclosure (*Verwerfung*) does not permit. In other words, foreclosure preempts the experiences that repression would conceal. For both Lacan and Freud, what makes the difference here is castration, or the acceptance of castration. If a child forecloses the idea of castration, he (or she) rejects the Name-of-the-Father in favor of the Desire-of-the-Mother. Rather than accepting the loss of the phallus, the child wishes to *be* the mother's phallus, the completion of her desire, thus rejecting the limits implied by castration: the Law of the Father, the network of social roles (language, kinship, prohibitions, gender roles) that make up what Lacan calls the symbolic order. Lacan calls this "the failure of the paternal metaphor,"[27] and predicts that the foreclosure of the Name-of-the-Father, of the constitution of the Law in the symbolic, can lead to psychosis, and to delusions.

> It is the lack of the Name-of-the-Father in that place which, by the hole that it opens up in the signified, sets off the cascade of reshapings of the signifier from which the increasing disaster of the imaginary proceeds, to the point at which the level is reached at which signifier and signified are stabilized in the delusional metaphor.
>
> But how can the Name-of-the-Father be called by the subject to the only place in which it

could have reached him and in which it has never been? Simply by a real father, not necessarily by the subject's own father, but by A-father.[28]

The failure of the paternal metaphor. This is not unrelated to what might be called paternal undecidability, or the undecidability of paternity—the fact, so often commented on in Shakespeare's plays, that the father is always a suppositional father, a father by imputation, rather than by unimpeachable biological proof. "I think this is your daughter," says Don Pedro to Leonato at the beginning of *Much Ado About Nothing*, and Leonato replies, "Her mother hath many times told me so" (1.1.97). (As if to underscore the point, Benedick interposes with interest, "Were you in doubt, sir, that you ask'd her?") Prospero speaks to the same paternal obsession when he replies to Miranda's question, "Thy mother was a piece of virtue, and / She said thou wast my daughter" (*The Tempest* 1.2.56–7). This doubt, on which paternity, legitimacy, inheritance, primogeniture, and succession all depend, is the anxiety at the root of the *cultural* failure of the paternal metaphor—that is, its failure because of its status as metaphor, its nontranslatability into the realm of proof.

And when the failure of the paternal metaphor is regarded, not from the standpoint of the father contemplating the horror of bastardy, but from the point of view of the son, we have the dilemma of Hamlet, who simultaneously seeks and denies the authority of the law, the imprint of the father, what he calls "thy commandment" and "my word," (1.5.102; 110)—the Ghost's word of command, "his speech, the word (*le mot*), let us say of his authority" the place reserved for "the Name-of-the-Father in the promulgation of the law."[29] The more the father is idealized, the more problematic is the presence of doubt, the gap in certainty that instates paternal undecidability:

> the ravaging effects of the paternal figure are to be observed with particular frequency in cases where the father really has the function of a legislator, or at least has the upper hand, whether in fact he is one of those fathers who make the laws or whether he poses as the pillar of the faith, as a paragon of integrity and devotion, as virtuous or as a virtuoso, by serving a work of salvation, of whatever object or lack of object, of nation or of birth, of safeguard or salubrity, of legacy or legality, of the pure, the impure or of empire, all ideals that provide him with all too many opportunities of being in a posture of undeserving, inadequacy, even of fraud, and, in short, of excluding the Name-of-the-Father from its position in the signifier.[30]

Confronted with an overplus, a superfluity of fathers (psychoanalytic readers all comment on the splitting of the father into Claudius, Polonius, even old Fortinbras and old Norway), Hamlet finds both too many fathers and too few—he is too much in the son, but where is paternity, where is the law? Displacing onto these easier targets complaints he is blocked from voicing to the Ghost (because the Ghost is his father? because the Ghost is a ghost? because the Ghost is dead? but he is not dead, otherwise he would not walk, and how can he be dead without ever really having been alive?), Hamlet encounters doubt. Indeed, as in the case of the Medusa, where a multiplicity of penises is imagined to cover the unimaginable horror of no penis, of castration, so here the multiplicity of fathers covers the fact of lack. Covers it, in *Hamlet*, by foreclosing rather than repressing it.

We have seen that Lacan, following Freud, sees doubt as the sign of resistance. The image that he chooses to describe this doubt in the case of dream narratives is that of the mark, spot, or stain: "that which marks, stains, spots the text of any dream communication—*I am not sure, I doubt*."[31]

The stain is the sign of uncertainty—of the fact that one cannot be certain. And this too seems to be the function of the spot or stain in *Hamlet*. When Hamlet challenges his mother in her bedroom to turn her eyes, her gaze, inward, she sees "such black and grained spots / As will not leave their tinct" (3.4.90–1). These spots are not certainties but gaps, doubts—what did she do? and why? Most centrally, in his soliloquy in Act 4 on thinking and "dull revenge," Hamlet says of himself, "How stand I then, / That have a father kill'd, a mother stain'd" (4.4.56–7), and the ambiguity of the grammatical construction is telling. He has a father who has been killed, a mother who has been stained—but by whom? Does he not also by the terms of this utterance assert, or acknowledge, that he has killed a father, stained a mother?

In his essay on *Hamlet*, Lacan thus concerns himself with Shakespeare's play as a remarkable example of the topology of human desire, "the drama of Hamlet as the man who has lost the way of his desire."[32] This is not the only case in which Lacan finds the way of his own theoretical desire by turning to a Renaissance artifact. On another occasion he examines one of the most striking of Renaissance paintings, a painting which has lately excited a good deal of commentary among literary theorists, Holbein's portrait of 1533 called *The Ambassadors*. The famous work, which contains a preeminent example of the optical device known as the anamorphosis, discloses another ghost.

> Begin by walking out of the room, in which no doubt it has long held your attention. It is then that, turning round as you leave—as the author of the *Anamorphoses* describes it—you apprehend in this form . . . What? A skull.[33]

The object half obscured beneath the feet of the ambassadors in the depiction of *vanitas*, the skull, cannot fail to remind us of the skull in *Hamlet*—which is itself, in Act 5, followed by what Lacan in fact identifies in the *Hamlet* essay as a *vanitas*: the objects wagered in the final duel scene, he writes, are "staked against death. This is what gives their presentation the character of, what is called a *vanitas* in the religious tradition."[34] Holbein's skull, which is not seen as a skull except from an exceptional or eccentric angle, is called "the phallic symbol, the anamorphic ghost."[35] Yet, Lacan insists, what we see here is "not the phallic symbol, the anamorphic ghost, but the gaze as such, in its pulsatile, dazzling and spread out function, as it is in this picture."[36] "Look here upon this picture, and on this" (3.4.53). "The King is a thing . . . of nothing" (4.2.27–9). The anamorphic ghost, the embedded, embodied, and distorted figure of a ghostly skull beneath the apparently solid feet of the ambassadors—what is this but an anamorphism of the ghost and the Ghost, the Ghost (once again, uncannily, inevitably) of Hamlet's father?

Lacan goes on:

> This picture is simply what any picture is, a trap for the gaze. In any picture, it is precisely in seeking the gaze in each of its points that you will see it disappear.[37]

"This picture is simply what any picture is, a trap for the gaze." What is *this* but the play-within, the "Mousetrap," "the image of a murder done in Vienna" (3.2.233–4). Long treated as a dramatic presentation that encodes misdirection, putting the real play in the audience, setting up Claudius and Gertrude as the real Player King and Player Queen, the "Mouse-trap," also known as "The Murder of Gonzago," appropriates the gaze and makes it the function of the play. Again Lacan's description (in *Four Concepts*) of *The Ambassadors* is apposite:

> In Holbein's picture I showed you at once—without hiding any more than usual—the singular object floating in the foreground, which is there to be looked at, in order to catch, I would almost say, *to catch in its trap*, the observer, that is to say us. . . . The secret of this picture is given at the moment when, moving slightly away, little by little, to the left, then turning around, we see what the magical floating object signifies. It reflects our own nothingness, in the figure of the death's head.[38]

> That is not how it is presented at first. . . . At the very heart of the period in which the subject emerged and geometral optics was an object of research, Holbein makes visible for us here something that is simply the subject as annihilated—annihilated in the form that is, strictly speaking, the imaged embodiment . . . of castration, which for us, centres the whole organization of the desires through the framework of the fundamental drives.[39]

Holbein's portrait shows "the subject as annihilated"—which is the subject of *Hamlet*, a play situated on the cusp of the emergence of what has come to be known as the modern subject.[40] For there is a way in which *Hamlet* performs the same operation as Holbein's painting upon the gaze and the trope of *vanitas*. Its final tableau of the death's head in the graveyard scene is another critique of the subject. What then is being caught in the trap Hamlet sets for the King, the King who is a thing of nothing? Is it Claudius who is caught in the "Mouse-trap," or Hamlet as the signifier of the modern subject, already marked by negation, already dressed in black?

Lacan's own theoretical fantasy of the distortion produced by an anamorphism is determinedly phallic:

> How is it that nobody has ever thought of connecting this with . . . the effect of an erection? Imagine a tattoo traced on the sexual organ *ad hoc* in the state of repose and assuming its, if I may say so, developed form in another state.
>
>   How can we not see here . . . something symbolic of the function of the lack, of the appearance of the phallic ghost?[41]

"My father, in his habit as he lived!" (3.4.137), "My father's spirit—in arms!" (1.2.255), "thou, dead corse, again in complete steel" (1.4.52). The anamorphic ghost of old Hamlet, erected to full form by the gaze, contrasts sharply with the same figure in the "state of repose," recumbent, passive, "sleeping within my orchard" (1.5.59), who receives the poison in the ear, the incestuous rape of a brother. The Ghost recounts the fantasy-nightmare of his own castration: "Thus was I, sleeping, by a brother's hand / Of life, of crown, of queen at once dispatch'd, / Cut off even in the blossoms of my sin" (1.5.74–6).

This is what Hamlet has already fantasized, what he recalls in his ejaculation, "O my prophetic soul!" (1.5.40). And as in the case of Julius Caesar, the dead man turned ghost is more powerful than he was when living, precisely because he crosses boundaries, is not only transgressive but *in* transgression, a sign simultaneously of limit and of the violation of that limit, the nutshell and the bad dreams. Thus the murder empowers the Ghost and his ghostly rhetoric, the language spoken in, by, and through the Name-of-the-Father. The Hyperion-father who obsesses Hamlet in his soliloquies and in his conversations with his mother is erected from this moment, from the moment of the father's absence and death, half-guiltily acknowledged as the son's desire. The castration fantasy of the sleeping father in the orchard enacts both Hamlet's desire and its repression, which are in this moment identical. Here again Lacan is suggestive, when he writes of the impossibility of not wanting to desire:

> what does *not wanting to desire* mean? The whole of analytic experience—which merely gives form to what is for each individual at the very root of his experience—shows us that not to want to desire and to desire are the same thing.
>
>   To desire involves a defensive phase that makes it identical with not wanting to desire. Not wanting to desire is wanting not to desire.[42]

This is the condition in which we encounter Hamlet for much of the play, the condition of desiring not to desire. Look where his desires have gotten him—or not gotten him. He walks out of Ophelia's closet and into Gertrude's. Here again we have closet drama, and of a high order—plays not meant to be acted. Hamlet's accusation of his mother catches her in the trap set for the gaze: "O Hamlet, speak no more! /

Thou turn'st mine eyes into my very soul, / And there I see such black and grained spots / As will not leave their tinct" (3.4.88–91). The black spot she sees is Hamlet, Hamlet as marker, Hamlet as floating signifier, as his blackness becomes metonymically a sign of mourning, of negation, of absence, of the impossible desire to tell the difference between desire and the repression of desire.

What would your gracious figure?

The ghostly phallus as anamorphosis—that is, as *form*—assumes a certain visibility, however veiled. The Name-of-the-Father, on the other hand, is a function of the signifier, of language as a system of signs rather than shapes. As we shall see, the ghost— in *Hamlet*, as well as in a number of other literary guises—presents itself not only as a trap for the gaze but also a trope for the voice.

In an influential essay on prosopopeia as the "fiction of the voice-from-beyond-the-grave," Paul de Man writes:

> It is the figure of prosopopeia, the fiction of an apostrophe to an absent, deceased, or voiceless entity, which posits the possibility of the latter's reply, and confers upon it the power of speech. Voice assumes mouth, eye, and finally face, a chain that is manifest in the etymology of the trope's name, *prosopon poiein*, to confer a mask or a face (*prosopon*). Prosopopeia is the trope of autobiography, by which one's name, as in the Milton poem, is made as intelligible and memorable as a face. Our topic deals with the giving and taking away of faces, with face and deface, *figure*, figuration and disfiguration.[43]

The quotation from Milton with which de Man is here concerned is, perhaps inevitably, the sonnet "On Shakespeare" as cited and discussed in Wordsworth's *Essays Upon Epitaphs*. De Man singles out the thirteenth and fourteenth lines of this sixteen-line sonnet for special commentary.

> Then thou our fancy of itself bereaving
> Dost make us marble with too much conceiving.

Here de Man observes that the phrase "dost make us marble," in the *Essays Upon Epitaphs*, "cannot fail to evoke the latent threat that inhabits prosopopeia, namely that by making the dead speak, the symmetrical structure of the trope implies, by the same token, that the living are struck dumb, frozen in their own death."[44]

Milton's sonnet "On Shakespeare" is dated 1630, and was published in the Second Folio of Shakespeare's Plays in 1632. Merritt Y. Hughes speculates that "Milton's questionable date, 1630, suggests that the poem was written some time before its publication, possibly with the expectation that the Stratford monument instead of the Droeshout portrait would be represented as the frontispiece of the

Folio."[45] Thus the reference to "Marble," as well as the "piled Stones" of line 2, the "Monument" of line 8 and the "Tomb" of line 16 would be pertinent to the memorial occasion, and to the illustration accompanying the memorial verses. "Dost make us Marble," as Hughes also points out in a note, closely resembles the apostrophe to Melancholy in *Il Penseroso*, who is urged to "Forget thyself to Marble" (1.42). In the sonnet, however—and this is part of de Man's point—it is the spectator, the reader, the mourner who becomes marble. As Michael Riffaterre comments, paraphrasing de Man's argument:

> Chiasmus, the symmetrical structure of prosopopeia, entails that, by making the dead speak, the living are struck dumb—they too become the monument. Prosopopeia thus stakes out a figural space for the chiasmic interpretation: either the subject will take over the object, or it will be penetrated by the object.[46]

But in the case of the Stratford monument (or indeed, though less neatly, the Droeshout portrait), this exchange of properties has already taken place. The voice of the dead Shakespeare pictured on the tomb (and in the sonnet) speaks through the plays that succeed them in the Folio.

Moreover, the same exchange has been prefigured and depicted in Shakespeare's plays themselves, most straightforwardly—if such a figuration is ever straightforward—in *The Winter's Tale*, where a statue comes to life and speaks. The awakening of Hermione, a true animation of the uncanny, is prepared for by a moment in the scene that precedes it, when an anonymous Third Gentleman reports the wonderment of the court at the reunion of King Leontes and his lost daughter Perdita. At the relation of the Queen's death, he reports, Perdita was so moved that "Who was most marble, there changed colour" (5.2.89–90). The intimation is the more pointed because of the specific moment at which it occurs in the narrative—"the relation of the Queen's death"—and it sets up, in dramatic terms, the mysterious finale, the revelation of a truth not known to the audience: that Hermione is alive.

The awakening of the Queen itself takes the form of apostrophe, as Leontes, Perdita, and Paulina all address the "dear stone" and offer to join her in her inanimate fate: "does not the stone rebuke me / For being more stone than it? O royal piece! / There's magic in thy majesty, which has / My evils conjur'd to remembrance, and / From thy admiring daughter took the spirits, / Standing like stone with thee" (5.3.37–42). Here a trope familiar from lyric "comes to life," as it were, in drama, and there occurs a double uncanniness. As the statue of Hermione moves and speaks, the figure of prosopopeia likewise comes alive.

The trope of the living and speaking statue, posing the question of "whether an object is living or inanimate"[47] as does the "statue of Hermione" is certainly not unique to Shakespeare. To broaden the context of this discussion of uncanny authority, I will here briefly wander through a larger sculpture garden of ghostly animation.

Molière's *Dom Juan, ou Le Festin de Pierre*, first acted in 1665,[48] includes a particularly "scandalous" (in Shoshana Felman's sense) example of the trope of the talking stone. Molière's subtitle depends on a punning doubleness in "Pierre," which means both "stone" and "Peter," the name of the Commander whose statue walks and talks in *El burlador de Sevilla y Convidado de Piedra*—a play by the Spaniard Tirso de Molina published in 1632, which was the principal source for *Dom Juan*. Molière's statue has no name—it is described as "the Statue of the Commander" in the list of *dramatis personae*, and is addressed formally by both Dom Juan and Sganarelle as "Your Excellency the Commander." In Molière's play the statue first "comes to life" in Act 3 when it nods in response to an invitation to dine with Dom Juan, then returns the compliment in Act 4, inviting Dom Juan to dinner, to the "stone feast" of the subtitle.

When it appears in Mozart's *Don Giovanni*, and especially in Peter Shaffer's recent drama on the life of Mozart, *Amadeus*, the statue becomes a reproving father, a revenger of his own death, a superego looming enormous over the philandering Dom Juan and bearing him off to hell. In Mozart's opera, with libretto by Lorenzo da Ponte, the Commendatore is killed by Don Giovanni when he discovers Giovanni attempting to seduce his daughter.[49] In Act 2 of the opera, the statue speaks, predicting Giovanni's death. The servant Leporello thinks its voice comes from another world, but Giovanni assumes it to be that of a mortal antagonist, and strikes out with his sword. The inscription on the statue proclaims its purpose of vengeance. When the statue nods, twice, in response to the invitation to supper tended by Leporello, Giovanni demands that it speak: "Speak if you can! Shall I see you at supper?" The statue answers affirmatively, and duly appears—accompanied by the portentous music of the Overture—in Giovanni's house, inviting Giovanni to sup with him in turn, and no longer seeking revenge, but rather repentance. Giovanni accepts the dinner invitation, but refuses to repent, and is engulfed in flames.

The statue is referred to several times in this act as "the stone man," and Leporello seems to draw attention to its stoniness and that of Giovanni when he remarks to Donna Elvira that his master "has a heart of stone." When it disappears, the statue of the Commendatore is also, interestingly, described as a ghost, as Donna Elvira concludes that "It is surely the ghost I met," when she left Giovanni's house, having failed—like the statue—to persuade him to repent.

In this version, the Commendatore is a punishing father figure, but specifically the father of a woman betrayed by the hero. Killed by inadvertence (as is Polonius, who occupies a similar paternal role), he reappears in the plot as an undecidable apparition who is read differently by the two spectators, Giovanni and Leporello. For all his differences from them, Leporello is in something of the place of Horatio and the sentries, crediting the other-worldly origin of the spectre, and eliciting only gesture —not language—from his invitation. Giovanni demands speech, responds to his intercourse with the statue with bravado, and is then disconcerted by a second visit.

The transferential mention of the "heart of stone," which is attributed not to the Commendatore, who is literally a stone man, but to Don Giovanni, who behaves like one, may remind us of Hermione and Leontes ("does not the stone rebuke me / For being more stone than it?" [*The Winter's Tale* 5.3.37–8]) and also of the language of *Othello* as characterized by Stanley Cavell:

> As he is the one who gives out lies about her, so he is the one who will give her a stone heart for her stone body, as if in his words of stone which confound the figurative and literal there is the confounding of the incantations of poetry and magic. He makes of her the thing he feels ("my heart is turned to stone" [4.1.178]). . . .[50]

An analogous transference is arguably taking place in *Hamlet*, as the son imputes to the Ghost commands and wishes he would like to receive from the father, and which have the dual authority of concurring with (because they personate) his own desires, and presenting themselves as externally (and paternally) motivated instructions, imposed *upon* rather than *by* the ambivalently situated son. Hamlet's word for this stony instruction is the appropriately chosen "commandment" ("thy commandment all alone shall live / Within the book and volume of my brain" [1.5.102–3]). As Moses received the stone tablets of the law, so Hamlet sets down in his tables the words he hears from—or the words he gives to—the Ghost.

There are some grounds for arguing a connection between Mozart and *Hamlet*. Mozart attended a production of *Hamlet* staged by a touring company in Salzburg in 1780, and subsequently wrote to his father, "If the speech of the Ghost in *Hamlet* were not so long, it would be far more effective." In calculating the effect of a subterranean ghostly voice in the theater—in this case for *Idomeneo*—he was concerned that the dramatic intervention be unearthly:

> Picture to yourself the theatre, and remember that the voice must be terrifying—must penetrate—that the audience must believe that it really exists. Well, how can this effect be produced if the speech is too long, for in this case the listeners will become more and more convinced that it means nothing. If the speech of the Ghost in *Hamlet* were not so long, it would be far more effective.[51]

In 1789 a German newspaper, reviewing a performance of *Don Giovanni*, commented that "Mozart seems to have learned the language of ghosts from Shakespeare—a hollow, sepulchral tone seemed to rise from the earth; it was as though the shades of the departed were seen to issue from their resting-places."[52] The comparison has also appealed to the imagination of modern Mozart scholars. William Gresser compares *Don Giovanni* Act 2 scene 7 explicitly to *Hamlet*, remarking on the problem of temporality in Mozart's second act, and on the belief that a ghost could only walk between midnight and dawn.[53]

Peter Shaffer's *Amadeus* points out the parallel. News of the death of Mozart's stern father Leopold is brought to him by two "venticelli," two "little winds," purveyors of gossip and rumor. Salieri, who is with Mozart at the time, consoles him with words that closely resemble Claudius' to Hamlet ("Do not despair. Death is inevitable, my friend")[54] and promptly transforms himself into a father substitute, opening his arms "in a wide gesture of paternal benevolence," as Mozart, eluding this embrace, falls on his knees and cries "Papa!" "So rose the Ghost Father in *Don Giovanni*!" comments Salieri, as the scene closes. The next scene (2.9) begins with "the two grim chords which open the overture to *Don Giovanni*," and which also accompany on the stage "the silhouette of a giant black figure, in cloak and tricorne hat. It extends its arms menacingly and engulfingly, toward its begetter"—that is, toward Mozart. And Salieri comments to the audience, as if completing his previous thought, "A father more accusing than any in opera."[55]

Mozart reports to Salieri that his wife thinks he's mad, and that he thinks so too. He has seen a "Figure in [his] dreams" (2.13) gray and masked, who instructed him "Take up your pen and write a Requiem" (2.17). And Salieri costumes himself, deliberately, in a cloak and mask of gray, "as—the Messenger of God!" "as the Figure of his dreams! [*Urging*] 'Come!—Come!—Come! . . .'" (2.15):

> Salieri: He stood swaying, as if he would faint off into death. But suddenly—incredibly—he realized all his little strength, and in a clear voice called down to me their words out of his opera *Don Giovanni*, inviting the statue to dinner.
> Mozart: [*Pushing open the "window"*] *O statua gentilissima, venite a cena!* [*He beckons in his turn*]
> Salieri: For a moment one terrified man looked at another. Then—unbelievably—I found myself nodding, just as in the opera. Starting to move across the street! [*The rising and falling scale passage from the Overture to Don Giovanni sounds darkly, looped in sinister repetition. To this hollow music Salieri marches slowly upstage.*] Pushing down the latch of his door—stamping up the stairs with stone feet. There was no stopping it. *I was in his dreams!*[56]

Shaffer, in describing the masked apparition, writes that "he was not a crudely melodramatic figure—a spooky, improbable Messenger of Death—but a more poetic and dangerous apparition, a messenger from God stepping out of Mozart's confessed dreams."[57]

From this father–son encounter, with its reminder of the way the father can personate both Death and the Law, we are led back to *Hamlet*, as Freud's walk through the provincial town in Italy led unerringly, and uncannily, back to the quarter inhabited by prostitutes. In his discussion of the Oedipus complex Freud stresses the fact that *Hamlet* was "written immediately after the death of Shakespeare's father (in 1601), that is, under the immediate impact of his bereavement and, we may well assume, while his childhood feelings about his father had been freshly revived."[58] Freud adds that Shakespeare had lost his own son, Hamnet, at an early age, and thus was in a double position of bereavement, a son mourning a father and a father mourning a son. (This, of course, is the doubled situation Joyce describes in *Ulysses*, and the occasion for the remarkable discussion of *Hamlet* in that novel: "Gravediggers bury Hamlet *père* and Hamlet *fils*. A king and a prince at last in death, with incidental music.")[59]

Hermione and the Commander—two stony "statues," both taken as monuments to (and representations of) the dead, the dead parent. One "statue" actually made of stone that nods and speaks, inviting a friend to supper, the other "statue" deservedly enrobed in its quotation marks, since it is actually the queen herself, Hermione masquerading as a statue, condemned to the "fate of stone" by her husband's skepticism. As Stanley Cavell remarks, "One can see this as the projection of his own sense of numbness, of living death . . . the man's refusal of knowledge of his other is an imagination of stone."[60] The Ghost in *Hamlet* resembles both of these monumental figures. Like them, he is specifically associated with the "fate of stone," with the marble sepulchre. "Tell," pleads Hamlet,

> Why thy canoniz'd bones, hearsed in death,
> Have burst their cerements, why the sepulchre
> Wherein we saw thee quietly inurn'd
> Hath op'd his ponderous and marble jaws
> To cast thee up again. (1.4.47–51)

The sudden animation of the monument, opening "his ponderous and marble jaws," underscores the uncanniness of the apparition which is not itself a statue but is, nonetheless, a similarly idealizing representation. And the key question about this apparition, as about the others, is whether it will speak.

The statue of the Commander in Molière first nods, startling the servant Sagnarelle, and subsequently speaks to Dom Juan, inviting him to supper. The final test for Hermione is articulated by Camillo: "If she pertain to life, let her speak too!" (*The Winter's Tale* 5.3.113). The question of whether the Ghost will speak is a central preoccupation of the whole first Act of *Hamlet*, and has a great deal to do with the way it is described and addressed. "It would be spoke to," says Barnardo. Horatio, as a "scholar," is asked to do the job. Popular belief had it that "A ghost has not the power to speak till it has been first spoken to; so that, notwithstanding the urgency of the business on which it may come, everything must stand still till the person visited can find sufficient courage to speak to it."[61] Horatio valiantly tries to interview it on two occasions in scene 1, urged on by Marcellus' apt invitation, "Question it, Horatio":

> *Horatio*:   What art thou that usurp'st this time of night,
>   Together with that fair and warlike form
>   In which the majesty of buried Denmark
>   Did sometimes march? By heaven I charge thee speak.
> *Marcellus*: It is offended.
> *Barnardo*:   See, it stalks away.
> *Horatio*:   Stay. Speak. Speak. I charge thee speak.
>   *Exit Ghost* (1.1.49–54)

> *Horatio*:   Stay, illusion:
>   If thou hast any sound or use of voice,
>   Speak to me.
>   If there be any good thing to be done
>   That may to thee do ease, and grace to me,
>   Speak to me;
>   If thou art privy to thy country's fate,
>   Which, happily, foreknowing may avoid,
>   O speak;
>   Or if thou hast uphoarded in thy life
>   Extorted treasure in the womb of earth,
>   For which they say your spirits oft walk in death,
>   Speak of it, stay and speak. (1.1.130–42)

The cock crows, and though Barnardo thinks "it was about to speak," it starts away. We may notice that the constant pronoun here is *it*, not *he*, and that the "apparition" is carefully described as "*like* the King," as one who "usurp'st" the time of the night (a loaded word in the circumstances) and the "fair and warlike form" of the dead King, "buried Denmark," was wont to appear. "It" = King Hamlet. "It" is a space of conjecture, to be questioned. But the proof is to come, with the imparting of this tale to "young Hamlet." "For upon my life," says Horatio, "this spirit, dumb to us, will speak to him" (175).

Cautiously, we may return to de Man's definition of prosopopeia, the master trope, the trope of tropes: "the fiction of the voice-from-beyond-the-grave,"[62] "the fiction of an apostrophe to an absent, deceased, or voiceless entity, which posits the possibility of the latter's reply, and confers upon it the power of speech."[63] This description not only coincides with the dramatic circumstances of the first scene of

Hamlet, it exemplifies it. "Our topic deals with the giving and taking away of faces, with face and deface, *figure*, figuration and disfiguration.[64]

When Hamlet is informed by Horatio of the appearance of "a figure like your father" (1.2.199) he asks, inevitably, "Did you not speak to it?" But the other question, on which he is curiously insistent, is whether the sentries saw the apparition's *face*: "saw you not his face?" "look'd he, frowningly?" "Pale, or red?" "And fix'd his eyes upon you?" (228–33). We know that the Elizabethans often used *its* and *his* interchangeably but still there is something striking about Hamlet's recurrent use of *he* and *his* after all the *its* of scene 1. Hamlet himself will return to the neuter pronoun after this exchange ("Perchance 'twill walk again" [243]; "If it assume my noble father's person / I'll speak to it" [244–45]) so that the brief gendering of the figure comes as a moment of achieved personating or animation, to be followed by a return to the objectification of *it*, which, as the *OED* tells us, is used "now only of things without life." Is the Ghost animate or inanimate? Certainly it is animated—but the he / it distinction marks an act of naming that is an act of choice, confirmed when Hamlet sees the Ghost face to face:

> *Horatio*:   Look, my lord, it comes.
> *Hamlet*: Angels and ministers of grace defend us!
>   Be thou a spirit of health or goblin damn'd,
>   Bring with thee airs from heaven or blasts from hell,
>   Be thy intents wicked or charitable,
>   Thou com'st in such a questionable shape
>   That I will speak to thee. I'll call thee Hamlet,
>   King, father, royal Dane. O, answer me.
>   (1.4.38–45)

Critical attention has usually been focused on the spirit / goblin, heaven / hell problem here—is this a false ghost or a true ghost, a delusion or a sign? But what seems equally central is the structure of address. Hamlet *chooses* to name the Ghost with those names which are for him most problematical: King, father, royal Dane.[65]

Hamlet addresses the "questionable shape" and brings it to speech, and therefore to a kind of life. Does he, in doing so, fulfill de Man's dire prophecy: "the latent threat that inhabits prosopopeia, namely that by making the dead speak, the symmetrical structure of the trope implies, by the same token, that the living are struck dumb, frozen in their own death?"[66]

In the fiction of address, what Jonathan Culler suggestively terms "this sinister reciprocity"[67] is always present *as* a threat. But if it is latent in lyric, it may become manifest in drama, and in *Hamlet* it does. *This* is the nature of revenge in *Hamlet*, the unremitting demand of the Ghost, leading to Hamlet's final paradoxical declaration,

"I am dead." De Man elsewhere points out that "the object of the apostrophe is only addressed in terms of the activity that it provokes in the addressing subject."[68] Our attention is focused on the *speaker*. Culler interestingly comments on this argument that "apostrophe involves a drama of 'the one mind's modifications,'"[69] and I would like to take his metaphor here seriously—for it is precisely a *dramatic* situation that is produced by this structure of address, which is why it is plausible to say that Hamlet constructs his own Ghost, makes use of the "gracious figure" of his father by utilizing the equally gracious figure of prosopopeia. Since apostrophe and prosopopeia so often involve a sensation of loss (not only in the post-Enlightenment lyric as observed by commentators like de Man, Culler, and Hartman, but in the elegaic tradition and the epitaphic texts of the Renaissance), the fiction of address itself performs a paradoxical function, not unlike that performed by Hamlet's "I am dead": it instates that which it mourns, makes present that which it declares absent and lost. "The poem," says Culler, "denies temporality in the very phrases—recollections—that acknowledge its claims," the narrator can "find, in his poetic ability to invoke [the mourned object] as a transcendent presence, a sense of his own transcendent continuity."[70] This is the transaction that takes place in *Hamlet*. "I am dead" and "I am alive to contemplate and mourn—and avenge—the dead" coexist in the same sensibility, in the same moment of naming. And this capacity, on the part of apostrophe and prosopopeia, is, exactly, *dramatic*: "Apostrophe is not the representation of an event; if it works, it produces a fictive, discursive event."[71] In *Hamlet* (as in *The Winter's Tale*) the effect of the dramatic mode is to dis-figure the trope of address to a dead or inanimate object, and ventriloquize its response as part of the ongoing dramatic action. "Marry, how tropically!" (*Hamlet* 3.2.237–8) The Ghost is not—or not only—an instance of the unmetaphoring[72] of prosopopeia. It is also the *manifestation* of that "latent threat" implicit in the trope itself. The rhetorical figure ("a figure like your father," 1.2.199), under the operation of the uncanny, comes to life, is dis- or un-figured ("then saw you not his face," 1.2.229), and exacts its sinister reciprocity: "that the living are . . . frozen in their own death."[73]

Begging the question

Uncanny reciprocity is thus created by the transference of death to the living and voice to the dead. But what does the dead voice say? What kind of commandment does the ghostly father in *Hamlet* hand down?

The Ghost's commandment comes in the form of a double imperative: "Remember me!" and "revenge!" What I will attempt to demonstrate here is that this double imperative is in fact a double bind. But first, a look at the first part of the commandment, the imperative to remember.

Hamlet is indeed a play obsessively concerned with remembering and forgetting. Not only does the Ghost in his first appearance call upon Hamlet to "Remember me," and provoke his son to take that "commandment" as his "word" (1.5.91–110); when he appears again in the Queen's closet he makes the same demand, this time in the negative: "Do not forget." (3.4.110). Claudius, the new King, acknowledges that "Though yet of Hamlet our dear brother's death / The memory be green" (1.2.1–2) and a fit circumstance for grief, yet insists that "we with wisest sorrow think on him / Together with remembrance of ourselves" (6–7). Hamlet, in soliloquy, is pained by the memory of his mother's passionate attachment to his father: "Heaven and earth, / Must I remember? Why, she would hang on him / As if increase of appetite had grown / By what it fed on" (1.2.142–5). And "O God, a beast that wants discourse of reason / Would have mourn'd longer" (150–1). In a sardonic mood he laments the frailty of memory two months after his father's death (and his mother's remarriage):

> O heavens, die two months ago and not forgotten yet! Then there's hope a great man's memory may outlive his life half a year. But by'r lady a man must build churches then, or else shall a suffer not thinking on, with the hobby-horse, whose epitaph is 'For O, for O, the hobby-horse is forgot'. (3.2.128–33)[74]

When he comes to her closet, Gertrude, chiding him for his flippancy, asks "Have you forgot me?" and receives a stinging reply: "No, by the rood, not so. / You are the Queen, your husband's brother's wife, / And, would it were not so, you are my mother" (3.4.13–15). When in the same scene, after the Ghost's injunction: "Do not forget!" Hamlet reminds her that he must go to England, she answers, "Alack, / I had forgot" (201).

Ophelia herself is constantly associated with the need to remember. Laertes urges her to "remember well" (1.3.84) his cautions about Hamlet's untrustworthiness as a suitor, and she answers that "'Tis in my memory lock'd" (85). In the scene where she is "loosed" to Hamlet in the lobby he says to her, "Nymph, in thy orisons / Be all my sins remember'd" (3.1.89–90) and she offers him "remembrances of yours / That I have longed long to re-deliver" (93–4). Her next offerings of remembrance will be the flower-giving, when she gives her brother "rosemary, that's for remembrance—pray / you, love, remember. And there is pansies, that for / thoughts" (4.5.173–5). "A document in madness: thoughts and remembrance fitted," he concludes (4.5.176–7).

Forgetting, and especially forgetting oneself, is closely connected to manners, but also to something more. Hamlet greets Horatio, whom he has not seen since

Wittenberg, with "Horatio, or I do forget myself" (1.2.161). Much later in the play
he apologizes for grappling with Laertes: "I am very sorry, good Horatio, / That to
Laertes I forgot myself; / For by the image of my cause I see / The portraiture of his"
(5.2.75–8). At the beginning of Act 5 scene 2 he takes up his tale of the voyage
to England, checking to see if Horatio "remember[s] all the circumstance" (2).
"Remember it, my lord!" Horatio exclaims (3). Hamlet describes the moment on
shipboard when he opened Claudius's death warrant, "making so bold, / My fears
forgetting manners, to unseal / Their grand commission" (5.2.16–18), and comments
on his pretense of aristocratic carelessness: "I once did hold it, as our statists do, / A
baseness to write fair, and labor'd much / How to forget that learning, but, sir, now /
It did me yeman's service" (5.2.33–6). "Antiquity forgot, custom not known"
(4.5.104), the rabble call for Laertes to be king. Hamlet presses Osric to forego
courtesy and to put his hat back on his head: "I beseech you / remember" (5.2.103–
4). Hamlet's dying request is for Horatio to tell his story, and in the final moments
Fortinbras asserts that he has "some rights of memory in this kingdom" (394) which,
with the support of Hamlet's "dying voice," he is now prepared to claim.

Recent critical discussions of the two Hegelian terms for memory, *Erinnerung*
and *Gedächtnis*, can shed light on the problem we are considering, the relationship
between memory and revenge. Initiated by Paul de Man in an essay on "Sign and
Symbol in Hegel's *Aesthetics*,"[75] the discourse on memory has since developed in a
number of provocative directions.[76]

Erinnerung ("recollection"), as de Man defines it, after Hegel, is "the inner gathering and preserving of experience,"[77] while *Gedächtnis* ("memory") is "the learning
by rote of *names*, or of words considered as names, and it can therefore not be
separated from the notation, the inscription, or the writing down of these names. In
order to remember, one is forced to write down what one is likely to forget."[78]

How can this distinction help us to understand the complexity of Hamlet's
mandate to turn his mourning into revenge?

When Hamlet first appears on stage, he is beset by *Erinnerung*, interiorizing
recollection, the consciousness of loss. Loss is what he thinks he *has*—not just "the
trappings and the suits of woe," but "that within which passes show" (1.2.85–6). He
will not relinquish this memory, which he hugs to himself. Claudius has a number of
motives for calling his "obstinate condolement" "a course / Of impious stubbornness"
(1.2.93–4), but he is not altogether wrong. Loss is what Hamlet has instead of both
mother and father—and loss is what he must lose, or learn to live with.

Freud describes such immersion, when it reaches the state of melancholia, as a kind
of fetishization, a privatizing and husbanding of grief, a refusal to let go.[79] In Hamlet this
condition is exemplified by the first soliloquy, "O that this too too sullied flesh would

melt" (1.2.129–58), with its longing for dissolution, its flirtation with self-slaughter, and its fragmented and particularized memory of both his father and his mother.

The encounter with the Ghost disrupts his absorption in the past as recollection. Abruptly Hamlet is wrenched from *Erinnerung* to *Gedächtnis*, from symbol to sign, or, to use de Man's terms, from symbol to allegory. From this point forward he is compelled to constitute the past by memorization, by inscription, by writing down:

> Remember thee!
> Ay, thou poor ghost, whiles memory holds a seat
> In this distracted globe. Remember thee!
> Yea, from the table of my memory
> I'll wipe away all trivial fond records,
> All saws of books, all forms, all pressures past
> That youth and observation copied there,
> And thy commandment all alone shall live
> Within the book and volume of my brain,
> Unmix'd with baser matter. Yes, by heaven!
> O most pernicious woman!
> O villain, villain, smiling, damned villain!
> My tables. Meet it is I set it down
> That one may smile, and smile, and be a villain—
> At least I am sure it may be so in Denmark.
>   [*Writes.*]
> So, uncle, there you are. Now to my word.
> It is, 'Adieu, adieu! remember me.'
> I have sworn't. (1.5.95–112)

The "tables" of Act I scene 5 are writing tables, somewhat like Freud's "Mystic Writing-Pad,"[80] which is, in turn, somewhat like the operations of memory as inscription of memory, *Gedächtnis*. Polonius alludes to a similar kind of table when he repudiates the role of "desk or table-book" (2.2.136) in his conversation with the Queen, announcing that he could not, like such inanimate objects, merely remain "mute and dumb" (137) when he learned of Hamlet's overmastering love for Ophelia. Polonius' choice of mute and dumb objects is suggestive, since both desk and table-book are surfaces for writing. His refusal to "play" the desk or table-book denies the possibility of prosopopeia, of a speaking record. Thus while Polonius declines to be such a table, Hamlet takes dictation from the Ghost so as to carry about with him the transcribed and inscribed "word," whether his "tables" are tables of wax, of paper, or of memory.[81]

The writing tables, then, must take the place of another kind of "table" in *Hamlet*, the table at which one eats and drinks, the kind of table associated not with *Gedächtnis* but with *Erinnerung*. For the language of *Erinnerung*, of interiorization, in this play is the language of digestion, of eating: "the funeral bak'd meats / Did coldly furnish forth the marriage tables" (1.2.180–1); "Heaven and earth, / Must I remember? Why, she would hang on him / As if increase of appetite had grown / By what it fed on" (142–5). Even the famous soliloquy on the sullied-sallied-solid flesh, the wish that the flesh would "melt, / Thaw and resolve itself into a dew" (1.2.129–30) reflects this burden of interiorization. Hamlet, unable either to escape or to complete the desired *Erinnerung*, is caught between cannibalism and anorexia, spewing forth in language what he cannot swallow,[82] taunting Claudius with a reminder of "how a king may go a / progress through the guts of a beggar" (4.3.30–1). Caught, that is, until he is catapulted into an even more difficult trap by the double pull of the paternal imperative, an imperative so indigestible that it must be written down. The feast, like the one to which the Commander invites Dom Juan, is a feast of stone.[83]

Jacques Derrida, writing on memory and mourning, writing in memory of and in mourning for Paul de Man, suggests that *Gedächtnis* and *Erinnerung* are central to "the possibility of mourning," and that "the inscription of memory" is "an effacement of interiorizing recollection."[84] In the "tables" speech, Hamlet limns precisely the efface-ment of *Erinnerung by Gedächtnis*. By writing down the Ghost's "commandment" he both inscribes and constitutes the paternal story of a past which, in its pastness, is necessarily fictive, since it is only experienced *as* past, as tale, as narrative. Thus Derrida writes,

> for Paul de Man, great thinker and theorist of memory, there is only memory but, strictly speaking, the past does not exist. It will never have existed in the present, never been present, as Mallarmé says of the present itself: "*un présent n'existe pas.*" The allegation of its supposed "anterior" presence *is* memory, and is the origin of all allegories. If a past does not literally exist, no more does death, only mourning, and that other allegory, including all the figures of death with which we people the "present," which we inscribe (among ourselves, the living) in every trace (otherwise called "survivals"): those figures strained toward the future across a fabled present, figures we inscribe because they can outlast us, beyond the present of their inscription: signs, words, names, letters, this whole text whose legacy-value, as we know "in the present," is trying its luck and advancing, *in advance* "in memory of . . ."[85]

Derrida's allusion to Mallarmé is pertinent, for Mallarmé was a great admirer of Shakespeare's *Hamlet*, describing it as *la pièce que je crois celle par excellence*, "what I consider to be *the* play."[86] And for Mallarmé Hamlet is already a ghost.

> *L'adolescent évanoui de nous aux commencements de la vie et qui hantera les esprits hauts ou pensifs par le deuil qu'il se plaît à porter, je le reconnais, qui se débat sous le mal d'apparaître.*
>
> [That adolescent who vanished from us at the beginning of life and who will always haunt lofty, pensive minds with his mourning, I recognize him struggling against the curse of having to appear.[87]]

We may notice not only his word *hantera*, "will haunt," but also the verb tenses in this passage: Hamlet "vanished," "will always haunt," "I recognize him," "struggling to appear." In this sentence, too, Hamlet himself is never present, is always a trace or an anticipation, haunting Mallarmé and other readers, other audiences.[88] He struggles not only against the curse of having to appear, but also with the very difficulty of appearing (*le mal d'apparaître*); in this too he is like a ghost, like the Ghost. Mallarmé's Hamlet is thus just what Derrida describes: "a figure strained toward the future across a fabled present." What makes Mallarmé's mind pensive is mourning—mourning *for* the vanished Hamlet as well as in appreciation of Hamlet's own loss.

But what, exactly, does Hamlet write? (Or does he write at all? Critics and editors divide on this question, as to whether he whips out a table or mimes the taking of dictation.)[89] What he claims to record is "thy commandment," and the conjunction of "table" and "commandment" is suggestive. Implicit in the scene, but not always explicitly noted, is its relationship to the moment in Exodus when God gives to Moses "two tables of testimony, tables of stone, written with the finger of God" (Exodus 31:18). In the Mosaic case, *God* writes, and Moses, angry with the idolatrous Israelites dancing about the golden calf, casts the tables out of his hands and breaks them. Moses then returns to God and pleads with Him to show him His glory. And God says to him, "Thou canst not see my face: for there shall no man see me, and live" (Exodus 33:20). Contrary to the case of prosopopeia, there must here be voice without face, speech without face. And God commands Moses to hew "two tables of stone like unto the first: and I will write upon *these* tables the words that were in the first tables, which thou brakest" (34:1). The tables that Moses brings to the Israelites, the foundations of the Law, are thus themselves copies, the second version written by God in substitution for the first, the originals, which were broken, which were lost. Moses breaks the tablets because the people were breaking the commandments they did not yet have. Even this law, the great original, is a copy and a substitution.

When we turn our attention once again to Hamlet's tables, we can see the operation of substitution here through erasure, the inscription on the tables of "thy commandment," which is—to revenge? to remember? to do the one through the agency of the other? We may notice that the same word, "commandment," is used to denote Hamlet's other act of inscription as substitution, the "new commission" that sends Rosencrantz and Guildenstern, instead of Hamlet, to be executed in England. The Ambassador from England arrives upon the bloody scene at the close of the play, and comments—in a figure that recalls the murder of King Hamlet—"The ears are senseless that should give us hearing / To tell him his commandment is fulfill'd, / That Rosencrantz and Guildenstern are dead" (5.2.374–6), and Horatio, taking "his commandment" to refer to Claudius' original intent, replies, "He never gave commandment for their death" (379).

Hamlet's writing is thus already a copy, a substitution, a revision of an original that does not show its face in the text. Whether it be the revisionary "tables," the interpolated "dozen or sixteen lines," or the redirected "new commission" signed with a usurped signature, Hamlet's writing is always, in fact, ghost writing.

Forgetting the hobbyhorse

Nietzsche's theory of historical repetition suggests that the world is itself a constructed fiction, so that what is "remembered" is in fact invented as a memorial object, and put in place in the past—put, perhaps, in the place of the past. J. Hillis Miller, describing "two kinds of repetition," the Platonic model based upon resemblance, and the Nietzschean model based upon difference, observes that "this lack of ground in some paradigm or archetype means that *there is something ghostly about the effects of this second type of repetition*"[90] and, again, that, "the second is not the negation or opposite of the first, but its 'counterpart' in a strange relation whereby *the second is the subversive ghost of the first, always already present within it as a possibility which hollows it out.*"[91] If my understanding of *Hamlet* is correct, the Ghost is itself a figuration of that "subversive ghost," that "something ghostly." Just as Shakespeare's *Richard III* figures the deformation of history through his own physical deformity and the deformations detectable in language and plot throughout the play, so the Ghost in *Hamlet* marks the text of that play as a belated harbinger of repetition as difference. The command to "Remember me!" encodes the necessity of forgetting.

Miller cites a very suggestive passage from Walter Benjamin's essay on Proust, in which Benjamin mulls the same relationship I have been exploring—that between memory and forgetting:

> the important thing for the remembering author is not what he experienced, but the weaving of his memory, the Penelope work of recollection. Or should one call it, rather, a Penelope work of forgetting? Is not the involuntary recollection, Proust's *mémoire involontaire*, much closer to forgetting than what is usually called memory? And is not this work of spontaneous recollection, in which remembrance is the woof and forgetting the warp, a counterpart to Penelope's work rather than its likeness? For here the day unravels what the night has woven.[92]

What, then, are we to make of the reminders of remembering, the cautions against forgetting, of which the Ghost's two visitations are the benchmarks? It might seem natural to assume that remembering would facilitate reparation, restitution, and recuperation—that the way to rectify an error, or expiate a crime, is through a memory of the act, and even of the historical circumstances that produced, provoked, or surrounded the act. Yet this is precisely what the play of *Hamlet* does *not* tell us. Rather than facilitating action, remembering seems to block it, by becoming itself an obsessive concern, in effect fetishizing the remembered persons, events, or commands so that they become virtually impossible to renounce or relinquish. Our contemporary sense of "hobbyhorse" as a constant preoccupation sums up this fetishizing instinct fairly well: the hobbyhorse must *be* forgot in order for action to follow.

Consider the Ghost's two visitations and his reiterated command. The Ghost asks Hamlet to do two things: to remember and to revenge. Repeatedly on the first occasion he urges revenge. "If thou didst ever thy dear father love . . . Revenge his foul and most unnnatural murder" (1.5.23–5). "Bear it not" (81). "Let not the royal bed of Denmark be / A couch for luxury and damned incest" (82–3). Hamlet is to "[pursue] this act" (84) to revenge his father's murder, while sparing his mother any punishment: "Taint not thy mind nor let thy soul contrive / Against thy mother aught" (85–6). But he is *to act*, he is *to revenge*. "Adieu, adieu, adieu. Remember me" (91). Remember and revenge. But these two injunctions are not only different from one another, they are functionally at odds. For the more Hamlet remembers, the more he meditates the "word" that he takes as the Ghost's "commandment" and inscribes on his tables, the more he is trapped in a round of obsessive speculation. Far from goading him to action, the Ghost's twice iterated instruction, "Remember me," "do not forget," impedes that action, impedes revenge. What Hamlet needs to do is not to remember, but to *forget*.

> Imagine the extremest possible case of a man who did not possess the power of forgetting at all and who was thus condemned to see everywhere a state of becoming: such a man would no longer believe in his own being, would no longer believe in himself, would see everything flowing asunder in moving points and would lose himself in this stream of becoming. . . . Forgetting is essential to action of any kind . . . it is altogether impossible to love at all without forgetting. Or, to express my theme even more simply: there is a degree of sleeplessness, or of rumination, of the historical sense, which is harmful and ultimately fatal to the living thing, whether this living thing be a man or a people or a culture.
>
> To determine . . . the boundary at which *the past has to be forgotten if it is not to become the gravedigger of the present*, one would have to know exactly how great the *plastic* power of a man, a people, or a culture is: I mean by plastic power the capacity to develop out of oneself in one's own way, to transform and incorporate into oneself what is past and foreign, to heal wounds, to replace what has been lost, to recreate broken moulds.[93]

The "boundary at which the past has to be forgotten if it is not to become the gravedigger of the present." This is Nietzsche, again in "The Use and Abuse of History." Nietzsche's gravedigger is also Hamlet's, a talismanic figure who digs up the pate of a politician, the skull of a lawyer, the bones of a great buyer of land, and jowls them indifferently to the ground (5.1.75–110). It is Hamlet, on this occasion, who "consider[s] too curiously" (199), who speculates about the noble dust of Alexander stopping a bunghole, and "Imperious Caesar, dead and turn'd to clay" who "Might stop a hole to keep the wind away" (206–9). Hamlet, who is still prey to the "rumination, of the historical sense, which is harmful and ultimately fatal to the living thing, whether this living thing be a man or a people or a culture."[94] The gravedigger himself marks Hamlet's boundaries. He came to his trade "that day that / our last King Hamlet o'ercame Fortinbras" (139–40), "the very day that young Hamlet was born" (143). Harold Jenkins in the Arden edition of *Hamlet* remarks,

> What matters is that when Hamlet came into the world a man began to dig graves and has now been at it for a lifetime . . . As Hamlet's talk with the grave-digger thus links the grave-digger's occupation with the terms of Hamlet's life, will it not seem to us that the hero has come face to face with his own destiny?[95]

Yet the gravedigger has the same uncanny valence as the Mower in Marlowe's *Edward II*;[96] he is the figuration of Hamlet's mortality, as the skull of Yorick is the fragmented emblem of that mortality. Re-membering is here reconstituted through a process of dismembering, of disarticulation of parts, of dislocation of bones and members.

But there is more that is uncanny in this passage of Nietzsche, for it seems throughout to be haunted by the ghost of *Hamlet*. "I have striven," he writes in the foreword to "The Use and Abuse of History," "to depict a feeling by which I am constantly tormented; *I revenge myself upon it* by handing it over to the public."[97] "It" is the abuse of history, the preoccupation with the past that can inhibit life, making it "stunted and degenerate."[98] Nietzsche's *revenge* is to be a "meditation" he describes as "untimely"—but then it must *be* untimely in order to be effective: "for I do not know what meaning classical studies could have for our time if they were not untimely—that is to say, acting counter to our time and thereby acting on our time and, let us hope, for the benefit of a time to come."[99] It is not, I think, entirely fanciful to wish to juxtapose these remarks to Hamlet's famous *cri de coeur*, "The time is out of joint—O cursed spite, / That ever I was born to set it right!" (1.5.196–7). And we may perhaps go further and suggest that Nietzsche in this exclamation, this profession of revenge—like Hamlet in his own professions of belatedness and determination—is himself a revenant, a ghost, a figure dislocated in and from history ("classical studies"; "earlier times") and constituted (or self-constituted) as not only critic but critique.

This is Hamlet's use of the classical past as well as Nietzsche's; the Pyrrhus play ("Aeneas's Tale to Dido") the constant reminders that his father was Hyperion

to Claudius' satyr, that he himself is confronted with a choice of Hercules—these
too are uses of history that verge upon the abusive because they place Hamlet rhetorically on the margins of history rather than in the midst of historical process. It is
only when he writes himself back into that process, with the agency of his father's
signet ring, later claiming his place in history ("This is I, / Hamlet the Dane."
[5.1.250–1]) by an act of self-naming, that he moves beyond untimely meditation,
the belatedness of soliloquy, toward action. For action is inextricably bound with
forgetting.

> Consider the cattle, grazing as they pass you by: they do not know what is meant by yesterday
> or today, they leap about, eat, rest, digest, leap about again, and so from morn till night and
> from day to day, fettered to the moment and its pleasure or displeasure, and thus neither
> melancholy nor bored. This is a hard sight for a man to see. . . . A human being may well ask
> an animal: "Why do you not speak to me of your happiness but only stand and gaze at me?"
> The animal would like to answer, and say: "The reason is I always forget what I was going to
> say"—but then he forgot this answer, too, and stayed silent: so that the human being was left
> wondering.
>   But he also wonders at himself, that he cannot learn to forget but clings relentlessly to the
> past: however far and fast he may run, this chain runs with him. And it is a matter for wonder:
> a moment, *now here and then gone*, nothing before it came, again nothing after it has gone,
> nonetheless *returns as a ghost* and disturbs the peace of a later moment.[100]

"'Tis here." "'Tis here." "'Tis gone." Nietzsche's meditation, Nietzsche's revenge,
incorporates (or "incorpses")[101] *Hamlet* as a manifestation of the haunting presentness
of the past. Hamlet remembers; Polonius forgets. "What was I about / to say? By the
mass, I was about to say something. / Where did I leave?" Reynaldo: "At 'closes in the
consequence'" (2.1.50–3). What Polonius forgets is precisely what closes in the
consequence: causality, history. "'The reason is I always forget what I was going to
say'—but then he forgot this answer, too." Polonius forgets: Hamlet remembers.
Hamlet's own meditation on revenge and bestial oblivion is so close to Nietzsche's
that we may wonder whether Nietzsche's complex of ideas, from revenge to the ghost
to the beast to the gravedigger, does not derive in some way from Shakespeare's great
untimely meditation, and in particular, from the soliloquy in Act 4 scene 4:

> How all occasions do inform against me,
> And spur my dull revenge. What is a man
> If his chief good and market of his time
> Be but to sleep and feed? A beast, no more.
> Sure he that made us with such large discourse,
> Looking before and after, gave us not
> That capability and godlike reason
> To fust in us unus'd. Now whether it be

> Bestial oblivion, or some craven scruple
> Of thinking too precisely on th' event—
> A thought which, quarter'd, hath but one part wisdom
> And ever three parts coward—I do not know
> Why yet I live to say this thing's to do,
> Sith I have cause, and will, and strength, and means
> To do't. (4.4.32–46)

Now, what does it mean to say that Nietzsche's meditation on revenge and forgetting situates itself as a rewriting of *Hamlet*? Is this merely a way of repositioning Shakespeare as the great authority, the great original, in whose work all ideas, all controversies, all contestations are already present? Is Shakespeare the *locus classicus* (or *the locus renascens*) of the move to place subversion within containment? And / or is *Hamlet*—as I have suggested above—the play that articulates, or represents, the construction of the modern subject?

I think that the last of these questions can be answered, tentatively, in the affirmative, and that this accounts at least in part for the befuddlement and irritation some contemporary critics demonstrate when they are asked to come face to face with this play. It is too close to us. What look like critiques, analyses, implementations of *Hamlet* to make some *other* point (philosophical, political, psychoanalytic) dissolve to bring us back to the play itself, not as referent, but as origin—or marker of the unknowability of origins, what Freud called the navel of the dream: "There is at least one spot in every dream at which it is unplumbable—a navel, as it were, that is its point of contact with the unknown":[102]

> There is often a passage in even the most thoroughly interpreted dream which has to be left obscure; this is because we become aware during the work of interpretation that at this point there is a tangle of dream-thoughts which cannot be unravelled and which moreover adds nothing to our knowledge of the content of the dream. This is the dream's navel, the spot where it reaches down into the unknown.[103]

When Terry Eagleton complains that "Hamlet has no 'essence' of being whatsoever, no inner sanctum to be safeguarded: he is pure deferral and diffusion, a hollow void which offers nothing determinate to be known" and that "Hamlet's jealous sense of unique selfhood is no more than the negation of anything in particular. How could it be otherwise, when he rejects the signifiers by which alone the self, as signified, comes into its determinacy?"[104] He is registering a protest (though a postmodern and somewhat satisfied protest) against this Alice's rabbit-hole quality in the play's text. Likewise when Jonathan Goldberg, in a characteristically rich and compressed three pages on Hamlet, suggests that "Hamlet's divided identity—and with it his delays and deferrals, his resistance to the ghostly plot, his inability to act and his compulsions to repeat—are the result of his *identification* with his father's words," and that "The depth of his interiority is his foldedness within a text that enfolds him and which cannot be unfolded,"[105] he is at once finding within Shakespeare's play the reflection of his own critical and theoretical moment, Derridean and Lacanian, and—at the same time, and through the same process—locating the play's power precisely in its capacity to assume the guise of contemporaneity and timely contestation. That critics write their own Hamlets, as, for example, Coleridge, Goethe, and T. S. Eliot, have done, is something of a commonplace for us. That they are *compelled* to do so—that this is *their* compulsion to repeat—because the play limns a preconscious moment that can only be retrieved *through* repetition and not through memory, reinscribes the paradox of the play as itself a *mise en abyme* without (exactly, precisely, without) the primal scene at which it is constantly hinting, and which we are constantly on the brink of remembering, falsely, fictively. The ghost of *Hamlet*—the ghost *in Hamlet*—is this illusion of the articulation of our own perception of desire and its denial, our own conviction that "the spot where it reaches down to the unknown" *can* be plumbed, even if it is found to be a hollow void. *Hamlet* is the play of undecidability. But / and it is the play of the uncanny, the play in which the *Heimlich* and the *Unheimlich* are opposite and identical, the play that demonstrates that you can't go home again. Why? Because you *are* home—and home is not what you have always and belatedly (from *un*home) fantasized it to be. Hence, once again, forgetting and remembering. And revenge. In other words, *transference*.

Freud is quite clear about the dynamic that links remembering, forgetting, and action. The patient forgets something because he / she represses it, and in order to retrieve that which has been repressed, he or she *acts*. The repetition-compulsion becomes a way of remembering, as well as a substitution for unretrievable or unretrieved memories. Consider this passage from the 1914 essay, "Recollection, Repetition, and Working Through":

> We may say that here the patient *remembers* nothing of what is forgotten and repressed, but that he expresses it in *action*. He reproduces it not in his memory but in his behaviour; he *repeats* it, without of course knowing that he is repeating it. . . .
>
> As long as he is under treatment he never escapes from this compulsion to repeat; at last one understands that it is his way of remembering.
>
> The relation between this compulsion to repeat and the transference and resistance is naturally what will interest us most of all. We soon perceive that the transference is itself only a bit of repetition, and that the repetition is the transference of the forgotten past not only on to the physician, but also on to all the other aspects of the current situation. We must be prepared to find, therefore, that the patient abandons himself to the compulsion to repeat, which is now replacing the impulse to remember, not only in his relation with the analyst but

also in all other matters occupying and interesting him at the time, for instance, when he falls in love or sets about any project during the treatment.[106]

Furthermore, the degree of resistance to the analyst and to quiescent remembering determines the degree to which acting out takes place.

> The greater the resistance the more extensively will expressing in action (repetition) be substituted for recollecting . . . if, then, as the analysis proceeds, this transference becomes hostile or unduly intense, consequently necessitating repression, remembering immediately gives way to expression in action. From then onward the resistances determine the succession of the various repetitions. The past is the patient's armoury out of which he fetches his weapons for defending himself against the progress of the analysis, weapons which we must wrest from him one by one.[107]

This last analogy sounds disquietingly like the end of *Othello* ("Take you this weapon / Which I have here recovered from the Moor" [5.2.238–9]: "I have another weapon in this chamber" [250]), but the pattern of resistance and repetition is uncannily like the plot of *Hamlet*. Indeed, it is not surprising to think of *Hamlet* as the story of an analysis, for what is analysis but a contemporary restaging of the pattern of deferral and substitution that we recognize in *Hamlet*? If our question, or one of our questions, concerns the relationship of memory and revenge, it is here answered, at least in part, by the compulsion to repeat. "As long as he is under treatment he never escapes from this compulsion to repeat; at last one understands that it is his way of remembering." This compulsion to repeat, "which is now replacing the impulse to remember," encompasses the killing (and not killing) of fathers, the accusation of women, the plays within the play, dumb show, and talking cure. The transference-neurosis is induced as a kind of therapeutic substitution, which *can* be cured or worked on because it is present rather than lost, and because it is, in some sense, play. "We admit it into the transference as to a playground."[108]

> The transference thus forms a kind of intermediary realm between illness and real life, through which the journey from the one to the other must be made. The new state of mind has absorbed all the features of the illness; it represents, however, an artificial illness which is at every point accessible to our interventions. It is at the same time a piece of real life, but adapted to our purposes by specially favourable conditions, and it is of a provisional character. From the repetition-reactions which are exhibited in the transference the familiar paths lead back to the awakening of the memories, which yield themselves without difficulty after the resistances have been overcome.[109]

This is a reasonably appropriate description of the role played by the play within the play in *Hamlet*, and also by Hamlet's role as chorus (analyst) of the "Mousetrap" (or even of the first Player's Pyrrhus speech). Real and provisional, "adapted to our purposes" with or without the addition of a dozen or sixteen lines, close enough to the original or originary situation (at least as it is fantasized or retold) yet safely "artificial" and thus able to be discounted or bounded, the play within the play does exhibit many of the symptoms of transference-neurosis, as in fact do the soliloquies that problematize the *activity* of others (Fortinbras, the First Player, Pyrrhus, even Laertes) as contrasted with the ruminative passivity of Hamlet.

The connection between repressed thoughts and memories and the compulsion to repeat is also strongly argued in *Beyond the Pleasure Principle* (1920), and it is not surprising that both of these Freudian texts have been used by narratologists to develop strategies of narrative displacement, substitution, and delay. In *Beyond the Pleasure Principle* Freud again states that "the compulsion to repeat must be ascribed to the unconscious repressed"[110] and comments on the odd but undeniable fact that people often compulsively repeat things that are not, and seem never to have been, pleasurable. How then is the compulsion to repeat related to the pleasure principle?

> The artistic play and artistic imitation carried out by adults, which, unlike children's, are aimed at an audience, do not spare the spectators (for instance, in tragedy) the most painful experiences and yet can be felt by them as highly enjoyable. This is convincing proof that, even under the dominance of the pleasure principle, there are ways and means enough of making what is in itself unpleasurable into a subject to be recollected and worked over in the mind."[111]

Tragedy—whether exemplified by *Hamlet* or by "The Murder of Gonzago"—thus can produce pleasure when it is received as a repetition. But if the illusion represented by the players conduces to pleasure when categorized as play, what of the kind of compulsion to repeat that results in a different sort of illusion—the terrifying spectacle of the ghost? "Stay, illusion" (1.1.130). Three times in *Beyond the Pleasure Principle* Freud evokes the image of some "daemonic" power produced by the repetition-compulsion:

> What psycho-analysis reveals in the transference phenomena of neurotics can also be observed in the lives of some normal people. The impression they give is of being pursued by a malignant fate or possessed by some "daemonic" power; but psycho-analysis has always taken the view that their fate is for the most part arranged by themselves and determined by early infantile influences.[112]

> The manifestations of a compulsion to repeat (which we have described as occurring in the early activities of infantile mental life as well as among the events of psycho-analytic treatment) exhibit to a high degree an instinctual character and, when they act in opposition to the pleasure principle, give the appearance of some "daemonic" force at work.[113]

> It may be presumed, too, that when people unfamiliar with analysis feel an obscure fear—a dread of rousing something that, so they feel, is better left sleeping—what they are afraid of at

bottom is the emergence of this compulsion with its hint of possession by some "daemonic" power.[114]

In the terms of *Hamlet*, this "daemonic" force or power, if it is to be ascribed to or even personified by the Ghost, is the compulsion to repeat which repression substitutes for remembering. Confronted with the Ghost's command, "Remember me!" Hamlet remembers that he is commanded to remember, but displaces that which he is unable to remember into compulsive behavior of a kind that translates *him* into a daemon, into a ghost. Thus he appears as a silent spectacle in Ophelia's closet, pale, sighing, as if "loosed out of hell" (2.1.83). The passivity of Hamlet, his apparent position of being acted on rather than acting, is also commensurate with the impression of being possessed, while in fact giving the name of "possession" to the repetition compulsion.

We may note that in both of these texts Freud represents the patient as male. Interestingly, however, when he comes to speak more closely of "transference-love" he shifts genders, to describe the circumstances of a female patient—and therefore, by implication, of a male analyst. And here again there is a ghost come from the grave—or from the unconscious. But from whose?

> To urge the patient to suppress, to renounce and to sublimate the promptings of her instincts, as soon as she had confessed her love-transference, would not be an analytic way of dealing with them, but a senseless way. It would be the same thing *as to conjure up a spirit from the underworld by means of a crafty spell and then to dispatch him back again without a question.* One would have brought the repressed impulses out into consciousness only in terror to send them back into repression once more. Nor should one deceive oneself about the success of any such proceeding. When levelled at the passions, lofty language achieves very little, as we all know. The patient will only feel the humiliation, and *will not fail to revenge herself for it.*[115]

The passion evoked by the analyst should rather be put in the service of the analysis, as the same kind of "playground" (or *play*-ground) occupied by the transference-neurosis described above. The "spirit from the underworld" is the patient's desire, and the denial or repression of that desire will send the ghost tunneling underground again, and prompt the analysand to *revenge*. But revenge upon what?

Turning the tables

For Hamlet himself, who or what is the Ghost? We could say that for Hamlet the Ghost is—or at least, is supposed to be—what Lacan calls the *sujet supposé savoir*, the subject who is supposed to know. "As soon as the subject who is supposed to know exists somewhere," says Lacan, "there is transference."[116] Who is, who *can* be, invested with such authority, such being-in-knowledge? For Lacan, "If there is someone to whom one can apply there can be only one such person. This *one* was Freud, while he was alive."[117] What a muted accolade is this—"This *one was* Freud, while he was alive." And now that he is dead? Lacan does not say, or does not say directly, who is the new *one*, the new *sujet supposé savoir*. But does he need to? The King is dead, long live . . . And so in *Hamlet*, also, the investment of authority is not without a sense of question and cost. Can the Ghost be the subject who is supposed to know only *because* he is dead? "O my prophetic soul," cries Hamlet (1.5.40). The Ghost is supposed to know—that is, to confirm—what Hamlet did not know he knew.

"The analyst," says Lacan, "occupies this place in as much as he is the object of the transference. Experience shows us that when the subject enters analysis, he is far from giving the analyst this place."[118] Then when does Hamlet enter into a trans-ferential relationship with the Ghost? When, precisely, he is given to think that his own authority is confirmed. Notice how much like an analytic situation is Hamlet's own response to this uncanny consultant:

> Given that analysis may, on the part of certain subjects, be put in question at its very outset, and suspected of being a lure—how is it that around this *being mistaken* something stops? Even the psycho-analyst put in question is credited at some point with a certain infallibility, which means that certain intentions, betrayed, perhaps, by some chance gesture, will sometimes be attributed even to the analyst put in question, *"You did that to test me!"*[119]

For Hamlet's testing of the Ghost ("The spirit that I have seen / May be a devil, and the devil hath power / T'assume a pleasing shape, yea, and perhaps, / Out of my weak-ness and my melancholy, / As he is very potent with such spirits, / Abuses me to damn me. I'll have grounds / More relative than this" [2.2.594–600]) is really in many ways the provision of a test for himself. Does he believe the Ghost, or not? Does the Ghost have authority?

The Ghost that comes "in such a questionable shape" (1.4.43) is immediately put in question, is in fact, as we have begun to see, the shape or sign of putting things in question. We could almost designate him as is done in Spanish with an inverted question mark before each appearance, before each utterance, and with another ques-tion mark following each. Plain as the Ghost's utterances may seem, Hamlet *wants* them to be a riddle, a problem, a question.

> Be thy intents wicked or charitable,
> Thou com'st in such a questionable shape
> That I will speak to thee. I'll call thee Hamlet,
> King, father, royal Dane. (1.4.42–5)

"Certain intentions, betrayed, perhaps, by some chance gesture" seem to provoke in Hamlet a wish to name, to pin upon his *sujet supposé savoir* the signifier Lacan has called "*le nom-du-père*" [the Name-of-the-Father]. Lacan's term derives in part from a critique of the traditional Christian invocation all too appropriate to *Hamlet*: "In the name of the Father, the Son, and the Holy Ghost." Coupling this formula with the biological indeterminacy of paternity, Lacan notes that

> the attribution of procreation to the father can only be the effect of a pure signifier, of a recognition, not of a real father, but of what religion has taught us to refer to as the Name-of-the-Father.
>
> Of course, there is no need of a signifier to be a father, any more than to be dead, but without a signifier, no one would ever know anything about either state of being.
>
> . . . insistently Freud stresses the affinity of the two signifying relations that I have just referred to, whenever the neurotic subject (especially the obsessional) manifests this affinity through the conjunction of the themes of the father and death.
>
> How, indeed, could Freud fail to recognize such an affinity, when the necessity of his reflexion led him to link the appearance of the signifier of the Father, as author of the Law, with death, even to the murder of the Father—thus showing that if this murder is the fruitful moment of debt through which the subject binds himself for life to the Law, the symbolic Father is, in so far as he signifies this Law, the dead Father.[120]

Lacan extends this view further by underscoring the homonymic double meaning of "*nom-du-père*," which in French sounds identical to the expression "*non-du-père*"— "no" of the father. The father—the dead father, the symbolic father—is the Law. For Freud, of course, this symbolic father is not the Christian father but the father of Jewish law. And the law commands, "thou shalt *not*": "If thou hast nature in thee, bear it *not*, / Let *not* the royal bed of Denmark be / A couch for luxury and damned incest. / But howsomever thou pursuest this act, / Taint *not* thy mind, *nor* let thy soul contrive / Against thy mother aught" (Ghost to Hamlet, 1.5.81–6, emphasis added); "Do *not* forget" (Ghost to Hamlet, 3.4.110, in Gertrude's closet, emphasis added).

Freud, it will be recalled, made much of the connection between the writing of *Hamlet* and the death of Shakespeare's father. In *The Interpretation of Dreams*, he cites the Shakespearean scholar Georg Brandes[121] to demonstrate that

> *Hamlet* was written immediately after the death of Shakespeare's father (in 1601), that is, under the immediate impact of the bereavement and, as we may well assume, while his childhood feelings about his father had been freshly revived. It is known, too, that Shakespeare's own son who died at an early age bore the name of "Hamnet," which is identical with "Hamlet."[122]

Yet there is another father involved here, as Freud's preface to the second edition of *The Interpretation of Dreams* (1908) makes clear. For that masterpiece of analytic invention was itself written right after the death of Freud's *own* father. In his preface, Freud writes:

> this book has a further subjective significance for me personally—a significance which I only grasped after I had completed it. It was, I found, a portion of my own self-analysis, my reaction to my father's death—that is to say, to the most important event, the most poignant loss, of a man's life.[123]

There may therefore be a connection between Freud's interpretation of Hamlet and the death not only of *Shakespeare*'s father but also of *Freud*'s father.

Similarities between Freud's story and Hamlet's have been noticed by recent revisionist biographers, often in connection with his recantation of (or "suppression of")[124] the seduction theory, which held that neuroses originated in actual sexual encounters—with adults, often parents, servants, or older children—experienced in childhood. Marianne Krüll, for example, argues that Hamlet's situation—"a son dwelling with impotent rage on the ruthlessness of his mother and his uncle—had parallels with Freud's own family."[125] The "uncle" in the Freud story was his half-brother Philip, called "Uncle" by Freud's niece and nephew, and represented in Freud's own dream associations in such a way as to suggest some real or imagined sexual relationship between Philip and his (Freud's) mother.[126] Krüll's book argues that Freud received from his father, Jacob, an ambivalent mandate: he was commanded to show filial piety, to honor his father as instructed by the Fifth Commandment, and above all not to inquire into his father's secrets, or his past; at the same time, he was commanded to seek success in the secular world, to become a great man. The son's resentment at this impossible double task was identical, says Krüll, to that felt by Jacob Freud toward *his* father, Schlomo (Sigmund's Hebrew name). "Neither of them rebelled against his father, and both shouldered the contradictory mandate of making his own way, even while remaining dutiful sons."[127] "To complete its hold over him" writes John Gross, "the mandate forbade him to acknowledge the feelings of resentment that it inspired, his rage against Jacob for saddling him with an insoluble problem."[128] This "mandate," we may notice, is very like the "word" Hamlet receives from the Ghost in the "tables" scene, together with the troublesomely ambivalent command, "Remember me!"

A dream mentioned by Freud in slightly different versions in the letters to Fliess and *The Interpretation of Dreams*[129] concerns the arrangements he made for his father's funeral, and the criticism he incurred from relatives for choosing "the simplest possible ritual"[130] though he did so in accordance with his understanding of his father's wishes. It is this dream that Krüll has in mind when she writes that like Hamlet,

> Freud too has been given orders by his late father in a dream which, though the subject was not revenge, as in Hamlet's case, nevertheless caused the son comparable qualms of conscience. Another reason for Freud, in my view, to feel so drawn to the Hamlet theme.[131]

Not only the funeral of old Hamlet, swiftly followed by Gertrude's remarriage, but even more particularly the "hugger-mugger" interment (4.5.84) of Polonius and the "maimed rites" accompanying Ophelia's obsequies (5.1.212; 219)—so disturbingly punctuated by Laertes's twice iterated demand, "What ceremony else?" (5.1.216; 218)—correspond to Freud's own anxieties about performing his duty to the dead.

In the dream—which he tells Fliess took place *after* his father's funeral, and which in *The Interpretation of Dreams* he describes as taking place *before*—he sees a notice-board inscribed with the phrase, "You are requested to close the eyes," which he interprets as an ambivalent statement; in *The Interpretation of Dreams* the ambivalence has made its way onto the notice-board itself, so that the sign reads "*either*

"You are requested to close the eyes"
or, "You are requested to close an eye."

I usually write this [says Freud] in the form:

"You are requested to close the eye(s)."[132]
                                     an

Closing the eyes is a funerary rite, a service performed on the eyes of the dead; closing *an* eye is winking at (overlooking) an offense or slight. As Freud writes to Fliess, "The sentence on the sign has a double meaning: One should do one's duty toward the dead (an apology, as though I had not done it and were in need of leniency) and the actual duty itself. The dream thus stems from the inclination to self-reproach that regularly sets in among the survivors."[133]

The generalization at the end denies any *particular* ambivalence occasioned by this specific bereavement, but the whole letter, like the ones preceding it during his father's illness, speaks openly of Freud's own feeling. Jacob Freud died on 23 November 1896. A little less than a year later, with affirmations of relief and release rather than "disgrace," Freud abandoned the seduction theory. Whatever else his motivations were for making this crucial change, the seduction theory came dangerously close to an accusation of the father, as is pointed out in the famous letter to Fliess of September, 1897. Jeffrey Mason, whose controversial book, *The Assault on Truth: Freud's Suppression of the Seduction Theory*, has occasioned much disputation among psychoanalysts, notes that the original English edition of the letters (itself provocatively entitled *The Origins of Psychoanalysis*)[134] omitted the reference to Freud's own father, by using an ellipsis: "in every case . . . blame was laid on perverse acts by the father." The three dots appear in the letter in place of the phrase Masson translates as "the father, not excluding my own." The editors, Marie Bonaparte, Ernst Kris, and Freud's daughter Anna, comment that their editorial principle was one of "omitting or abbreviating everything publication of which would be inconsistent with professional or personal confidence . . . Omissions have been indicated by dots."[135] Even translation, here, acts out the story of suppression. Thus the discarding of the seduction theory, and the substitution of the Oedipus complex, not only opened the way for the discovery of the inner life of the child and the foundations of modern psychoanalysis, but also paid a kind of filial duty, honoring the memory of the father, and of fathers. The child's (Freud's own) fantasies, not the parent's actions, were to blame. Or if no blame was to be attached, at least there was no accusation against the parent. Are we—and were Freud's fellow analysts—being requested to close an / the eye(s)?

The story by means of which Freud substitutes infantile fantasy for child abuse is the story of Oedipus, who, by killing his father and marrying his mother, acts out in reality what every man is said to live in fantasy. Oedipus, then, becomes a paradigm for every man. Or does he? In the course of a discussion of the differences between *Oedipus* and *Hamlet*, Freud indicates that the later play represents a cultural advance: "the changed treatment of the same material reveals the whole difference in the mental life of these two widely separated epochs of civilization: the secular advance of repression in the emotional life of mankind."[136] What Oedipus *does* (kills his father, marries his mother), Hamlet *fantasizes* but *represses*, so that "we only learn of [this fantasy's] existence from its inhibiting consequences."[137] And yet this, to Freud, is very much more interesting than the straightforward enactment of the desire. Oedipus gives his name to the complex Freud discovered in every child's fantasy life, but it is Hamlet rather than Oedipus who engages Freud's own fascination, and his most extended discussion on the subject.

It is therefore not entirely clear which of the two dramas is "closer to home." *Hamlet* looks like a repressed version of the Oedipus story but in being a story *of* repression, it may in fact be closer to the story of "modern" man. There may, in other words, be *two* originary stories in Freud's mind, *both* of which are too close for comfort, and between which the story of Oedipus emerges as a compromise formation: the story of the father's sins, to which Freud dutifully closes his eyes by abandoning the seduction theory; and the story of repressed filial ambivalence, hesitation, and resentment towards an impossible paternal mandate, which Freud relegates to the status of secondary revision. The story of killing the father, which would seem to express Freud's filial ambivalence, in fact represses it: the murdered father can forever remain innocent while the son shoulders the guilt. The Oedipus story does not account for filial love.

While Freud thus confers upon Oedipus a primacy he denies to Hamlet, Hamlet remains a half-hidden center of preoccupation throughout Freud's work. *Hamlet* is of course the Shakespearean text that has most intrigued psychoanalysts and psychoanalytic critics after Freud. But the writings of Freud himself seem uncannily to circle back upon the subject—and subjects—of *Hamlet*. Consider some of these titles: *The Interpretation of Dreams* (1900); "On Narcissism" (1914); "Mourning and Melancholia" (1917); "Negation" (1925); "A Note Upon the 'Mystic Writing-Pad'" (1925).

In "Mourning and Melancholia" (1917), for example, we find a fascinating treatment of the relationship between narcissism and mourning, and the need for the relinquishment of mourning to free the ego. Here Freud comments on "the mental faculty called *conscience*"[138] on the way in which "the self-reproaches are reproaches against a loved object which have been shifted onto the patient's own ego,"[139] especially the kind of self-reproach in which "the mourner himself is to blame for the loss of the loved one, *i.e.*, desired it."[140] Freud explicitly makes a connection in this essay between mourning and revenge, suggesting that both melancholics and obsessional neurotics "usually succeed in the end *in taking revenge*, by the circuitous path of self-punishment, on the original objects and in tormenting them by means of the illness."[141]

"The tendency to *suicide* which makes melancholia so interesting—and so dangerous"[142] is, according to Freud's argument, occasioned by the element of sadism intrinsic to such object loss. "In the two contrasting situations of intense love and suicide," Freud writes (still ostensibly on the general case of melancholia), "the ego is overwhelmed by the object, though in totally different ways . . . The most remarkable peculiarity of melancholia, and one most in need of explanation, is the tendency it displays to turn into mania accompanied by a completely opposite symptomology."[143] And here both the "antic disposition" (1.5.180) and Hamlet's disconcertingly "merry" tone in the "Mousetrap" scene can be located. Hamlet, in short, is a textbook melancholic. Or is he the textbook itself, disclosing in the "book and volume of [his] brain" (1.5.103) the very symptomology Freud describes, the "three conditioning factors in melancholia—loss of the object, ambivalence, and regression of libido into the ego," of which, as Freud points out, "the first two are found also in the obsessional reproaches arising after the death of loved persons"?[144] Is this to commit the naive error of early psychoanalytic criticism, to diagnose a literary character as if he were a person? or is it, rather, to diagnose the symptomology of the *play*, and to see that symptomology informing the book and volume of *Freud's* brain?

The essay on "Mourning and Melancholia" itself contains a ghost that points the way, if not to the answers to such questions, at least to the questions themselves. For the case of Hamlet is cited, here, in an essay otherwise devoid of concrete examples—but cited in an oblique way, as a glancing analogue rather than an animation of the condition being described. Here is Freud's text, again, on the general case of the melancholic:

> When in his exacerbation of self-criticism he describes himself as petty, egoistic, dishonest, lacking in independence, one whose sole aim has been to hide the weaknesses in his own nature, for all we know it may be that he has come very near to self-knowledge; we only wonder why a man must become ill before he can discover truth of this kind. For there can be no doubt that whoever holds and expresses to others such an opinion of himself—one that Hamlet harboured of himself and all men—that man is ill, whether he speaks the truth or is more or less unfair to himself.[145]

Hamlet's cameo appearance in this passage, where he is evoked (and quoted in a footnote—"Use every man after his desert, and who shall 'scape whipping") comes in connection with one of the least particularized "symptoms" the essay will discuss. In effect he is used as a marker of typical melancholia. *His* repressions and ambivalences are nowhere cited, nor is the extraordinary aptness of his situation for a discussion of the *difference* between mourning and melancholia.

It begins to become clear that for Freud, the text of *Hamlet* occupies the place both of the patient (the entity to be analyzed) and of the *sujet supposé savoir* (the storehouse of psychoanalytic knowledge). The axis of authority from analyst to patient or analyst to text is commutative and reversible, as Shoshana Felman has shown in the case of literature and psychoanalysis: "With respect to the text, the literary critic occupies thus at once the place of the psychoanalyst (in the relation of interpretation) *and* the place of the patient (in the relation of transference)."[146] Lacan, in a celebrated axiom, declared that "the unconscious is structured like a language."[147] Felman adds that "*literature, in its turn, is the unconscious of psychoanalysis*, that the unthought-out shadow in psychoanalytic theory is precisely its own involvement with literature; that literature *in* psychoanalysis functions precisely as its 'unthought'; as the condition of possibility *and* the self-subversive blind spot of psychoanalytical *thought*."[148]

For Freud, *Hamlet*—the play, not the Prince—becomes not the analyzed but the analyst, the *sujet supposé savoir*, the ur-text of the Oedipus complex and not the other way around. *Hamlet* is, we might say, the navel of Freud's dream—the place of origination that marks the undiscoverable fact of origin, the "one spot in every dream that is unplumbable," "its point of contact with the unknown."

Later in life, Freud found an ingenious way of taking revenge on the authority both of his father and of Shakespeare. In *Moses and Monotheism* (1927–39), he wrote a family romance for the entire Jewish tradition, in which he claimed that Moses was not a Jew but a noble Egyptian—a text that Marianne Krüll describes as "Freud's last will and testament, in which he both accounts to his father and also settles accounts with him."[149] It was in those same years that Freud decided that Shakespeare was not, after all, the author of the Shakespeare plays. "The man of Stratford . . . seems to have nothing at all to justify his claim."[150]

But the ghost of *Hamlet* was not to be laid to rest so easily. Witness the following letter from one of Freud's own ambivalent "sons," C. G. Jung:

> Dear Professor Freud,
> I accede to your wish that we abandon our personal relations, for I never thrust my friendship on anyone. You yourself are the best judge of what this moment means to you. "The rest is silence."[151]

Post Ghost

Ghosts always pass quickly, with the infinite speed of a furtive apparition, in an instant without duration, presence without present of a present which, coming back, only *haunts*. The ghost, *le re-venant*, the survivor, appears only by means of figure or fiction, but its appearance is not nothing, nor is it a mere semblance.

Derrida, "The Art of Mémoires"

—What is a ghost? Stephen said with tingling energy. One who has faded into impalpability through death, through absence, through change of manners. Elizabethan London lay as far from Stratford as corrupt Paris lies from virgin Dublin. Who is the ghost from *limbo patrum*, returning to the world that has forgotten him? Who is king Hamlet?

James Joyce, *Ulysses*

I

Whatever else it is, the *Hamlet* Ghost is an animation of the earlier theatrical genre known as revenge tragedy, come to summon protagonist and play to a genre already beginning to fade. Ghosts always come back, but they are always already belated when they come—it is only when they return, *re-venant*, that they *are* ghosts, and carry the authority of their own belatedness. The Ghost comes to summon Hamlet—and *Hamlet*—to a dramatic world which is no longer present. If Hamlet as a character is located in the place of the emergence of the modern subject, so *Hamlet* as a play is located on another, and equally indeterminate and undeterminable boundary.

Between Hamlet and the Ghost, there is not only a conflict of generations but also a conflict of genres. The Ur-*Hamlet*, Belleforest, the *Spanish Tragedy, A Warning for Fair Women, Der bestrafte Brudermord*—all these precursors and schoolfellows, themselves interrogated by the scholar and critic of *Hamlet* for clues as to Shakespeare's sources, Shakespeare's authority—such texts are the Rosencrantzes and Guildensterns of this quest for an understanding of how the present text came to be as it is. The diagnosis of *madness* so earnestly alleged by Polonius, so gratefully received by Claudius, is a diagnosis of the play's dislocation from its origins, or rather, the play's repudiation of the obligations and possibilities of origin or origination, of paternity, of knowing one's father. As Shoshana Felman writes,

> In the play of forces underlying the relationship between philosophy and fiction, literature and madness, the crucial problem is that of the subject's *place*, of his *position* with respect to the delusion. And the position of the subject is not defined by *what* he says, nor by what he talks *about*, but by the place—unknown to him—*from which* he speaks.[152]

"A little more than kin, and less than kind" (1.2.65) is a statement about genre and its conceptual limitations akin to, and of a more radical kind than, Polonius's canonical remarks on "tragical-comical-historical-pastoral" (2.2.394–5). By the time the actors arrive the genre of revenge tragedy has already been put in question by the questionable shape of the Ghost, of whose injunctions neither Hamlet nor the play are ever entirely free, but whose iterated command to revenge prompts a revenge upon revenge tragedy rather than a compliance with all its "forms, all pressures past" (1.5.100). It is no accident that Hamlet speaks to the players of "form and pressure" (3.2.24), as he has spoken of them to the Ghost:

> Suit the action to the word, the word to the action, with this special observance, that you o'erstep not the modesty of nature. For any thing so o'erdone is from the purpose of playing, whose end, both at the first and now, was and is to hold as 'twere the mirror up to nature; to show virtue her feature, scorn her own image, and the very age and body of the time his form and pressure. . . . O, there be players that I have seen play—and heard others praise, and that highly—not to speak it profanely, that neither having th'accent of Christians, nor the gait of Christian, pagan, nor man, have so strutted and bellowed that I have thought some of Nature's journeymen had made men, and not made them well, they imitated humanity so abominably. (3.2.17–35)

"Neither having th'accent of Christians nor the gait of Christian, pagan, nor man"—"[having] so strutted and bellow'd"—"imitated humanity so abominably"—this reads curiously like a critique of the older forms of revenge tragedy—and even of the Ghost. Thomas Lodge's 1596 report of the "ghost which cried so miserably at the theatre, like an oyster-wife, *Hamlet, revenge*"[153] in a performance of what scholars usually call the Ur-*Hamlet*, and Hamlet's own comment on the "Mousetrap" play, "Come, the croaking raven doth bellow for revenge" (a conflation of two lines from *The True Tragedy of Richard III*: "The screeking Raven sits croking for revenge. / Whole heads of beasts come bellowing for revenge") both situate the cry for revenge in the realm of the melodramatic, and accord with Hamlet's apparent views about bad theater.

Whether the *Hamlet* Ghost is Christian, pagan, or man is a question that has much vexed the academic community—prompting studies like Eleanor Prosser's influential *Hamlet and Revenge*[154]—and, indeed, the question troubled scholars, readers and audiences even before there was an academic community. Prosser notes that "throughout the Restoration and most of the eighteenth century, the Ghost was treated as a terrifying figure,"[155] that in the nineteenth century, "the questionable spirit that had so terrified Betterton and Garrick became transmuted by sentimentalism into an unquestioned spirit of health who aroused not horror but reverence," and that "as a result the Ghost became a pompous bore."[156] "The traditional view that the Ghost's command is to be obeyed," Prosser concludes, "has, indeed, held the stage since the Restoration, but this view has been made possible only by changing stage business, by modifying the interpretation of the Ghost, and, above all, by cutting contradictory lines and scenes."[157] Prosser, who believes that the play is Christian and that the Ghost is not to be obeyed—that revenge is un-Christian—tries to exorcize these changes, cuts and modifications by restoring the play to its original meaning, maintaining that "our attitude toward revenge is almost the same as the Elizabethan attitude, and it is doubtful that human nature has changed,"[158] and that "we find the tragic issue to be rooted in an ethical dilemma [revenge] that is universal."[159]

The difficulty of holding an essentialist view of the Ghost, or of *a* ghost, is implicit in and intrinsic to the nature (if that is the word) of ghosts themselves. To instate a meaning, or a dramatic effect, is to divest it of some of its power, the power that inheres in the sequence "'Tis here!" "'Tis here!" "'Tis gone!". It is the nature of ghosts to be gone, so that they can return. When they are predictable, when they are no longer uncanny, they are no longer ghosts, but characters, capable of being inscribed in stage history.

Prosser's long and learned book is put to the service of one central purpose: to prove that the Ghost is an evil spirit that should not be trusted or obeyed. In this she goes counter to the received wisdom of critics like Bradley, who assume that the Ghost is trustworthy, or at least assume that Hamlet—and the Elizabethans— thought so. To write *against* the Ghost, as Prosser does, seems a curious thing to do, especially when the ranks of apologists *for* it go out of their way to rationalize revenge, discounting any hints of the daemonic. Prosser is not alone in this contention, as she herself points out.[160] Nonetheless, the project is interesting as a gesture of demystification, and even of defiance. Prosser denies the authority of the Ghost, and summons alternative authorities to bolster her denial. This is very like the project of scholars (and others) who write books demonstrating conclusively that Shakespeare is not the author of the plays. In both cases authority is flouted and rejected, under the comfortable visor of scholarship. The undecidability of paternity is here decided in the negative, allowing an unconflicted, authorized rebellion against authority. But to do this *requires* an essentialist reading of the Ghost, since if it behaves like a ghost, only in traces and belatedly, taking on "meanings" in a demonstrably delusive and subjective way, it can neither support the energy of rebellion, nor gratify the survivor.

II

Why do we still maintain the centrality of Shakespeare? Why in a time of canon expansion and critique of canonical literature does Shakespeare not only remain unchallenged, but in fact emerge newly canonized, as the proliferation of new critical anthologies—*Alternative Shakespeares, Political Shakespeare, Shakespeare and the Question of Theory*[161]—attests? Why does Harold Bloom exempt Shakespeare from the anxiety of influence, Geoffrey Hartman coedit with Patricia Parker an anthology of Shakespeare criticism, J. Hillis Miller bolster his argument about narrative theory with a reference to *Troilus and Cressida*?[162] Why does Terry Eagleton, who usually writes metacriticism, devote a book to William Shakespeare? Why does Elaine Showalter, who usually writes on nineteenth- and twentieth-century feminist topics, select Ophelia as the focus of a recent study?[163] Why with the current renaissance in Renaissance studies, is Shakespeare still the touchstone for new historicists, feminists, deconstructors? Why, in other words, do those who criticize canonical authority so often turn to Shakespeare to ratify the authority of their critique?

If anything is clear, it is that the Ghost is not—or not merely—Shakespeare *père* or Shakespeare *fils*, the son of John Shakespeare or the father of Hamnet—but rather "Shakespeare" itself. The ambiguous and ambivalent pronoun of Act 1 is appropriately used here, because Shakespeare is a concept—and a construct—rather than an author. We thus hear of the Shakespeare establishment, and of "Shakespeare" as a corpus of plays—a corpus "incorpsed" in innumerable authoritative editions, yet one that breaks the bounds—the margins—set to contain it, stalking the battlements of theory:

>   tell
> Why thy canoniz'd bones, hearsed in death,
> Have burst their cerements; why the sepulchre
> Wherein we saw thee quietly inurn'd,
> Hath op'd his ponderous and marble jaws
> To cast thee up again.

The Ghost is Shakespeare. He is the one who comes as a revenant, belatedly instated, regarded as originally authoritative, rather than retrospectively and retroactively canonized, and deriving increased authority from this very instatement of authority backward, over time. "The ghost, *le re-venant*; the survivor, appears only as a means of figure or fiction, but its appearance is not nothing, nor is it a mere semblance." This "presence without present of a present which, coming back, only *haunts*" haunts Freud, haunts Nietzsche, haunts Lacan, haunts postmodern England and postmodern America. The Ghost's command, his word, is "Remember me!" and we have done so, to the letter, *avant la lettre*, moving our remembrance further and further back until it becomes an originary remembrance, a remembrance of remembrance itself. "Remember me!" cries the Ghost, and Shakespeare is for us the superego of literature, that which calls us back to ourselves, to an imposed, undecidable, but self-chosen attribution of paternity. "Remember me!" The canon has been fixed against self-slaughter.

    "A little more than kin and less than kind." Hamlet's bitter phrase inflects not only the problem of a ghostly genre, the unwriting and rewriting of revenge tragedy, but also the continuous attempt to render Shakespeare both kind and kin, of our time, our contemporary, always already postmodern, decentered. "Yet his modernity too, like Nietzsche's, is a forgetting or a suppression of anteriority."[164] This is de Man on Baudelaire. But it could be said of Hamlet—and of Shakespeare. This Baudelairization is not Bowdlerization, but transference, con-texting. We know that Shakespeare played the part of the Ghost in *Hamlet*. What could not be foreseen, except through anamorphic reading, was that he would *become* that Ghost. "Remember me!" the Ghost cries. "Do not forget." And, indeed, we do not yet seem quite able to give up that ghost.

Macbeth: The Male Medusa 3

Freud provided the formula: remembering, repeating, and working through. For Lady Macbeth, this tidy progress toward resolution seems arrested midway, condemned to the cyclical pattern of repetition without end. Oppressed by nightmares, she herself becomes the belated author of *Macbeth*. Here is the scene in which her astonished audience, a doctor and a gentlewoman, describe her as she writes, seals, and performs the play—repeatedly, night after night.

> *Gentlewoman*: Since his Majesty went into the field, I have seen her rise from her bed, throw her night-gown upon her, unlock her closet, take forth paper, fold it, write upon't, read it, afterwards seal it, and again return to bed; yet all this while in a most fast sleep.
>
> *Doctor*: A great perturbation in nature, to receive at once the benefit of sleep and do the effects of watching! In this slumbery agitation, besides her walking and other actual performances, what, at any time, have you heard her say?
>
> *Gentlewoman*: That, sir, which I will not report after her. (5.1.4–14)
>
> *Lady Macbeth*: Out, damned spot! out, I say!—one; two: why, then 'tis time to do't.—Hell is murky.—Fie, my lord, fie! a soldier, and afeard?—What need we fear who knows it, when none can call our power to accompt? Yet who would have thought the old man to have had so much blood in him? (33–8)
>
> *Doctor*: Go to, go to: you have known what you should not.
>
> *Gentlewoman*: She has spoke what she should not. (44–5)
>
> *Doctor*: My mind she has mated, and amaz'd my sight.
> I think, but dare not speak. (75–6)

Is *Macbeth*, then, a tale told by a sleepwalker, capable of striking its audience blind and dumb? What can be made of this *mise en abyme*, this uncanny reenactment of the play's composition and "actual performances," which repeat but do not exorcise its traumatic events?

What is striking about this scene is not only that it offers a perfect miniature of the play's action and the audience's response, but that it represents the medium of representation itself as a sleepwalker—someone who, in the very act of dramatic composition and performance, personifies the transgression of a boundary. *Macbeth* is, of course, a play *about* things "unnatural, / Even like the deed that's done" (2.4.10–11)—the murder of a king, the slaughter of innocent women and children, bearded women who know the future, a moving grove, a child not born of woman, horses that eat each other ("to th'amazement of mine eyes / That look'd upon't" (2.4.19–20). But to what extent can the play itself be seen as transgressive? Is this a mere figure of the play's power to unsettle, or does the play *literally* let something loose that stalks with uncanny sureness, compelled to repeat what it can neither repress nor cure? Let us look at stage history.

"towards his design
Moves like a ghost"

By the superstitious on and off the stage, *Macbeth* has always been considered an unlucky play. Actors have been known to refuse to wear a cloak or carry a sword that has been used in a *Macbeth* production.[1] Inside the theatre, it is said, even in the wings and dressing rooms, they will not mention the name of the play, or the names of any of its characters. They call it "the Scottish play" or "that play" or "the unmentionable." Macbeth's death is referred to as "the death," and Lady Macbeth as "the Queen." Those who unwittingly or carelessly break these unspoken rules, and quote from the "Scottish play" behind the scenes, are obliged to perform a time-honored ritual to remove the "curse." The offender must go out of the dressing room, turn around three times, spit, knock on the door three times, and beg to be admitted. It may be that this ceremony of exorcism derives in some way from the knocking at the gate in the Porter scene (2.3), or from the witches' custom of cursing in threes, or perhaps from the incantation of those same witches when Macbeth approaches them on the heath: "By the pricking of my thumbs, / Something wicked this way comes.—Open, locks, / Whoever knocks." (4.1.44–47). An alternative method of removing the curse is said to be to quote from *The Merchant of Venice*—especially Lorenzo's benison to the departing Portia: "Fair thoughts and happy hours attend on you!" (3.4.41). *Merchant* is considered a particularly lucky play, and thus to provide an antidote for the malign powers of *Macbeth*.

Interestingly enough, if we are to believe in stage history, those powers seem to have been considerable. In the first production of the play outside England, in 1672, the Dutch actor playing Macbeth was at odds with the actor playing Duncan over the affections of the latter's wife—who was cast in the role of Lady Macbeth. One evening the murder scene was particularly bloody, and "Duncan" did not appear for his curtain call. Afterwards it was discovered that a real dagger had been used. The former "Macbeth" served a life sentence for murder.

In more modern times the curse has apparently been equally lively. Laurence Olivier played the title part in 1937. First he lost his voice. Then the sets were found to be far too large for the stage. Finally he narrowly escaped death when a heavy weight plummeted from above and demolished the chair in which he had just been sitting. The show went on.

In the 1942 production starring—and directed by—John Gielgud there were no fewer than four fatalities. Two of the witches, the Duncan, and the scenic designer all died in the course of its run. The set was then repainted and used for a light comedy, whereupon the principal actor of that play promptly died.

Orson Welles filmed the play in 1946. When the film was finished, he discovered that the Scots accent he had insisted his actors acquire was totally incomprehensible to the audience. The entire sound track had to be recorded again.

When Charlton Heston played the part he had a serious motorcycle accident during rehearsals, after which there was much backstage murmuring about the "curse." The production was staged outdoors, and Heston was required to ride a horse in the opening scene. At the first performance he rushed from the stage, clutching his tights and whispering urgently, "Get them off me. Get them off me." The tights, it seemed, had been dipped in kerosene, either accidentally or on purpose, so that the heat from the horse inflicted painful burns. To add insult to injury, the audience responded to the play as if it were a comedy, laughing uproariously throughout the last act, and redoubling their laughter when Macduff appeared with Macbeth's severed head, which had been closely modeled on Heston's own.

Actors have occasionally been tempted to defy the curse, chanting lines from the play in unison in their dressing rooms just to see what would happen. This occurred in 1974 at the Bankside Theater, which was then performing in a tent. The result was a huge and sudden rainstorm, which short-circuited the electricity and made the entire stage a deathtrap. Then the canvas roof of the tent collapsed—fortunately just after the audience had made its way out. The entire theatrical season for the following year had to be cancelled.

On another occasion the young actress playing Lady Macbeth declared shortly after the dress rehearsal that she did not believe in the curse. The next day she decided she had been playing the sleepwalking scene wrong, keeping her eyes open when they ought properly to be shut. At the first performance she entered with her eyes closed and fell fifteen feet into the orchestra pit. She climbed back to the stage and continued the scene.

But the show has not always gone on. The great Russian director Constantin Stanislavski, who greatly admired *Macbeth*, mounted an elaborate production for the Moscow Arts Theater. During the dress rehearsal the actor playing Macbeth forgot his lines and—as was the custom in the Russian theater—came down to the prompt box at the front of the stage to get his cue. There was no word from the prompter. Irritably he tried again; still no word. A third try; nothing. At last he peered into the box, only to find the aged prompter dead—but still clutching the script. Stanislavski, no less a fatalist than his countrymen Chekhov and Dostoevsky, cancelled the production immediately. It—like the prompter—was never revived.

Stories of this kind are legion. People have been injured or killed, and productions seriously disrupted. The play is not only thought to be unlucky—on the face of things it actually has been unlucky, and actors today continue to believe in the curse. Recently, a tourist visiting the Stratford Festival in Ontario, Canada, innocently mentioned the name of the play while standing on the stage; the tour guide, a member of the company, quickly crossed himself.

What is there about Shakespeare's *Macbeth* that provokes so strong a response, and so heightened a defense? The answer is not hard to locate, for the play is itself continually, even obsessively, concerned with taboo, with things that should not be heard and things that should not be seen, boundaries that should not be crossed—and are. One of the principal themes of *Macbeth* is the forbidden, the interdicted, that which a man (or woman) may not with safety see or do. As much as it seeks to repress this acknowledgment, the play's *subject* is the uncanny and the forbidden—and its ancillary, covering subject is the need to repress or deny that fact. There *is* something uncanny going on here. Thus attempts to explain away the evidence of stage history have about them an engagingly overdetermined air of rationalization—a deliberate insistence upon finding the "facts"—as if these would dispel the numinous effect. Thus it is asserted that the role of Macbeth is so large, and the stage action so busy, with swordfights, entrances and exits (especially at the end of the play, when Birnam Wood comes to Dunsinane) that accidents are just bound to happen—an explanation that explains nothing at all.

"Research" has also been brought to bear on the suppression of this troubling history of performance. We are informed, for example, that the witches' brew concocted in Act IV was based on an actual recipe known to the witches of Shakespeare's native Warwickshire—a region famous for its practice of witchcraft.[2] Since the public enunciation of these secret ingredients—"fillet of a fenny snake," "eye of newt and toe of frog," not to mention "liver of blaspheming Jew" and "finger of birth-strangled babe"—would constitute a kind of inverse blasphemy, like the use of Christian artifacts in the Black Mass, disastrous or "unlucky" events might well ensue.

Ingenious "solutions" of this kind, with their spurious but reassuring documentation (the "real" recipe; the "original" witches, now safely dead) invite us to take refuge in the happy bromide that "accidents are bound to happen," as if such uncomfortable formulae could, by their very familiarity, produce comfort—or at least eliminate the sneaking suspicion that there is more going on in *Macbeth* than is dreamt of in anyone's philosophy. But such deferrals will not stay in place. The play is itself transgressive, and insists upon the posing of pertinent thought-troubling questions.

What is the relationship of the play to its stage history? In what sense can *Macbeth* be said to be about this kind of transgression and dislocation? Are these seeming "accidents" part of the play's affect—and also of its subject?—something let out to wander, to cross the borders between safety and danger, play and "reality," like a sleep-walker or a persistent wandering ghost: Lady Macbeth's somnambulistic nightmare, or Banquo's unsettling, extraneous and persistent presence at the banquet? The more we wish to pack her safely offstage and thus to bed, to banish him from his usurped place at table the more we see how much the play resists such easy resolutions, such comfortable conclusions about the dramatic role of dramatic presentations. The story *of* the play reflects the story *in* the play.

"wicked dreams abuse
The curtain'd sleep"

Macbeth presents us with what is in effect a test case of the limits of representation. The boundary between what is inside the play and what is outside it (in its performances, in its textual resonances) is continually transgressed, and marked by a series of taboo border crossings: sleep / waking, male / female, life / death, fair / foul, heaven / hell, night / morning. It is perhaps no accident that the Porter scene, itself a theatrical presentation of the transgressive limit or boundary, has aroused so much critical interest. It may indeed be the case that all stories about the uncanny are stories about the repression of the uncanny. In his essay on "The Uncanny" Freud discusses the strategy of the writer who lulls his reader into a false sense of security which he then deliberately transgresses or violates: "He takes advantage, as it were, of our supposedly surmounted superstitiousness; he deceives us into thinking that he is giving us the sober truth, and then after all oversteps the bounds of possibility."[3] Something of the same emotion is reflected in De Quincey's famous remarks "On the Knocking at the Gate in *Macbeth*" (1823), and even more acutely in Mallarmé's, "La Fausse Entrée des Sorcières dans *Macbeth*" which takes De Quincey as a point of departure. Mallarmé is fascinated by the witches' uncanny presence, so different from the bold transgressive knock at the gate. "*Rien, en intensité, comparable aux coups à la porte réper-cutés dans la terreur; mais ici, au contraire, un évanouissement, furtif, décevant la curiosité.*"[4] "Something comes only to vanish, furtive, disappointing all curiosity." He lays stress on the fact that the witches do not *enter*, are not described as entering the scene in the ordinary way of actors—instead they *appear: extra-scéniquement*, uncannily present.

> *Overture sur un chef-d'oeuvre: comme, en le chef-d'oeuvre, le rideau simplement s'est levé, une minute, trop tôt, trahissant des menées fatidiques.*
>
> *Cette toile qui sépare du mystère, a, selon de l'impatience, prématurement cédé-admis, en avance sur l'instant réglementaire, la cécité commune à surprendre le geste éffarouché de comparses des ténèbres—exposé, dans une violation comme fortuite, pour multiplier l'angoisse, cela même qui parassait devoir rester caché, tel que cela se lie par derrière et effectivement à l'invisible: chacun scrute et dérange, parmi l'éclair, la cuisine du forfait, sans le chaudron futur aux ingrédients pires que des recommandations et un brusque au revoir.*

[The overture to a masterpiece: as if, in the masterpiece, the curtain had simply risen a minute too soon, betraying fateful goings-on.

That canvas that separates mystery off has somehow, through some impatience, prematurely given way—admitted, anticipating upon the regulation moment, the common blindness to surprise the startled gesture of the cronies of darkness—exposed, in a seemingly fortuitous violation, so that anxiety is compounded, the very thing that seemed to have to remain hidden, such that *that* is knotted up from behind and effectively to the invisible; everyone examines and disturbs, in the lightning, the kitchen in which the deed is cooking, without the future cauldron with its ingredients worse than recommendations, admonitions, prophecies and a brusque vow to meet again.]

In Mallarmé's vision of the scene, we have a *theatrical* transgression—the curtain lifts too soon, the witches and their malign powers are prematurely exposed in a "fortuitous violation." Like an antemasque, the first encounter of the witches seems indecently to invite the spectator behind the scenes, into the kitchen, to the source of creative energy and dramatic power before it unfolds in its proper place. "The very thing that seemed to have to remain hidden" is revealed, examined, and disturbed. The spectator sees—indeed is compelled to see, by the timely-untimely lifting of the curtain—what should not be seen. *Une violation comme fortuite*—a fortuitous, but also a somehow fortunate violation.

Macbeth is full of such moments of transgressive sight and concomitant, disseminated violation. Repeatedly the play—through its chief protagonist—theorizes about the uncanny, while at the same time resolutely determining to ignore it, to cover it over or repress it.

> This supernatural soliciting
> Cannot be ill; cannot be good:
> If ill, why hath it given me earnest of success,
> Commencing in a truth? I am Thane of Cawdor:
> If good, why do I yield to that suggestion
> Whose horrid image doth unfix my hair,
> And make my seated heart knock at my ribs,
> Against the use of nature? Present fears
> Are less than horrible imaginings.
> My thought, whose murther yet is but fantastical,
> Shakes so my single state of man,
> That function is smother'd in surmise,
> And nothing is, but what is not. (1.3.130–42)

"Supernatural soliciting"; "function . . . smother'd in surmise"; "nothing is but what is not." Yet in the next moment Macbeth resolves that "If Chance will have me King, why, Chance may crown me, / Without my stir" (144–5). Notice that it is a horrid "image" that transfixes him (by "unfixing" his hair and setting his heart to "knocking"—a physiological anticipation of the unnatural knocking in the Porter scene). The boundary between a thing and its reflection is constantly being transgressed, here and elsewhere in the play. Good / ill; natural / supernatural; single / double; function / surmise; is / is not. "Nothing," a present absence, emerges from this internal debate as the one palpable substantive. But as much as Macbeth tries to contain these speculations, to know and dissemble the uncanny, it will out. Murder will out.

Consider another key passage about boundary transgression, knowledge and identity. Prior to the murder of Duncan, Macbeth is still vacillating, debating the trajectory of murder and the priority of particular taboos: against slaying a kinsman; against slaying a king; against slaying a guest; tacitly against parricide, the double murder of king and father.

> If it were done, when 'tis done, then 'twere well
> If were done quickly: If th'assassination
> Could trammel up the consequence, and catch
> With his surcease success; that but this blow
> Might be the be-all and the end-all—here,
> But here, upon this bank and shoal of time,
> We'd jump the life to come.—But in these cases,
> We still have judgment here; that we but teach
> Bloody instructions, which, being taught, return

> To plague th'inventor: this even-handed Justice
> Commends th'ingredience of our poison'd chalice
> To our own lips. He's here in double trust:
> First, as I am his kinsman and his subject,
> Strong both against the deed; then, as his host,
> Who should against the murtherer shut the door,
> Not bear the knife myself. (1.7.1–16)

"Shut the door"; but it is precisely this door, this portal, threshold, or boundary, which cannot be shut. The keen knife that, in Lady Macbeth's pregnant phrase, must "see not the wound it makes" (1.5.52) will pierce the blanket of the dark—and the limits of the stage. The stage history of the play is in effect the acting out of the play's own preoccupation with boundary transgression. It is not extrinsic or anecdotal; it is the matter of the play itself.

A particularly striking instance of this transgressive violation occurs, as we have noticed, in the sleepwalking scene, which encodes an onstage audience: Lady Macbeth's Waiting-Gentlewoman, horrified by the events of previous nights, has called a Doctor of Physic to observe her lady's actions. "What, at any time, have you heard her say?" asks the Doctor (5.1.12–13). "That, Sir," replies the Waiting-Gentlewoman, "which I will not report after her" (14). "Neither to you," she answers, "nor any one; having no witness to confirm my speech" (16–17). What she has heard is unspeakable, unrepeatable. At this point the sleeping Lady Macbeth appears, tries to wash invisible blood from her hands, and in half a dozen other words and actions reveals that she and her husband are guilty of the murders. Not only Duncan, but Banquo and the family of Macduff have all been their victims. And the response of the Doctor and Waiting-Gentlewoman is once again expressed in terms of taboo. "You have known what you should not," he reproaches her (44), and she replies roundly, "She has spoke what she should not, I am sure of that: Heaven knows what she has known" (45–6). Notice "should not" here—not "cannot." The unspeakable knowledge is transgressive, interdicted. The audience in the theater, which has experienced these horrors once, now relives them through new eyes and ears. As the scene closes the Doctor confirms the sense of impotent dismay that is felt by both audiences, onstage and off, declaring, "My mind she has mated, and amaz'd my sight. / I think, but dare not speak" (75–6).

"My mind she has mated"—that is, checkmated, stunned, stupefied—"and amaz'd my sight." Consider how very frequently in the play this kind of perturbation in nature takes place. As we have seen, Macbeth is paralyzed when he contemplates the murder of Duncan. Having committed the murder, he cannot bear to look upon his victim: "I am afraid to think what I have done; / Look on't again I dare not" (2.2.50–1). The vision of the dagger he sees before him (2.1.33), the blood-boltered

ghost of Banquo (which, like the dagger, is invisible to everyone on the stage save
Macbeth himself), and the apparitions produced by the witches are all literally amazing sights, sights that are taboo, forbidden, dangerous. "Seek to know no more"
(4.1.103) counsel the witches. But Macbeth is deaf to their instruction. "I will be
satisfied: deny me this, / And an eternal curse fall on you!" (104–5). With extraordinary hubris he threatens to lay a curse upon the very creatures who themselves
possess the power of malediction. And when they ironically comply with his demands
he misinterprets what he sees and hears, and brings upon himself defeat and death.
The whole play is in one sense at least a parade of forbidden images gazed upon at
peril, and it inscribes an awareness of this, a preoccupation with it. Through "the
sightless couriers of the air" it "blow(s) the horrid deed in every eye" (1.7.23–4). "My
mind she has mated, and amaz'd my sight." There is one dramatic moment, early in
the play, in which the act of gazing on the taboo is explicitly described, and it is a
moment which I think has a crucial significance for the pattern and meaning of
Shakespeare's play. I refer to the moment—and the manner—in which Macduff
announces the death of Duncan.

The time is early morning. Macduff and Lennox, two loyal liegemen, have arrived
to see the King at his request. They knock on the Porter's door, waking him and
prompting the famous and disquieting comparison of Macbeth's castle to hell itself.
"If a man were Porter of Hell Gate, he should have old turning the key" (2.3.1–2). For
Macduff and Lennox the crossing of this threshold is a transgressive act, a fatal journey
from the familiar to the forbidden, a rite of dreadful passage from which they will
return greatly changed.[5]

Admitted, they are welcomed by their host, Macbeth, who shows them the way
to the king's chamber. And it is from that chamber that Macduff emerges, a moment
later, with words of horror on his tongue. "O horror! horror! horror! / Tongue nor
heart cannot conceive, nor name thee!" (62–3). Again the event is said to be unspeakable—it cannot be told. But equally important, it cannot be looked upon.

> Approach the chamber, and *destroy your sight*
> *With* a *new Gorgon.*—Do not bid me speak:
> See, and then speak yourselves.—
>   Awake! awake!—
> Ring the alarum-bell!—Murther and treason!
> Banquo and Donalbain! Malcolm, awake!
> Shake off this downy sleep, death's counterfeit,
> And look on death itself!—up, up, and see
> The great doom's image!—Malcolm! Banquo!
> As from your graves rise up, and walk like sprites,
> To countenance this horror!
>   [*Bell rings.* (2.3.70–9, emphasis added)

The Gorgon of classical mythology turned those who looked upon her to stone. To Macduff the sight of the dead king is a "new Gorgon" that will do the same to Duncan's subjects—a monstrous vision that will amaze their sight. What is this reference to "a new Gorgon" doing in the play?

"our rarer monsters"

The most famous of the Gorgons was Medusa, one of three sisters in Greek mythology, whose hair was said to be entwined with serpents, whose hands were brass, their bodies covered with scales, their teeth like boars' tusks.[6] When gazed upon, they turned the onlooker to stone. The first two Gorgons, Stheno ("The Mighty One") and Euryale ("Wide-leaping") were immortal, and seem to have nothing really to do with the myth beyond multiplying the fearsome power of the terrible and petrifying female image from one to the favorite number for monstrous females, three, as with the Graiai, or Spirits of Eld; the Moirai, or Fates; and the Charities, or Graces. The two supernumerary Gorgons disappear almost immediately from most accounts, leaving the focus on the third, the mortal Gorgon, Medusa, whose name—significantly enough for *Macbeth*—means "The Queen."

I arrive to talk about Medusa at a moment when considerable attention has been paid to this myth—particularly by Freud and by theorists influenced by him. I will therefore first run briefly through the myth in such a way as to highlight those aspects of it that are important for my purposes, then touch upon the readings of Freud and others, and how they pose, or counterpose, some difficulties and unresolved questions in contextualizing the Medusa story within *Macbeth*. Once again I hope to show that the unresolved questions are precisely at issue in the play. Specifically, the initial difficulty of applying Freud's reading of the Medusa head as a fearful sighting of the female genitals indicates a site of resistance and underscores the way in which gender undecidability and anxiety about gender identification and gender roles are at the center of *Macbeth*—and of Macbeth.[7]

In classical mythology the story of Medusa is one of the exploits of the hero Perseus, the son of Zeus and of a mortal woman, Danae. For reasons that need not concern us here mother and son were exiled from their native country and came to the land of a certain king, Polydectes. Polydectes lusted after Danae, and sent her inconvenient son Perseus off to fetch the head of Medusa, hoping—and expecting—that he would never return from this dangerous exploit. But Perseus was favored by the gods, especially Athena, the virgin goddess of wisdom and war, who advised him how to proceed. To gain access to the Gorgons (still described as three, although only Medusa's head was his object) he first visited another triad of figures, the Graiai, who are thought to be either the sisters or the sentries of those Gorgons. The Graiai, gray-haired from birth, are considered by modern commentators to represent the personified spirits of old age. They had only one eye and one tooth among them, and by trickery Perseus stole both, agreeing to return them only when he received in exchange a magic cap, which made him invisible; magic shoes, which made him swift; and a magic wallet, in which he might carry the severed head. When the time came he approached Medusa with his back turned, looking at her image as it was reflected in his shield rather than directly, and was thus able to decapitate her without being turned to stone. Once he achieved this feat he made use of the head as a weapon, turning to stone those who dared to oppose him. Ultimately he gave the head to his patroness, Athena, who wore it thereafter on her aegis.

Thus the head of Medusa, so horrible in life, becomes in death an apotropaic talisman, a means of warding off evil. Throughout Greek and Roman art the Medusa head—with grinning mouth, staring eyes, and protruding tongue—appears as a protective ornament, whether worn on armor, carved on statues of Athena, or incised on tombstones. In fact the head as a talisman seems to have preceded the myth, and perhaps to have generated it. Jane Ellen Harrison writes persuasively that

> in her essence Medusa is a head and nothing more; her potency only begins when her head is severed; she is in a word a mask with a body later appended. The primitive Greek knew that there was in his ritual a horrid thing called a Gorgoneion, a grinning mask with glaring eyes and protruding beast-like tusks and pendant tongue. How did this Gorgoneion come to be? A hero had slain a beast called the Gorgon, and this was its head. Though many other associations gathered round it, the basis of the Gorgoneion is a cultus object, a ritual mask misunderstood. The object comes first; then the monster is begotten to account for it; then the hero is supplied to account for the slaying of the monster.[8]

Thus Homer speaks of the Gorgon as a disembodied head, whether he is describing an ornament or an actual monster. Agamemnon carries a shield embossed with the staring face of the Gorgon (*Iliad* 11.36), Hector glares with the Gorgon's stark eyes (*Iliad* 8.349), and Odysseus fears lest Persephone send a Gorgon-head from deeper hell to affright him, and flees to his ship (*Odyssey* 11.634).

If the Gorgon's heads in effect precede and preempt the bodies that support them, in what sense can we say of Macbeth that *his* real potency only begins when his head is severed, and he becomes an apotropaic object? Before we come to consider the terrifying heads of Shakespeare's *Macbeth*, it may be useful to consider what some of his contemporaries thought of the Medusa myth, and the degree to which there was a consciousness of that myth in Western Europe, and especially in England.

Renaissance mythographers, when they contemplated the story of Medusa, saw plainly allegorical meanings. The influential Italian mythographer Caesare Ripa, in his *Iconologia*, interpreted the head of the Medusa as "a symbol of the victory of reason over the senses, the natural foes of 'virtu,' which like physical enemies are petrified when faced with the Medusa."[9] The real battle was within the warring elements of the self. Thus Mantegna represents *Philosophia* in the form of Minerva with a shield bearing a Medusa mask, to represent wisdom's control of the senses.[10] The degree to which this interpretation accords with the spirit of *Macbeth* is made manifest in the two speeches we have already considered: Macbeth's first long aside, which begins, "This supernatural soliciting / Cannot be ill; cannot be good" (1.3.130–1), and the remarkable soliloquy that begins Act 1 scene 7, ("If it were done, when 'tis done, then 'twere well / It were done quickly" [1–2]). Like Lady Macbeth's open eyes and closed sense in the sleepwalking scene, this speech refuses to look where it is going, to see where it is headed—and so in effect it beheads itself, and "falls on th'other" (28), yielding to the very transgressive energy it struggles so hard to contain.

Francis Bacon, in a treatise called *De sapientia veterum*, or *The Wisedome of the Ancients*, titled his interpretation of the Medusa story "Perseus, or Warre." The Medusa was an emblem of tyranny, against which the just warrior should fight.

> There must bee a care that the motives of Warre bee just and honorable; for that begets an alacrity . . . in the soldiers that fight. . . . But there is no pretence to take up arms more pious than the suppression of Tyranny, under which yoake the people loose their courage, and are cast downe without heart and vigour, as in the sight of Medusa.[11]

Bacon also has interesting things to say about the Graiai, whom he identifies as "treasons which may be termed the Sisters of Warre." They are "descended of the same stocke, but far unlike in nobilities of birth; for Warres are generall and heroicall, but Treasons are base and ignoble."[12] "Perseus [Bacon continues] therefore was to deale with these Greae for the love of their eye and tooth. Their eye to discover, their tooth to sowe rumors and stirre up envy, and to molest and trouble the minds of men."[13] Once again, we have forbidden sight and forbidden language. The Graiai in this reading bear a suggestive resemblance to the weird sisters, similarly consulted, and similarly—though again reluctantly—helpful to the hero in his quest. The Old English word *wyrd* means Fate, and it has been conjectured by Holinshed and others that the weird sisters may represent the "goddesses of destiny"; Holinshed also reports that they resembled "creatures of elder world."[14] In any case the threeness of the witches, (and indeed the murderers) calls to mind the ritual trios of Graiai and Gorgons, all relentless and unrepentant in their dealings with mortal men.

Another English mythographer, Alexander Ross, sees Medusa as an emblem of the dangerous power of women: "the sight of these Gorgones turned men into stones; and so many men are bereft of their sense and reason, by doting too much on women's beauty."[15] Ross also comments on the fact that not only Perseus but his entire family were made into constellations, remarking that by this fact it was possible to see "how one worthy person doth enoble a whole family."[16]

For James I the allegorization of the Medusa story would have had potentially disquieting political—and personal—implications. In his political writings James continually recurred to the image of the King as head of state: thus he writes in the *Basilikon Doron* of the King as a "publicke person" to whose "preseruation or fall, the safetie or wracke of the whole common-weale is necessarily coupled, as the body is to the head";[17] in a speech to the first English Parliament (19 March 1603) he declared, "I am the Husband, and the whole Isle is my lawfull Wife; I am the Head, and it is my Body",[18] and in *The Trew Law of Free Monarchies* (1598) he likewise articulates, and embellishes, this figure:

> And for the similitude of the head and the body, it may very well fall out that the head will be forced to garre cut off some rotten members (as I haue already said) to keep the rest of the body in integritie: but what state the body can be in, if the heade, for any infirmitie that can fall to it, be cut off, I leaue it to the readers judgement.[19]

The decapitation of the state, the severing of the head from the body politic, was at the same time unimaginable, and offered to the reader (or audience) to imagine. Yet in James' own recent memory there had been such a beheading and such a severance, of a monarch "set upon a skaffolde"—or, as later editions of the *Basilikon Doron* would emend the phrase, "on a stage, whose smallest actions and gestures, all the people gazingly doe behold":[20] the public beheading of his mother, Mary Queen of Scots, on February 8, 1587. The fate of Mary haunts the *Basilikon Doron*, so much so that in his introduction to later editions the King felt it necessary to excoriate the "malicious" critics who claimed that "in some parts [of the *Basilikon Doron*] I should seeme to nourish in my minde, a vindictive resolution against *England*, or at the least, some principals there, for the Queene my mothers quarrell";[21] in the treatise itself he urges Prince Henry to pay particular heed to the Fifth Commandment, to honor his father and his mother, alluding to the just retribution that had fallen upon "all them that were chiefe traitours to my parents . . . I mean specially by them that serued the Queene my mother."[22] (The editor of James' political writings comments without irony that the religious and civil disorders of the time "had been brought to a head by the execution of Mary Stuart in 1587."[23])

In the *Basilikon Doron*, addressed to his son as presumptive heir, James distinguishes—in passages that have often been linked to *Macbeth*—between the characteristics of the "good King" and those of the "vsurping Tyran."[24] For James, a usurping tyrant like Macbeth, who deserves to have his head struck off and exhibited to the people ("live to be the show and gaze o'th'time: . . . Painted upon a pole, and underwrit, / 'Here may you see the tyrant.'" 5.8.24–7) would indeed be a sort of male Medusa. The play covers over and represses or displaces the figure of the decapitated Mary, so offensive and so omnipresent to the King's imagination, "set high upon a skaffolde," and substitutes for it the appropriate and politically necessary decapitation of Macbeth: "Behold, where stands / Th'usurper's cursed head" (5.9.20–1).

Not only mythographic and political but also archaeological evidence speaks to these questions. The architectural remains of Roman Britain include a remarkable number of Medusa heads.[25] Coffins, tombstone pediments, antefixes, floor mosaics and pottery all bear Medusa masks, as do bronze jugs, jug-handles, and visor-masks, skillets intended for religious and sacrificial use, rings, coins, pendants, and *phalerae* (small glass or metal disks, often awarded as gifts to soldiers of the Roman armies)—to say nothing of statues and relief carvings of the goddess Minerva (the Roman counterpart of Athena) with the head of Medusa displayed on her aegis. The function of these decorations, like those of their Greek predecessors, is in most cases clearly apotropaic; the figured jet pendants, for example, were obviously intended to ward off evil from their wearers, the *phalerae* to protect the soldiers in battle, and the tomb and coffin Medusas to safeguard the dead.

But among these numerous Medusas there were a few which differed crucially from the traditional representation, for they are manifestly *male*. Three certain examples of the male Medusa have been found in England, and others have been tentatively identified. Carved on a pediment for a tombstone at Chester is a bearded and moustached male head with severely patterned hair and eight writhing snakes framing its face. "It is, in fact," writes J. M. C. Toynbee, "a kind of male Medusa."[26] An antefix or roof ornament from Dorchester bears the mask of another bearded Medusa, and coins from the reign of Tincommius (ca. 20 B.C.–5 A.D.) carry full-faced Medusa masks which are "very probably bearded."[27] But the most celebrated of the British male Medusas is the second or third century sculpted pediment on the Temple of Sulis-Minerva at Bath. Toynbee, cataloguer of the 1961 London Exhibition of Art in Roman Britain, asserts

That the glaring mask on the boss of the central, dominating shield of the Bath pediment is, to some extent, at any rate, intended, despite its masculinity, to depict the Medusa of Minerva is certain. Of this the wings and snakes in the hair are clinching evidence; the owl beside the shield was specifically Minerva's bird; the temple was dedicated to her as conflated with the Celtic Sulis; and to Minerva, as the child of Jupiter, oak-wreaths are appropriate. The Bath face, with its trap-like mouth, lined, scowling brows, and huge, deeply drilled, and penetrating eyes, is, indeed, very different from the normal, feminine Medusa of Hellenistic and Roman art. All the same, wild, glowering, frowning faces, sometimes set on round shields, were not unknown in Roman art in Mediterranean lands.[28]

Indeed, other representations of the male Medusa are to be found in the Mediterranean area, specifically at Rome, Petra, and Hatra in Mesopotamia (now Al Hdr, Iraq).[29]

Toynbee's description of the striking mouth, brows, and eyes on the pediment at Bath bring sharply to mind another decorative architectural motif that also involves a glaring male beard, often with gaping mouth and protruding tongue. I refer to the foliate head or leaf mask which gained enormous popularity in England and throughout Western Europe during the Romanesque and medieval periods. These remarkable images, with leaves sprouting from their faces, can be found virtually everywhere in English medieval churches, from fonts to tombs, corbels and capitals to armrests. Known in Britain chiefly as the Green Man, this often sinister and frightening figure appears among other places, in Exeter, Ely, Lincoln, and Winchester Cathedrals, and in the Church of the Holy Trinity in Coventry, Warwickshire—not a great distance from Shakespeare's home in Stratford-upon-Avon.[30] The Green Man, although he seems in some ways an odd choice for ecclesiastical ornamentation, in fact embodies a warning against the dark side of man's nature, the devil within: "For all flesh is as grass, and all the glory of man as the flower of grass. The grass withereth, and the flower thereof falleth away" (1 Peter 1:24).

Foliate head and Medusa head, one monster with hair and beard of leaves, the other with snaky locks; both are in effect conquered, tamed, and appropriated as symbols by religions to which they were originally antipathetic. Medusa was considered Athena's antitype, "a hostile Pallas who could sometimes be united with her . . . and sometimes regarded as an antagonist being detested by the goddess herself."[31] So closely are they associated that Euripides calls Athena "Gorgon" twice in his plays. The rational goddess can also be an irrational monster; wisdom can be transformed to war: "There's no art / To find the mind's construction in the face" (Macbeth 1.4.11–12). As for the Green Man, a type of the male Medusa, he is terrifying precisely because he is, and is not, man. And, as I hope to show, Macbeth too becomes a male Medusa. To see why, it may be helpful to return to Freud.

"Bloody instructions, which, being taught, return
To plague th'inventor"

Freud's essay on "The Uncanny" is uncannily pertinent to *Macbeth*, although—as we have already seen—Freud repeatedly denies or represses that pertinence by disclaiming any direct relationship between the literary appearance of ghosts and apparitions and the *Unheimlich* or uncanny. The affect of uncanniness, we have noted, is for Freud a kind of "morbid anxiety" that derives from "something repressed which *recurs*"; this uncanny is in reality nothing new or foreign, but "something familiar and old-established in the mind that has been estranged only by the process of repression."[32] Thus he is moved to agree with Schelling that the uncanny is something which ought to have been kept concealed but has nonetheless come to light—something concealed because of the protective mechanism of repression.

Associated with such sensations as intellectual uncertainty whether an object is alive or not, the fear of the evil eye and of "the omnipotence of thoughts,"[33] instantaneous wish-fulfillment, secret power to do harm, and the return of the dead,[34] the uncanny is nothing less than the thematized subtext of Shakespeare's *Macbeth*. For example, the "moving grove," Birnam wood en route to Dunsinane, is precisely the kind of phenomenon about which it is difficult to judge—is it animate or inanimate, natural or unnatural? The audience knows, because it is told directly in Act 5 scene 4, that the soldiers have hewn down boughs, and carry them before them—not as an uncanny spectacle but as military camouflage, that they may better scout out the numbers of the enemy, and hide their own troop strength. The rational explanation is given to us directly, and apparently explains the strategem. But does it? With the witches' prophecy inevitably in mind, we may count the ironic fulfillment as itself uncanny. Macbeth's appalled presentiment of doom identifies the moving grove as a reified, dramatized catachresis.

> I pull in resolution; and begin
> To doubt th'equivocation of the fiend,
> That lies like truth: "Fear not, till Birnam wood
> Do come to Dunsinane";—and now a wood
> Comes toward Dunsinane. (5.5.42–6)

The uncanny, says Freud, is also linked to the well-documented phenomenon of the double—whether through telepathic communication between persons, so that one "identifies himself with another person, so that his self becomes confounded, or the foreign self is substituted for his own"—as in the case of Macbeth and Lady Macbeth—or through the "constant recurrence of similar situations, a same face, or character-trait, or twist of fortune, or a same crime, or even a same name recurring throughout several consecutive generations." Manifestations of the uncanny appear in the witches' riddling prophecies, the puzzling, spectacular apparitions, the walking of trees and sleepers, the persistent sense of doubling that pervades the whole play: two Thanes of Cawdor; two kings and two kingdoms, England and Scotland themselves doubled and divided; two heirs apparent to Duncan; the recurrent prefix "Mac" itself which means "son of"; the sexually ambiguous witches replicated in the wilfully unsexed Lady Macbeth; Macbeth and Banquo on the battlefield "As cannons overcharg'd with double cracks; / So they / Doubly redoubled strokes upon the foe" (1.2.37–9); Duncan as the Macbeths' guest, "here in double trust" (1.7.12), their ostentatious hospitality as Lady Macbeth points out, "in every point twice done, and then done double" (1.6.15). Macbeth believes the witches' prophecies (and believes that he interprets them correctly), but he will "make assurance double sure" by killing Macduff, thus bringing down sure disaster upon himself. The witches or weird sisters, he will later assert, are "juggling fiends" "that palter with us in a double sense," (5.8.19; 20), and we hear them chant their litany of "double, double toil and trouble" (4.1.10; 20; 35). The mode of involuntary repetition, which we saw embodied in Lady Macbeth's futile acting out of the events of the play, determines dramatic action from Macbeth's first reported action to his death at the close. In Act 1 scene 2 a "bloody man," the sergeant just returned from battle, reports Macbeth's valiant victory over a traitorous rebel, "the merciless Macdonwald." "Brave Macbeth," says the sergeant,

> (well he deserves that name),
> Disdaining Fortune, with his brandish'd steel,
> Which smok'd with bloody execution,
> Like Valor's minion, carv'd out his passage,
> Till he fac'd the slave;
> Which ne'er shook hands, nor bade farewell to him,
> Till he unseam'd him from the nave to th'chops,
> And fix'd his head upon our battlements. (16–23)

The play thus begins with the (offstage) head of a rebel fixed upon the battlements, as it will end with another rebellion, another battle, and "the usurper's cursed head" held aloft by Macduff. The sergeant's phrase, "bloody execution" encapsulates the doubleness, since execution here means both deed and death, and points ahead to the "If it were done" soliloquy (1.7.1). Thus, Macbeth performs in the first, offstage battle what might be aptly described as "bloody instructions, which, being taught, return / To plague th'inventor" (1.7.9–10), imagistically "carv[ing] out" the patterns of his own retributive death.

Significantly, Freud singles out as well a series of metonymic objects, dislocated body parts—several of which appear as prominent stage properties in Elizabethan and Jacobean drama: "Dismembered limbs, *a severed head*, a hand cut off at the wrist, feet which dance by themselves—all these have something peculiarly uncanny about them . . . As we already know, this kind of uncanniness springs from its association with the castration-complex."[35] For Freud, indeed, the castration-complex is intrinsic to uncanniness wherever it appears. The severed head so central to *Macbeth* (and its Medusa associations) is only one instance of this pervasive pattern of underlying meaning. Doubling, too, is linked to castration anxiety: "the 'double' was originally an insurance against destruction of the ego . . . This invention of doubling as a preservation against extinction has its counterpart in the language of dreams, which is fond of representing castration by a doubling or multiplication of the genital symbol."[36] Again, he comments that "It often happens that male patients declare that there is something uncanny about the female genital organs."[37] Later, in his essay on "Medusa's Head" (1922), he will point out that the representation of Medusa's hair by snakes in works of visual art is another manifestation of the castration complex:

> however frightening they may be in themselves, they nevertheless serve actually as a mitigation of the horror, for they replace the penis, the absence of which is the cause of the horror. This is a confirmation of the technical rule according to which a multiplication of penis symbols signifies castration.[38]

The "Medusa's Head" essay has achieved a certain prominence in recent theoretical discussions, in part because of Neil Hertz's provocative article "Medusa's Head: Male Hysteria under Political Pressure" in the Fall 1983 issue of *Representations*, and the replies to it by Catherine Gallagher and Joel Fineman in the same issue of that journal.[39] The key passage here is Freud's explanation of "the horrifying decapitated head of Medusa":

> To decapitate = to castrate. The terror of Medusa is thus a terror of castration that is linked to the sight of something. Numerous analyses have made us familiar with the occasion for this: It occurs when a boy, who has hitherto been unwilling to believe the threat of castration, catches sight of the female genitals, probably those of an adult, surrounded by hair, and essentially those of his mother.
>
> The hair upon Medusa's head is frequently represented in works of art in the form of snakes, and these once again are derived from the castration complex. It is a remarkable fact that, however frightening they may be in themselves, they nevertheless serve as a mitigation of the horror, for they replace the penis, the absence of which is the cause of the horror. This is a confirmation of the technical rule according to which a multiplication of penis symbols signifies castration.
>
> The sight of Medusa's head makes the spectator stiff with terror, turns him into stone. Observe that we have here once again the same origin from the castration complex and the

same transformation of affect! For becoming stiff means an erection. Thus in the original situation it offers consolation to the spectator: he is still in possession of a penis, and the stiffening reassures him of the fact.

If Medusa's head takes the place of a representation of the female genitals, or rather if it isolates their horrifying effects from the pleasure-giving ones, it may be recalled that displaying the genitals is familiar in other connections as an apotropaic act. What arouses horror in oneself will produce the same effect upon the enemy against whom one is seeking to defend oneself. We read in Rabelais of how the Devil took to flight when the woman showed him her vulva.

The erect male organ also has an apotropaic effect, but thanks to another mechanism. To display the penis (or any of its surrogates) is to say: "I am not afraid of you. I defy you. I have a penis." Here, then, is another way of intimidating the Evil Spirit.[40]

The desire to rewrite the female first as castration then as erection has seldom been so clearly expressed. In *Macbeth*, too, gender assignments are constantly in doubt, in flux, and in the way.

We may note that the brief 1922 piece on "Medusa's Head," the 1927 essay on "Fetishism," and the longer essay on "The Uncanny" (1919) all return or double back upon this fear of castration and its relationship to the sight of the female genitals, the mythologized version of which is Medusa's severed head. In this context it is particularly interesting to take note of Freud's own implicit strategy of repression or denial in "The Uncanny" as manifested in his gentle but firm correction of E. Jentsch's interpretation of Hoffmann's tale with which "The Uncanny" begins. Jentsch had maintained, in what is described as "a fertile but not exhaustive paper,"[41] that uncanny effects in literature are produced by uncertainty as to whether a particular figure in the story is a human being or an automaton. This, says Freud, is not in fact what produces uncanniness in "The Sand-Man." It is not, or not only, "the theme of the doll, Olympia, who is to all appearance a living being" that gives Hoffmann's tale its "quite unparalleled atmosphere of uncanniness," but rather "the theme of the Sand-Man who tears out children's eyes,"[42] and the Sand-Man's association with fears of castration and the castrating father. Yet when he turns to the subject of other imaginative literature, Freud makes a similar move in the direction of a misleading detail. Twice in his essay he specifically mentions Shakespeare's plays, and prominent among them, *Macbeth*; on both occasions, as we have seen, he denies that the presence of "spirits, demons and ghosts"[43] or "ghostly apparitions" in themselves impart to the play an aspect of the play's uncanniness. I quote again:

The souls in Dante's *Inferno* or the ghostly apparitions in *Macbeth* or *Julius Caesar*, may be gloomy and terrible enough, but they are no more really uncanny than is Homer's jovial world of gods. We order our judgement to the imaginary reality imposed on us by the writer, and regard souls, spirits and spectres as though their existence had the same validity in their world as our own has in the external world. And then in this case too we are spared all trace of the uncanny.[44]

What Freud in effect denies here, in the case of Shakespeare, is the real uncanniness at the center of the play, which is provoked not by the ghosts and apparitions in *Macbeth* but rather by the "morbid anxiety" produced by "something repressed which *recurs*"[45]—an idea, fear, or fantasy that is continually undergoing a process of repression or denial. "This uncanny is in reality nothing new or foreign, but something familiar and old-established in the mind that has been estranged only by the process of repression."[46] Summing up his findings, Freud catalogues them, and in doing so names practically every major theme in *Macbeth*: "animism, magic and witchcraft, the omnipotence of thought, man's attitude to death, involuntary repetition, and the castration-complex comprise practically all the factors which turn something fearful into an uncanny thing."[47] By the terms of this anatomy, *Macbeth* is *the* play of the uncanny—the uncanniest in the canon.[48]

For Macbeth the dramatic character, uncanniness, the "something repressed which recurs," is figured not only in the witches and Banquo's ghost, but also, perhaps most strikingly, in the fear of castration, which he repeatedly expresses in the form of gender anxiety:

> *Macbeth*: I dare do all that may become a man;
> Who dares do more is none.
> *Lady Macbeth*:   What beast was't then
> That made you break this enterprise to me?
> When you durst do it, then you were a man;
> And to be more than what you were, you would
> Be so much more the man. (1.7.46–51)

Lady Macbeth's sexual taunts here and elsewhere in the play have about them the painful familiarity of an old story, an efficacious and destructive strategy of attack upon his masculinity, his male identity.[49] "You would / Be so much more the man." But what is *more* than man? Is it, in this play of border transgressions, equivalent to being woman? or some androgynous combination of the genders, like the bearded witches or the "unsexed" Lady Macbeth herself?

This same conversation repeats itself in a yet more agonized form when Macbeth is confronted by the Medusa head of Banquo at the banquet in Act 3 scene 4:

> *Macbeth*:   Thou canst not say I did it; never shake
> Thy gory locks at me . . . (49–50)
> *Lady Macbeth*:   —*Are you a man?*
> *Macbeth*:   Ay, and a bold one, *that dare look on that*
> *Which might appall the devil.*
> *Lady Macbeth*:   O proper stuff!
> This is the very painting of your fear;
> This is the air-drawn dagger which you said

	Led you to Duncan. O, these flaws and starts
	(Impostors to true fear) would well become
	A woman's story at a winter's fire,
	Authorized by her grandam. Shame itself,
	Why do you make such faces? When all's done
	You *look* but on a stool. (57–67)
Macbeth (*to Ghost*):	Avaunt, *and quit my sight!* let the earth hide thee!
	Thy bones are marrowless, thy blood is cold;
	Thou hast no speculation in those eyes
	Which thou dost glare with!
Lady Macbeth (*to assembled lords*):	Think of this, good peers,
	But as a thing of custom. 'Tis no other;
	Only it spoils the pleasure of the time.
Macbeth:	*What man dare, I dare.*
	Approach thou like the rugged Russian bear,
	Th'armed rhinoceros, or th'Hyrcan tiger,
	Take any shape but that, and my firm nerves
	Shall never tremble. Or be alive again,
	And dare me to the desert with thy sword;
	If trembling I inhabit them, protest me
	The baby of a girl. Hence, horrible shadow!
	Unreal mock'ry, hence! (Exit Ghost)
	Why, so; *being gone*
	I am a man again. (92–106)
Macbeth (*to Lady Macbeth*):	You make me strange
	Even to the disposition that I owe,
	When now I think you can behold such sights,
	And keep the natural ruby of your cheeks
	When mine is blanch'd with fear. (111–15)

"Daring" here becomes the play's trope of transgression, and also Macbeth's desperate and self-defeating rhetorical equivalent of masculinity in action. Lady Macbeth taunts him with "Letting 'I dare not' wait upon 'I would,' / Like the poor cat in th'adage" (1.7.44–5), giving the word an aphoristic context; the "poor cat" contrasts ironically with the "beast" that broke the murder plan to her, and also to the Hyrcan tiger, the Russian bear and the armed rhinoceros, just as "the baby of a girl" contrasts with the bold "man" he claims to be. Lady Macbeth's scathing reference to female storytelling, womanish narrative, and female authority and lineage neatly encapsulates all his fears, providing a devastating alternative to the bold male historical chronicle in which he would like to act, as well as to the paternal authority symbolized by Duncan, by the desire for heirs to the throne, and by the tacit and powerful figure of the father-king James I. Likewise the references to proliferation of dangerous gazings and forbidden sights in this scene ("never shake thy gory locks at me"; "a bold one, that dare look on that / Which might appall the devil"; "Avaunt, and quit my sight"; "Thou hast no speculation in those eyes / Which thou dost glare with"; "take any shape but that, and my firm nerves / Shall never tremble"; "Hence, horrible shadow! / Unreal mock'ry, hence!"; "you can behold such sights, / And keep the natural ruby of your cheeks, / When mine is blanch'd with fear") calls attention to the underlying theme of the Medusa complex. Notice that Lady Macbeth can, in his view, look with impunity on that which reduces him to unmanned fright. Why? Because she is "unsexed"? Because she is a woman? Because she has no "manhood" to protect?

"Unsex me here"

With its gaping mouth, its snaky locks and its association with femininity, castration, and erection, Medusa's head ends up being the displacement upward neither of the female nor of the male genitals but of gender undecidability as such. *That* is what is truly uncanny about it, and it is that uncanniness that is registered in the gender uncertainties in *Macbeth*. Yet Freud (along with virtually all other commentators on Medusa as well as on *Macbeth*, including recent feminist critics) enacts the *repression* of gender undecidability. Freud's text is positively acrobatic in its desire to reassign decidable difference, to read the Medusa figure in terms of castration anxiety and penis display, and to locate fetishism as an identifiable variant of this same anxious and repressive process. Shakespeare's play, however, resists such assignment, resists even the present-day tendency to see the play in terms of male homosocial bonding or anxiety about female power.[50] Power in *Macbeth* is a function of neither the male nor the female but of the suspicion of the undecidable. The phallus as floating signifier is more powerful than when definitely assigned to either gender.

The presence of gender anxiety and its contiguity to border crossings and boundary transgressions has been evident from the opening moments of the play, when the three witches, the weird sisters, gloatingly plot their revenge upon the sailor's wife through their designs upon her husband, the "master o' the Tiger." The witches, who physically exhibit signs of their gender undecidability, as Banquo notes ("you should be women, / And yet your beards forbid me to interpret / That you are so" [1.3.45–7]), are in a sense pluralized, replicative dream-figures for Lady Macbeth. Both they and she whisper plots and hint at the glorious future for Macbeth, goading him on to "dare." We may remember also that Medusa, whose name means "the Queen," was originally one of three. Wherever Macbeth goes, to the castle or to the heath, he encounters the same powerful female presence that lures him to destruction.

As for the witches, their language early in the play is what we might now recognize as Medusa language, the language of gender undecidability and castration fear. "Like a rat without a tail" the First Witch will "do"; in glossing this zoo-logical peculiarity the eighteenth-century editor George Steevens noted a belief of Shakespeare's time "that though a witch could assume the form of any animal she pleased, the tail would still be wanting, and that the reason given by some old writers for such a deficiency was, that though the hands and feet by an easy change might be converted into the four paws of a beast, there was still no part about a woman which corresponded with the length of tail common to almost all our four-footed creatures."[51] Again the woman comes up short—a Renaissance witch, it seems, could not even aspire to mimetic rathood, but instead had to content herself with a curtailed or foreshortened version of that condition. The gleeful assertion, "I'll drain him dry as hay" (1.3.18) may refer to unshakable thirst, a common affliction of sailors, but it is also plausibly a description of a man exhausted ("drained dry") by excessive sexual demands made upon him. "Sleep shall neither night nor day / Hang upon his pent-house lid . . . Weary sev'n-nights nine times nine, / Shall he dwindle, peak and pine" (1.3.19–23).[52] The transgressive and usurping androgynous power of the witches seems to justify, indeed to invite, a reading of these lines as sexually invasive and demeaning; the drained husband will not, unlike the weird sisters, be capable of "doing." "Look what I have," the First Witch cries delightedly.

> 2 *Witch*: Show me, show me.
> 1 *Witch*: Here I have a pilot's thumb,
>   Wrack'd, as homeward he did come. [*Drum within.*
> 3 *Witch*: A drum! a drum!
>   Macbeth doth come. (26–31)

This dismembered "pilot's thumb" culminates the implicit narrative of sexual disabling and castration. The repetition of the word "come" to describe the progress of both Macbeth and the hapless "pilot" reinforces the metonymic association of the two figures, especially since Macbeth is also on his way home to be "wrack'd." (He uses the word in a similar context of storm and disaster just before his own decap-itation at the play's close: "Blow, wind! come, wrack! / At least we'll die with harness on our back" [5.5.51–2]). Nor can we entirely ignore the possibility that "look what I have" can function as a gleeful, childlike announcement of sexual display. Just as the Medusa head incorporates the elements of sexual gazing (scopophilia) and its con-comitant punishment, castration, so the First Witch's exhibition of a prize, coming as it does in the narrative just after the account of the "drained" sailor, invites a similar transgressive sight. The morphological similarity between thumb and phallus needs no elaboration, and the possession by the witches of a thumb / phallus as a fetishistic object would emphasize their ambiguous, androgynous character, shortly to be remarked by Banquo. The witches' chortling exchange, aptly described by Coleridge as exhibiting "a certain fierce familiarity, grotesqueness mingled with terror,"[53] introduces the entrance of Macbeth and Banquo, and marks Banquo's questions of them as appropriate descriptions of the uncanny:

> What are these,
> So wither'd and so wild in their attire,
> That look not like th'inhabitants o'th'earth,
> And yet are on't? Live you? or are you aught
> That man may question? . . .
> you should be women,
> And yet your beards forbid me to interpret
> That you are so. (1.3.39–47)

The "Medusa complex," if we may continue to call it that, persists throughout the play, from Macduff's horrified cry to the final scene. Macbeth's first act is to display a severed head. Even before the murder there is a muted anticipation of the myth, in an image that seems localized but will recur: Macbeth's curious insistence on the phenomenon of his hair standing on end as if it were alive. Learning that he is Thane of Cawdor, and therefore that the witches' other prophecies may come true, he contemplates the murder of Duncan and is terrified at the thought. "Why," he wonders aloud,

> do I yield to that suggestion
> Whose horrid image doth unfix my hair,
> And make my seated heart knock at my ribs,
> Against the use of nature? (1.3.134–7)

The word "horrid" comes from a Latin word meaning "to bristle with fear," and is used to mean "bristling, shaggy," throughout the Renaissance. Metaphorically, at least, Macbeth's hair stands on end, "unfixed" by the "horrible imaginings" that flood his mind. Significantly, his imagined physiological response occurs in a key passage about undecidability and the sensation of the uncanny. The "supernatural solicitings" are the text of transgressive doubt, when "nothing is but what is not."

Much later in the play he makes use of the same image, this time to emphasize not his emotional distraction but the numbness that has succeeded it. Hearing the distressful cry of women, he speculates on its source, but does not otherwise respond.

> I have almost forgot the taste of fears.
> The time has been, my senses would have cool'd
> To hear a night-shriek; and my fell of hair
> Would at a dismal treatise rouse, and stir,
> As life were in't. I have supp'd full with horrors. (5.5.9–13)

Notice "as life were in't." Hair that stands on end is occasionally mentioned elsewhere in Shakespeare, notably when Brutus beholds the ghost of Caesar and addresses it as a "monstrous apparition." "Art thou any thing?" he asks. "Art thou some god, some angel, or some devil, / That mak'st my blood cold, and my hair to stare?" (*Julius Caesar* 4.3.276–8). Never, however, does this figure appear with the imaginative intensity that it does in *Macbeth*. Occurring once near the beginning of the play and once near the end, the picture of the man with horrid, bristling hair frames the dramatic action in an oddly haunting way.

Like Brutus, Macbeth is also visited by the ghost of a man he has murdered, and that encounter provides the opportunity for another, more substantial evocation of the Medusa story. On this occasion Macbeth is the horrified onlooker, and the ghost of Banquo the instrument of his petrification.

The scene is the banqueting-hall, where the Scottish lords are gathering to feast with their new king. Macbeth has just learned of the successful murder of Banquo—"his throat is cut" (3.4.15). It is therefore with some complacency that he addresses the assembled lords, expressing the disingenuous hope that "the grac'd person of our Banquo" (3.4.40) is merely tardy rather than fallen upon "mischance" (42). But no sooner has he said these words than he turns to find the ghost of his old companion seated in the king's place. His shock is profound, and his language significant. In effect he is petrified, turned to stone.

Desperately he resolves to visit the weird sisters and compel them to show him the future. But when they do, it is only to present him with another Gorgon, one he will neither recognize nor interpret correctly. For the first apparition summoned by the witches is "an armed Head," prefiguring Macbeth's own ignoble decapitation. Had he read the apotropaic warning in the disembodied head, or in its words, his story might have ended differently. But his failure to "beware the Thane of Fife" (4.1.72), like his inability to comprehend the limits of his own power and knowledge, spell his doom. It remains for the Thane of Fife to transform him into yet another "new Gorgon," a warning sign to Scotland and to the audience of tragedy.

When Macduff confronts Macbeth on the field of battle, he offers, unwittingly, an explanation of the second apparition displayed by the witches, the bloody child. The apparition had proclaimed that "none of woman born / Shall harm Macbeth" (4.1.80–1) so that Macbeth departed confident of his safety. But now Macduff reveals that he "was from his mother's womb / Untimely ripp'd" (5.8.15–16). Macduff's Caesarean birth recalls the moment before the play began when, according to the sergeants' report, Macbeth "carv'd out his passage" (1.2.19) through the rebels and "unseam'd" Macdonwald "from the nave to th'chops" (22).[54] To be "not of woman born" is at least rhetorically to be exempt from the gender anxiety that so torments Macbeth—to be a man born only from a man. And the image of parthenogenesis suggested by this deliberately "paltering" phrase may also bring to mind the figure of Athena, the virgin war goddess, bearer of the Gorgon shield, who sprung full grown, armed and shouting from the head of her father, Zeus. Both of these births avoid the normal "passage" through the female body. Both avoid a disabling identification with the mother and with female weakness, empowering the figures thus begotten as appropriate emblems of retribution. Hearing this phrase—"from his mother's womb / Untimely ripp'd"—Macbeth's courage begins to fail. "I'll not fight with thee," he declares (5.8.22). "Then yield thee, coward," retorts Macduff,

> And live to be the show and gaze o'th'time!
> We'll have thee, as our rarer monsters are,
> Painted upon a pole, and underwrit,
> "Here may you see the tyrant." (5.8.23–7)

"Monster," a word which for the Renaissance carried the modern meaning of an unnatural being, also retained the force of its Latin root, monēre (to warn), and hence meant a divine portent or sign. In Macduff's scenario the picture of Macbeth is to become an object lesson, a spectacle, a warning against tyranny, a figure for theater and for art. Like the head of Medusa, this painted figure would serve a monitory role, much in the manner of the dead suitors whose severed heads were to adorn the walls of Antioch in *Pericles*. Ultimately, however, taunted by so inglorious a fate, Macbeth decides to fight—and it is at this point that the next "new Gorgon" appears. Macbeth is slain, and in the next scene we find the stage direction, "Enter Macduff with Macbeth's head."

On the stage this is, or should be, an extremely disturbing moment. The head is presented to the spectators, both the onstage Scottish troops and the audience in the theater, and it is reasonable to suppose that before Macduff's speech of homage to Duncan's son, Malcolm ("Hail, King! for so thou art" [5.9.20]) there should be a brief silence. Even though this is a bloody play, and the soldiers are engaged in bloody battle, the sudden appearance of a severed head—and a recognizable one, at that—might give one pause. The audience, if not turned to stone, is at least likely to be taken aback. Macduff the avenging Perseus, Macbeth the horrified Medusa head, are presented as if in allegorical tableau. And since there is no stage direction that indicates departure, the bloody head of the decapitated king must remain onstage throughout all of Malcolm's healing and mollifying remarks. In his final speech he refers to "this dead butcher" (5.9.35), presumably with some sort of gesture in the direction of the head. However complete Malcolm's victory, however bright the future for Scotland under his rule, the audience is confronted at the last with a double spectacle; the new king and the old tyrant, the promising future and the tainted past.

Yet just as the head of Medusa became a powerful talisman for good once affixed to the shield of Athena, so the head of Macbeth is in its final appearance transformed from an emblem of evil to a token of good, a sign at once minatory and monitory, threatening and warning. Not in the painted guise foreseen by Macduff, but in its full and appalling reality, the head of the monster that was Macbeth has now become an object lesson in tyranny, a demonstration of human venality and its overthrow—"the show and gaze o'th'time."

The severed head, the gory locks of Banquo, and the armed head that appears as the witches' first apparition—all these have an iconographic congruence to the "new Gorgon" Macduff announced. But there is yet one more episode in the play which, to me at least, suggests associations with the Gorgon story, and which is, in its way, the most remarkable version of that story in the play. I refer to the final apparition displayed for Macbeth on the heath, at his importunate insistence. You will recall that the witches had told him to "seek to know no more" and that he had nonetheless insisted on an answer to his final question, "shall Banquo's issue ever / Reign in this kingdom?" (4.1.102–3). As we have seen, he threatens to curse them if they do not reply, and is answered by a chorus that makes plain that the ensuing vision is taboo, not to be gazed upon: "Show! / Show! / Show! / Show his eyes, and grieve his heart; / Come like shadows, so depart" (4.1.107–11). Now there appear what the stage directions describe as *A show of eight Kings, the last with a glass in his hand; BANQUO following.* Macbeth's anguished response is worth quoting in full because of its relevance to our line of inquiry:

> Thou art too like the spirit of Banquo: down!
> Thy crown does sear mine eye-balls:—and thy hair,
> Thou other gold-bound brow, is like the first:—
> A third is like the former:—filthy hags!
> Why do you show me this?—A fourth?—Start, eyes?
> What! will the line stretch out to th'crack of doom?
> Another yet?—A seventh?—I'll see no more:—
> And yet the eighth appears, who bears a glass,
> Which shows me many more; and some I see,
> That two-fold balls and treble sceptres carry.
> Horrible sight!—Now, I see, 'tis true;
> For the blood-bolter'd Banquo smiles upon me,
> And points at them for this.—What! is this so?
>
> 1 Witch: Ay, Sir, all this is so:—but why
>   Stands Macbeth thus amazedly? (112–26)

"Why stands Macbeth thus amazedly?" We could answer with the Doctor's words from the sleepwalking scene: "My mind she has mated, and amaz'd my sight." Notice Macbeth's words: "Sear mine eyelids"; "start, eyes"; "horrible sight." Once again Macbeth is a man transfixed by what he has seen, once again in effect turned to stone. His murders have been for nothing; Banquo's sons will inherit the kingdom. This is his personal Gorgon, the sign of his own futility and damnation.

But the form of this particular apparition has more to tell us. The eighth king appears with "a glass," which shows us many more kings to come. A glass is a mirror—in the context of the scene a magic mirror, predicting the future, but as a stage prop quite possibly an ordinary one, borne to the front of the audience where at the first performance King James would have been seated in state. James, of course, traced his ancestry to Banquo, a fact which—together with his interest in witchcraft—may have been the reason for Shakespeare's choice of subject. The "glass" is another transgression of the inside / outside boundary, crossing the barrier that separates the play and its spectators.

Moreover, the word "glass" in Shakespeare's time meant not only "mirror" but also "model" or "example." Thus Hamlet is described as "the glass of fashion and the mould of form" (*Hamlet* 3.1.155); Hotspur as "the glass / Wherein the noble youth did dress themselves" (*King Henry IV, Part 2* 2.3.21–2), and King Henry V, in a variant of the figure, as "the mirror of all Christian kings" (*King Henry V* 2.0.6). For the apparition of the eighth king to reflect such a "glass" (in the person of James I) with the glass he bears would therefore approximate in metaphorical terms the optical phenomenon of infinite regress when two mirrors face one another. Banquo's line would indeed "stretch out to th' crack of doom." Implicitly this trope is already present, since the king reflects all his ancestors. In this sense as well he is "a glass / Which shows [Macbeth] many more." James himself would later explicate this figure of the king as mirror in a speech to Parliament on 21 March, 1609:

> Yee know that principally by three wayes yee may wrong a Mirrour.
>
> First, I pray you, look not vpon my Mirrour with a false light: which yee doe, if ye mistake, or mis-vunderstand my Speach, and so alter the sence thereof.
>
> But secondly, I pray you beware to soile it with a foule breath, and vncleane hands: I meane, that yee peruert not my words by any corrupt affections, turning them to an ill meaning, like one, who when hee hears the tolling of a Bell, fancies to himself, that it speakes those words which are most in his minde.
>
> And lastly (which is worst of all) beware to let it fall or breake: (for glass is brittle) which ye doe, if ye lightly esteeme it, and by contemning it, conforme not your selues to my perswasions.[55]

What I would like to suggest here is that the reflecting glass or mirror in this scene is the counterpart of Perseus's reflecting shield, another transgression of the boundary between stage and reality. Perseus, we are told, was able to gaze on the reflection of Medusa without harm, although had he looked at her directly he would have been turned to stone. But the reflection or deflection of the dreadful image made it bearable. When the head was presented to Athena, and its image fixed on her aegis, it became a positive force, allied with the goddess and the virtues for which she stood. In the context of *Macbeth* the reflecting glass is the binary opposite of Macbeth's severed head: the glass is a happy spectacle demonstrating the long line of kings descended from Banquo, a line which James would doubtless hope to have "stretch out to th' crack of doom"; the head is a dismal spectacle signifying the end of a tyrant's solitary reign. Both are displaced versions of the Gorgon myth, "new Gorgons," since what horrifies Macbeth gratifies King James and the Jacobean audience. Indeed it may not be too extreme to suggest that James himself is the Athena figure here, to whom the head of the slain Macbeth is offered as a talisman and sign. The code of flattery which attended the theater of patronage would surely have allowed such a trope, and the apotropaic function of the severed head, warding off evil, would have been entirely consonant with the play's other compliment to English kings, the mention of the "healing benediction" (4.3.156)—the sovereign's ability to cure scrofula ("the evil") with the "king's touch," a custom which dated from the reign of Edward the Confessor, and was still in practice at the time of James I. Yet the fact that the "glass" transgresses the boundary of representation implies once again that tranquil containment is not possible without opening a new rift.

"There's no art
To find the mind's construction in the face"

What is reflected in the mirror is thus, on the one hand, the king, and on the other hand, the sexually ambiguous head of the Medusa. There are in fact historical reasons why it should come as no surprise to find that gender undecidability in Shakespeare is profoundly implicated in power. England had recently been ruled by a Queen who called herself a Prince, used the male pronoun in all her state papers, and was widely rumored to possess some of the anatomical features of the male sex. In a famous passage in her speech to her troops at Tilbury—when she appeared in the costume of an androgynous martial maiden—she declared:

> I know that I have the body but of a weak and feeble woman, but I have the heart and stomach of a king, and a king of England, too.[56]

Louis Montrose puts the matter of the queen's two bodies clearly when he remarks that "As the female ruler of what was, at least in theory, a patriarchal society, Elizabeth incarnated a contradiction at the very center of the Elizabethan sex / gender system."[57] "More than a man, and, in troth, sometimes less than a woman," as Cecil wrote to Harington.[58]

As for King James, he was known to have not only a wife but also male favorites. A preacher at St. Paul's Cross spoke openly in a sermon about the King and "his catamites." Sir Walter Raleigh, discussing the King's special friend, the Duke of Buckingham, is reported to have said that royal favorites "were frequently commanded to uncomely, and sometimes unnatural, employments,"[59] and James himself wrote longingly to Buckingham as his "sweet child and wife," while expressing in his poems and letters his desire for "sweete bedchamber boyes."[60] "The love the king shewed," wrote Francis Osborne, "was as amorously conveyed, as if he had mistaken their sex, and thought them ladies."[61] Historically as well as dramatically, then, one can ask: was the Queen a man? Was the King a queen?

Elizabeth and James, in other words, themselves encoded boundary transgression at precisely the point of maximum personal and political power. This play marks the gender undecidability of monarchs. But if the curtain rises too soon on the bearded witches, revealing a scene of gender undecidability, is the final scene a restoration of decidability? Does Macbeth's brandished head apotropaically dismiss uncertainty, or reinscribe it? *That* is what remains uncertain. The attempts of feminists and others to reassign gender and power in *Macbeth* merely replicate the fundamental resistance we have seen in Freud, the refusal to regard the enigma as such, to gaze upon the head of the Medusa, to recognize the undecidability that may lie just beneath the surface of power—and perhaps of sexuality itself.

The prevalence of the Medusa image and its own uncanny propensity for appearing at moments of aesthetic or representational crisis underscores the aptness of the figure's obsessive presence in *Macbeth*. Linked repeatedly to gender and to threatening sexual manifestations, it is also found again and again in the context of poetic anxiety and the anxiety of narrative completion. John Freccero has convincingly shown that the Medusa against which the furies warn Dante's pilgrim in *Inferno* (9.52–63) represents "a sensual fascination and potential entrapment, precluding all further progress,"[62] the danger of narcissistic fascination with the poet's own creation. "Petrification by the Medusa," Freccero argues, "is the real consequence of Pygmalion's folly."[63] This kind of self-conscious poetic idolatry, "a refusal to go beyond, a self-petrification"[64] is both the risk and the triumph of secular poetry, as exemplified in the appropriately named poet Petrarca, who acknowledges the risk of turning to stone in the idolatrous adoration of his own creation, *Laura / lauro*, the poetic subject and the poetic garland: "*Medusa e l'error mio m'han fatto un sasso.*"[65] Such a reification immortalizes the poet as much as it does his ostensible subject.

Gender undecidability is here a figure for the anxiety of art. Dante's Virgil covers the pilgrim's eyes to protect him from the sight of the Medusa, and the poet turns, immediately to warn the reader:

> O voi ch'avete li 'ntelletti sani,
> Mirate la dottrina ch s'asconde
> Sotto 'l velame de lie versi strani. (9.61–3)
>
> [O you possessed of sturdy intellects,
> observe the teaching that is hidden here
> beneath the veil of verses so obscure.]

Here Dante substitutes his own apotropaic warning for the sight of the Medusa—a warning produced and engendered by the absence, refusal, or denial of that sight. The reader, in fact, is invited not to look away, but to look at, *mirate*, to observe that which is veiled or displaced by the Medusa. The text presents itself as a legible sight, a survivable alternative to the petrification of the Medusa gaze, which would prevent a return to the world above (*nulla sarebbe di tornar mai suso*).

The word "apotropaic," so frequently associated with the power of the severed Medusa head, means "turning away" or "warding off," and derives from the same root as "trope," and also as Atropos, the third of the Moirai or Fates—Atropos whose name means the Inflexible or the Inexorable, she who cannot be turned away. Like the Gorgons, the Fates were three in number; they are represented in myth as old women, and probably originated not as abstract powers or destiny but as birth-spirits, telling the story of a child's future. The thread they spin, the tale or plot they weave, is the individual's destiny, the life line or the plot line. Atropos is variously described as spinning or singing, both creative arts, then as cutting the thread of life short. The Latin word *Fata* itself is probably an adaptation of the singular *fatum*, "that which is spoken." In fact, the Fates seem from the first to have been connected with narrative, and perhaps also with prophetic powers, as are Shakespeare's Weird Sisters. It is not entirely surprising, therefore, that an apotropaic object like the Medusa head, especially when represented in visual art or poetry, would have a doubled message to deliver, a message at once seductive and dangerous, enabling and disabling.

Not only in antiquity and the Middle Ages, but also in the Renaissance, the image of Medusa exercised a powerful fascination over visual artists. Cellini's famous statue of *Perseus* in the Bargello Museum in Florence holds aloft a rather romanticized head of Medusa with attractive classical features, and Rubens's Baroque version of the head (in the Picture Gallery in Vienna) wears an anguished expression and a plenitude of writhing snakes. But the two most provocative renderings of the subject in the period are probably a lost work by Leonardo da Vinci described in Vasari's *Life of*

Leonardo, and Caravaggio's arresting painting now in the Uffizi Gallery. Both illustrate the transgressive representational powers of the Medusa, as well as the durability of the myth.

Vasari tells a remarkable and pertinent anecdote about the Leonardo Medusa. When the artist was still a very young man, his father, Ser Piero, gave him a round panel of wood (Vasari's word is *rotella* which, it is interesting to note, means a round shield) and asked him to paint something on it. Leonardo, says Vasari,

> resolved to do the Head of Medusa to terrify all beholders. To a room to which he alone had access, Leonardo took lizards, newts, maggots, snakes, moths, locusts, bats, and other animals of the kind, out of which he composed a horrible and terrible monster. . . . When it was finished Leonardo told his father to send for it when he pleased, as he had done his part. Accordingly Ser Piero went to his rooms one morning to fetch it. When he knocked at the door Leonardo opened it and told him to wait a little, and, returning to his room, put the round panel in the light on his easel, which he turned with its back to the window to make the light dim; then he called his father in. Ser Piero, taken unaware, started back, not thinking of the round piece of wood, or that the face which he saw was painted, and was beating a retreat when Leonardo detained him and said, "This work is as I wanted it to be; take it away, then, as it is producing the effect intended."[66]

The disembodied head, placed as if on a shield, terrifies and repels, while its creator wields the power of his creation, which is also the (suspended) power of parricide.

The life of Leonardo da Vinci held a particular fascination for Freud, whose 1910 essay on the painter's development attempts to explore the "peculiarity of [his] emotional and sexual life . . . in connection with Leonardo's double nature as an artist and as a scientific investigator,"[67] and concludes that "after his curiosity had been activated in infancy in the service of sexual interests he succeeded in sublimating the greater part of his libido into an urge for research"[68]—an extension and displacement of the "intense desire to look, as an erotic instinctual activity" which occurs in infantile development "before the child comes under the dominance of the castration-complex."[69] In this early essay on "Leonardo da Vinci and a Memory of his Childhood" Freud explicitly connects Leonardo's homosexuality to his desire to see his mother's penis, and his "disgust" at the appalling discovery that she lacks one. The theories of narcissism, fetishism and castration which would be elaborated in later works are here directly applied to the "youthful investigator"[70] who deflected his sexual desires into artistic creation, but even more centrally, into scientific curiosity, into *looking*. That Leonardo was an illegitimate child suggests a further nuance in Vasari's anecdote. The apotropaic head, the disembodied emblem and threat of castration, the sign of the androgynous mother, is displayed to the artist's father and produces "the effect intended," the consternation and repulsion of the father. Thus the son asserts control over his disconcerted parent, sending him away with the painted Medusa head, the son's own repellent and fascinating "work." In this image of the independent youthful investigator it is perhaps possible to see a self-portrait of Freud the analyst as creator and scientist, exhibiting his own Medusa head, the concept of the castration-complex, to an audience simultaneously fascinated and horrified.

To portray the head of Medusa as if on a shield, round or oblong, was not uncommon in the fifteenth and sixteenth centuries. The head is directly conceived as an apotropaic object that will protect the shield-bearer from harm. This seems also to be the case in the striking Caravaggio *Medusa*, which is painted on canvas and stretched over a round convex shield.[71] Her mouth is open as if crying out, blood streams from her neck, and her head is wreathed in a profusion of lively snakes. Presumably this work, like other similar representations, is intended to depict the aegis of Athena (or Minerva). It is in essence the Renaissance equivalent of those Roman Medusa masks discovered by archaeologists.

However, one other factor in the rendering of the Caravaggio *Medusa* may be of some interest in the light of our discussion. We know that for the *Medusa* as well as for his *Bacchus* and the decapitated Goliath in *David with the Head of Goliath* (and possibly for *Judith Beheading Holofernes*) Caravaggio reproduced by reflection his own face in a mirror. It therefore seems possible to consider Caravaggio's painting as a representation not—or not only—as Athena's shield, but also as Perseus's. Instead of being mounted on the shield, the head would in that case be reflected in it, and the viewer would share the immunity of Perseus. Since he gazes not directly upon the head of Medusa—which would by convention turn him to stone—but rather on its reflection, he can contemplate horror in safety. As Lady Macbeth points out in chiding Macbeth for his fears, "'tis the eye of childhood / That fears a painted devil" (2.2.51–2).

Whether the Medusa of the Caravaggio painting is considered a deflected image (and the shield that of Perseus) or a displaced image (and the shield Athena's), the result for the spectator is largely the same. He beholds a terrifying spectacle which, if it were encountered in the flesh, would be devastating to him—but he beholds it, as it were, from a safe distance, insulated by art. It would be tempting to conclude that the same is true of the Gorgon's heads in Shakespeare's play, that Shakespeare permits us to gaze at the face that should turn us to stone. This is indeed the conclusion to which Joyce Carol Oates comes in an essay that clearly articulates the theory of displacement and vicarious purgation:

> Critics who chide me for dwelling on unpleasant and even bloody subjects miss the point: art shows us how to get through and transcend pain, and a close reading of any tragic work (*Macbeth* comes immediately to mind) will allow the intelligent reader to see how and why the

tragedy took place, and how we, personally, need not make these mistakes. The more violent the murder in *Macbeth*, the more relief one can feel at *not* having to perform them. Great art is cathartic; it is always moral.[72]

Yet in the very wording of this passage we find an uncanny doubleness that exposes the fragility of such a reassuring formulation. "The more violent the murders in *Macbeth*, the more relief one can feel at *not* having to perform them." Notice Oates's word, *perform*. Murders, she implies, must be *performed*—that is, both committed and theatrically acted. This instability in language, this double sense of performance, makes it impossible to know exactly where to locate the boundary between stage and reality. In order to work apotropaically, tragedy *must* cross that boundary. The action may be an imitation, but the purgation is real—the emotion must be felt. The curtain rises too soon, and will not fall on cue. The danger seemingly foreclosed by art may be unleashed by the shifting, transgressive status of representation itself. The voyeuristic act which is the role of the audience in the theater has us coming and going; the desire to look, which is itself transgressive, cannot be dismissed as merely the disinterested glance of a spectator, the "objective" view of the "scientific investigator," displacing our passion—and our danger—as Freud's Leonardo displaced his.

In its self-conception, in its stage history, in the doubleness of its final tableau, *Macbeth* seems almost paradigmatically to be a play that refuses to remain contained within the safe boundaries of fiction. It is a tragedy that demonstrates the refusal of tragedy to be so contained. As it replicates, it implicates. Things will not remain within their boundaries: sleepers and forests walk, the dead and the deeds return, the audience stares at forbidden sights. This is what the plot of *Macbeth* is about. Yet what is most uncanny about the play is perhaps that it is *both* apotropaic and atropic, *heimlich* and *unheimlich*, faltering with us constantly in a double sense. It is as though we too can in the end only cry, with Lady Macbeth's doctor, "A great perturbation in nature, to receive at once the benefit of sleep and do the effects of watching!"

Shakespeare
as Fetish
4

Why is Shakespeare fetishized in Western popular—as well as Western high—culture? Who does the fetishizing, and what work does that fetishization do? What is the relationship of Shakespeare as fetish to current debates about Shakespeare in the academy, including the role of Shakespeare as the anchor of the canon, the Bloomingdales or Neiman Marcus (or, as we'll see shortly, the Wanamakers) of the upscale shopping mall which is the present-day English department? What has the fetishization of Shakespeare to do with recent critical emphases on colonialism, imperialism, undecidability, feminism, and the discourse of subjectivity?

I want to address these questions by briefly considering the phenomenon of fetishizing Shakespeare in one case involving a literary critic, one case involving a theatrical (and cultural) audience, and one case involving a government bureaucrat. But let me start by posing a simple question, which will be familiar to all who have been engaged with teaching and writing about Shakespeare and poststructuralism in the wake of the explosion of new work on Shakespeare in the last several decades. Why is it that parents who would be appalled to find their college-age children studying the same chemistry textbooks, or economic theorems, that they themselves were taught 20 years ago, fully expect that those children will learn the same things about Shakespeare that they learned when they themselves were in college? What is it about the humanities in general, and Shakespeare in particular, that calls up this nostalgia for the certainties of truth and beauty—a nostalgia which, like (I would contend) *all* nostalgias, is really a nostalgia for something that never was? Here I mean something as trivial as imagery and thematics ("What about the animal images in *King Lear*?" one alumnus asked me after a public talk. By not mentioning them I had, inadvertently to be sure, taken away something of his treasured childhood, or rather, his treasured memories of that childhood), or as loaded as politics: Caliban as the hero of *The Tempest*? cried an academic traditionalist. "Then I wouldn't know what the play would *mean*." By definition, the fetish and the circumstances of its narrative or enactment must always be the same.

That Shakespeare *is* the dream-space of nostalgia for the aging undergraduate (that is to say, for just about everyone) seems self-evidently true, and, to tell the truth, not all bad. He is—whoever he is, or was—the fantasy of originary cultural wholeness, the last vestige of universalism: *unser Shakespeare*. From the vantage point of a hard-won cultural relativism, a self-centered de-centering that directs attention, as it should and must, to subject positions, object relations, abjects, race-class-and-gender, there is still this tug of nostalgia, the determinedly secularized but not yet fully agnosticized desire to believe. To believe in something, in someone, all-knowing and immutable. If not God, then Shakespeare, who amounts to a version of the same thing.

Here is one of the most intelligent and influential of contemporary Shakespeareans, Stephen Greenblatt, fantasizing this wholeness-through-humanism.

> I began with the desire to speak with the dead.
>   . . . If I never believed that the dead could hear me, and if I knew that the dead could not speak, I was nonetheless certain that I could re-create a conversation with them . . . conventional in my tastes, I found the most satisfying intensity of all in Shakespeare.
>   I wanted to know how Shakespeare managed to achieve such intensity, for I thought that the more I understood this achievement, the more I could hear and understand the speech of the dead.[1]

By the end of this moving, almost incantatory introduction, itself a return to the rhetoric of high humanism despite (or because of) its emphasis on social energy and modes of production, Greenblatt has "corrected" his "dream": "the mistake," he says, "was to imagine that I would hear a single voice, the voice of the other. If I wanted to hear one, I had to hear the many voices of the dead. And if I wanted to hear the voice of the other, I had to hear my own voice."[2] But the voice he dreams of is still the voice of Shakespeare: Shakespeare the fetish.

There are two things I'd like to say about this barely secular invocation. The first thing to say is that Greenblatt picks up, in this confessional beginning ("I began with the desire to speak with the dead"), a narrative that he let drop at the end of his previous book, *Renaissance Self-Fashioning*; the anecdote about the man whose son— whose grown son—was in the hospital with an incapacitating illness which made it impossible for him to articulate words. The man therefore asked the Greenblatt of the Epilogue (a Greenblatt who was planning, with professional detachment, to "finish rereading Geertz's *Interpretation of Cultures*") to "mime a few sentences so that he could practice reading my lips? Would I say, soundlessly, 'I want to die. I want to die'?" But Greenblatt found that he could not say these words, even soundlessly. "Couldn't I say, 'I want to live'?" Better still, he suggested that the man might "go into the bathroom, and practice on himself in front of a mirror." "It's not the same," the man replied. And clearly it wasn't.[3]

From the unvoiced, taboo pronouncement (who would say it when a plane was taking off?) "I want to die, I want to die," to the professed desire to speak with the dead (and to acknowledge that to do so he had to hear his own voice) is not, after all, so far to go. It is, if you like, to go from the Hamlet of Act 1 scene 2 to the Hamlet of Act 1 scene 5. It is still a long distance to the enunciation of what Derrida has called "the impossible sentence," Hamlet's declaration, "I am dead, Horatio" (*Hamlet* 5.2.338). But the movement from the secular text (Geertz's *Interpretation of Cultures*) back to the fetishized universal Shakespeare is striking. "Conventional in my tastes, I found the most satisfying intensity of all in Shakespeare."

Remember—and this is my second and last point about Greenblatt as re-fetishizer of Shakespeare—that it is he who, in the last essay of *Shakespearean Negotiations*, tells the story of H. M. Stanley's canny burning of a copy of Shakespeare's plays. Stanley substituted this handy volume, easily replaceable in an English bookstore, for his irreplaceable field-notebook, to palliate the members of an African tribe who regarded his note-taking as taboo. "We will not touch it. It is fetish. You must burn it."[4] And so—if Stanley is to be believed—his field research was saved by Shakespeare.

Greenblatt puts a lot of distance between himself and this anecdote, once he has told it. "For our purposes, it doesn't matter very much if the story 'really' happened. What matters is the role Shakespeare plays in it." That role is described, characteristically, as two-edged; on the one hand, the field-notes were more powerful than Shakespeare's plays, and the plays had to be sacrificed for them; on the other hand, "Shakespeare *is* the discourse of power," whose agency in fact intervened to save Stanley's notes. In a footnote, which credits the finding of the anecdote to Walter Michaels, and the printing of it to William James, Greenblatt speculates on "the actual fetishism of the book" which he is willing to see in Stanley, "the attribution of power and value and companionship to the dead letter."[5] Thus Greenblatt is able to preserve, once again, his own divided subjectivity; he is at once the rational observer of discourses of power and the genial admirer of the numinousness of that power, both the desperate man on the plane and his dismayed, abashed, and finally unwilling Horatio. Yet "the attribution of power and value and companionship to the dead letter" is clearly what Greenblatt's opening gambit is all about. "I began with the desire to speak with the dead."

What has happened here, it seems to me, is that the dead metaphor of commodity fetishism has come back to life through the commodification of Shakespeare *as* a fetishized commodity. But what of the psychoanalytic understanding of the fetish, that the fetish is a substitute for the mother's penis (or phallus)? Here is Freud's description:

> the boy refused to take cognizance of the fact of his having perceived that a woman does not possess a penis. No, that could not be true: for if a woman has been castrated, then his own possession of a penis was in danger; and against that there rose in rebellion the portion of his narcissism which Nature has, as a precaution, attached to that particular organ. In later life a grown man may perhaps experience a similar panic when the cry goes up that Throne and Altar are in danger.[6]

The fetishist, says Freud, at once disavows and affirms the castration of women. To quote the famous little boy cited by Octave Mannoni, "Je sais bien, mais quand même" ("I know, but still. . . ."). "When the cry goes up that Throne and Altar are in danger"—so says Freud, writing in the Austria of 1927. We may hear, from a time and place when neither Throne nor Altar hold sway, the academic's (and the alumnus') cry, "then I wouldn't know what the play would *mean*." Shakespeare is the phallus of the mother, the guarantor of (impossible) originary wholeness.

And the phallic mother is England. Not any old merrie olde England, but the fantasy space of "early modern" England, the England of Elizabeth and James, in which we are busily discovering all kinds of behaviors and social practices, from colonialism to imperialism to transvestism to sodomy, that make it the mirror of today. Elizabethan England as phallic mother—"this sceptered isle," in John of Gaunt's famous speech about just such a nostalgia for originary wholeness (*King Richard II* 2.1.40)—the place of "the balm, the sceptre and the ball" (*King Henry V* 4.1.257) as signatures of office. Elizabeth herself as a man, perhaps physiologically a blurred gender, certainly appearing as that famous androgynous martial maiden before the troops at Tilbury, Elizabeth as Amazon, as Prince, as, precisely the phallic mother who is *the* fetish object, the object of fetishism.

Let us consider, briefly, some material evidence for the fetishizing of Shakespeare through the body of the phallic mother, on our way back to that quandary I noted a few moments ago. Consider, for example, the recently completed project to rebuild the Globe Theatre on the Bankside, a slick, professional campaign spearheaded by an expatriate American character actor, Sam Wanamaker, who put together a dynamite coalition of Hollywood celebrities, wealthy socialites, and bemused British (and Anglophilic) academics, with the goal of exactly reproducing, with surveyor's plans from period engravings, the dimensions, orientation, and furnishings of the old Globe. Naturally it would have been an American who longed for this, who made it his dream: to wrest the territory from a commercial brewery which owned the rights to the land, and rebuild, not just a building, but Shakespeare himself. Like the

Rockefellers rebuilding colonial Williamsburg, or Disney reconstituting the psychic realms of Fantasyland, Frontierland, and Tomorrowland in the conservative suburbs of Los Angeles, this plan longed for origins, for the moment when the dream began, for the navel of the dream.

The desire to return to a place one has never been, this very particular return of the repressed, animated the Wanamaker project of rebuilding the Globe. But the claim to return through reconstruction, the origin as located in and through representations of what the Globe once was, gave way for the moment to a claim of return through archaeology, the excavation of the site of the Rose Theatre, yet another brouhaha in a London attuned to Prince Charles's obsession with traditional architecture. "Dig Unearthing the Bard's World," trumpeted an early *Boston Globe* article on the excavation. The name of Shakespeare was repeatedly invoked to explain the importance of the project. "At the Rose, Shakespeare's *Titus Andronicus* was first performed. . . . It's fairly certain, scholars say, that Shakespeare himself acted minor roles in Ben Jonson plays at the Rose before turning to writing plays full-time."[7] On the night of May 14, 1989, 500 people, including "many prominent actors," camped out on the Rose site "listening to the likes of Dame Peggy Ashcroft and Ian McKellen" recite Shakespearean exhortations to hold firm. McKellen wore a shirt that said, "Will Power." Now, the Rose is not exactly *Shakespeare's* theater. The name (and fledgling acting career) of Shakespeare is here invoked to sanctify the site against incursion. "No other nation on the face of the Earth would allow the destruction of the theatrical home of the world's greatest playwright," declared Dame Peggy Ashcroft "as she trod the ruins with Hollywood's Dustin Hoffman, who was in London to appear in *The Merchant of Venice*." Even if it is not the Globe, it is still, somehow, "the world of the Bard."

I want to tie this kind of fetishizing of Shakespeare as maternal phallus in with the other major Shakespearean event in the London news during that period, the death of Lord Olivier. Now Olivier's death, quite simply, was celebrated, or mourned, or commemorated, as if it were the death of Shakespeare himself—only this time, much more satisfyingly, *with* a body. At a memorial service in Westminster Abbey, where, famously, Shakespeare is *not* buried, although a portrait bust represents him, "the casket," according to the *Boston Globe*, "was surmounted with a floral crown . . . studded with flowers and herbs mentioned in Shakespeare's works: from lavender and savory to rue and daisies."[8] The parade of dignitaries who moved up the aisle to the fanfare from Sir William Walton's music to "Hamlet," included Douglas Fairbanks, Jr., carrying the Order of Merit on a gold-fringed, blue velvet pillow, Michael Caine, carrying Olivier's Oscar (awarded not for any single role, but for "lifetime achievement"), and a host of other actors and actresses (Maggie Smith, Paul

Scofield, Derek Jacobi, Peter O'Toole, etc. etc.) bearing such relics as the crown used in the film of *Richard III*, the script of the film *Hamlet*, the laurel wreath in the stage production of *Coriolanus*, and the crown used in the television production of *King Lear*, as well as silver models of the Royal National Theatre and the Chichester Festival Theatre. That impossible event in literary history, a state funeral for the poet-playwright who defines Western culture, doing him appropriate homage—an event long-thwarted by the galling absence of certainty about his identity and where-abouts—has now at last taken place. Through a mechanism of displacement, the memorial service for Olivier became a memorial service for Shakespeare.

What I would like to argue here, riding my own hobbyhorse for a moment, is that under these cultural circumstances it is no accident that the Olivier eulogized (even before his death in commemorative essays) is a transvestite Olivier.

At first it might seem surprising that in both print and television obituaries for Olivier he was repeatedly pictured in drag, and described as "girlish." A photo of Olivier as Katherina in a school production of *The Taming of the Shrew* appeared on the NBC Evening News to mark the actor's passing. *Time* magazine commented that "From a list of his acting credits at school (Maria in *Twelfth Night*, Kate in *The Taming of the Shrew*), one imagines that his teachers had already spotted what director Elia Kazan would later cite as Olivier's 'girlish' quality. Throughout his career . . . Olivier would bat his eyes at the audience, soliciting its surrender. But belying those feminine eyes were the cruel, pliant lips, and on them the smile of a tiger too fastidious to lick his chops in anticipation of a tasty meal."[9]

"I may be rather feminine but I'm not effeminate," Olivier once declared, and critic Michael Billington remarks that "he can be masculine and feminine but never neuter."[10] He has been compared to Garbo and Dietrich in his sexual ambiguity—a quality, it is claimed, of great actors, though what this asserts it does not explain. Nor is Olivier as woman merely an artifact of the transvestite theater of his same-sex public school. The "definitive" biography by Anthony Holden ("author of *Prince Charles*," says the dustjacket) devotes a page of photographs to the great actor in drag, including a full-length photo of a serious-faced, middle-aged Olivier in a girdle, high heels, stockings, and padded bra.[11] Olivier's Malvolio at Stratford in 1955 is said to have been marked by a "dainty, fairy-footed progress across the stage and a skittish, faintly epicene lightness," like that of Jack Benny.[12] (Jewish and working-class, this Malvolio, with his crinkly hair and his uncertainty about pronunciation, invoked stereotypes about Jewish effeminacy that are part of the stage heritage of category crisis in ethnic- and gender-crossover, an essential element in what I call the "transvestite effect.") Kenneth Tynan described Olivier's Richard III, admiringly, as "a bustling spinster" in his dealings with Clarence,[13] and one critic aptly recalled Neil Simon's lampoon of a flamboyantly gay

Richard III in *The Goodbye Girl* as the obverse of Olivier's "sinister amalgam of male-power-hunger and female seductiveness."[14] The mechanism of displacement in category crisis deployed in and by transvestism is never more acutely emblematized than in Olivier's *Othello*; as Billington notes, "[e]ven at his butchest Olivier slips in hints of a dandified vanity: one remembers that astonishing first entrance in *Othello* with a red rose held gently between thumb and forefinger and with the hips rotating slightly in a manner half way between Dorothy Dandridge and Gary Sobers."[15]

This odd emphasis on the feminine and girlish Olivier comes despite—or, perhaps, because of—the fact that Olivier is frequently described as an exceptionally "athletic" Shakespearean actor, and his three marriages are extensively chronicled, as is his career as a movie heartthrob modeled after John Barrymore. As Billington in the same proto-posthumous appreciation recalls, "Olivier's fops leave you in no doubt as to their ultimate masculinity. . . . It is a modern fallacy that fops are homosexual. Olivier's two Restoration performances reminded us that in the seventeenth-century finery of apparel and frivolity of manner were compatible with balls."[16]

It is not, then, that Olivier is revealed in these representations as effeminate or gay (although biographer Donald Spoto would later publish disclosures about Olivier's sexual relationships with Danny Kaye and Peter Finch, and perhaps also with Noel Coward and critic Kenneth Tynan)[17] but rather that he becomes the portrait of triumphant transvestism—no closet queen, but the Queen Elizabeth of his age, and thus a figure for (who else) Shakespeare himself. If it is the case—and I believe it is—that the transvestite makes culture possible, that there can be no culture without the transvestite because the transvestite marks the entrance into the Symbolic, then the eulogizing of Olivier as on the one hand a matinee idol who began his career as a girl (or a "boy actress"), and on the other hand as Shakespeare makes a compelling, if at first counterintuitive, cultural sense.[18]

The nature and the point of that sense can perhaps best be seen by looking—briefly—at my last example of the fetishizing of Shakespeare, which comes from a report issued at about the same time to "the President, the Congress, and the American People" of the then-chairman of the National Endowment for the Humanities, Lynne Cheney. Cheney's 1988 report, *Humanities in America*, was at pains to point out that every cultural custodian *except* the university was doing its job right. High schools, libraries, museums, theater companies all came in for praise, but colleges and universities were letting America down by politicizing literature, opening up the canon, and teaching third world and ethnic studies rather than "the ideals and practices of our [which is to say, Western] civilization."[19]

"The humanities," declared Cheney, "are about more than politics, about more than social power. What gives them their abiding worth are truths that pass beyond time and circumstances; truths that, transcending accidents of class, race, and gender, speak to us all."[20] This paean to timeless and transcendent truths was guaranteed, it is almost needless to say, by a reference to Shakespeare, and in this case a very clever one, an apparent preemptive strike at the race-class-and-gender crowd: a quotation from a speech given in 1985 by a black woman writer, Maya Angelou, in which she declared that Shakespeare was a black woman.

In this address (entitled, doubtless to Cheney's gratification, "Journey to the Heartland"), Angelou told her audience in Cedar Rapids, Iowa, that when she was growing up in Stamps, Arkansas, she announced to her grandmother her intention to read "Portia's speech from *The Merchant of Venice*" to her church congregation. Her grandmother admonished her not to read the works of a white author, but rather one from her own tradition, like Langston Hughes, Countee Cullen, or Paul Laurence Dunbar. But years afterward, Angelou recalled, "I found myself and still find myself, whenever I like, stepping back into Shakespeare. . . . He wrote it for me. 'When in disgrace with fortune and men's eyes, / I all alone beweep my outcast state. . . .' Of course he wrote it for me; that is a condition of the black woman. Of course, he was a black woman. I understand that. Nobody else understands it, but I *know* that William Shakespeare was a black woman. That is the role of art in life."[21]

Now, let us pass over the ironic fact that Angelou's original choice of presentation piece, "Portia's speech in *The Merchant of Venice*," is spoken by one of the few Shakespearean characters to openly disparage a black man for his race and color, in ways that even sympathetic editors have not been able to explain away. ("Let all of his complexion choose me so," Portia remarks with satisfaction, when the Prince of Morocco chooses the wrong casket and fails to win her hand [*Merchant of Venice* 2.7.79].) Let us concentrate, instead, on Angelou's humanistic claim that "William Shakespeare was a black woman," and the ways in which that assertion is offered by Cheney as a validation of her own claim that "the humanities are about more than politics . . . [and] social power," that they are about truths transcending time, circumstance, and "accidents" of race, class, and gender.

What makes Angelou's appropriation of Shakespeare as a black woman acceptable—and a fitting climax to Cheney's indictment of ideologues in the academy—is the same thing that makes the figure of Olivier as a woman acceptable: the fact that this is *only* a figure, an allegory, a "transcendent" "truth." Shakespeare's identity is shrouded in mystery, and rival factions have warred for centuries over the competing claims of Oxford, Bacon, Queen Elizabeth, Christopher Marlowe, and the mysterious "William Shakespeare of Stratford." What would happen if it were *in fact* discovered that Shakespeare was a black woman, not through a ventriloquizing voice lamenting an archetypal "outcast state," but through some diligent feat of archival research? Just the same thing, I would suggest, that would happen if it were *in fact* discovered that Laurence Olivier was a woman. If morticians had revealed to the world days after his death that Olivier had actually, anatomically and biologically, been a woman, what would have happened, of course, would have been a massive campaign of disavowal. The man, after all, had wives, and children, and, to recall the Secretary of State's word, *cojones*.

Shakespeare as fetish *is* Shakespeare as phallus. The mother's phallus, to be sure—the imagined phallus of the child's universalizing vision of the world. But what makes Shakespeare fetishized and fetishizing, a scenario of desire that has to be repeated with exactitude for every generation, is the way in which he has come to stand for a kind of "humanness" which, purporting to be inclusive of race, class, and gender, is in fact the neutralizing (or neutering) of those potent discourses by appropriation and by a metaphysical move to the figure.

Race, class, and gender. If Maya Angelou can be convinced that Shakespeare speaks for her, at the cost of acknowledging vestiges of racism, sexism, and classism in his own works (that is, if she can be persuaded to believe that he speaks for her even—or precisely when—he is in fact speaking against her) then the ideological danger of fetishizing Shakespeare becomes clear and present. If Olivier's voice, recorded on tape, can again be heard echoing through Westminster Abbey in the most blatantly nationalistic and chauvinistic of English calls to arms, the Crispin Crispian speech from *Henry V* with which a living Olivier exhorted his fellow citizens to arms during World War II from that same Abbey—a call to arms that came, not coincidentally, on the eve of Britain's loss of most of its colonies—it is worth stopping to think what the political implications are of this kind of speaking with the dead. If Stephen Greenblatt can conclude that "the open secret of identity—that within differentiated individuals is a single structure, identifiably male—is presented literally in the all-male cast" of a Shakespearean play[22]—that, in effect, women are an artifact of male culture—then the danger of a critical refetishizing of Shakespeare is overt, and disturbing. What is much less clear is how we can get beyond this particular ideology. For Shakespeare as fetish has, in this time of perceived crisis in the humanities, become the ideology of our age.

Character Assassination: Shakespeare, Anita Hill, and JFK 5

Great men are more distinguished by range and extent than by originality.
—Ralph Waldo Emerson, "Shakespeare"

1st VOICE: Oh no!
2nd VOICE: Can't be!
3rd VOICE: They've shot the President!
5th VOICE: Oh, piteous sight!
1st VOICE: Oh, noble Ken O'Dunc!
2nd VOICE: Oh, woeful scene!
6th VOICE: Oh, traitorous villainy!
2nd VOICE: They shot from there.
1st VOICE: No, that way.
3rd VOICE: Did you see?
4th VOICE: Let's get the facts. Let's go and watch TV.
                    —Barbara Garson, *Macbird* (1966)

In the Fall of 1991, the televised Senate hearings on the confirmation of Clarence Thomas as Justice of the U.S. Supreme Court yielded an unexpected and fascinating benefit for the student of literature and culture: the voice of Shakespeare ventriloquized, speaking through our nation's lawmakers and those called to testify before them.

Senator Alan Simpson of Wyoming, one of Judge Thomas's most ardent supporters, declared roundly as he addressed the assembled gathering that "Shakespeare would love this. This is all Shakespeare. This is about love and hate and cheating and distrust and kindness and disgust and avarice and jealousy and envy." To reinforce his point, that the Bard had a word for it, he then went on to cite in defense of Clarence Thomas what he felt was a particularly apposite and telling passage:

> Good name in man and woman, dear my lord.
> Is the immediate jewel of their souls.
> Who steals my purse, steals trash; 'tis something, nothing;
> 'Twas mine, 'tis his, and has been slave to thousands;
> But he that filches from me my good name
> Robs me of that which not enriches him,
> And makes me poor indeed.

To underscore the depth of his feeling, Senator Simpson added "What a tragedy! What a disgusting tragedy!"—a remark I take to be a comment on the Thomas-Hill events, and not on the play from which he had just quoted.[1]

Let us pause for a moment to consider what any psychoanalytic critic would recognize as the overdetermined nature of this choice of text. For the quotation, as Simpson noted to his learned colleagues, comes of course from *Othello*, a play about a black man whose love for a white woman, Desdemona, leads his detractors to describe his passion—or rather, their fantasies about his passion—in the most graphic and vivid terms. It is not, that is to say, only a telling passage about sexual jealousy, but also a passage chosen from a play with a peculiar pertinence—or impertinence— to the events narrated in the Senate chamber.

Whether Senator Simpson had, in fact, the thematic relevance of *Othello* firmly in mind when he quoted from it, however, must remain a little in doubt. For the passage that he quoted, in ringing tones, is not the voice of the injured Othello, but rather that of his Machiavellian manipulator, Iago, the very man who sets in motion the plot against him, the man whose own "hate . . . and distrust . . . and jealousy and and envy"—to quote the Senator's eloquent peroration—leads him to falsify evidence and to twist the facts. Needless to say, Iago has no use at all for "good name," nor for the quality he calls, in an equally famous interchange with another victim of his innuendo, "reputation."

The whole speech (*Othello* 3.3. 158–64), as any student knows, is an example of the most blatant *hypocrisy*. The audacity of Iago in taking what he pretends to be the high road while secretly manipulating his dupes (Othello and the unsuspecting, gullible Venetians) is, in dramatic context, breathtaking. In his next lines, Iago will invoke—and invent—the "green ey'd monster," "jealousy," which is the very quality that typifies *his*, and not Othello's, behavior throughout.

What is it that Senator Simpson thought he perceived in this dollop of the classics, this soupçon of Shakespeare, that somehow would make his point? Perhaps it is no accident that the Venetian deliberative body are themselves called Senators—

"most grave senators" (*Othello* 1.3.230). Yet Iago's audience, like that of Senator Simpson, is a wider one. By citing Shakespeare this "most grave Senator" was in effect giving moral weight to his own position. Shakespeare said it: therefore it must be true. True, somehow, to human nature, whatever that is. Universally, transhistorically true.

This penchant for quoting Shakespeare out of context, as a testimony simultaneously to the quoter's own erudition and the truth of the sentiment being uttered, is itself a time-honored trick of American public oratory. In some quarters, although not on the fundamentalist right, it has come to replace the Bible, since Shakespeare is regarded as both less sectarian and less sanctimonious. For many years one of the most quoted passages of Shakespeare in the *Congressional Record* was a set piece equally wrenched out of context, Polonius's advice to his son in *Hamlet*: "This above all: to thine own self be true, / And it must follow as the night the day / Thou canst not then be false to any man" (*Hamlet* 1.3.78–80). That this is the same passage that begins "Neither a borrower nor a lender be" may testify to the Congress's ability to disregard, as well as to regard, the timeless "wisdom" of Shakespeare.

For Polonius, like Iago, is being presented in an ironic context. His utterances on this occasion are bromides, sententiae, used wisdom, the *Bartlett's Quotations* of his day, spilled forth helter-skelter in a speech that many in Shakespeare's audience would have recognized as the mark of a puffed-up public man delighted with the sound of his own voice.

But let us return to Senator Simpson. For Senator Simpson emerged in the course of the hearings as in some sense the voice, and the guardian, of Shakespeare. When the Chairman of the Judiciary Committee, Senator Joseph Biden, mis-attributed another quote to Shakespeare, Simpson quickly corrected him: "One of the things that has been indicated here," as Biden summarized the proceedings for his colleagues, "is this notion of maybe that the witness, Professor Hill, really was basically the woman scorned . . . and that after being spurned she took up the role in the way that Shakespeare used the phrase, 'Hell hath no fury like' and that's what's being implied here."[2]

But the ever-vigilant Senator Simpson was on hand to set the record straight. "My friend from Wyoming," Biden reported genially, "in an attempt to save me from myself, has suggested to me that it was not William Shakespeare who said 'Hell hath no fury. . . .' I still think Shakespeare may have said it as well, but he says, William Congreve said it and the phrase was, 'Heaven has no rage like love to hatred turned, / Nor hell a fury like a woman scorned.' I want the record to show that."

Biden was good-natured enough to add a further self-deprecating quip: "I must tell you—I have my staff researching Shakespeare to discern if he said [anything like that]. Not that I think Mr. Congreve would ever plagiarize Shakespeare."[3] This last reference is to his own history of quotation without citation from the political speeches of British politician Neil Kinnock. But then, as Emerson reminds us in his essay on "Shakespeare," "Great men are more distinguished by range and extent than by originality." And though "a certain awkwardness marks the use of borrowed thoughts," "as soon as we know what to do with them they become our own."[4]

The Congreve passage comes from a play called *The Mourning Bride*, not neces- sarily standard American curricular fare even in Wyoming, which is why I am guessing that *Bartlett's Familiar Quotations*, not Congreve, was Senator Simpson's source.[5] And *Bartlett's Quotations*, that *disjecta membra* of famous, disembodied voices, is the repository of conventional wisdom, of what we, and our Senators, purport to know about "human nature." This use of quotation from the literary classics—quotation, especially, from Shakespeare—had, then, bipartisan appeal. Why did Biden think that "hell hath no fury like a woman scorned" was by Shakespeare? Because it was famous—and because he thought it was true. Indeed, many if not all of the most grave Senators seemed to think it was true, was a given, was a foregone conclusion. If Anita Hill *was*, or could be said to be, a scorned woman, then it would be clear that she was animated and motivated by fury, had become, in effect, one of the Furies, who were themselves regarded by the wise ancients as female. A "scorned" woman or a "spurned" woman? The Senators seemed unsure as to the exact quotation—how many of them had read *The Mourning Bride* recently?—but the phrase echoed, ghost- like, throughout the hearings. Hell had no fury like one of them; Shakespeare had— almost—said so.

Why Shakespeare? Well, for one thing Shakespeare is "safe"; neither too high nor too low. He is not an author whom Lynne Cheney or her colleagues then at the National Endowment for the Humanities could have accused of being the property of narrow specialists,[6] but rather the abiding, ventriloquized voice of us all, of disem- bodied wisdom. Emerson wrote in 1850 about the way in which Shakespeare's works underlay political and moral thought in America and Europe: "literature, philosophy, and thought," said Emerson, "are Shakspearized. His mind is the horizon beyond which, at present, we do not see. Our ears are educated to music by his rhythm."[7]

Emerson's Shakespeare is enhanced rather than diminished by the fact that so little is known about his life. Like some of George Bush's political and judicial appointments, whose past opinions are nonexistent, retracted, or under erasure, he is therefore free to be everything, to know everything, to tell us what we want to know, or what we already think we know. "The wise Shakespeare and his book of life," "inconceivably wise," a "poet and philosopher" who teaches the king, the lover, the sage, and the gentleman—this is the Shakespeare whom Emerson calls a "genius" and a representative man.[8] This is the Shakespeare whom Thomas Carlyle, in a book written a few years earlier, called a "Hero," an object of "Hero-Worship." "A thousand years hence," Carlyle wrote in 1840, "From Paramatta, from New York, wherever English men and women are, they will say to one another, "Yes, this Shakespeare is ours; we produced him, we speak and think by him; we are of one blood and kind with him!"[9]

We speak and think by him.

The power of this kind of disembodied, free-floating quotation is considerable. Sometimes the quotation itself can perform an implicit act of commentary, less overt than Senator Simpson's grumpy (and un-Shakespearean) off-stage (but on-mike) complaint that people were afraid to tell the supposed "truth" about Anita Hill because of "all this sexual harassment crap."[10] (The shift in tonal register in the learned Senator's language from the earlier heights of "Good name in man and woman . . . is the immediate jewel of their souls" was, perhaps, not wholly lost upon a discerning audience.) The faxes supposedly hanging out of his pockets were another kind of *disjecta membra*, foul papers that had come in over the transom.

Yet the Thomas hearings provided all-too-glaring evidence of how the Shakespeare quote, lifted out of context, could be like a double-edged sword, turning back upon the wielder. During the floor debate on the day of the Senate vote, Patrick Leahy, Senator from Vermont, attempting to reclaim the high ground from the Republicans, noted that "Senator Simpson quoted Shakespeare the other day," and added, "let me paraphrase from *Hamlet*, 'Judge Thomas doth protest too much.'"[11] Leahy thus inadvertently cast himself as Queen Gertrude and Clarence Thomas as the Player-Queen whose over-fervent claims of innocence and fidelity were—or so Hamlet remarks to the audience—themselves grounds for suspicion. Notice the gender roles implicit in this allusion. Thomas, Senator Leahy's reference seemed subliminally to suggest, had appropriated to himself the "female" role, the role of impossible virtuousness and chastity. If he were in a locker room or a sports bar his language among men, Thomas asserted, would be as pure as tea party conversation with a roomful of Republican ladies. But the *Hamlet* context, of course, is doubled. The spectator who sees through this language of protesting too much is the very person whose own innocence the play-within-the-play is set up to question. Was Senator Leahy, among the most staunch and, to my mind, admirable, of Anita Hill's supporters, subconsciously offering a comment on the Senate's own holier-than-thou position—on, for example, Orrin Hatch's horrified claim that any man who watched pornography or talked about his own body was a psychopathic monster?

But this may be, to cite the Bard once more, to consider too curiously. My favorite of all the Shakespeare citations in the Thomas hearings, however, has, apparently, very little of the subconscious or inadvertent about it. I refer to the accusation leveled by

Thomas character witness J. C. Alvarez, who had worked with him in the office of Education, at Anita Hill, whom Alvarez characterized directly as aggressive, aloof, and, above all, *ambitious*. Alvarez, whom right-wing columnist Peggy Noonan unforgettably described as "the straight-shooting Maybellined J. C. Alvarez," "the voice of the real, as opposed to the abstract, America," sneered self-righteously,

> What is this country coming to when an innocent man can be ambushed like this, jumped by a gang whose ringleader is one of his own protégées, Anita Hill. Like Julius Caesar, he must want to turn to her and say "Et tu, Brutus? You too, Anita?"[12]

Thus the voice of the real America spoke, not entirely surprisingly, in and through the voice of Shakespeare. Can it be a total accident that her cryptic initials, J.C., are the initials of the Shakespearean figure she is quoting, Julius Caesar? Caesar who became the most famous case of literal character assassination in ancient history, or, indeed, in Shakespeare's plays?

The phrase "Et tu, Brute"—you too, Brutus—is "a quotation of a quotation, a quotation which has *always* been 'in quotation,' ultimately a quotation of nothing."[13] It has no source in ancient texts, and though it is set off in Shakespeare's play as apparently "authentic" by the fact that the dying Caesar speaks it in Latin, it is in fact not a sign of authenticity but its opposite, "a back-formation from Elizabethan literary culture, a 'genuine antique reproduction.'"

"Et tu, Brute"—or, to quote the voice of America, J. C. Alvarez, more exactly, "Et tu, Brutus." That Ms. Alvarez has small Latin (and, I think it is fair to assume, perhaps even less Greek) makes her appropriation of Shakespeare, and Shakespeare's cultural power, even more striking. "You too, Anita." The bathos, as with Senator Simpson's rhetorical tumble into "sexual harassment crap," is imperceptible to the speaker. For she is speaking "Shakespeare"—never mind that the Shakespeare she speaks is, to a large extent, made-up. (Peggy Noonan, you may recall, contrasted J. C. Alvarez favorably with "the professional, movement-y, and intellectualish [Judge] Susan Hoerchner," who, said Noonan disparagingly, wore no makeup.) Alvarez is speaking "Shakespeare," as "Shakespeare" has come to be spoken in the public sphere of American politics. Out of context, de-professionalized, timeless, transcendent, and empty, the literary version of the American flag, to be waved at the public in an apparently apolitical gesture toward universal wisdom.

Indeed, had Anita Hill wished to reply in kind, she too could have found prescient authorization and authority in the disembodied voice of Shakespeare. Turning to *Richard III*, his play of Machiavellian statecraft, she might have quoted a familiar passage from the episode known as Clarence's dream: "Clarence is come: false, fleeting, perjur'd Clarence, / That stabb'd me in the field by Tewksbury" (*King*

Richard III 1.4.55–6). The dreamer, and the speaker, in this case is in fact the Duke of Clarence himself, recalling a moment in his earlier career.

The saving remnant for the reader of Shakespeare is that the context is, in fact, so often telling, that the play's language does, so often, to quote Brutus on the spirit of Caesar, walk abroad, and "turn our swords / In our own proper entrails," stabbing or undercutting the speaker. Senator Simpson as Iago will long linger in my mind as one of the most revealing moments of the hearings. Honest, honest, honest Iago. The play's the thing.

Emerson himself was not immune to the nicking of this two-edged sword. Both his chapter on "Shakespeare: Or the Poet" and the more general introductory essay on the "Uses of Great Men" in *Representative Men* reproduce the same pattern of quotation undercutting—we used to say subverting—the apparent argument of the text. The overtly presiding spirit of Emerson's essay is that of Hamlet. His observation that literature, philosophy, and thought are "now" "Shakspearized" is presented in the context of a praise of German Romantic Shakespeare criticism: "It was not until the nineteenth century, whose speculative genius is a sort of living Hamlet, that the tragedy of Hamlet could find such wondering readers."[14]

This privileging of *Hamlet* as the key text of the age is as expectable for Emerson as it is common to writers of the period. The same semi-autobiographical impulse that led him to claim that great geniuses all plagiarize from one another (a teaching that might have been some comfort to Senator Biden, had one of his staffers, or the staffers of the indefatigably learned Senator Simpson, called it to his attention)—that same impulse to write *himself* into his praise of Shakespeare surfaces again in the "identification" with Hamlet and his problems.

Emerson tacitly casts himself as Hamlet when he tells the story of his visit to the theater to see a great tragedian play the part, "and all I now remember of the tragedian was that in which the tragedian had no part; simply Hamlet's question to the ghost":

> What may this mean,
> That thou, dead corse, again in complete steel
> Revisit'st thus the glimpses of the moon?[15]

It needs no ghost come from the grave to tell us that the "dead corse" here is Shakespeare, or the avid questioner, Emerson; the "great" tragedian, a mere transitional object, is conveniently erased and forgotten, remains nameless in the essay, and will not be numbered among the "great men."

Hero-worship, and character assassination.

The question of "character assassination" and the phrase itself did, needless to say, come up in the course of the Thomas hearings. Thomas's protest against what he viewed as racial stereotyping of black male sexuality, his suggestion that he was undergoing a "high-tech lynching," was reinforced by this declaration: "I would have preferred an assassin's bullet to this kind of living hell that they have put me and my family through."[16] And Senator Edward Kennedy spoke out sharply against the "dirt and innuendo" that had been cast upon Anita Hill: "We heard a good deal about character assassination yesterday, and I hope we're going to be sensitive to the attempts of character assassination on Professor Hill. They're unworthy. They're unworthy."[17]

For Kennedy, the image of the assassin's bullet had, undoubtedly, a special and painful relevance. The difference (and the relationship) between assassination and character assassination, between the bullets that had killed his brothers and the innuendo aimed at him by the press, was doubly clear in his case, since his own "character" (and, indeed, the "question of character" raised by Thomas C. Reeves's moralizing JFK biography of that name) was tacitly on trial, or at least on view.[18] And ironically, the chief defense counsel for Judge Thomas, the point man for innuendo against Anita Hill, was also a key figure in the story of the Kennedy assassination and its aftermath.

To make the irony more precise, and to introduce what will be, inevitably, a strong and ghostly Shakespearean subtext to *that* story of character and assassination, we may note that the name of the counsel, the hardnosed senior Senator from Pennsylvania, was "Specter": Arlen Specter.

> What may this mean,
> That thou, dead corse, again in complete steel
> Revisit'st thus the glimpses of the moon?

Uncannily, this same Arlen Specter was the aggressive and ambitious junior counsel for the Warren Commission, the man who proposed the famous "magic bullet" theory that enabled the Warren Commission to claim that Lee Harvey Oswald had acted alone. In doing so he warded off any implications of the sort that Oliver Stone brings forward in his 1991 blockbuster film, *JFK*: that "spooks" from the C.I.A. had foreknowledge of, much less any hand in, the assassination. Is this specter an "honest ghost"? or a "damned ghost"? Or just "an affable familiar ghost"—the return of the repressed?

It will probably not surprise you at this point to learn that Stone's film contains not one or two but five Shakespeare quotations, all performing cultural work of a kind which should now be familiar. *Hamlet*, inevitably, is the play of choice for this dramatization of the moral musings of a man who regards himself as the conscience of the nation—whether that part is being played by Jim Garrison (Kevin Costner) or

Oliver Stone. "One may smile and smile and be a villain," Garrison / Costner reflects, as he ushers the urbane and elusive Clay Shaw (Tommy Lee Jones) out of his office, shortly to charge him with conspiracy in the murder of JFK, whom he will characterize as a "slain king." In a long and (mostly) moving speech to the jury at the end of the film he tells them "we are all Hamlets, children of a slain father-leader whose killers still possess the throne." Since considerations of spurious "national security" have allowed the government to classify the relevant documents for a conspiracy trial, he tells the jury he himself will have "shuffled off this mortal coil" before they are unsealed, but he will urge his son to examine them when they are opened in fifty years. *Julius Caesar*, too, is, perhaps inevitably, invoked and cited, as Garrison asks a staff member whether he's read it; this is how a conspiracy works, he says, Brutus and Cassius and all the others united in a plot against the innocent leader. "Do you read Shakespeare?"

But the oddest and most piquant Shakespearean touch, as you will remember if you've seen the film, is the final epigraph, starkly lettered in white against a field of black: "What is past is prologue," it says. Not "what's past is prologue" (*Tempest* 2.1.253): "what is past is prologue." Is it that Shakespeare is not, on so solemn an occasion, to seem colloquial? Does mis-quotation here seem more authentic, more like a real quotation. Does it seem more like what Shakespeare—our Shakespeare— would have, should have, said?

The citation from *The Tempest*, itself a play of revenge, is spoken in the voice of the usurping Duke of Milan, Prospero's brother. The context is his suggestion to Sebastian that he kill his own brother, the king, and rule Naples in his stead, appropriate enough, we might think, in a film that paints a dark picture of the motivations of Lyndon Johnson. But Stone preempts this scenario, disembodies the text, to make the line an ominous pledge: like Garrison he will continue to fight the good fight, seek the truth, uncover the character assassination of the single "patsy," Oswald, that is hiding the real story of the assassination of JFK by a mega-conspiracy of agencies, generals, and politicians. What is past is prologue.

A very similar set of concerns was brought forward in Barbara Garson's 1966 play *Macbird*, the source of the stichomythic dialogue I have cited at the beginning of this chapter. ("Oh, no!" / "Can't be." / "They've shot the President," etc.) *Macbird*, a pastiche of parodied Shakespearean passages from plays like *Richard II, Henry V, Hamlet, Julius Caesar*, and *Othello*, as well as *Macbeth*, was written, as is doubtless clear from this excerpt, in the chaotic time after the Kennedy assassination, and was published in Berkeley, California in 1966, by an outfit calling itself the Grassy Knoll Press. It tells the story of the murder of Ken O'Dunc by the ambitious Macbird and Lady Macbird, who then escalate the war in Vietland and are finally defeated by Ken

O'Dunc's surviving brothers Robert and Teddy "when burning wood doth come to Washington."[19]

But the role played by Shakespeare in Stone's *JFK* is a slightly different one from the one he plays in *Macbird*. Stone's Shakespeare is present not overtly as analogue and pretext but covertly as a glancing subtext, as 1) a sign that educated discourse in this country is Shakespeare-literate; and 2) a ghostly evocation of Shakespeare as the cultural voice of revenge and retribution, of values and of conscience; and 3) as yet further evidence that Shakespeare quotation can be an uncanny, double-edged sword—if not a magic bullet.

Furthermore, as is perhaps needless to say, Garson's *Macbird* was a coterie production of the antiwar movement, while Stone's *JFK* is a $40 million film bankrolled by Time Warner and ballyhooed on the pages of mass circulation magazines and newspapers from *Esquire* to *Newsweek* to the *New York Times*. And the question raised in journal after journal has been: is Stone, like Shakespeare's comic and self-important vicar, an "Oliver Mar text"?[20] What right does he have to make so public and political a statement of his own interpretation of historical events, and to buttress that opinion with manufactured footage, cross-cuts, grainy color, and black-and-white reenactments of "historical events"—meetings between conspirators, the planting of Oswald's hand-print on the rifle, admirals intervening at the autopsy of JFK—"events" that may never have occurred?

Here is Oliver Stone's defense, or explanation: "I consider myself a person who's taking history and shaping it in a certain way. Like Shakespeare shaped *Henry V*." "Like Hamlet we have to try and look back and correct the inaccuracies."[21] D. A. Jim Garrison may have suffered from hubris and made serious mistakes, but that "only makes him more like King Lear." This is indeed the official story from Stone headquarters, that Stone is today's Shakespeare. Here is entertainment lawyer Bert Fields, whose firm represents the director: "If you are doing what purports to be a book or film about history, it's hardly rare for an author or film maker to take a position. Look at *Richard III*. There was a violent controversy between those who believed Richard was a tyrant who murdered his two nephews. And those who think he was a wonderful king. Shakespeare represented one view, the view that was acceptable to his Queen. Nobody faulted Shakespeare."[22]

Leaving aside this last observation ("nobody faulted Shakespeare"), the argument seems fairly joined. *Newsweek*'s cover story decried "The Twisted Truth of 'JFK': Why Oliver Stone's New Movie Can't Be Trusted."[23] Headlines like "When Everything Amounts to Nothing,"[24] "Oliver Stone's Patsy,"[25] and Stone's Op-Ed page challenge, "Who is Rewriting History?"[26] (all printed on the same day in the same newspaper) are obviously good publicity for the film, but they are also something more. A *New*

York Times reporter named Michael Specter—no relation, presumably, to the Senator from Pennsylvania—noted skeptically that many filmgoers seem to have "succumbed to Mr. Stone's Grand Unified Conspiracy Theory, a gaudy, frenetic fiction."[27] These ghosts are all around us.

"Stone has always required a hero to worship," wrote *Newsweek*'s arts columnist, David Ansen. "He turns the D.A. into his own alter ego, a true believer tenaciously seeking higher truth. He equally idealizes Kennedy, seen as a shining symbol of hope and change, dedicated to pulling out of Vietnam and to ending the Cold War."[28] A hero to worship. Stone's heroes are not two but three: Jim Garrison, John F. Kennedy, and Shakespeare. And here he is in formidable company. Consider again the view of Shakespeare put forward by the man who popularized the term "hero-worship" (a term invented, it would seem, by David Hume)[29] more than one hundred and fifty years ago, Thomas Carlyle. "How could a man delineate a Hamlet, a Coriolanus, a Macbeth, so many suffering heroic hearts, if his own heroic heart had never suffered?"[30]

Of Shakespeare's "Historical Plays," Carlyle asserts that "there are really, if we look to it, few as memorable Histories. The great salient points are admirably seized; all rounds itself off into a kind of rhythmic coherence; it is, as Schlegel says, *epic*." Art, not history, is thus the measure of hero-worship; to Carlyle, Shakespeare's "veracity" lies in his "universality."[31]

For Carlyle—as for Emerson—Shakespeare was cramped, even demeaned, by the material circumstances of cultural production in his time: "Alas, Shakespeare had to write for the Globe Playhouse; his great soul had to crush itself, as it could, into that and no other mould. It was with him, then, as it is with its all. No man works save under conditions. . . . *Disjecta membra* are all that we find of any Poet, or of any man."

Disjecta membra. Familiar quotations. Disembodied voices. In the Thomas-Hill hearings, in Oliver Stone's *JFK*, in *Bartlett's Familiar Quotations*, everywhere in the corridors of power, Shakespeare authorizes a rhetoric of hero-worship and character assassination based upon this Orphic dismemberment of the text. "Et tu, Brutus." "What is past is prologue." Perhaps it is well for us to remember in these times how uncannily the "familiar" can be de-familiarized—and that a "familiar" can also be a demon, a spirit, a Specter, a "spook," or a ghost.

Out of Joint | 6

Cursed be he that moves my bones.
Epitaph on Shakespeare's grave, Holy Trinity Church, Stratford

If anything, the linkage is just as natural the other way around.
Peter Elbow, "The Question of Writing"[1]

The elephant, medieval scholars believed, had no joints. When Pope Leo X was presented with an elephant in 1514, the animal was made to kneel, partly as a sign of respect, and partly to show that it could do so.

Fifteenth- and sixteenth-century observers began to refute the legend. "I must explain that these animals have knees, which they bend when walking,"[2] wrote one Italian commentator. The Frenchman André Thevet explained, likewise, that "They have joints in their knees, so that when their master commands them to kneel down, they kneel down promptly, which is contrary to the opinion of many who have described the Nature of the Elephant . . . I myself saw them kneel down several times in the town of Cairo."[3] By the seventeenth century Sir Thomas Browne could scoff at the "absurdity": "for first, they affirm it hath no joints, and yet concede it walks and moves about; whereby they conceive there may be a progression or advancement made in Motion without inflexion of parts."[4]

> The hint and ground of this opinion might be the gross and somewhat Cylindrical composure of the legs, the equality and less perceptible disposure of the joints, especially in the former legs of this Animal: they appearing when he standeth, like Pillars of flesh, without any evidence of articulation.[5]

"The elephant hath joints, but none for courtesy; / His legs are legs for necessity, not for flexure," observes Ulysses tartly in Shakespeare's *Troilus and Cressida* (2.3.103–4). Like a proud man, said the proverb, the elephant will not kneel.

Knee-jerk responses

All day long,
My heart was in my knee.

George Herbert, "Deniall"

Genuflect! Genuflect! Genuflect!

Tom Lehrer, "The Vatican Rag"

Of all early modern joints, the knee is arguably the most distinguished, at least in literary terms. The knee is an important articulation of the physical body politic, especially if the physical body politic is male.[6] As David Bevington points out in his account of the language of stage gesture, "kneeling is a profound gesture of acknowledgement of the claims of hierarchy."[7] To bend the knee is to give homage, to assent to a political and social contract. Thus the knee in Shakespeare is often a figurative as well as a literal joint, appearing disproportionately (so to speak) in the history plays, both English and Roman. Indeed, it "can serve as the dominant expressive gesture at the point of dramatic reversal"[8]—functioning allegorically, we might say, as a joint of the dramatic action. A double joint. A hinge. Why this should be so, and what it has to do with the knee as a physical joint of the body, can be seen in the much-noticed and overdetermined function of kneeling in *Richard II*, Shakespeare's play of articulated and disarticulated homage.

Is patriotism a knee-jerk response? Should it be? Where does loyalty properly reside? The knee-plot of *Richard II* stages these questions in vivid terms.

Bolingbroke affects homage and deference to the king in public ("let me kiss my sovereign's hand / And bow my knee before his majesty" [1.3.46–7]) but Richard scornfully describes his courtship of the common people: "Off goes his bonnet to an oyster-wench. / A brace of draymen . . . had the tribute of his supple knee" (1.4.31–3). Acting as regent in Richard's absence from England, the loyal York clearly reads through this knee language when Bolingbroke drops to his knees before him: "Show me thy humble heart, and not thy knee, / Whose duty is deceivable and false" (2.3.83–4). By the time Richard returns from Ireland and greets his opponents from the walls of Flint Castle, the rebellion of the knee—the unjointed jointure of English hierarchy—is legible even to him. "We are amazed," he says to Northumberland,

> and thus long have we stood
> To watch [i.e., to wait for] the fearful bending of thy knee
> Because we thought ourself thy lawful king.
> And if we be, how dare thy joints forget
> To pay their awful duty to our presence? (3.3.72–6)

By the end of the scene Bolingbroke's gesture of kneeling to authority is frankly repudiated:

> Fair cousin, you debase your princely knee
> To make the base earth proud with kissing it . . .
> Up cousin, up. Your heart is up, I know,
> Thus high at least, although your knee be low. (190–5)

This encounter has been traditionally understood by critics and audiences as a symbolic turning point of high and low, anticipating Richard's image of the dipping well as a scale in the deposition scene (4.1). But the lying knee, the low knee, the knee whose duty, in York's phrase, is "deceivable and false," is also part of an articulated language of disarticulation, the breakdown, the dislocation, of a ceremonial culture of the body. The disturbingly comic scene of mass kneeling in Act 5 scene 3, in which the entire York family, the elderly Duke and Duchess and their rebellious son Aumerle all kneel before Bolingbroke with a virtually audible creaking sound, extends this language to its inevitable and ludicrous conclusion, as the embarrassed and discomfited new king tries in vain to get these old people to rise up.[9]

   "For ever will I walk upon my knees,"declares the doughty Duchess, sinking to the ground.[10] "Upon my mother's prayers I bend my knee," cries the son, hurling himself down. But York, professing loyalty to the king over loyalty to flesh and blood, claims that his own kneeling means something different—means obeisance rather than supplication, compliance rather than revolt: "Against them both my true joints bended be." York, who has begun his entreaty by describing his son as a "fest'red joint" that should be amputated for the health of the body politic ("This fest'red joint cut off, the rest rest sound"), announces that he possesses "true joints"—joints that join rather than put asunder or "out of joint." He thus raises the question of the joint moralisé—the signifying knee.

   But the Duchess suggests that her husband's real sentiments lie with the private body rather than the public one, while her and her son's posture should be read as both entreaty and homage: "His weary joints would gladly rise, I know; / Our knees still kneel till to the ground they grow." Desperate to get them *all* to rise—especially his aunt, whose age and sex both render her kneeling deeply unsuitable ("Good aunt, stand up," he says twice more, helplessly, as she continues to plead, volubly, from a kneeling position), Bolingbroke finally capitulates, pardoning Aumerle. "O, happy vantage of a kneeling knee!" exults the Duchess (*King Richard II* 5.3.104–31), perhaps now at last laboriously hauling herself to her feet. In these scenes, as indeed throughout Shakespeare's staging, public / private hierarchies are troubled by the knee-work.[11]

In later literature the knee, obedient or rebellious, bent or straight, would be used to reinforce the sense of hierarchy through a reanimation of the theory of the body politic. Spiritual size could be achieved not only in direct but also in inverse proportion to the physical. George Herbert's "Deniall" located the rebellious or resistant heart in the knee, the outward show of an obedient grace not yet achieved within. Herbert is here following a passage of Church liturgy which itself derived from Clement and ultimately from the apocryphal *Oratio Manassae: et nunc flecto genua cordis mei*, "and now bow I the knees of my heart."[12] The phrase "the knees of my heart"—disarticulated from its liturgical context—became a common citation, almost a cliché, in later years. Heinrich von Kleist who—as we will see—plays a pivotal role in the story of the language of joints—used it both in his play *Penthesilea* and in a letter to Goethe in which he encloses a recent publication: "I present it to you [writes Kleist] 'on the knees of my heart.'"[13]

"It is so truly the mystery of the kneeling, of the deeply kneeling man; his being greater, by his spiritual responses, than he who stands!" wrote the poet Rilke in a letter to his mother. "He who kneels, who gives himself wholly to kneeling, loses indeed the measure of his surroundings, even looking up he would no longer be able to say what is great and what is small. But although in his bent posture he has scarcely the height of a child, yet he, this kneeling man, is not to be called small. With him the scale is shifted. . . ."[14] Rilke's observations could stand as a brilliant gloss on the fourth act of *King Lear*, when, as we have just noted, the formerly imperious king kneels to Cordelia, and she gently admonishes him: "No, sir, you must not kneel" (*King Lear* 4.7.59).

But the knee as body part does not always connote homage or prayer. Although it is *metaphorically* a sign of linkage and thus of obeisance, *metonymically* the knee rebels. "How long is't ago, Jack, since thou sawest thine own knee?" asks Prince Hal of Falstaff (*King Henry IV, Part 1* 2.4.318–19). Part of a continuing series of jokes about Falstaff's present girth (he responds by reminiscing about the tiny waist he had as a boy), this is also one of Hal's recurrent gibes about Falstaff's indifferent loyalty and questionable potency, since the knee was not only the bodily instrument of homage but also a location proximate to the genitals, often invoked as a kind of euphemism. Can you look down past your waistline at your lower body, Hal seems to be asking, and if so, what—if anything—do you see? The knee—the joint that bends, or not, obediently or rebelliously—becomes in Hal's little joke the unseen sign of Falstaff's unreliability.

Not for the first time, Falstaff becomes the "joint" or point of articulation between male and female. For—perhaps unsurprisingly, given the differential logics of power and hierarchy—joints like the knee often function *metaphorically* in men, who are part of the body politic, but *metonymically* in women, who derive their standing (or their kneeling) from adjacency. Women do use the supplicant knee in the ordinary way to petition grace or favor: Volumnia kneels to Coriolanus, and Isabella to Angelo. But the knee is a tricky joint, and a "trick knee" (from *trichier*, to deceive) is weak, deceptive, and liable to fail. Especially when it is the woman who is suspected of turning tricks.

More often than not, in early modern usage, the proximity of the knee to the genitals is noted in *women* rather than in men. An old man in *Iacke of Dover* (1604) keeps his wife in fancy stockings as a compensation: "Because I can not please her above the knee, I must needes please her below the knee." A seventeenth-century ballad describes a gardener who touched a carpenter's wife "a little above the knee," (*Five Merry Wives of Lambeth*, Williams), and another suggests that pregnancy may result from "tickl[ing] my knee" (*Young Man's Frolicks*). Defloration and impregnation are often figured in this period as a breaking of joints—most often knees, but occasionally elbows: "She has broken her leg above the knee (broken her elbow)" according to Tilley's proverbs, means "she has lost her virginity," or "she has become pregnant."[15] These "breaks" in jointed limbs both injure the connection and reinforce it.

When Freud describes fetishism as "com[ing] to life" when "some process has been suddenly interrupted," he instances "the circumstance that the inquisitive boy used to peer up the woman's legs towards her genitals." For Freud, of course, the *absence* of the "longed-for penis" in women, the disappointed fantasy of the phallic woman, produces—by metonymy—the fetishization of the part nearby. In Freud's Vienna that "part" was often a foot or (its further metonymic emblem), the shoe; velvet or fur, he says, are acknowledged as signs of pubic hair. The woman's body is named by contiguity.

Contiguity, association, linkage—these elements of what is fundamentally metonymic logic are also (and not by accident) themselves joining or jointed functions, cognitive moves that depend upon a presumed coherence, not only of parts, but of connection. Early modern man kneels to demonstrate his entire connectedness to the body of the state. His knee is a hinge of rule. But the woman's knee is often a stand-in for her sexual parts, and women who kneel in homage like men are often, in literary terms, a cause of consternation.

Elbow room

No man lives without jostling and being jostled; in all ways he has to elbow himself through the world, giving and receiving offense.
                                                Thomas Carlyle, "Sir Walter Scott"

Our horizon is never quite at our elbows.
                                Henry David Thoreau, *Walden*, "Solitude"

The elbow, unlike its bodily equivalent the knee, was and continues to be a relatively comical joint, linked to lower-class activities and to superstitions: To be out at elbow is to be threadbare, to shake one's elbow is to play at dice, to rub or scratch the elbow was, apparently, a sign of pleasure or satisfaction. In Shakespeare's *Love's Labour's Lost* an offstage rehearsal of the disastrous Masque of the Muscovites meets with the approval of the commons: "One rubbed his elbow thus, and fleered, and swore / A better speech was never spoke before" (5.2.109–10). An itchy elbow was a sign, though of what was not certain. When Conrade, summoned by the villain Borachio in *Much Ado About Nothing*, materializes "at thy elbow," Borachio observes with his customary elegance, "my elbow itched; I thought there would a scab follow" (3.3.97–8). Elbow grease, then as now, was a sign of industry, and may even (this is a guess) have meant "sweat," since it seemed to "smell."[16] (Modern pranksters, long after Shakespeare, would often tell a rube to go out and buy a container of "elbow grease" at the hardware store.)

In a suggestive essay on "The Renaissance Elbow," Joaneath Spicer chronicles the "rise and apogee of the male elbow" as a sign of protectiveness and control in paintings—mostly portraits—in the period 1500 to 1650. Spicer argues that "the elbow in its most perfectly evolved form—the arms akimbo" will achieve in Holland "the status of a national attribute," marking the "alert, on guard, proud regent class."[17] In German and Italian painting, and in conduct books and manuals of gesture, the arm akimbo was often a sign of pride. Erasmus, among the first to comment on this attribute of male display, spoke slightingly of those who "stand or sit and set [the] one hand on [the] side which maner to some semeth comly like a warrior but it is not forthwith honest."[18] Bonifacio's *L'arte de' cenni* (1616) regards the elbow and arm akimbo as signs of strength, useful for pushing one's way through crowds, but consequently "pushy" in a negative way, and John Bulwer's *Chironomia* of 1644 is similarly dismissive: "to set the arms agambo or aprank, and to rest the turned-in back upon the side is an action of pride and ostentation, unbeseeming the hand of an orator."[19] For soldiers and standard-bearers, however, the gesture was appropriate. Thus, presumably, the remark of Shakespeare's King John on his deathbed: "now my soul hath elbow-room" (*King John* 5.7.28).

Male portraits of the period, especially in Holland, displayed a hand on hip as a sign of cultural or military power. The same configurations can be found in Dutch group or corporate portraits, where artfully disposed limbs could produce a literalization of the "joint-stock company." Women, by contrast—unless they were monarchs or allegories—kept their elbows to themselves, and, in the language of the nursery rhyme (addressed to a hypothetical, ill-mannered "Mabel, Mabel") "off the table." These days the gesture—especially with *both* hands on hips, what Plautus called "handle men"—is most frequently found among women (and gay men) in musical comedy, where it appears to mark a certain kind of soubrette figure as waggish or scolding, and often appears as a prelude to breaking into song.

While the knee is often aligned with ascent and descent, with movements up and down, the elbows seem to work—literally and metaphorically—by a pushing in, out, and around. Thus the knee becomes connected to the tragic, the divine, and the narrowly hierarchical, while the elbow extends itself to the realm of the comic, the secular, and the broadly expansive. It is only when elbows are in a fixed position that they can work as emblems of power; it is the multidirectional mobility of the elbow which gives it its comic potential.[20] In terms of the social system elbows can be in or out of joint. Oddly, though they are "above the knee" in anatomical terms they are often below it in status: displacement, we see, does not always go upward, after all.

Taking joint stock

The joint is jumpin'.

Fats Waller

Remove the joint!

Lewis Carroll, *Through the Looking-Glass*

Twentieth-century readers tend to think of the phrase "out of joint" as a philosophical observation, a dead metaphor, a cliché.

"The time is out of joint. O cursed spite, / That ever I was born to set it right." The most familiar of quotations, this observation—made by Hamlet to his companions after the visitation of the Ghost—is glossed by Arden Shakespeare editor Harold Jenkins as "in utter disorder."[21] "Out of joint" in this sense is indeed something of a political cliché, embodying—and thus in a sense disembodying—the old image of the body politic.[22] The *Oxford English Dictionary* lists this example under "Out of joint," *phrase, figurative*, meaning "disordered, perverted, out of order, disorganized. (Said of things, conditions, etc.; formerly also of persons in relation to conduct)." Reviewing French translations of the phrase, Jacques Derrida finds "time is off its hinges" (*Le temps est hors de ses gonds*), "time is broken down, unhinged, out of sorts" (*Le temps est détraqué*), "the world is upside down" (*Le monde est a l'envers*), "this age is dishonored" (*Cette époque est déshonorée*).[23] Derrida notes that the *OED*, unsurprisingly, "gives Hamlet's phrase as example of the ethico-political inflection."

For theorist Slavoj Žižek, "out of joint" is an ontological and a philosophical condition, a matter of consciousness and of history. Reading F. W. J. Schelling and Fredric Jameson together, Žižek suggests that by their reasonings "every narrative eventually endeavours to provide an answer to the enigma of how things got out of joint, how the old 'authentic' ties disintegrated," how traditional societies became "modern, 'alienated,' unbalanced."[24] The logic of Schelling's thought, claims Žižek, "compels him to assert the inevitability of the 'out-of-jointness' and of man's Fall."[25] And elsewhere Žižek will use the same phrase to explain "the impossibility of locating the subject in the 'great chain of being,'" since "subject is in the most radical sense 'out of joint'; it constitutively lacks its own place."[26]

"In the most radical sense 'out of joint.'" But there is a different kind of "radical" sense that goes to the root of this oft-cited phrase. For right above "out of joint," *phrase, figurative*, the diligent *OED* browser will encounter, as he or she might expect, "out of joint," *phrase, literal*. "Said of a bone displaced from its articulation with another; dislocated; also of the part or member affected."

A glance at the 1611 King James translation of the Bible reveals that it regularly describes body parts as "out of joint": (Genesis 32:25: "and the hollow of Jacob's thigh was out of joint"; Psalm 22:14: "I am poured out like water, and all my bones are out of joint"; Proverbs 25:19: "Confidence in an unfaithful man in time of trouble is like a broken tooth, and a foot out of joint"). Donne's "First Anniversary" blends the two frames of reference, political / philosophical and bodily: "So is the worlds whole frame Quite out of joynt, almost created lame." Likewise in *Troilus and Cressida* Ajax is described as a man who "hath the joints of everything, but everything so out of joint that he is a gouty Briareus, many hands and no use" (1.1.127–9).

"Ha! What news here?" demands the bastard Spurio in *The Revenger's Tragedy*. "Is the day out o' the socket, / That it is noon at midnight, the Court up? / How comes the guard so saucy with his elbows?" Here is the familiar and officious "handle-man" again, his elbows at the ready. "Out o' the socket" seems like a disturbingly literal and anatomical version of "out of joint."[27] The power of this image derives in part from its re-literalization. "Out o' the socket" sounds painful: we can almost supply the torturer and the rack. When Hamlet remarks that the time is out of joint and laments that he "was born to *set* it right," we may wonder, perhaps, whether that word "set" itself carries a strong or a weak meaning, a figurative or a literal one. A "bone-setter," after all, was a surgeon, responsible for "setting" dislocated or broken bones. "Can honor set to a leg?" asks Falstaff, rhetorically. Bones in Shakespeare may ache, rattle, be mocked, ground, gnawn or hacked asunder, or, more peacefully, lie either in a tent or a grave. They are not usually "set," but they may indeed be "out of joint."

(It may be worth recalling that Heminge's and Condell's prefatory letter to the First Folio uses a similarly literal anatomical figure, describing Shakespeare's plays, restored to wholeness in their edition, as once "maimed, and deformed" but now "cur'd, and perfect of their limbes."[28] The texts of the plays, once out of joint, are now properly realigned, in effect, "set" ["to place (type) in the order in which it is to be printed from; to compose, set up (type); hence, to put (manuscript) into type" *OED* sense 72, 1530; "to place in a certain sequence in a literary work" *OED* sense 15, 1535; "to put (a broken or disclosed bone) in a position adapted to the restoration of the normal condition" *OED* sense 79, 1572].)

Strikingly, the bodily member the *OED* singles out for special attention under the heading "out of joint" is "the nose," not a part that is normally thought of, these days, as being or having a joint at all. ("*To put one's nose out of joint*; see NOSE.") A modern slang dictionary notes that to "put someone's nose out of joint" = to make someone envious or jealous, but the use of the phrase goes back at least as far as Barnaby Rich in 1581. Dekker and Marston's *Satiromastix* uses the phrase ("Yonder bald Adams, is put my nose from his joint"), as does Robert Armin's *Fool upon Fool* ("The thought of the new come Foole so much mooved him . . . that he would put his nose out of ioynt"[29]).

"Nose" for penis in Western literature and culture goes at least as far back as Ovid (Publius Ovidius *Naso*) and as far forward as Pinocchio and Freud. Eric Partridge observes the frequency with which the nose in Shakespeare became a penis. "If you were but an inch of fortune better than I," asks Cleopatra's waiting-woman Charmian to her colleague Iras, "where would you choose it?" and Iras retorts, "Not in my husband's nose." (*Antony and Cleopatra* 1.2.62–3). "Here," Partridge instructs firmly, "*nose* = proboscis = trunk = dangling projection."[30]

Metaphors of articulation are often generated by the physical functions, limitations, and possibilities of individual joints. Even joints that don't seem to *have* joints. But could the "joint" be out of joint?

A "joint" in modern slang is a penis; a piece of meat. It is also a marijuana cigarette, a low dive, and a hangout.[31] To "unlimber the joint" is to urinate.[32] In the early modern period "joint" as "cut of meat" seems to have had a sexual flavor, too, both male and female. In *Pericles* a pimp and a bawd bicker about Marina's maidenhead: "Mistress, if I have bargain'd for the joint,—" "Thou mayst cut a morsel off the spit" (4.2.128–30). But "joint" also regularly meant "penis," presumably because it bent, connected, and joined. In George Chapman's *Widow's Tears* the widow of the title laments to her companion, "One joint of him I lost was much more worth / Than the rack'd value of thy entire body"; the retort, not so sotto voce, is "I know what joint she means." In Sampson's *Vow-Breaker* (1625–26) an old man rues his lack of potency: "I have daunc'd till every joynt about me growes stiffe but that which should be" (2.2.183)—obviously a familiar form of the joke—and there are dozens of similiar references, especially in the plays of the time.[33] Holofernes the pedant in *Love's Labour's Lost* announces that Costard the clown will play the part of a Roman hero: "this swain, because of his great limb or joint, shall pass Pompey the Great" (5.1.119–20). This is a laugh-line if ever I heard one; "or joint" functions like an elbow in the ribs, and the jest is clearly dependent on the proverbial notion that fools and "naturals" were especially well-endowed.

In Shakespeare's plays, however, when the term "out of joint" is explicitly physical, it is often used in reference to the shoulder. "Thou hast drawn my shoulder out of joint," complains Hostess Quickly to the officers who arrest her and Doll Tearsheet at the end of *King Henry IV, Part 2* (5.4.3–4). The rogue Autolycus, disguised as a robbed and beaten man and grovelling in the dirt to cozen the clown in *The Winter's Tale*, complains (perhaps with equal falsehood), "I fear, sir, my shoulder-blade is out" (4.3.73–4). In Shakespeare the shoulder is a site of honor ("which gently laid my knighthood on my shoulder" [*King Richard II* 1.1.79]), fellowship ("they clap the lubber Ajax on the shoulder" [*Troilus and Cressida* 3.3.140]), male beauty and heroism (Coriolanus is wounded "i'th'shoulder, and i'th'left arm," and will have scars to show the people [2.1.146]; Pelops' ivory shoulder was a paradigm of perfection [*Two Noble Kinsmen* 4.2.21]). But dislocated shoulders—claimed, perhaps significantly in these examples by rebellious and socially marginal characters (the brothel Hostess and the rogue)—are signs of something else: of, in fact, a social world "out of joint," signified by the *pretense* or excuse of forcible bodily dislocation.

As the case of Pelops suggests, the shoulder was a quintessentially "human" joint. As John Donne pointed out in a sermon, "God is never said to have shoulders." Why? Because in essence he is "all shoulder," according to the Scriptures: "shoulders are the subjects of burdens, and therein the figures of patience, and so God is all shoulder, all patience."[34] Like the elephant without knees, the God without shoulders (or the God who was all shoulder) demarcated the limits of a body at once allegorically and physiologically conceived.

What do joints do? They articulate and connect; they facilitate movement. Ulysses says with scornful lust that even Cressida's foot speaks; "her wanton spirits look out / At every joint and motive of her body" (*Troilus and Cressida* 4.5.57–8). A joint "out of joint" is dislocated, disarticulated—and highly painful. "Let him die, /

With every joint a wound" (*Troilus and Cressida* 4.1.30–1) "to th'rack with him!—We'll touse you / Joint by joint" (*Measure for Measure* 5.1.309–10); "By heaven I will tear thee joint by joint, / And strew this hungry churchyard with thy limbs" (*Romeo and Juliet* 5.3.35–6). "Animals use joints like a centre," declared Aristotle, "and the whole member, in which the joint is, becomes both one and two, both straight and bent, changing potentially and actually by reason of the joint."[35]

Syntax

and as I prophesied, there was a noise, and behold a shaking, and the bones came together, bone to his bone.

Ezekiel 37:7

the whole body fitly joined together and compacted by that which every joint supplieth, according to the effectual working of the measure of every part
Paul to the Ephesians 4:16

Only connect!

E. M. Forster, *Howards End*

The word "syntax" originally meant a systematic arrangement of parts and elements, like—and including—the constitution of the body. Thus Helkiah Crooke's *Microkosmographia, A Description of the Body of Man* (1615) asserted that,

> The universal compage of coagmentation of the bones is called a Syntax, and the backe of bones so fitted together is called a Sceleton.
> The manner of this Syntax or composition is double, for it is made either by Articulation or by Coalition. Articulation we define to be a Naturall structure of the bones, where in the extremities or ends of two bones do touch one another. So that the whole Nature of Articulation consisteth of the Contraction of extremities or ends.[36]

A "compage" is a framework or system of conjoined parts, a complex structure, a means of joining. So *syntax*, in modern usage most frequently considered as an aspect of grammar, and *articulation*, frequently regarded as an aspect of speech, thus each inhabit, in their early modern forms, an intellectual and conceptual space modelled on the body, and, quite specifically, on its "connexions" or joints. "Their articulation doth not differ from the Syntax or coniunction of other parts," says Crooke,[37] and John Edwards would declare in 1690 that, "This single [argument] from the fabrick and syntax of man's body is sufficient to evince the truth of a Deity."[38] Physical motion becomes evidence of divine motion. As Aristotle had noted, ". . . this is our meaning when we speak of a point which is in potency one, but which becomes two in actual exercise. Now if the forearm were the living animal, somewhere in its elbow-joint would be the movement-imparting origin of the soul." It is by a logic of connectedness that order is perceived, and, for a Christian like Edwards, "the Existence and Providence of God" deduced from the "naturalness" of order. The hip bone's connected to the thigh bone, the thigh bone's connected to the knee bone, the knee bone's connected to the leg bone, the leg bone's connected to the ankle bone . . . In the case of the body and its joints, it was the joints that were articulate, that connected, that spoke.

But if they spoke, they also sometimes misspoke. In two key instances of inadvertent malapropism in Shakespeare's plays we can see how the expectation of organic form is disarticulated—how (as in the earlier example of Falstaff's invisible and rebellious knee) the very logic of bodily coherence and obedience can be challenged by the language of the joints. The dramatic episodes I have in mind, striking to modern as well as to early modern audiences, are the verbal miscues of Elbow the Constable and the language lesson of Princess Katherine of France.

A personification of the out-at-elbow "handle man," Shakespeare's "simple" Constable Elbow in *Measure for Measure*, is the butt of constant jokes about his name. "He's out at elbow," says Pompey the bawd, and the constable himself offers an early gloss on his comical "handle": "my name is Elbow. I do lean upon justice" (2.1.48–9). "Elbow," I should point out, is a not-uncommon English surname; Harvard's Widener library lists works not only by Peter Elbow, cited above, but also by Gary, Linda, and Matthew Elbow, among others. Shakespeare is not being merely allegorical, but also what a later age might call ethnographic, in giving his policeman this bare-bones name. Present-day authors by the name of Ankles, Shoulderblade, Knee and Kneebone likewise testify to the propensity of various cultures to tag their populations by anatomical features. But Elbow the constable's name performs itself not only in what may be characteristic postures of physical assertion, but also in the way his character articulates—or rather, disarticulates—language. He speaks of "my wife whom I detest [for *protest*] before heaven" (68) who "if she had been a woman cardinally [for *carnally*] given" (78–9); his malapropisms persist, with growing consequence, throughout the play, for example "respected" for "suspected" (165). "Do you hear how he misplaces?" says the councillor Escalus to Angelo, the deputy. "Misplacing" here becomes a nonce rhetorical term for dislocation, and significantly, it is what might be called the "joints" of language, the prefixes and suffixes that alter meaning, that Elbow "misplaces," to produce meanings the contrary of what he (apparently) intends.

That such "misplacement" is, in Shakespeare, an articulate language of disarticulation, can perhaps be seen even more clearly when language itself is the topic. In her comically pertinent (and impertinent) English language lesson, Katherine of

France persistently mispronounces the word "elbow," first as "bilbow" and then as "ilbow." In the early modern period a "bilbo" was both a sword and an iron bar with sliding fetters, used to shackle the feet of prisoners (probably from the town of Bilbao in Spain, famous for its ironworks). So the elbow as bilbow invokes another kind of joint, binding together prisoners who (to literalize Aristotle), though formally two "become one in actual exercise." The word "bilbo" appears elsewhere in Shakespeare in both senses.[39]

But what of "ilbow"? There is no such word in English; unlike "bilbo," it is not a verbal joke. Or is it? The princess, being French, gives the word its proper preposition: she says not "ilbow" but "de ilbow"; or dilbo; or—in this escalating feast of naughty half-rhyming words, dildo.

Malapropism is itself a kind of dislocation, as is clear from some of Katherine's other inadvertent *mots*: *nick* for neck, *sin* for chin, and, most notoriously, *coun* (cunt) for gown and the homonym *foot* (= French foutre, fuck) for English foot. What is dislocated here is not only a word from its socket of meaning, but the sense of language itself as firmly jointed and joint. At once compound and complex, these are fractures of language ("fractured French" is indeed a modern term for fumbling attempts at Gallic speech). When the malapropism produces meaning, despite itself, it is said that the unconscious is speaking. The Princess of France, speculating about the swashbuckling "enemy" king who is destined to be her husband, misplaces foot, gown, chin, and elbow, and replaces them with foutre, coun, sin, and dildo. Her English has "english" on it; it spins out of control; it is out of joint.

We have been considering the dependence of certain implicit theories of language and structure upon the notion of organic form. The so-called "body politic" became the model for coherence and rule; mimesis, imitation, resemblance, and metaphor gave order and suggested "natural" hierarchies. The joint of the body could stand for the part-ness of the individual (again, normatively the male individual) in the unitary whole. But other theories of language which bear upon this same rhetoric of the joint and the body are, importantly, *not* based on organic form. Ferdinand de Saussure's theory of modern linguistics was based on a structuralist system of differences, not on resemblance or identity: a word is an element in a system. The "arbitrary nature of the sign" meant that the relationship between the signifier and the sign is never necessary or "motivated." The body—the natural body—was not the inevitable tenor for which particular words would be vehicles. Instead, it was the point of articulation itself, the relation, the joint, that gave meaning.

"Language might be called the domain of articulations," suggests Saussure in his *Course in General Linguistics*. "Each linguistic term is a member, an *articulus* in which an idea is fixed in a sound and a sound becomes the sign of an idea."[40] And again,

"In Latin *articulus* means a member, part, or subdivision of a sequence; applied to speech, articulation designates either the subdivision of a spoken chain into syllables or the subdivision of the chain of meanings into significant units; *gegliederte Sprache* is used in the second sense in German."[41] *Geglierdert* means "jointed; articulate; constructed organically, organized." *Glied* is limb or member, and *Gliederpuppe* is puppet, marionette, or jointed doll. What has the jointedness of puppets to do with the jointedness of language?

Pulling strings

O excellent motion! O exceeding puppet! Now will he interpret to her.
Two Gentlemen of Verona **(2.1.89–90)**

Fie, fie, you counterfeit! You puppet you!
A Midsummer Night's Dream **(3.2.288)**

Come, children, let us shut up the box and the puppets, for our play is played out.
Thackeray, *Vanity Fair*

In Heinrich von Kleist's story "Über das Marionettentheater" ("On the Puppet Theater," 1810) the narrator converses with a celebrated dancer, Mr. C, whom he has often encountered at "a puppet theater which had been hammered together in the marketplace, to entertain the crowds with little mock-heroic dramas." Dancers, says Mr. C., have much to learn from puppets about the graceful disposition of their own bodies.

The narrator is surprised "that he should signify with serious consideration this toy version of a high art":

> I inquired about the mechanism . . . and how it was possible, without myriad strings on the fingers, to control the separate members and their tie points as the rhythm of their movements or dances required.
>
> He answered that I must not imagine that each member, in the various motions of the dancer, had to be placed and pulled individually by the puppeteer.
>
> Each movement, he said, had its center of gravity; it would suffice to control that center, on the inside of the figure; the limbs, which are really nothing but pendulums, follow of themselves, in a mechanical way, without further aid.
>
> He added that this movement was a very simple one, that even when the center of gravity was directed in a *straight* line, the limbs began to describe *curves*; and that often, when shaken in a quite random way, the whole puppet assumed a kind of rhythmic motion that was very much like a dance.
>
> [. . .]

> The line that the center of gravity must describe is indeed very simple and, as he believed, in most cases straight. When it happens to be curved, the law of its curvature seemed only the first, and at most of the second order: and even in the latter case only elliptical, which form of movement happens to be the natural one for the extremities of the human body (because of the joints) and which would demand no great skill on the part of the puppeteer to describe.
>
> This line, however, considered from another point of view, is something very mysterious. For it is nothing less than *the path of the dancer's soul*.[42]

Mr. C. describes to the narrator with admiration the "mechanical legs that English craftsmen manufacture for hapless accident victims." Equipped with these prostheses, recipients not only "manage to dance," but dance with an extraordinary "lightness . . . serenity . . . and gracefulness that must amaze every thinking person." Such mechanically-aided dancers, like the puppets that the same gifted English craftsman "could doubtless construct" to Mr. C.'s specifications, would have a key advantage over ordinary dancers, in that their members "are, as they should be, dead, pure, pendulums"—unlike, for example, the young dancer F., who, playing the part of Paris and extending an apple, finds that "his soul . . . actually settles in his elbow." The elbow here stands as emblem of all that is merely human: off-balance, intrusive, particular rather than general and ideal. These are "blunders," says Mr. C., unavoidable since the fall of man.

As Scott Shershow observes, Kleist's dialogue, with its "distrust of the animate body," is "both the earliest example of what would become a virtual obsession with the puppet in the theory and practice of European drama.[43] The modernist concern with the machine as an aesthetic object so intensely contemplated as to become a virtual subject enlisted the puppet, or the marionette, as part of a critique of naturalistic acting. William Butler Yeats, attending the premiere of Alfred Jarry's *Ubu Roi* in 1896, remarked that the actors were "hopping like wooden frogs" and looked like "dolls, toys, marionettes."[44] Maurice Maeterlinck in France and Gordon Craig in England were among others who saw the modernist puppet theater as a commentary on the impossibility of verisimilitude, the destabilization of authorship, and, ultimately, the vexed status of the subject.

We might recall Slavoj Žižek's observation that "subject is in the most radical sense 'out of joint': it constitutively lacks its own place." This quintessentially postmodern perception is, as Žižek shows, traceable back through Kant to Descartes, whose "I think" introduces "a crack in the ontologically consistent universe" by conjuring up the possibility of the "Evil Genius (*le malin genie*) who, behind my back, dominates me and pulls the strings of what I experience as 'reality.'"[45] To be "out of joint" is thus, for the human subject, to be subject to the machinations of an invisible puppeteer: "the prototype of the Scientist-Maker who creates an artificial man."

Žižek's concern is with borderline "human" figures evoked by modern science, like the replicants in *Blade Runner* or the monster in *Frankenstein*. But his metaphor—"pulls the strings of what I experience as 'reality'"—returns "out of joint" to the time of its most familiar iteration: early modern England.

The early modern term for puppet show was "motion,"[46] which also became a shorthand word for puppet. Thus Ben Jonson's irritable Morose is reproved by the suddenly loquacious "silent woman" (actually a boy in disguise) he has taken for his wife: "why, did you thinke you had married a statue? or a motion, onely? one of the French puppets, with the eyes turn'd with a wire?"[47] As Scott Shershow notes, in the early modern period "the word *motion* constantly slips between the two sides of the physio-psychological opposition which it also predicates, linking biology and behavior, rhetoric and theater, within a transparent system of correspondences."[48] A curious reversal or inversion of meaning seems to have taken place in the process, however, where the puppet show was called a "motion" presumably because in it the inanimate moved, the puppet (or, as frequently, the human being compared to a puppet) was so-called because he or she did *not* move, or show animation.

Touring companies of Italian puppet-masters were popular in England and throughout Europe in the late sixteenth and seventeenth centuries, and the shows they presented were often related to the *commedia dell'arte*. Marionettes were not unknown in the period, especially in Italy, where an arrangement of rods and silk or cords were used to manipulate the arms and legs, "permitting all kinds of backward-bending joints,"[49] and some English references take note of them.[50] Beaumont and Fletcher's *The Woman Hater* compares a sexually unresponsive man to "dead motions moving upon wires,"[51] and a stage direction in a Cornish mystery play of 1611 calls for the appearance of "spirits on cords."[52] The famous *Hero and Leander* puppet show in Ben Jonson's *Bartholomew Fair* seems to have been of glove puppets, made to move by the action of the fingers, wrist, and thumb since they are brought out in a basket. "Here is young Leander, is as proper an actor of his inches," says Leatherhead proudly, "and shakes his head like an ostler" (*Bartholomew Fair* 5.3.95–7). Even glove puppets had "joints," both human ones, inside the gloves, and represented ones. A character in Jonson's *Poetaster* asks derisively, "What's he with the half arms there, That salutes us out of his cloak, like a motion?"[53]

In *Bartholomew Fair* the puppet-master Leatherhead acts as "interpreter" for Littlewit's "motion" of *Hero and Leander*. "I am the mouth of 'em all," he declares (5.3.74). Deploring the fact that the time is "out of joint," Hamlet in effect proposes himself as the interpreter for the puppet government of the Claudius court. "I could interpret . . . if I could see the puppets dallying." Rejoining the old notion of the "body politic" with the perception that language itself was radically unstable and duplicitous, even the voice liable to be ventriloquized, the motion of the limbs (to borrow Kleist's terms) naturally elliptical ("which form of movement happens to be the natural one for the extremities of the human body [because of the joints]"), the early modern puppet marks the crisis point of articulation and disarticulation which is the theoretical space of the joint.

The unsettling movements of such "motions" can have their effect in the modern (and postmodern) theater as well. In the fall of 1995, for example, a series of Shakespeare plays performed by marionette companies played to sold-out houses in Berlin.[54] Presenting Shakespeare through puppet "actors" paradoxically brought the dramatic tensions closer to the surface, by de-familiarizing and estranging the realm of the psychological, and even the mimetic language of face and voice. In a comparable piece of spectacle, the 1995 George C. Wolfe production of *The Tempest* at New York's Public Theater, starring Patrick Stewart as Prospero, used puppets and stiltwalkers to produce a major part of the magical stage action. Naked "human" puppets like ventriloquists' dummies presided over the banquet scene, wielded by "unseen" Kuroko figures, actors dressed in black. The very limber jointedness of the puppets (designed by Barbara Pollitt), together with their human facial expressions and glistening nakedness (*not* a characteristic of most ventriloquists' dummies— imagine Charlie McCarthy with no clothes on), brilliantly and uncannily suggested both the living and the dead. We may recall that Freud's essay on the "Uncanny" took as one of its starting points Hoffmann's fantastic tale about the wooden doll Olympia, and the "impression made by waxwork figures, ingeniously constructed dolls, and other automata"; Freud singles out "dismembered limbs, a severed head, a hand cut off at the wrist, . . . feet that dance by themselves"—all enabled by the movement of the joints—as "peculiarly uncanny . . . especially when, as in the last instance, they prove capable of independent action."[55]

The Wolfe / Public Theater *Tempest* also included a number of "stiltwalkers," quite literally actors walking on stilts,[56] both to generate expressionistic stage action (in the opening storm the Neapolitans' ship was "tossed" on the waves of long cloth strips held at each end, and loosely fluttered, by an "invisible" figure on stilts) and, once again, to mark the uncanny. The wedding masque of Juno, Iris, and Ceres, often a ho-hum event in modern production, became a vivid and witty spectacle generating wonder because the three goddesses were all gigantic, walking on stilts. Moreover, the "feet" of the stilts wore dancers' toe shoes (rather like the feet of the original Barbie doll). The effect was to render the audience, in Freud's terms, uncannily uncertain as to whether the legs they were looking at were "alive" (were these tall apparitions really two people, one on another's shoulders, the head and torso of the lower one hidden by the goddess' skirts?) or "dead" (the lower limbs not "human" but wooden, the "feet" not feet at all but painted poles). If the effect was not precisely that of Freud's "feet that dance by themselves," it was, nonetheless, powerfully uncanny, precisely because of the unjointed "joints"—the "ankles" and "toes" that seemed to flex as they bore the goddesses' weight.

The word "stilt" was also used to mean "crutch," and may derive from a German word for "limp." Yet the novelist Thackeray would associate "stilts" with the larger-than-life appearance of figures on the stage when he described "the actors in the old tragedies, . . . speaking from under a mask, and wearing stilts."[57] Limb or prosthesis? Human or puppet? Psychoanalyst Jacques Lacan described the "fragmented body-image" of the child (and the "aggressive disintegration" of the analysand) as manifesting itself "in the form of disjointed limbs."[58] The deliberate un-jointing and re-jointing of these super-human figures, goddesses and "invisible" stagehands, produces the prosthetic joint as irreducible supplement to the human body, at once mimetic and fantasmatic.

Skeleton keys

The word of God is quick, and powerful, and sharper even than any two-edged sword, piercing even to the dividing asunder of soul and spirit, and of the joints and marrow.
The Epistle of Paul the Apostle to the Hebrews, 4:12

He knew the anguish of the marrow
The ague of the skeleton.
T. S. Eliot, *Whispers of Immortality*

"If hee had been made of one continuall bone," Helkiah Crooke wrote of mankind, at the beginning of the seventeenth century, "how could he have bent or extended or compassed his body? how could he have apprehended any thing or moved him-selfe forward to attayne it? No; he must have stood like a trunke or a blocke." In this section of the *Microkosmographia*, called "of the structure and connexion of Bones," Crooke seems to suggest that the "connexion," the joint, was, in a sense, that which made human creatures human. Being not only conscious but jointed, man was enabled to "receive infinite images of Sensible things, and to flye and apply himselfe to the divers objects of his appetite." "Notwithstanding though this connexion be divers, yet it is so strangely fitted together that al seeme to be but one; one I say either by Continuity or by Contiguity at least." Continuity and Contiguity are themselves tropes here, and indeed most familiar ones: we know them by names like metaphor and metonymy.[59] Metaphor is the seeming-to-be-one; metonymy is the linkage, the chain of associations, the joint. To be out of joint, to have the capacity to dislocate and be dislocated, is to recognize the fragility of the join, the point of vulnerability (call it an Achilles' heel) that is the corollary of the gift of movement, and in the register of language, the ambivalent task of the interpreter.

Paul de Man draws a connection between the uncanniness of the puppet figures in Kleist's allegorical tale and the political problematic of "the aesthetic," describing what he calls "the articulated puppets":[60]

> The puppets have no motion by themselves but only in relation to the motions of the puppeteer, to whom they are connected by a system of lines and threads. . . . The aesthetic power is located neither in the puppet nor in the puppeteer but in the text that spins itself between them. This text is the transformational system. . . . Tropes are quantified systems of motion.[61]

What de Man notes here is the illusion of freedom and universal order produced by an "ideology of the aesthetic" that encodes restriction and formalization under the sign of perfect art. His comparison text is a letter of Schiller that extolls the traditional "English dance, composed of many complicated figures and turns" as "the perfect symbol of one's own individually asserted freedom" in a system in which "everything has [already] been arranged." "Caught in the power of gravity, the articulated puppets can rightly be said to be dead, hanging and suspended like dead bodies: gracefulness is directly associated with dead, albeit a dead cleansed of pathos. But it is also equated with a levity, an un-seriousness which is itself based on the impossibility of distinguishing between dead and play."[62] "The puppet's ground is not the ground of a stable cognition."[63] Gravity and levity; "dead and play." "I could interpret between you and your love," says Hamlet to Ophelia, "if I could see the puppets dallying."[64]

The aesthetic is a principle of articulation, de Man suggests. "It is as a political force that the aesthetic still concerns us as one of the most powerful ideological drives to act upon the reality of history," he wrote. "But what is then called . . . the *aesthetic*, is not a separate category but a principle of articulation between various known faculties, activities, and modes of cognition."[65] In the essay on Kleist's marionette theater, one of his few explicitly anti-fascist texts, de Man perceived that the idea of the "aesthetic state" in Schiller was the preference for the prosthetic grace of puppets or dead bodies in a harmony that can only be totalitarian. (Significantly, perhaps, Kleist's wonder-worker is an "English craftsman," who, like Schiller's "English dance," replaces the human member with a mechanical prosthesis.) The "aestheticization of politics" about which Walter Benjamin would speak so forcefully was precisely this kind of new, "improved" body politics in which prostheses, perfect, regular, and predictable, replaced the flawed and the human. And here too what was crucial was the logic, or pseudo-logic, of the joint.

Consider, as calculated theatrical examples, two signifying gestures from the political aesthetics of German fascism: the goose step and the Nazi salute. Both involve locking a joint—the knee, the elbow—rather than bending it (as for example in the parade march and bent-arm military salute favored by some other nations). In the goose step and Nazi salute the body aspires to the condition of a machine, or a prosthesis, through the simulation of an unjointed limb that levitates, almost of its own accord, in response to the presence of the hero or the apparatus of state. (It is this automatism that Stanley Kubrick parodies, to such good effect, in *Dr. Strangelove*, and that Ian McKellen would later recall in his brilliant restaging of *Strangelove* as Shakespeare's *Richard III*.[66]) When thirty thousand hands were raised in the Nazi salute at the Nazi Party Congress in Nuremburg on September 4, 1934, Hitler had one of his officers proclaim: "The German form of life is definitely determined for the next thousand years. The Age of Nerves of the nineteenth century has found its close with us."[67] Nerves had been replaced by a "form of life" that aestheticized and mechanized the body: not a body without organs but a body without joints.

Characteristically, de Man's essay on Kleist cautions the reader against succumbing to pathos. "One should avoid the pathos of an imagery of bodily mutilation and not forget that we are dealing with textual models, not with the historical and political systems that are their correlate. The disarticulation produced by tropes is primarily a disarticulation of meaning; it attacks semantic units such as words and sentences."[68] Disarticulation—what later commentators on "deconstructive 'performativity'" have called "dislinkage"—is a product of figure itself: "the *dislinkage* precisely of cause and effect between the signifier and the world."[69] (Here we might perhaps usefully recall Peter Elbow's comment about writing: "If anything, the linkage is just as natural the other way around.") This dislinkage is not a failure of reference but rather an estrangement, a "torsion."[70] Or, to put it in other words—in very familiar words—things are out of joint. Relations "between the signifier and the world" are strained—or sprained. Can they be set right? "Can honour set to a leg?" asked Falstaff, a performative deconstructor *avant la lettre*. "No. Or an arm? No. . . . Honour hath no skill in surgery, then? No. What is honour? A word. What is in that word 'honour'? What is that 'honour'? Air" (*King Henry IV, Part 1* 5.1.131–5).

"One should avoid the pathos of an imagery of bodily mutilation." In early modern drama this is not so easily done. For to avoid the pathos of an imagery of bodily mutilation is, in effect, to avoid the theater and its peculiar power. We might recall Romeo's over-the-top threat to Paris, "By heaven I will tear thee joint by joint, / And strew this hungry churchyard with thy limbs" (*Romeo and Juliet* 5.3.35–6).

Achilles, encountering Hector for the first time, remarks that he has looked his fill: "I have with exact view perus'd thee, Hector / And quoted joint by joint" (*Troilus and Cressida* 4.5.232–3). The "quote" comes from the register of language, but it parses a manifest threat in action: "I will . . . As I would buy thee, view thee limb by limb" (237–8); "Tell me, you heavens, in which part of his body / Shall I destroy him? Whether there, or there, or there?" (242–3). Pathos is not an incidental affect of theatrical representation; it is a key element of theatricality, ultimately inseparable from the words that produce it. What is torn is both body *and* words. The "joint" as body part and as the connective tissue of language is always *double-jointed*, figurative and literal at once. Which is the figure and which is the ground? Syntax or skeleton, homage or knee?

In Marlowe's *Doctor Faustus* the actor playing Faustus is furnished at one point with a prosthesis—a wooden leg:

> Horse-courser: Master doctor, awake and rise. . . . Master doctor! *He pulls off his leg.* Alas, I am undone; what shall I do? I have pulled off his leg . . . now he has but one leg I'll outrun him, and cast this leg into some ditch or other. [*Exit*]
>
> Faustus: Stop him, stop him, stop him—ha, ha, ha! Faustus hath his leg again.
>
> (4.4.28–36)[71]

Although the doctor exults at his deception, this comic scene prefigures his own later dismemberment: "See, here are Faustus' limbs, / All torn asunder by the hand of death. . . . We'll give his mangl'd limbs due burial" (5.3.6–7;17).

The disarticulation of language from "historical and political systems," of the syntax of the sentence from the syntax of the skeleton, threatens to dislocate literature from culture, to put them "out of joint." But neither in early modern culture nor in dramatic literature more generally can one finally "avoid the pathos of an imagery of bodily mutilation." The materiality of the body and its vulnerable articulations not only exemplifies, but constitutes, the semantics of performance. Dismemberment is the hard connective tissue of drama, the skeleton beneath its scrim. Bodily pathos (and for that matter, bodily levity, too) manifested through the eloquent syntax of the jointed body has been the spectacular and articulate engine of theater since the *sparagmos* of Pentheus in Euripides' *Bacchae*, since the piecemeal excavations of a gravedigger in the *Hamlet* churchyard, since the cozened Horse-courser pulled the leg of Doctor Faustus—and the leg came off.

Roman Numerals | 7

I love not only you yourself. I love your name. And your numeral.
Jenny Cavilleri to Oliver Barrett, IV, in Erich Segal's *Love Story*

Menance II Society
Title of a 1993 film

I

In late September 1985, during the height of Hurricane Gloria, the purchaser of a New England house built in 1790 went up to the rafters to check for leaks in the roof. Shining his flashlight above his head, he discovered a "large Roman numeral six" carved near the end of one of the rafters. Nearby rafters were similarly marked with Roman numerals not by Romans, of course," he assures us, "but by people from long ago."[1]

The timbers for a post-and-girt house might be hewn by its 18th-century builder over the period of many months. To keep track of the pieces, the incised Roman numerals would indicate where in the finished structure this particular beam or post would go. "In the attic of a log cabin built in Illinois near Lake Michigan a hundred years ago," another observer reported, he discovered on the roof beams "carpenter's marks, I II III and so on, cut with mallet and chisel, as a guide for their order of placing."[2] I have myself seen similar markings in the wideboard pine floors of a house in Nantucket—boards that were taken from the attic of one building and recently re-laid as a floor in another, using the colonial-era numerals as a guide.

"The scratched lines from which Roman numerals supposedly arose, require only primitive tools and skill," notes a historian of typography. "Arabic numerals predicate a brush and a hand trained in calligraphy. Nevertheless, they are casual and demotic, while the Roman are formal, inscriptional, hieroglyphic."[3] A French account of the "universal history of numbers" commented in 1981 that "the Roman numerals we sometimes still use today . . . now seem old-fashioned and quaint."[4]

Old-fashioned and quaint. Formal, inscriptional, hieroglyphic. What are the implications of Roman numerals today?

This inquiry began as an exploration of the relationship between anachronism and nostalgia—specifically, my own nostalgia for the days when act and scene numbers to Shakespeare's plays were written in Roman numerals. For me, these glyptic capital letters and curly minuscules once conveyed the very spirit of canonicity—an effect, of course, not of "authentic" or "original" sixteenth- or seventeenth-century notation, but rather of subsequent scholarship and editorial practice. Act III, scene iv, seemed quite different from plain old Act three, Scene four.

For the record, the First Folio gives act and scene numbers in Latin words (*Actus Secondus, Scena Tertia*), marks the date of publication in Arabic numbers (or, more properly, Hindu-Arabic numbers) (*1623*), paginates the leaves in Arabic numbers, and spells out the names of Kings in English words, using ordinals ("King Henry the Fourth," "Fift," "Sixt," and so on).[5] Francis Meres's famous praise of Shakespeare in *Palladis Tamia* (1598) uses Arabic numbers: "for Tragedy his *Richard the 2.*, *Richard the 3.*, [and] *Henry the 4.*"[6] So—as we might by now expect about virtually any object of nostalgia—the original is absent. This is a nostalgia, like all nostalgias, for something that never was. The only Roman numerals *per se* in the First Folio are to be found in the tavern bill Prince Hal discovers in Falstaff's pocket, for ii.s, ii.d. for a capon, and v.s, viii.d for two gallons of sack (*King Henry IV, Part 1* 2.4.535ff.).

But by the time of Nicholas Rowe's edition of 1709, based largely on the Fourth Folio, many key elements have already been converted to Roman numerals, which are used for Act and Scene numbers (which Rowe attempted to systematize), for the title pages of the plays, and in some references to dramatis personae ("Richard II," "Henry V"). So also with the editions of Pope (1723) and Theobald (1733), who even give the year of publication in Roman numerals (Rowe used Roman numerals for the title pages of volumes, and Arabic numerals on the title pages of plays). Thus begins a textual and cultural practice that has over the years become naturalized as the very sign of Shakespearean reference until the advent of computers, and computerized concordances, in the present day.[7]

For it is largely, I think, computers that we have to thank (or blame) for the recent changes in notation. Marvin Spevack's *Harvard Concordance to Shakespeare*, which has rendered so much formerly painstaking literary detective work now into a matter of instant (and consequently devalued) knowledge, boasts in its 1973 Preface that it is "based on the most advanced Shakespeare scholarship and produced by means of computer technology." Spevack's Preface, of course, like most modern Prefaces, is paginated in minuscule or lower-case Roman numerals. And his multi-volume *Complete and Systematic Concordance to the Works of Shakespeare*, published in Germany, uses majuscule or upper-case Romans to number the volumes. But the concordance entries themselves, as all latter-day Shakespeare scholars know, are given in Arabic numbers, as are the abbreviations to the play titles.

Spevack's concordance, which promised in those optimistic days to "exemplif[y] the latest thinking on what may be called the 'true text' of Shakespeare" based on the newly published modern-spelling *Riverside Shakespeare* of 1973, inevitably revolutionized notation in Shakespearean publishing practice. For though the Riverside itself used Roman numerals to mark Act and Scene numbers (as well as in the running titles of the English history plays and the names of the English kings), scholars working with that edition, and with the Ardens and other Shakespearean texts of record, began increasingly post-Spevack to give Act, Scene, and line references in Arabic numbers.

The first book of Shakespeare criticism I remember noticing with this distinctively "modern" touch (this is sheer anecdotal memory, not any point of origin) was Janet Adelman's *The Common Liar: An Essay on Antony and Cleopatra*, itself published (like Spevack's concordance and the *Riverside Shakespeare*) in 1973. Adelman did not use the Riverside as her text (she could hardly have done so even if she had wanted to, since her book was published in the same year), but rather cited M. R. Ridley's Arden edition of *Antony* from 1954, which, like all the other "new Ardens"—it is perhaps needless to say—used Roman numerals to mark the Acts and Scenes, with the notation at Act I Scene I (given in Roman numerals) that *Acts and scenes [were] not marked, save here, in F.* (As we have noticed, in the First Folio the initial designation was in Latin words, not numbers: "Actus Primus. Scena Prima.") But today the new "new Ardens" of the third series have replaced the Roman numerals with Arabic ones without comment on the change, noting only that "Act and scene divisions (seldom present in the early editions and often the product of eighteenth-century or later scholarship) have been retained for ease of reference, but have been given less prominence than in the previous series."[8] (We may note that this information from the "General Editors' Preface" can be found in the new new Arden *Antony and Cleopatra* on page xi. Some conventions are more enduring than others.)

The Arden is not the only recent edition to convert to Arabic numbers for acts and scenes; the popular paperback Bantam made the switch in 1988. On the other hand, the new (1996) edition of the Riverside retains Roman numerals, which the editors have deemed more attractive and "official"-looking—and which would have cost a great deal to change.

Economics, aesthetics, and cultural authority thus—as usual, we might think—reinforce one another to produce anachronism as tradition. But why should a Roman numeral look either more attractive or more "official"? And to whom? Let me offer a hint in the form of an unscientific observation: it's scholars, today, who use the Hindu-Arabic notations in their citations. Journalists, politicians, and students—at least my students—hanker (like my younger self) after the iconic Roman numerals, the sign of otherness. The sign (to them) of the real Shakespeare. These Roman numerals are the equivalent of "genuine antique reproductions"—the kind of classy notations Shakespeare *would* have used if he had only thought to do so.

II

There's a lot I never knew about Roman numerals. Like the fact that in the medieval period and the Renaissance, they are often described not as Roman but as German. And the fact that, despite all appearances, "Roman numerals" do not derive from letters. C and M were not, that is to say, originally abbreviations for *centum* and *mille*, no matter what you were taught at school.

The Roman number symbols seem to have developed over time, in fits and starts, probably from tally sticks, groups of notches, much as we put a cross stroke through four 1s on the blackboard to count 5. (Thus an I for a 1, not an I for a "I.")

Comparative anthropological research suggests that in Switzerland and in parts of India, as well as in ancient Rome, "a crossing of straightline symbols means 10."[9] V is pictographically the top half of an X. (Ancient coins show that the Romans used the *top* half to signify 5; the Etruscans, the *bottom* half.) Alternatively (this is the theory of Theodore Mommsen and others), V is a kind of hierography representing the open hand with its five fingers. Two such Vs combined produced an X, the sign for ten.[10]

The pictographic view based on anatomical gesture has been dismissed recently as both "banal" and "stretch[ing] visual credibility" (how likely is it that two open-hand Vs would be used to make an X? Try it yourself and see.)[11] Alphabet historian Johanna Drucker, commending the Romans for "the adaptation of letter forms to represent number values," argues that "the conventions which brought these forms into conformity with letters within the Latin alphabet were the effect of convenience, rather than necessity, and other signs would have functioned equally well—even better since they would have stood less chance of confusion."[12] But of course the confusion became part of the process—became, in fact, one of its most valued attributes.

The Romans never wrote M for 1000; instead they used a single vertical stroke enclosed in what look to modern eyes like parentheses. M (for *mille*) was a medieval contribution. An alternative notation for 1000 was a horizontal stroke above the number, a mark known as the *titulus* in the Middle Ages and as *vinculum* in classical Latin.[13] This horizontal stroke was different from the stroke that served to distinguish numbers from letters, and does appear in classical times: that stroke is the origin of our present-day practice of enclosing Roman numerals within horizontal strokes, above and below.

German authors of the sixteenth century, and others in Europe as well, called these "German numbers," not "Roman numerals." An arithmetic book of 1514, for example, gives its fractions in Roman numerals (I over IIII, VI over VIII, and so on), with the genial notation, "To make this little book of computations agreeable and useful to its reader, who will find numerals hard to learn at first, I have used the common German numbers throughout."[14]

But what about those letters and numbers? An early Etruscan figure for 1000 was a circle with an oblique cross in it, which gradually became an upright cross and then dropped its horizontal bar, leaving something that looked like a circle cut in half by a straight vertical line. (Some historians theorize that this figure may have been derived from the Greek *phi*, which it resembles.) The Roman numeral C, for 100, has been traced to the left half of this old form for 1000, and the Roman numeral D, for 500 (half of 1000), to the right half. To indicate larger numbers, like 5,000 or 100,000, additional hoops or curves were added, in effect multiplying the numbers by ten or a hundred, and producing, as we've noted, an image like a capital I enclosed in several sets of parentheses. The central point here, though, is that the pictograph that looks like C, and, indeed, the pictograph that looks like M, were both derived, scholars believe, from symbols that had, originally, nothing to do with the words *centum* and *mille*, Latin for one hundred and one thousand. The verbal equivalence, the verbal match between symbol and word, between C and a hundred, M and a thousand, is, historically speaking, a back-formation. (An analogous modern instance is the American slang word "sawbuck" for ten-dollar bill, from the resemblance of the Roman numeral X—found on pre-Federal Reserve Bank currency—to the ends of a sawhorse. And "sawbuck," in turn, seems to be unrelated, etymologically speaking, to the word "buck" for a single dollar, which comes, say the dictionary-makers, from "buckskin." Go figure.) Likewise, the Roman numeral that looks like the letter L "coincidentally resembles" it but "has nothing to do with the letter L," according to mathematician Karl Menninger.[15]

Nothing to do with it *historically*, that is to say. Nothing to do with it developmentally. Nothing to do with it etymologically, in terms of origins and intentions. But in other registers we might want to claim that it has *everything* to do with it.

The very fact that numbers and letters *could* be confused or interchanged would lead to a kind of visual punning or riddling, a cryptography that would have its uses even in the modern day. Thus the "chronograms" or "date riddles" that used capital Ls, Vs (for Us), Ms, and Ds to spell out a second message. *LVtetIa Mater natos sVos DeVora VIt,* "Mother Lutetia has devoured her own children," encoded the date 1572 in Roman numerals to commemorate the Massacre of St. Bartholomew's Night, when Huguenots were slaughtered in Paris."[16] A rhyme memorializing the Council of Constance in 1416 declared,

> The council was held
> In Costnitz; that happened when we counted
> a ring, 4 horseshoes too,
> a ploughshare, a hook, and an egg.

The ring is a buckle (a circle with a line through it, looking like the letter M), the horseshoes are Cs (open at one end), the ploughshare is the iron tip of the plough, shaped like an X, the hook is a V, and the egg (despite its rounded shape) a time-honored symbol for "one." Thus 1416.

Nor is letter-and-number magic using Roman numerals exclusively a thing of the past. A recent Internet contribution, headed "Barney is Satan," took the phrase "Cute Purple Dinosaur," converted all the Us to Roman-equivalent Vs, extracted the Roman numerals CV, V, L, DI, and V, added up their decimal equivalents (100 5 5 50 500 1 and 5) and revealed that the total was 666, the notorious Biblical "number of the Beast" (Revelation 13:16–18). Voila! Barney is Satan.[17]

Just as Roman numerals were sometimes read as, taken for, or thought to be derived from letters in the medieval and early modern periods, so letters could be, after a fashion, derived from numbers. In 1463, a scholar-printer felicitously named Felice Feliciano wrote a manuscript setting forth rules governing the construction of a Roman capital alphabet by geometrical means. In 1509, the mathematician Luca Pacioli, said to be the inventor of double entry bookkeeping, printed his own set of rules, and several other scholars, mathematicians and artists (including Albrecht Dürer) did the same.[18] It seems that Renaissance geometricians, designing capitals or majuscules, rather than copying "the forms which at that mid-15th century period existed about them in great numbers on the classical monuments scattered throughout Western Europe,"[19] instead imagined, quite falsely, that the Roman forms derived from the harmonious proportions of the circle and the square, and developed, in consequence, elaborate theoretical models based on this mistaken historical notion. The revival of the classical letters, both in stone inscriptions and medals and in manuscripts, drew energy from these elaborate systems, whether or not they were ever fully put into practice.

This change came on the cusp of the shift from manuscript to print, and from Roman to Hindu-Arabic numerals. As Elizabeth Eisenstein observes, "The way letters, numbers, and figures were pulled and pushed into new alignments by early printers and engravers is worth further thought. Human proportions were made to conform with letters once inscribed on ancient Roman arches, even while Roman numerals were being replaced by Arabic ones."[20] As we will see, the volatility of the cultural moment led to both over- and under-valuation of the Roman forms. Number and letter magic, familiar in necromancy, in ciphers and in the process of Biblical decoding known as gematria, found another way into Elizabethan culture through the over-determined site of the Roman numeral.

Consider now a little complex of charts from the pages of a late sixteenth-century manuscript.

	A	T	G	C	L	V	Li	SCO	SA	CAP
	.1.2	345	678	9.10	11.12.13	14.15	16.17	18.19.20	21.22	23.24
	Aq		P							
	25.26.27		28.29							

take the name of Chilld m or wom & the name of the

.m A thowsan — mother her owne naturall name & the chylldes name

.C A hundred — & then youe moste take owt all the m & c & l & x &

.d v hundred — & d & v & n & J [the take] & owt of & m & owt of

.l for fifte — & l & a n & J & JJ owt of 100 owt of 40 ^{4}owt of 30 owt

.x for tenne — 2   2   1   2   2[4]   4   6

.v for five — of 20 owt of 500 owt o (2) 800 owt of 700 owt of 400 owt of 200 owt of

                  8   8   8   4   4   8

n for two — 160 owt of 140 owt of 80 owt of 50

.J for one — 4   8   8   2

JJ for two

Across the top of the page are abbreviations for the signs of the zodiac. Below to the left, running vertically down the side of the leaf, is a chart of Roman numeral equivalences: ".m A thowsan," ".C A hundred," ".d v hundred," and so on. And to the right of this listing is an instruction for what looks like the casting of a nativity.

"take the name of Chilld m or wom & the name of the mother her owne naturall name & the chylldes name & then you moste take owt all the m & c & l & x & & d & v . . ." and so on. This is one of several sets of instructions or recipes clustered together in this part of the manuscript: those that follow on the next two pages include charms "to drive away a grievous ague," "for a great ache or strain in the back," "to make a bird fall down," "to know wher a thing is stolen," and so on.

What's so striking to me here, in the instructions for casting the nativity, is the way in which the letters listed on the left—the letters corresponding to Roman numerals—are the ones to be subtracted or taken from the letters in the names of the child and its mother. I'm reminded of the telltale elixirs in Middleton and Rowley's seventeenth-century play *The Changeling*, one in glass C (to detect whether a woman is with child or not) and the other in glass M (to detect whether she is a maid). That C = child and M = maid once seemed a sufficiently revealing if seriocomic code. But clearly these letters that are also numbers carry with them, potentially, an even greater kind of power.

What is the sixteenth-century manuscript from which this nativity spell is taken? It is not, as it happens, one of the works of mathematical sages like John Dee or John de Sacrobosco. It is a page of Philip Henslowe's *Diary*, more properly described as a book of accounts and memoranda kept by Henslowe (and by his predecessor, the book's first owner, John Henslowe) from 1579 to 1609. Philip Henslowe, theater manager, pawnbroker, moneylender, and entrepreneur, kept accounts of the daily receipts of performances in the several theatres, together with records of loans made on behalf of the theater company, payments made in connection with the building and repair of the Rose and the Fortune theaters, and lists of costumes, properties, and other items and transactions. He was not a magus; he was a bookkeeper.

During the course of Henslowe's record-keeping, the mathematical notations in his *Diary* change from lower case (minuscule) Roman numerals to pounds-shillings-and-pence. This was a period of transition in early modern accounting. It was not unusual for these two methods of notation to coexist or cross. In 1596, for example, Henslowe recorded a series of sums lent to his son-in-law, the actor Edward Alleyn. The sums are noted in a kind of demotic Roman numeral system, what could almost be described as pidgin numbers: xj (meaning "eleven") with a superscript li (short for Latin *librae*, "pounds"); xxxs meaning "thirty shillings," followed by xxxx with a superscript s, meaning "forty shillings." At the bottom of this set of "items lent" Henslowe reckons up the total, in Hindu or Arabic numbers: 21 pounds, 13 shillings, 04 pence. It's clear that Henslowe had no difficulty making the transition from one number system to another, any more than we have difficulty "translating" from Roman to Arabic numerals on the dial of a clock.

Throughout the *Diary* the same kind of casual multinumeracy obtains: items are recorded in Roman numerals and then the totals are given in pounds, shillings, and pence. Since. "li" for pounds and "d" for pence are also Roman numeral notations, and since Roman numerals are retained throughout the *Diary* for operations like itemization (for example, the famous list of stage properties for the Lord Admiral's Men, "j rocke, j cage, j tombe, j Hell mought . . . viij lances, j payer of stayers for Fayeton, . . . iij marchepanes, & the sittie of Rome"),[21] what we have in the book known as *Henslowe's Diary* is a snapshot of a cultural practice, or set of cultural practices, in the process of being overwritten.

Far from being exclusively a "formal, inscriptional, hieroglyphic" mode, then, the Roman numerals of the medieval and Renaissance periods were, indeed, casual and demotic. They were used by bookkeepers and shopkeepers. So the Roman numerals of the middle ages and the Renaissance were "low" not "high" culture, the tools of "counter-casters," bookkeepers, debitors and creditors, at the same time they were enjoying a kind of double life as magical and mystical symbols, as notations for mathematicians, and (in some places) as ordinals after the names of monarchs.

In 1300, the use of Hindu-Arabic numerals was *forbidden* in commercial documents and in the banks of certain European cities, since it was thought that they could be more easily forged or changed (a 0 turned into a 6 or a 9 by a single stroke, for example). In fact, Roman numerals were commonly used in bookkeeping in European countries through to the eighteenth century, and Hindu-Arabic numbers were not generally accepted by the English public until the seventeenth.[22]

One reason bookkeepers preferred the Roman system—other than the conservatism inherent in any business practice—was that addition and subtraction were easier in it, though multiplication and division were more difficult. (Two Cs plus one C was CCC; XXV minus X was XV, and so on.)[23] For multiplication and division, the ancient Romans used the abacus—as did early modern (human) calculators.

Brian Rotman points out that "the Roman way of notating numbers, like those languages that express the plural by repeating the singular, did not detach itself from the iconic mode," but "introduced an order into the syntax through the subtractive principle," so that three Is in a row could make a three, while an I before an X indicated the operation of subtraction. But as he is also careful to note, this complex syntax produced "an overcomplicated grammar," so that calculations with Roman numerals were "laborious, byzantine, impractical," and, in fact, apparently seldom attempted, since "throughout its history there is no evidence that the system of Roman numerals was used or ever intended to be used for calculation."[24] Instead, those who wrote in Roman numerals calculated on an abacus.

The abacus appears in Shakespeare as a "counter"—thus Iago, who scorns Cassio as a "great arithmetician" (a book-soldier or armchair warrior) also calls him a book-keeper (this "debitor and creditor. This counter-caster" [*Othello* 1.1.18; 30]). The Clown in *The Winter's Tale* can't calculate his profit "without counters" (4.3.36), and Posthumus' jailer entertains him with some hangman's wit: "your neck, sir, is pen, book, and counters" (*Cymbeline* 5.4.170–1). (Arithmetic books, we might notice, were not apparently held in universally high regard in early modern England. The dying Mercutio sneers at Tybalt as "a villain, that fights by the book of arithmetic" [*Romeo and Juliet* 3.1.103–4], and Hamlet out-Osrics Osric with a riddling remark about "dozy[ing] th'arithmetic of memory" [*Hamlet* 5.2.114]. Arithmetic in these usages means something abstract and useless, like "theory," as well as something practical and useful, like bookkeeping.)

But, despite their popularity, Roman numerals are actually not very good for mathematics, though they are excellent for literature. "When considering views of antiquity," suggests Elizabeth Eisenstein, "the discarding of Roman numerals, or of Galen's anatomy or of Aristotle's physics, deserves at least as much emphasis as does the survival of theorems established by Pythagoras, Euclid, or Archimedes." And she notes, crucially, that "this discarding had not occurred until after a century of printing."[25] And again, "The discarding of Roman numerals . . . represented changes that cut across town-gown divisions and penetrated college halls. These changes are well reflected in the new printed materials turned out by applied mathematicians."[26]

Roman numerals were still in general use at the time of the invention of printing—though the Hindu-Arabic numeral, which took up less space on the printed page, had begun to come into fashion. Manuscripts were generally cited by chapter and verse, as is still done with the Bible (since no two copies would necessarily have the same pages). Chapters were given Roman numerals, a practice that continues today. Manuscript books were foliated, the leaves were counted, and numbers (in Roman numerals) appeared only on the recto pages. Pagination, which numbered the pages, recto and verso, came in later, and tended to use Hindu-Arabic numbers, again, because they saved space and were less ponderous. But the pagination of prefaces in lower-case Roman numerals, and the giving of chapter (and volume) titles in Roman capitals, is a practice that still persists today. We've seen this in the Roman-numeraled prefaces of learned books and editions of Shakespeare. One of my favorite instances, again nicely overdetermined, is a page from a modern book called *The Development of Arabic Numerals in Europe* that contains 64 tables of examples culled from the twelfth to the sixteenth centuries, with both the tables and the centuries meticulously numbered—in *Roman* numerals.[27]

The other obvious belated venue for Roman numerals is the clock or watch dial, where position rather than inscription allows the numbers to be "read" even by those who can't read. (Think of your driver-ed instructor telling you to "put your hands at ten of two" on the steering wheel.) This may be one reason why Roman numerals remained on clock faces long after Hindu-Arabic numbers replaced them in commercial use. Decorative, familiar, and iconic, the numerals on a clock did not need to be computed. It was only in the nineteenth century that Hindu-Arabic numbers began to appear with regularity upon clock dials—shortly to be followed, in this century, by the digital clock that did away with the notion of the dial altogether.[28] The striking clock in *Julius Caesar*, as editors never tire of pointing out, was always already an anachronism—what we might call an "original anachronism," in contradistinction to the modern use of Roman numerals as genuine antique reproductions, used to denote a spurious "originality."

One problem with the "German numbers" had been the absence of a zero; another, related problem was the increasingly inconsistent way in which place-value notation was given. The number 600 might be written, by authors in the medieval and early modern periods, as DC (500 + 100) or as vi.c (6 × 100). The English mathematician Robert Recorde, in the middle of the sixteenth century, wrote vj.C for 600 and CCC.M for 300,000.[29] What looked like abbreviations were actually evidences of a conceptually different mode of notation.

In the sixteenth and seventeenth centuries, therefore, enormous interest arose in developing a system of mathematical symbols as a kind of common language. François Viète used vowels for unknown quantities and consonants for known quantities. Descartes used letters from the beginning of the alphabet for known quantities and those from the end of the alphabet for unknown quantities. In England, Robert Recorde introduced the equals or equality sign, and William Oughtred experimented with more than 150 symbols. In this intellectual climate, the Roman numeral, with all its limitations, was destined for anachronism. Its days, we might say, were numbered. But with change came—as always—resistance. And with resistance, overvaluation. And with overvaluation, iconicity.

"Uniform mathematical symbols," says Elizabeth Eisenstein, "brought professors closer to reckon-masters. They did not separate academicians from artisans, although they did move scientists away from poets. To the warfare between scholastics and humanists was added a new schism, between the party of number and the party of words. Print insured a victory of the 'algorists' over the 'abacists.'"[30] The abacists wrote Roman numerals and calculated with the abacus. The algorists recorded and calculated with Hindu numerals. Eisenstein is here describing a shift in the practice of writing and printing mathematics; but she could equally well be describing C. P. Snow's two cultures.

In short, the shift from Roman to Hindu numerals was a revolution. It produced the important possibility of *zero*, aptly described by Brian Rotman as "a sign about names, a meta-numeral."[31] It allowed the registration of the concept of an absence—unrecordable in Roman numerals. And it regularized the crucial idea of place-value, first described by the mathematician Thomas Harriot (1560–1621), the founder of the English school of algebra, rather curiously known to a generation of post-New Historicist critics chiefly as the author of *A Brief and True Report of the New Found Land of Virginia* (1588).[32]

But this change was not achieved all at once, or without effort. "At our present stage," writes Karl Menninger, "we can scarcely imagine the extreme difficulty of abandoning the highly satisfactory visual quality of the number groupings in order to adopt the more sophisticated principle of place-value." Charts and tables for comparing "the German numbers and the cipher numerals" appeared in countless arithmetic texts, while verbal comparisons of the two systems also circulated widely. ("Cipher" originally meant "zero," and then came to refer to the entire number system. "Zero," short for the Latinized *zepharino* ["cipher"], thus came to denote 0.)[33] Polixenes in *The Winter's Tale* has learned the lesson perfectly: "And therefore, like a cipher / (Yet standing in rich place) I multiply / With one 'We thank you' many thousands moe / That go before it" (*Winters Tale* 1.2.6–9). He himself, of course, was shortly to become an absence, to take his hasty leave of the "rich place."

An elementary lesson in cultural capital was also about to be learned. For as the practical prestige of the Roman numerals fell, their iconic and esthetic value rose. They were now excess value rather than use. For some time they retained their customary utility among that most conservative of classes, the shopkeepers, whose ledgers continued to blossom with cursive ls, vs, is, and js. But in a development that will seem quite familiar to observers of culture, the Roman numerals became correspondingly (and as if in consequence of their loss of utility), emblems of monumentality and authority. Always "iconic" in a mathematical sense, they now became icons of a somewhat different sort. Their prestige as bearers of high culture increased as their arithmetical function decreased. They became, like the "Rome" whose borrowed name they bore, self-referential indices of their own defunct and therefore unassailable greatness. In their comparative uselessness they acquired a new and enduring use.

The Roman numeral—especially but not exclusively the capital Roman numeral—was now the perfect sign of anachronism and nostalgia, the perfect vehicle of what might be termed "the greatness effect."

III

The architects of the French Revolution renamed not only the months but also the years, starting over with the year I—in Roman numerals. The "great campaign of de-Christianization"[34] no longer dated the modern era from the birth of Christ, but rather from the fact of the Revolution. Thus in the autumn and winter of Year II, peoples' festivals abounded; the Constitution of Year III was approved on what we would call August 22, 1795; and the Directory government began after the elections of Year IV, in what we would call October of 1795.[35] At once monumentalizing and classicizing, this use of the Roman numeral recalled—as the Revolution did so often—the fantasmatic model of ancient Rome. "In the revolutionary view of history," as historian Lynn Hunt notes, "the republicans of Greece and Rome had invented liberty, and the mission of France was to bring that good news to all men."[36] But the choice of Roman numerals also struck a pose, historically speaking, instantiating what Hunt calls a "mythic present."[37] Perhaps unsurprisingly, the Statue of Liberty that stands in New York harbor, a gift of the people of France in 1886, bears the cast-iron date JULY IV MDCCLXXVI (July 4, 1776). In these cases, I would like to suggest, the Roman numeral becomes a sign of myth. Its iconicity is primary: an icon rather than an index, displaying itself rather than pointing to a referent, the Roman numeral is a sign of a sign.

In his charming essay on "The Romans in Films" Roland Barthes reads the little bangs worn by all the characters in Joseph Mankiewicz's 1953 *Julius Caesar* as "simply the label of Roman-ness." These "insistent fringes," as he delights in calling them, are transhistorical signs of historicity: "cross the ocean and the centuries, and merge into the Yankee mugs of Hollywood extras," these "Romans are Romans thanks to the most legible of signs: hair on the forehead."[38] Barthes hasn't much respect for this kind of sign, which is neither "openly intellectual," a kind of "algebra," nor "deeply rooted" (note the mathematical language here). The "fringe of Roman-ness" is an "intermediate sign," a "degraded spectacle," a hypocritical hybrid characteristic of bourgeois art, "at once elliptical and pretentious."

What would Barthes think, I wonder, of the *typographical* "fringe of Roman-ness" which is the Roman numeral today? What are the fringe benefits of the Roman numeral as monument to monumentality? Let us count the ways.

Perhaps the most visible worldwide use of Roman numerals to designate rulers today is that of the popes of the Roman Catholic Church. (Another overdetermined relationship, since they are styled the Vicars of Rome.) Julius II, Innocent IX, Pius XII, and John XXIII are familiar designations, indicating a tradition that is ages old. Some observers were taken aback when, in 1978, Albino Cardinal Luciani chose the name of John Paul I, indicating his reverence for his two predecessors, but also his expectation that there would be successors of that name. (Popes, of course, have no heirs of the body, at least officially.) Vatican loudspeakers boomed the announcement: "He . . . has taken the name of John Paul the First (Joannes Paulus Primus)."[39] This was the first double-name ever for a pope, and the first new name in a thousand years. But *Newsweek* speculated that "the Roman numeral 'I' in his chosen name may turn out to be more significant than his decision to be called John Paul." The newsmagazine saw this as a sign "that he intends to govern the church in a fresh manner." Within 34 days he was dead. (And in due course succeeded by John Paul II.)

Before John Paul I, the last pope to select an "original" name was Lando (913–14), who did not call himself "Lando I." Actually, the custom of appending an ordinal number to the pope's name dates only to the eighth century (with Gregory III [731–41]), and became common practice only in the tenth. Since Leo IX (1049–54), the lead seal of the papacy has borne the ordinal number. Earlier popes who chose the same names as their predecessors were—you will be interested to know—known as *junior*, or, for the third in line, *secundus junior*.[40]

In America, lacking (and perhaps secretly longing for) a hereditary elite, the Roman numeral after the name has been secularized into a version of American aristocracy: John D. Rockefeller III and IV, Henry Ford II (never a "junior," since he was the grandson of the original Henry), the novelist Lucian K. Truscott IV, an army officer who is the son and grandson of army officers. The British, who have their hereditary kings and queens, can be more cheeky about them; thus the sixties hit song from Herman's Hermits, "I'm Henry VIII," told the story of a man whose wife had married seven previous 'Eneries, making him "'Enery the Eighth."

But the real "hereditary" lineage in American culture is found in the spectacles of popular culture, in film and in sport. The greatness effect, the signifying function of the capital Roman numeral as spectacle, is evidenced in public entertainments from the Rocky films to the Super Bowl. *Rocky I, Rocky II, Rocky III, Rocky IV*, and *Rocky V* are the *Richard II, Henry IV*, and *Henry V* of today.[41] In fact, the Roman-numeraled sequel, from *Airplane II* to *The Godfather, Part III* and *Friday the 13th, Part VIII* has become so much of a cultural convention that when Alan Bennett's 1991 London hit *The Madness of George III* was adapted for the screen in 1994, the "people at Goldwyn" thought the play's title sounded like a sequel. They changed the title of the film to "The Madness of King George."[42] Even the *dates* of Hollywood films are given in Roman numerals: an on-screen equivalent of the architectural cornerstone, and another sign of grandeur (or at least, *delusions* of grandeur). In all of these contexts a Roman numeral means "greatness," historicity, cultural endurance, and authority. No matter that they can often not be read. Like celebrities, they are there to be seen.

As with Hollywood, so—quintessentially—with the Super Bowl. Under the apt head-line, "Supernumerary," a Russell Baker column in the *New York Times* for January 1988, Baker jokingly lamented the advent of "Roman numerology" in an era when no one any longer remembers what Roman numerals are, or how they work.[43]

The titles of the early Super Bowls were satisfactorily macho, he thought. "Those great numerals V, X and I looked so absolutely football. They looked like numerals a coach could use to diagram a rock 'em, sock 'em play on the blackboard," or a quarterback could use to call a play. But in the assumed persona of a public relations meister of the future, Baker speculated about the unfortunate Super Bowl XLIX, which would look "like a name for a laxative," and Super Bowl LI, which would remind viewers of "a Chinese general." The point of his little spoof was that the "youthful moneybags" who now owned all the professional sporting teams knew nothing about Roman numerals as numerals, regarding these weird combinations of Xs, Vs, Is and Ls instead as a peculiar semiotic of sports discourse.

Another newspaper's treatment of Super Bowl XXX took a similar—and similarly facetious—view. "Those three X's should convey to you the bigness here. Roman numerals are big. They were first used by the Romans, who were very big for a while until they collapsed. Now Roman numerals are used exclusively for very big things like Super Bowls, World Wars, Olympic Games, King Georges, King Henrys, Queen Elizabeths, popes, 'Death Wish' movies, and Wrestlemanias."[44] Facetious—and true. We live in a desperate cult of greatness, in which even olives are "Colossal."

The Roman numerals of today can be encountered in unexpected places, some-times still as a result of the confusion, or conflation, of letters and numbers. That magic, and those portents, remain uncannily vivid. (I'm sure I'm not the only Shakespearean to do a double-take when confronted, these days, with the standard abbreviation for *Henry the Fourth*: HIV.) The Roman numeral II in the title of the 1993 film *Menace II Society* is a manifestly postmodern Roman numeral, "readable" as a word, demotic and iconic at once, a defiant sign of greatness on its own terms. And in the aftermath of a wave of celebrity trials and retrials the news media began to refer to them with Roman numerals. One columnist made casual mention of "the Simpson II trial" and the "verdict in Simpson I."[45] "Last year brought Menendez II and Goetz II," reported the *New York Times*, "1997 is off to a fast start with O.J. II, and Crown Heights II. . . . Probably coming to newsstands this spring: Alex Kelly II."[46] Such show trials, it might be said without too much exaggeration, are the public theater of our day, the "abstract and [not so] brief chronicles" of our time.

Surely the putative "Romanness" of the numerals is itself part of the greatness effect; "German numbers," however correctly described, would not carry the same monumental weight. But "Romanness" is also, these days, part of the wistful joke—like the postmodern quotation of architectures of the past. Thus the contemporary Roman numeral can present itself as a witticism that monumentalizes even as it seems to undercut itself, like the advertisement for *A Funny Thing Happened on the Way to the Forum* that cautioned potential Broadway theatergoers that tickets were only available till February IX. Or—my favorite example—the 1941 Chon Day cartoon in which a placid Roman skater nonchalantly finishes off tracing a figure VIII. That the standard "figure eight" is a sign for infinity, proposed as such by the English mathematician John Wallis in 1655, but already in use in Rome as another numeral for 1000, adds something piquant (I can't help thinking) to the scene.[47]

What is fascinating, as we have observed, is the way in which the use of Roman numerals *increased* in literary and cultural contexts as it decreased in arithmetical or mathematical contexts. They have become, that is to say, iconic signs of *something else*. Something desired, and something lost.

Some are born great, some achieve greatness, and some have greatness thrust upon 'em." Fans of Shakespeare's Malvolio are already predisposed to find rebuses everywhere, magical combinations of letters and numbers that conjure a monumental identity. ("What should that alphabetical position portend? . . . 'M'! Why that begins my name" [*Twelfth Night* 2.5.119–26].) "Greatness" is an effect of dislocation and decontextualization. The decontextualizing of the sign produces an anxious fantasy of originary wholeness—of great heroes and great texts. Produces, that is to say, greatness as an effect of nostalgia and anachronism. Thus the attractive and "official" Shakespeare with its Roman numeraled acts and scenes is the Great Book to end all Great Books. No wonder it is only scholars who have made the democratizing cultural shift to the more "demotic" Hindu-Arabic act and scene citations, the ordinals of ordinary language, the numerals of everyday life. Everyone else has too much to lose.

Second-Best Bed ⋮ 8

^ Itm I gyve vnto my wief my second best bed wth the furniture Itm I gyve &
bequeath to my saied daughter Iudith my broad silver gilt bole All the Rest of
my goodes Chattels Leases plate Iewels & househod stuffe whatosoever after my
dettes and Legassies paied & my funerall expences discharged I gyve devise &
bequeath to my Sonne in Lawe Iohn Hall gent & my daughter Susanna his wief

Shakespeare's will

If others have their will Ann hath a way.

James Joyce, *Ulysses*

During a meal at a Chinese restaurant, critic Terry Castle once taught me an invaluable lesson about what might be called situational grammar. Any fortune-cookie fortune could be immeasurably altered, and enriched, she pointed out, by simply adding to it the phrase "in bed." (Try this yourself and you will see.)

When Shakespeare left his "second-best bed" to his wife Anne Hathaway in his will, he left, as well, a seductive historical conundrum. Is the phrase "second-best" a sign of his estrangement from the marriage, or was the "best" bed in the house given to guests, so that the "second-best" was the connubial couch—the one, as Shakespeare biographer Sam Schoenbaum remarks with deadpan wit, "rich in tender matrimonial associations?"[1]

Jane Cox, a specialist in old legal documents at the Public Records Office in London, recently described the second-best bed forthrightly as a "miserable souvenir." "This was no 'affectionate little bequest,'" she remarked, "neither was it usual for a seventeenth-century man, of any rank, to make no overt provision for his wife in his will. Of [a] sample of 150 wills proved in the same year . . . about one third of the testators appointed their wives as executrixes and residuary legatees. None left his wife anything as paltry as a second-best bed. Bedsteads and bedding were without doubt valuable and prized items and they were normally carefully bequeathed, best beds going to wives and eldest sons."[2]

But Shakespeareans are an ingenious lot, and much ingenuity has been expended in explaining, or explaining away, the problem of second-bestness in bed—or in beds. First there is the matter of "dower, right," the provision of English common law that automatically entitled a widow to a life interest in her husband's estate. Since this was the law, and known to be the law, there was no reason for Shakespeare to make a specific bequest to his wife at all. The diary of the Reverend John Ward, vicar of Stratford-upon-Avon during the lifetime of Shakespeare's daughter Judith, poses and answers the question to at least his own satisfaction:

> But why, it has been asked, leave the wife of his youth "his second best bed," and not his first best bed? It will not, I think, be difficult to give a most satisfactory answer to this query. Shakspeare had expressly left to his daughter, Susanna, and her husband, Dr. John Hall, "all the rest of his goods, chattels, leases, plate, and household stuffe whatsoever;" and supposing, as is most probable, Mrs. Shakspeare to have resided with them after her husband's death at New Place, she would there have the use and benefit of every article, as in her husband's lifetime. There is, I presume, a special reason why the second best bed was deemed by him so precious a bequest "to his wief"; few, if any, either in London or in the country, are themselves in the habit of sleeping on the first best bed;—this was probably by Shakspeare reserved for the use of Jonson, Southampton, the aristocratic Drayton, or for other of those distinguished persons with whom he is known to have been in habits of intimacy. The second best bed was, doubtless, the poet's ordinary place of repose,—the birthplace of his children; and on these and many other grounds it must have been, to Mrs. Shakspeare, of more value than all the rest of his wealth.[3]

Still, some modern commentators have privately—and not so privately—mused, he might have spared her a tender word. "Most of the wills of this period are personal and affectionate," writes biographer Marchette Chute, but "Shakespeare was one member of [his acting] company whose will does not show a flicker of personal feeling."[4]

G. E. Bentley complained that the will's single and possibly slighting proviso for Anne Hathaway had "given rise to many romantic or lurid tales."[5] E. K. Chambers, the great historian of the Elizabethan stage, declared that "A good deal of sheer nonsense has been written about this." Chambers and others, taking recourse (or refuge) in historical fact, suggest that "Mrs. Shakespeare would have been entitled by common law to her dower of a life interest in one-third of any of the testator's heritable estates in which dower had not, as in the case of the Blackfriars property, been legally barred"[6]—thus raising the inconvenient fact that the Blackfriars house *had* been left away from Shakespeare's wife, and by legal means.

And there was the undeniable and unhappy fact that the bequest of the bed was not even part of the original text, but was instead interlineated, inserted (perhaps, with Hamlet, we could say "popped in") after the fact. Like the wedding itself, it was, apparently, an afterthought.

"It is observable," noted the eighteenth-century Shakespeare editor Edmond Malone in a famous commentary, "that his daughter, and not his wife, is his executor; and in his Will, he bequeaths the latter only an old piece of furniture; nor did he even think of her till the whole was finished, the clause relating to her being an interlineation. What provision was made for her by settlement, does not appear."[7]

The context of Malone's remark is a reading of Sonnet 93, and Malone's contention is that the poet is writing "from the heart" about sexual jealousy. "That our poet was jealous of the lady," rejoins rival editor George Steevens with some asperity, is "an unwarrantable conjecture. Having, in times of health and prosperity, provided for her by settlement (or knowing that her father had already done so), he bequeathed to her at his death, not merely *an old piece of furniture* but perhaps, as a mark of peculiar tenderness,

> 'the very bed that on his bridal night
> Receive'd him to the arms of Belvedira.'"

And why did Shakespeare initially omit to leave her anything? "His momentary forgetfulness as to this matter, must be imputed to disease."

Malone, of course, will have none of this. His riposte is meant to be withering; it is clear to him that Shakespeare felt, and exhibited, nothing but contempt.

> His wife had not wholly escaped his memory; he had forgot her—he had recollected her—but so recollected her, as more strongly to mark how little he esteemed her; he had already (as it is vulgarly expressed) cut her off, not indeed with a shilling, but with an old bed.

"However," Malone goes on to remark, astringently, "I acknowledge, it does not necessarily follow, that because he was inattentive to her in his Will, he was therefore jealous of her. He might not have loved her; and perhaps she might not have deserved his affection."

Scholars and sentimentalists of the following centuries struggled to resist or overturn this uncharitable assessment. The author of *Shakespeare's True Life* (1890), once again citing dower right as the reason why the playwright made no express provision for his wife's maintenance, observes that "The bequest which he makes to her in his will, of his 'second-best bed,'—doubtless that in which as husband and wife they had slept together, the so-called 'best' being reserved for visitors—is intelligible enough, and needs none of the disquisitions of the would-be wise."[8] In

Shakespeare's Marriage (1905), Joseph William Gray is similarly confident: "It is difficult to believe that the bequest of the 'second-best bed' was intended for a slight, as is sometimes asserted. Even if feelings of dislike had been rankling in his mind, it is questionable whether he would have adopted such a contemptible method of expressing them."[9] We could hardly call this a "psychoanalytic" approach to the problem, but it does struggle toward the psychological, though here too it uses "history" (or "lore") to shore up its claims: "The only tradition which indicates Anne Shakespeare's opinion of or regard for her husband is that she 'greatly desired to be buried with him.'" (The "tradition" dates from Dowdall's *Traditional Anecdotes of Shakespeare, Collected in Warwickshire in the Year 1693*.)[10] The *grave* thus becomes the first-best bed, to which all others are second.

In 1918, Charlotte Scopes offered an argument based on sentiment and the humbleness of Anne Hathaway Shakespeare's origins, assuring her readers that "There is nothing derogatory in the legacy of the second-best bed; it was evidently her own last request. She was sure of her widow's *third*; she was sure of her daughters' love and care, but she wanted the bed she has been accustomed to, before the grandeur at New Place came to her."[11]

The authors of *Shakespeare's Town and Times* give a halcyon picture of the final years in Stratford: "At the time of the poet's death, we may imagine his wife, then over sixty years of age, as a brisk and kindly dame, her hair shot with silver and her step less firm than when she was wooed in Shottery fields, but with eyes still bright and cheeks still ruddy."[12] And Shakespeare biographer A. L. Rowse, a hundred years later, offers an equally benevolent view: "Most of his Will is concerned with the disposition of property among his family, most of it going to his heir, his elder daughter Susanna. She and her husband, Dr. John Hall, would naturally have the best double bed, so it was characteristically considerate of Shakespeare to specify that his widow, Anne, should have the next best bed for herself."[13]

From Malone's time to our own, then, we have moved from a characteristically cruel Shakespeare motivated by sexual jealousy to a characteristically considerate one motivated by fine family feeling, both predicated on the evidence of that second-best bed.

These explanations, or excuses, or explainings-away, had become so notorious by the beginning of this century that James Joyce could not resist mocking them in *Ulysses*: Stephen Daedalus and his friends are discussing Shakespeare and the neglected, patient "Mrs S." "He was a rich country gentleman, Stephen said, with a coat of arms and a landed estate at Stratford and a house in Ireland yard, a capitalist shareholder, a bill promoter, a tithefarmer. Why did he not leave her his best bed if he wished her to snore away the rest of her nights in peace?" Stephen's friend, the

Englishman John Eglinton, is inclined to defend the playwright, and Joyce has him
do so in Shakespearean blank verse:

> You mean the will.
> But that has been explained, I believe, by jurists.
> She was entitled to her widow's dower
> At common law. His legal knowledge was great
> Our judges tell us. . . .

But Stephen, whose sympathies are with the wife, will have none of this. His mordant
reply picks up the rhythms of Eglinton's verse and then breaks into mocking pseudo-
Elizabethan song:

> And therefore he left out her name
> From the first draft but he did not leave out
> The presents for her granddaughter, for his daughters,
> For his sister, for his old cronies in Stratford
> And in London. And therefore when he was urged,
> As I believe, to name her
> He left her his
> Secondbest
> Bed.
> *Punkt.*
> Leftherhis
> Secondbest
> Leftherhis
> Bestabed
> Secabest
> Leftabed.
> Woa!

Eglinton has recourse to the other stock answer: beds were valuable, "pretty coun-
tryfolk had few chattels then," but again Stephen's curiosity is piqued by Anne
Hathaway: "She lies laid out in stark stiffness in that secondbest bed, the mobled
queen, even though you prove that a bed in those days was as rare as a motorcar is
now and that its carvings were the wonder of seven parishes."[14]

There have been other skeptics, enough to generate an entire philosophy of
Shakespearean furniture. Samuel Neil's 1847 guide to *The Home of Shakespeare*
describes the appointments of Anne Hathaway's cottage, including "Shakespeare's
courting chair," so-called by Shakespeare enthusiast Samuel Ireland (the father of
William Henry Ireland, shortly to become famous for his forgeries). The chair, the
author admits, is not the same one that was there in the sixteenth century—the latter

having been bought for a stiff price by a central European princess—but it is "a very old chair," nonetheless, and the "absence of the genuine chair was not long felt." "It is but fair to add, that those who are sceptical are not met by bold assertions of its genuineness, although there be no denial of its possible claim to that quality; but all credulous and believing persons are allowed the full benefit of their faith."

And there was "an old carved bedstead, certainly as old as the Shakesperian era," which "has been handed down as an heirloom with the house. . . . Whether there in Anne's time, or brought there since, it is ancient enough for her and her family to have slept in, and adds interest to the quaint bed-room in the roof."[15] Any bed that Shakespeare—or his wife—or both—might have slept in had become a vital accessory after the fact.

But it was the famous "second-best bed" that had the first claim on the public's, and the scholars', attentions. The bed—that elusive and phantasmatic bed—has often seemed, in fact, something that could be fixed by history, by scouring the archives and the annals. Much energy has been expended on a search for other similar bequests to normalize or contextualize the apparent oddity of Shakespeare's interlineation. Thus, for example, scholars have located a number of other "second-best beds" in legal documents, including wills. In 1573, one William Palmer of Leamington left his wife Elizabeth his "second-best fetherbed for hir selfe furnished, And one other meaner fetherbed for her mayde. . . . And that I wolde have hir to live as one that were and had bien my wife."[16] So the second-best bed could be not only an affectionate bequest but, apparently, a status symbol. Palmer's will was seen by Schoenbaum as a knife that cut both ways, since by contrast the Shakespeare bequest "is unaccompanied by any expression of testamentary emotion, as in the Palmer will"; Schoenbaum promptly speculates that "perhaps his lawyer did not encourage, or permit, such embellishments."[17] Like Steevens's earlier conjecture that Shakespeare was too far gone with illness to think up any pretty thoughts for the occasion, this exculpatory speculation raises as many questions as it answers.

The best bed would technically qualify as an heirloom, an article of personal property handed down with the estate. Richard Marley in 1521 left his son his "best fetherbed," and, as historian Frederick Emmison suggests, "it is the eldest son, and not the widow, who gets the best bed."[18] In a will dated December 22, 1608, Thomas Combe left all bedsteads to his wife "except the best," which was bequeathed, "with the best Bedd and best furniture thereunto belonging" (that is, the sheets, pillows, linens, and so forth) to his son.[19] John Harris, a notary residing in Lincoln, left his wife two beds: "the standing bedstead in the little chaumber, with the second-best feath-erbed I have, with a whole furniture therto belonging and allso a trundle-bedsted with a featherbed, and the furniture therto belonging."[20]

"A second time I kill my husband dead, / When second husband kisses me in bed," intones the Player Queen in *Hamlet* (3.2.179–80), echoing the advice of Sir Walter Raleigh to his son: "leave thy wife more than of necessity thou must, but only during her widowhood, for if she love again, let her not enjoy her second love in the same bed wherein she loved thee."[21] Here the problem is that of the second *becoming* the first: the second love threatens to render the first husband's bed retroactively (and posthumously) second-best.

Scholar Joyce Rogers concludes from her own examination of medieval and Renaissance legal documents that many items other than beds are described in wills as "best" or "second-best," and makes a persuasive argument that this practice is linked to the medieval legal traditions of heriot and mortuary: the "best" things were given to the lord as a kind of tithe; after this the "second-best," or next-best, chattel was reserved to the church as a "mortuary," or reparation for the soul. Thus the jurist Sir William Blackstone, lamenting the passing of "the old common law," saw among those rights disappearing both the dower law or dower right and the "custom of many places . . . to remember his lord and his church, by leaving them his two best chattels."[22] "After the lord's heriot or best good was taken out, the second best chattel was reserved to the church as a mortuary."[23] Here, as Rogers points out, is quite a different valuation for "second-best." Instead of connoting something like "second-rate," or "second-hand"—something, that is, near the notional *bottom* of the heap, it instead repositions the "second-best" close to the *top*. "Thus the infamous phrase, 'second-best,' so often taken as an intentionally malicious slur, may be understood in ancient context as a parting tribute of profound meaning."[24]

Does this recourse to history "resolve" the problem of the "second-best bed"? On the one hand, we have learned that the surviving son—or, in Shakespeare's case, daughter—often got the best bed. On the other, we have seen that "second-best" (especially "with the furniture") is actually pretty good, and that its standing in law was traditional and honored. This would seem to be a "solution," of sorts, to the "problem" of Shakespeare's misogyny, or jealousy, or licentiousness, or homosexuality, or—at the very least—flight from the marriage and from Stratford, of which the "second-best bed" has been such a potentially tantalizing clue. In fact, there is no problem.

Or is there? The fact is that these "facts" will not make the problem go away, because Shakespeareans, professional and amateur alike, do not wish it to go away, however much they may protest to the contrary. We prefer the problem to any answer. The second-best bed, that perfect tester for the intersection and mutual embeddedness of historicism and psychoanalysis, is an overdetermined site for critical curiosity. The bed functions eroto-historically as the equivalent, in material culture, of the navel of the dream. Locus at once of procreation, legitimate and illegitmate (born on which side of the blanket?), inheritance and sexual fantasy, the scene of the primal scene. It is not an accident—as psychoanalytic critics like to say—that of all the elements in the Shakespeare story, and the Shakespeare will, the "second-best bed" has excited so much interest and controversy—interest and controversy that will not be quieted, or subdued, by a simple "answer" from history. For we do not want just the history— we want the story.

One evidence for this is the frequency with which the second-best bed has figured *in* a story. A 1993 novel by Robert Nye, *Mrs. Shakespeare, The Complete Works*, discloses that the "first best bed" was in fact the playwright's bed in London, where he engaged in sexual relations with Southampton (whom we may recall the Rev. Mr. Ward to have imagined visiting New Place and sleeping there in the household's "first best bed") and also with his wife when she came to visit. Initiated into sodomy ("what men do") by her husband, the delighted Mrs. Shakespeare finds a newly erotic pleasure in their marriage (as indeed does Mr. Shakespeare). The bequest of the "second best bed," she understands, is not "an insult" but a tribute to the memory of "that other bed, in every sense the best one,"[25] in which she had the best sex of her life. This queer narrative of female eroticism is a Shakespeare bedtime story for the 1990s. But it also—and this is perhaps more pertinent—conjures the scenario that lies behind the cultural fascination of the bequest: the spectacle of Shakespeare—our Shakespeare, *unser Shakespeare*—in bed. (Remember Castle's law of the prurient prepositional suffix: what was Shakespeare really like—in bed? What *did* Shakespeare really like—in bed?)

An earlier attempt at fiction offers a wry "historicist" approach. *No Bed for Bacon*, a 1941 comic novel by Caryl Brahms and S. J. Simon, evokes an Elizabethan England in which Raleigh longs chronically for a new cloak, Shakespeare for a perfect play (*Love's Labour's Won*), and Bacon for a bed. Sixteenth-century monarchs and great landowners took their own beds with them on their progresses, and Elizabeth, according to the novel's plot, is in the habit of presenting her favorites with "country bedsteads slept on by the Queen."[26] The comic conceit of *No Bed for Bacon* is that Bacon wants an Elizabethan trophy bed. But Bacon's longing is destined, of course, to go unsatisfied. The elusive bed is periodically glimpsed offstage: reports suggest that it has been delivered to Anne Hathaway's cottage; Shakespeare changes the subject whenever Bacon brings it up. The second-best bed is the *objet petit a* for both Bacon and the Shakespeare scholars gently satirized in the text.

No Bed for Bacon takes a creative approach to history, beginning with a "Warning to Scholars" that "This Book is Fundamentally Unsound," and a prefatory page that cites the great American pragmatist Henry Ford:

It was Henry Ford who is said to have remarked that "History is Bunk." The authors of this book have in a number of works set out to prove the point.

But if "History is Bunk," in the context of our inquiry we may be moved to ask whether it might also be said that "History is Bunk Beds." Indeed, a little reflection suggests that it is not only the "*bunk* bed" but the "*queen* bed," the "*king* bed," the "*California* king bed" (suitable for watching Kenneth Branagh's and Al Pacino's Shakespeare movies?), and perhaps especially, in light of Shakespeare's family, the "*twin* bed" that have some relevance for Shakespearean clinophiles.

"Shakespeare's will would not have been thought funny if his second-best bed had been a singleton," observes Reginald Reynolds in a 1952 book on the social history of the bed.[27] But if the bed had been a twin? The decade of the fifties, the decade of *Pillow Talk*,[28] was the modern heyday of the twin bed (a cultural innovation that dates, in point of fact, to a Sheraton design in the late eighteenth century, when they were invented "to keep lovers cool during the hot summer months").[29] Here are some striking statistics: the percentage of twin beds relative to all beds purchased in the U.S. in the pre-war period was 25 percent; by 1950—according to a number of studies—they had risen to 68 percent. And the scuttlebutt on twin beds was that— far from producing twins, as Shakespeare's bed had done (with some help from its tenants), twin beds produced divorce. Or so said the Director of the [American] Family Relations Institute in 1947: "This movement towards twin beds must stop. . . . The change from a double bed to twin beds is often the prelude to a divorce."[30]

"Twin Beds for Divorce," read the title of an article published in the previous year. But a British judge, called upon to rule in a 1950 divorce case as to whether a married couple sleeping in twin beds were sharing "the matrimonial bed" or occupying "separate sleeping accommodation" decided emphatically that the former was the case. Are twin beds one "bed" or two? Identical—or fraternal? It depends upon the nature of the (legal) case. If they slept in twin beds, neither could be said, for legal purposes, to have left the other's "bed and board." "I cannot," declared the judge, "regard twin divan beds in a married couple's bedroom as being otherwise than the matrimonial bed."[31] "The bed," in the terms of this ruling, henceforth could mean "the beds": when there were two in the same room, neither, presumably, was second-best.

Here we may seek further corroboration from an important and neglected work on beds by the early Marx—the early *Groucho* Marx. In a 1930 volume called *Beds* (described on the back cover as "the sleeper of the year!"), Groucho notes that "couples often become confused and get into the same twin bed by mistake, which explains why one bed is worn out more quickly than the other."[32] But if in life twin beds could cause divorce, in the Hollywood of the 1950s they were the very sign of marriage. "Twin bed marriages," writes Parker Tyler, a historian of sex in films, "actually mark a whole Hollywood epoch of bedroom customs." One of the ironclad rules was that, though a man and a woman could be shown alone together in a bedroom, even in their nightclothes, "there couldn't be a double bed waiting to accommodate their conjugal embraces; rather, there had to be *twin beds*."[33]

Hollywood, the "California king bed," and Groucho Marx may lead us to a consideration of a more recent manifestation of the second-best bed in public culture, the controversy about President Bill Clinton's use of the Lincoln bedroom. This hallowed White House chamber, where Lincoln never slept (but in which he was autopsied and embalmed, and where some say his spirit still walks abroad) has become the centerpiece in an American political scandal. ("Hark! Who lies i' th' second chamber?")

"Ready to start overnights right away," wrote Clinton in a memo to his staff. It turned out that some 938 supporters and friends had availed themselves of the opportunity to stretch out on the long and lumpy mattress of the Lincoln bed. *Newsweek*, unable to resist the obvious witticism, headlined its article on the Presidental bed-trick "Strange Bedfellows."[34]

Best bed? or second-best? For the guests of the Clintons—like, presumably, the guests of the Lincolns—the best was not good enough.

Some denizens of the Lincoln bedroom had more spectral expectations. Though Lincoln never slept there, it was an office in his lifetime and he is asserted to have visited, post mortem, when the fancy took him. Winston Churchill is said to have encountered the Great Emancipator's ghost, and Queen Wilhelmina of the Netherlands once saw "an ectoplasm in a stovepipe hat."[35] The most numinous encounter with Lincoln was imagined, perhaps not surprisingly, by Ronald Reagan, who confided his excitement to a group of junior high school students. "If he is still there, I don't have any fear at all! I think it would be very wonderful to have a little meeting with him, and probably very helpful."[36] It seems that Hillary Clinton's chats with Eleanor Roosevelt may have had Republican—and Presidential—precedent.

The seemingly inconsequential saga of the Lincoln bedroom, then, engages not only history but also, and even more crucially, psychoanalysis: narratives of the ghost, the revenant, the father, the family romance, the unattainable object of desire—and, perhaps even more crucially, the undecidable question of how we can tell first-best from second-best. Is the first-best bed the bed slept in by the First Family, or the bed that has come to signify—though, as we have seen, it never cradled—the most beloved President of them all?

On the key question, the question of how to distinguish the "first-best" from the "second-best" bed and what is at stake in that distinction, we may get some assistance from Plato. Let us turn for a moment to that controversial section of the *Republic* in which he speaks of the role of the poet and artist. For the object that Socrates holds up to Glaucon as an exemplary "thing" is the *bed*. And what we discover if we do so is that there are for our consideration not two beds, but three:

> Here we find three beds; one existing in nature, which is made by God, as I think that we may say—for no one else can be the maker?
>
> No one, I think.
>
> There is another which is the work of the carpenter?
>
> Yes.
>
> And the work of the painter is a third?
>
> Yes.
>
> Beds, then, are of three kinds, and there are three artists who superintend them: God, the maker of the bed, and the painter?
>
> Yes, there are three of them.
>
> God, whether from choice or from necessity, made one bed in nature and one only; two or more such beds neither ever have been made nor ever will be made by God.
>
> Why is that?
>
> Because even if He had made but two, a third would still appear behind them of which they again both possessed the form, and that would be the real bed and not the two others.[37]

"Very true," says Glaucon, obediently, and so we may perhaps say, as well. The third bed, the spectral bed—the bed, we may say, of Goldilocks, the bed that is (but only in fantasy) "just right"—appears "behind."

Plato's "third" bed is the *form* of the bed: "that would be the real bed and not the two others." But the thirdness of the bed disrupts, in what is by now a familiar fashion, the unsatisfactory binary of the carpenter's bed and the painter's bed, the material object-in-history and the object-in-representation. And it is the third which, according to Plato, is the "real" one.

The carpenter is a maker and the painter an imitator. Of their two beds, which is the "second-best"? That of the artist, the "imitator of that which others make"? Or is it in fact the case that the "third bed" is—by its very nature—the "best bed," so that the artifacts of both carpenter and painter are—again, by their very nature—only "second-best"? The "real" is the one that we *cannot* see. "The essential object which isn't an object any longer, but this something faced with which all words cease and all categories fail."[38] And this, needless to say, is not Plato's real but Lacan's.

Furthermore, this central passage from the *Republic* that we have been considering, about the three beds, comes from Benjamin Jowett's translation of Plato. But this is not the only way to construe the passage, or its key word. The Greek word here is *kline*, from *klinein*, to slope or lean—the word from which we get "recline," "incline," and "decline." And in Paul Shorey's translation of Plato for the Bollingen Series, the word (or concept) is translated as not *bed* but *couch*.

The resulting rhetorical questions have a special resonance for a twentieth-century reader.

> What of the cabinetmaker? Were you not just now saying that he does not make the idea or form which we say is the real couch, the couch in itself, but only some particular couch?[39]

"Some particular couch." With this we arrive at the scene of psychoanalysis, ground zero for Freudians, that celebrated piece of furniture that Freud historian Peter Gay repeatedly calls "the famous couch."

Freud's couch, the centerpiece of the doctor's office, the gift of a grateful patient,[40] was draped with Persian carpets, one of which hung behind the couch like an Elizabethan arras. Biographer Gay pictures the expansive founder of psychoanalysis "look[ing] around his consulting room from his comfortable upholstered armchair behind the couch."[41] When Freud became virtually deaf in his right ear as a result of operations on his oral cavity "the couch was moved from one wall to another so that he could listen with his left."[42] (Shakespeareans will recall that Julius Caesar had a complementary infirmity, being deaf in his left ear rather than his right.) The couch was moved once again near the end of Freud's life when the family was forced to leave Vienna and to resettle in London. "The possessions he had had to ransom from the Nazis—his books, his antiquities, his famous couch—were placed in the new house at 20 Maresfield Gardens so that the two downstairs rooms resembled, as closely as possible, the original consulting room and study in Berggasse 19."[43] In a fascinating essay on the architecture and symbolism of Freud's office, Diana Fuss and Joel Sanders suggest that "the sexual overtones of the famous couch—the sofa as bed . . . discomforted Freud's critics and, if Freud himself is to be believed, no small number of his patients."[44] Once, in its earliest history, Freud's couch had been used for hypnosis, a technique he abandoned, but the couch itself remained as a relic or "remnant" of "psychoanalysis in its infancy."[45] Fuss and Sanders aptly describe the office as "the birthplace of psychoanalysis."[46]

Here we might think of that other Birthplace, now held in trust for the nation: "The Holy of Holies of the Birthplace was the low, the sublime Chamber of Birth," writes Henry James.[47] "It was as empty as a shell of which the kernel had withered. . . . It contained only the Fact—the Fact itself." *The* Fact is the fact of the unnamed Shakespeare's birth, though to give it a name is to destroy the wicked subtlety of James's parlor-trick prose. In guidebooks of the period—to which James may well have had recourse—words like "relic" regularly appear,[48] and even the most current twentieth-century guidebook calls the house and the birthroom a "shrine." Though

the room James visited was empty and evocative, today's Shakespeare birthroom, out-
fitted for our more literal age, contains not only a period bedstead standing in for the
Fact of his conception, but also a cradle.

The relations between Freud and Shakespeare are complicated, and in fact revolve
around two versions of the second bed: the second marital bed of Hamlet's mother,
and the marital bed (indeed, the identity) of Shakespeare himself.

    Freud's take on *Hamlet* (like that of his disciple, Stephen Daedalus) had placed
the mother's bed squarely front-and-center. As Gary Taylor notes, what had been
"the closet scene" now became, in Dover Wilson's *What Happens in "Hamlet,"* "the
bedroom scene." By the 1940s the bed had become a standard prop, and in 1948
Laurence Olivier brought the Sigmund Freud-Ernst Jones *Hamlet*—and the maternal
bedroom—to the world screen.[49] "Let not the royal bed of Denmark be / A couch
for luxury and damned incest" (1.5.82–3), enjoins the Ghost-King in *Hamlet* to the
conflicted son. In this parental prohibition, bed and couch, those two Freudian props,
again function as not-quite synonyms. But exactly whose incest is being prohibited—
the uncle's, or the son's?

    In classic Freudian readings the eavesdropping scene in Gertrude's closet or
bedroom is another thinly-disguised wish appearing as a projection: Polonius ("that
great baby" [*Hamlet* 2.2.378]) takes the place of the child in the primal scene, who
wants to spy on his parents' lovemaking in bed—and perhaps even, in fantasy, to
witness his own conception.[50] Takes the place, that is, of Hamlet. Or of Freud.[51]
Freud had famously written to his friend Fliess that he had found, "in my own case,
too, [the phenomenon of] being in love with my mother and jealous of my father,"
and his conviction that this was "a universal event in early childhood," tied, once
again, to his reading of *Hamlet* as a confessional text. So, for Freud, the story of Hamlet
was overtly and self-evidently the story of Shakespeare. "It can of course only be the
poet's own mind which confronts us in Hamlet."[52]

    By 1919, about twenty years later, Freud was referring readers, in a footnote, to
Jones's fuller psychoanalytic account of Hamlet and Oedipus, where we are told in a
chapter called "The Hamlet in Shakespeare," that "the poet himself . . . had been
hastily married, against his will. . . .—an act for which he never forgave his wife, and
to which we may ascribe some part of his misogyny."[53] But by 1930, in another
footnote (his favorite mode of self-interrogation), Freud quietly disavowed his entire
biographical reading: "Incidentally, I have in the meantime ceased to believe that the
author of Shakespeare's works was the man from Stratford."[54] "Shakespeare wrote
Hamlet very soon after his own father's death," he had asserted in his *Autobiographical
Study* (1925). But in 1935 he inserted a footnote that caused great consternation to

his English translator: it read, "This is a construction which I should like explicitly to withdraw."[55] Shakespeare was not the author of the plays.

And here we have a good theoretical instance of what might be called the logic of the second-best bed. This disavowal of Shakespeare's authorship (about which I have commented at some length elsewhere)[56] may be usefully compared to that other famous Freudian disavowal, the disavowal of the seduction theory. In the latter, Freud revised his early view that the origins of neurosis lay in "infantile sexual scenes" or "sexual intercourse in childhood." But now Freud claimed that the "seduction theory" was not grounded in historical fact—that is, that his patient's intimations of "sexual intercourse in childhood" had not really taken place. Rather, these "seductions" were fantasies: "I was at last obliged to recognize that these scenes of seduction had never taken place, and that they were only fantasies which my patients had made up."[57] The "real" bed of incest or seduction was second best to the fantasy—indeed, it was now only the fantasy that was "real."

With the concept of the primal scene Freud had a similar problem: were these mental images of parental coitus memories or fantasies? "Real" or "imagined"? Psychoanalysis or history? The question was, he thought, undecidable in the general case: his account of the Wolf Man story emphasizes the degree to which the reality of the primal scene is only grasped by the child after the fact, by "deferred action"; on the other hand, retrospective fantasies are triggered by some real-world clues or symptoms, like familiar noises or the sexual encounters of animals.[58]

That the primal scene itself should be poised between—or overlap across—the boundaries of so-called reality and so-called fantasy is, for the terms of my argument, crucial. For what I propose is not just that the bequest of the second-best bed inserted, belatedly, into Shakespeare's will is a good example of the interpretative tensions between psychoanalysis and historicism, but rather that it embeds those tensions in a cultural icon—Will's will, "what he hath left us"—that is the primal scene of poesis, the primal scene of our literature. In other words, the second-best bed as cultural legacy is an overdetermined instance of primal rivalry between psychoanalysis and history. This is what accounts for its fascination. Psychoanalysis, as we can see from the examples of the seduction theory and the primal scene, is itself about, precisely, the relationship between history and psychoanalysis.

In revising his "seduction theory" Freud decides in favor of fantasy over history, and thus, as many have remarked, through this very act of disavowal creates the discipline of psychoanalysis. What I am suggesting here is that in revising his identificatory relationship with "Shakespeare" Freud performs a very similar act of disavowal, though apparently in the opposite direction (seeming, that is, to choose "history" over "fantasy").

When he accepted the Goethe Prize from the City of Frankfurt, Freud directly addressed the rival claims of history and psychoanalysis, acknowledging both the limits of biographical knowledge and the psychoanalytic reasons that lay behind the quest for historical details. Biographers, even the best of them, cannot explain either the artist or his work. "And yet there is no doubt that such a biography does satisfy a powerful need in us. We feel this very distinctly if the legacy of history unkindly refuses the satisfaction of this need—for example, in the case of Shakespeare."

Was "the author of the Comedies, Tragedies and Sonnets" the "untutored son of the provincial citizen of Stratford" or the "nobly-born and highly cultivated" aristocrat, Edward de Vere? How can we justify "a need of this kind to obtain knowledge of the circumstances of a man's life when his works have become so important to us?" Freud's answer is that we are in quest of father figures, teachers, and exemplars—and also that we need to think them finer than ourselves. Biographical research often produces unwelcome bits of information that tends toward the "degradation" of the same great man we so wish to admire.[59] "The man of Stratford," wrote Freud in a fan letter to the most vigorous proponent of the Oxford theory, "seems to have nothing at all to justify his claim, whereas Oxford has almost everything."[60] History is the phantasmatic sign of the family romance Freud elects to believe as truth.

So where we saw, a moment ago, that psychoanalysis was itself founded on the borderline between history and psychoanalysis, we can see now that the same is the case with history. The family romance of Oxford as the better Shakespeare reverses the pattern of fantasy as the better seduction. History itself is about the relationship between history and psychoanalysis.

Neither historicism nor psychoanalysis, in short, will benefit from a Procrustean view. What becomes most evident is the difficulty of making a bed while lying in it—a task, perhaps, beyond even the talents of Procrustes.

Shakespeare's Dogs | 9

When the eminent bibliographer and English scholar Fredson T. Bowers retired from the University of Virginia in 1975, the title pages of two of his works were reproduced in the commemorative program. One was from Bowers's landmark book *Principles of Bibliographical Description* (1949); the other was from an earlier work, *The Dog Owner's Handbook* (1936). Bowers, who "came to symbolize the fields of analytical and descriptive bibliography, textual criticism, and scholarly editing,"[1] and whose other hobbies included stamp collecting, cryptography, classical music, bridge, and single-malt Scotch, was also a former breeder of Irish wolfhounds and a respected dog show judge. At one time Bowers wrote a regular column for the *American Kennel Gazette*. Of his initial encounter with Irish wolfhounds[2] he wrote simply, "It was a case of love at first sight."

The Irish wolfhound might be regarded as a good Shakespearean choice. Hotspur may have owned one; he tells his wife he'd rather hear "Lady, my brach, howl in Irish" than Mortimer's wife sing in Welsh (*King Henry IV, Part 1* 3.1.232). But Bowers's *Dog Owner's Handbook* does not mix its registers in the manner of modern cultural criticism: it is all canine business, no Shakespearean (dog) tags in sight. The index headings under "S" are straightforward: "Scratching, Sealyham Terrier, Shedding, Shetland Sheepdog, Show dogs, Shredded Wheat"—no "Shakespeare" anywhere.

One of Fredson Bowers's early publications in the field of analytical bibliography was greeted by Alfred Harbage as "earnest conviction doggedly presented."[3] His very first scholarly article, in the March 1930 issue of *Modern Language Notes*, concerned the anonymous poetic satire *Machiavells Dogge* (1617). But (despite these plain hints) no one, so far as I know, has bothered to point out that "Bowers" was an easy anagram (or a printer's error) for "Bowser."

Is there any relationship between dog ownership, or dog breeding, and bibliography? Bowers's *Handbook* for dog owners moves briskly past the "mongrel" to the "pure-bred" to the "show dog." "Never be impressed by just one or two champions four or five generations back," he writes. "Finally, the word 'champion' is at times meaningless unless one knows how and when the dog won his title." Beware of "cheap champions" who won their laurels at inferior dog shows. "It is therefore better to admire the pedigree, but not to pay a fancy price for a puppy on the strength of a line of ancestors studded with champions. . . . If you are interested and if the dealer is a truly intelligent and worthwhile breeder, ask him to go over the breeding and show you how the particular dogs have been picked to offset weaknesses and strengthen good points. . . . But don't be over-impressed by pedigree alone."[4]

Bowers's work on descriptive and analytical or critical bibliography offered advice of a very similar kind. "No matter what the field of study," he remarked to an audience at the University of Pennsylvania in 1949, "the basis lies in the analysis of the records in printed or in manuscript form."[5] Descriptive bibliography is the description of a book as a physical object; textual bibliography is the critical examination of the book and its production history to determine the authority of the text. Both systems of analysis have homologies with the pedigree in dog breeding, and the (nonetheless crucial) necessity, as Bowers points out, to examine the individual specimen oneself, measuring it against the American Kennel Club Standard with the advice of a trained and reliable expert. As G. Thomas Tansell notes, the revision of the Kennel Club breed standard for the wolfhound, in which Bowers actively involved himself, "was not unlike the bibliographical question he later addressed concerning the description of 'ideal' copies of books."[6] In an address to the Irish Wolfhound Club of America in 1935 (a year after finishing his thesis on revenge tragedy), Bowers praised "the friendliness of the English breeders" and their desire "to popularize the very finest specimens possible of the noblest of all dogs, the love of which makes any nation kin."[7]

The idea that dog hierarchy, dog culture, and dog society offer a pattern for human status and degree is, of course, famously articulated by Macbeth in his rather testy reply to the First Murderer. The murderer had protested his own "common humanity."

First Murderer: We are men, my Liege.
Macbeth: Ay, in the catalogue ye go for men;
             As hounds, and greyhounds, mongrels, spaniels, curs,
             Shoughs, water-rugs, and demi-wolves, are clept
             All by the name of dogs: . . . (3.1.90–4)

That the society of dogs could be seen as a model for the society of humans in the Renaissance is clear from John Caius's treatise *Of English Dogges*, published in Latin in 1570, translated in 1576.[8] (His English translator warned against those who would "snarr and snatch at the English abridgement, and tear the Translator, being absent, with the teeth of spightfull envye"—"there eloquence is but currishe.")[9] In *De Canibus Britannicis*, Caius, a humanist, physician, and cofounder of Gonville and Caius College at Cambridge, describes at least six main varieties of dogs: greyhounds, true hounds, bird dogs, terriers, mastiffs, and shepherd dogs. His book contains sections like "Of the Dogge called the Fisher, in Latine *Canis Piscator*," "The Dogge called the Setter, in Latine *Index*," "Of the delicate, neate, and pretty kind of dogges called the Spaniel gentle, or the comforter, in Latine *Melitoeus* or *Fotor*" (lap dogs "sought for to satisfie the delicatenesse of daintie dames, and wanton womens wills . . . to contente their corrupted concupiscences with vaine disport" [18]), and "In Latine *Canis Mandatarius*, A Dogge messinger or Carrier," "because at his masters voyce and commaundement, he carrieth letters from place to place, wrapped up cunningly in his lether collar" (26), and so on. All dogs, in other words, are not alike.

But something very interesting has happened between that time and this, something quite relevant to "Shakespeare and the Twentieth Century."

I began with Fredson Bowers, and his twin lifelong preoccupations with Shakespeare and with dogs, to point out what seems to me to have been an under-noticed fact: that in the late twentieth century the twin guarantors of "humanism," conceived as a set of fast-vanishing values, are these very same two entities: Shakespeare and dogs. At a time when modes of analysis like feminism, poststruc-turalism, historical materialism, and identity politics all urge the situatedness of particular human subjects, calling attention to defining characteristics of difference, a popular nostalgia for humanism, for the universal "us" of midcentury criticism, has led to a recentering of the canine in, and as, the canon. In short, Shakespeare, long in the popular estimation a guarantor of "human nature" and our chief descriptor of "the human condition," is being used, these days, as the way of locating and describing true humanness—and humanism—in the place where it is paradoxically to be found: not among people but among dogs. On this view, all the world's a doghouse, and all the men and women merely spaniels; or beagles; or bichons frisés.

"Ay, in the catalogue ye go for men," says Macbeth contemptuously. (As hounds and greyhounds—the pets of aristocrats—mongrels, curs, and demi-wolves all go "by the name of dogs.") The universal claim to humanity is here dismissed as a self-serving fiction that ignores differences of nature and status. But in the late twentieth century the desire to universalize the subject persists. The claim that "we are men" continues to be made. And very often outside the academy, especially in fiction, popular culture, and certain realms of social sciences, this essential humanness is demonstrated, not through *human* examples of the transcendence of social category, but rather through a fascinating conjunction of Shakespeare and the dog. Uncannily (un-kennel-y?), in fact, wherever there is discussion of humanism's key topics—philosophy, love, and death—we are likely to find the track of Shakespeare's dogs.

Let me give you some examples. *Shakespeare's Dog*, a 1983 novel by Leon Rooke, is written in the voice of the dog, Hooker, who speaks a kind of Elizabethan dog-English (cognate to dog-Latin?): "woof-woof, grr and growl. . . . [T]ake this and that, demented beast, thou feast of a cesspool!"; "Agh and etch (blech and blah), you piddler, you leaf-sniffing pooch!"; "Blech and blah, woof and rar—oh you mangy huffers with pig's feet for brains." Hooker is contemptuous of Anne Hathaway, "my master Two Foot's kicksy wicksy, the noxious Hathaway,"[10] and of the literary aspirations of his master, Will. Written from the same household-retainer perspective as *Lord Byron's Doctor* or, indeed, the legendary *Lincoln's Doctor's Dog, Shakespeare's Dog* affords a cur's-eye (and curbside) glimpse of the world: "I remember once, talking with Will and him saying dogs were lower than the low. I'd pointed out even Aristotle had noted favorably the link between dog and man: how each shed his teeth similarly and had a single stomach that daily required replenishment. 'Who?' he'd said—and taken out his pen to write it down. 'Aristotle who? What's he done?'"[11]

As with philosophy and natural history, so also with love and family values. Best-selling dog author Elizabeth Marshall Thomas, in her unabashedly anthropomorphic book *The Hidden Life of Dogs*, describes a dog "marriage" between the huskies Misha and Maria:

> Popular prejudice might hold that romantic love, with its resulting benefit of fidelity, sexual and otherwise, is not a concept that can be applied to dogs, and that to do so is anthropomorphic. Not true. Fully as much as any human love story, the story of Misha and Maria shows the evolutionary value of romantic love. The force that drove Romeo and Juliet is no less strong or important if harbored by a nonhuman species, because the strength of the bond helps to assure the male that he, instead of, say, Tybalt or Bingo, is the father of any children born and that both parents are in a cooperative frame of mind when the time comes to raise those children.[12]

Notice that Shakespeare is here evoked as the humanistic "evidence" of an emotional standard: "the force that drove Romeo and Juliet" appears here as a fact, not a fiction, while the beguiling fantasy of a litter of baby Montagues sired by Romeo on his Capulet "mate" serves to corroborate "the evolutionary value of romantic love." In fact any analogy here would break down on the level, so to speak, of the breed: presumably the genetic purity and continuation of the Capulet line would profit more directly from marriage—or "mating"—between Juliet and her cousin Tybalt (what Bowers calls inbreeding and linebreeding in *The Dog Owner's Handbook*) than from the transgressive Montague-Capulet cross. *Romeo and Juliet*, in fact, is in this regard less like Misha and Maria than it is like *Lady and the Tramp*.

As it happens, elements of Shakespeare's *Romeo and Juliet* also turn up in another contemporary love story between dogs, Ivan Reitman's film *Beethoven's Second*. This popular family movie featuring a romance between two Saint Bernards has more than a little in common with *The Hidden Life of Dogs*. Missy the Saint Bernard, imprisoned by her wicked stepowners on a first-floor apartment house balcony, is wooed by the love-struck Beethoven, and—in a move Juliet might have envied—she leaps over the railing to join him for an afternoon on the town. Once again the reference to Shakespeare (rather more accurate here than in Thomas' account) is used as a shorthand for "romantic love."

The PBS children's television show *Wishbone* features a dog who sometimes dresses in "human" clothes to act out social roles. In a recent episode he donned tights and Elizabethan ruff to woo his beloved—using, as a script, Shakespeare's *Romeo and Juliet*. Somewhat to (at least) one viewer's surprise, the object of his affections was not another dog, but a (human) woman, who spoke Juliet's lines.

"What's in a name?" Juliet famously inquires. The other day I came upon an ad for dog biscuits that featured two irresistible golden retriever puppies. In tiny type by the side of each puppy were printed their names: "Goneril" and "Regan." Presumably these were female (okay, little bitches), and the owner was casting about for cute literary names for a pair of sisters. Never mind the context. On the other hand, perhaps the owner recalled that Lear had alluded to his "dog-hearted daughters," and took the phrase as a compliment. (The ad appeared, after all, not in a literary journal but in *Dog Fancy*, the journal of "dog care for the responsible owner.") As it turned out, someone in Triumph Pet Industries had a penchant for the Bard. Other advertisements for Triumph Products featured a Bernese mountain dog pup named Prince Hal, another golden puppy named Phebe, and two handsome adult dogs (collie and golden) named Fitzwater and Willoughby—as well as a complement of cats called Mariana, Claudio, Kate, and Paris.[13]

Naming your dog after a character in Shakespeare is probably an occupational hazard among *Shakespeareans* and other literary types (how many of you have dogs, or pets, named after characters in the plays?). Paul de Man had a dog called Puck, as did gay novelist and writer Paul Monette. Monette's moving essay about Puck, comparing the lives of gay men living in the time of the AIDS crisis with "dog years" ("seven for every twelvemonth"), clearly establishes this beloved canine companion, like his (unmentioned) Shakespearean namesake, as the guardian of the threshold.[14]

In George Sand's novel *Indiana* (1832) there is a beautiful hunting dog named Ophelia, who, perhaps inevitably, given her name, comes to an unhappy end. Tracking the heroine Indiana to the river Seine in time to prevent *her* from drowning, Ophelia later finds a watery grave herself. When the dog swims after Indiana (who is escaping from the clutches of an old and brutal husband and fleeing to join a young but faithless lover), she is beaten to death by the oars of sailors. Even when alive Ophelia suffers pangs of empathetic pain. "Down, Ophelia, down!" commands her master, when she puts her forepaws on his shoulders. And when the brutal Colonel Delaware threatens her with a hunting crop she "whimper[s] . . . with hurt and fear."[15]

A highly successful pop psychology book called *Reviving Ophelia*, this decade's answer to *The Peter Pan Syndrome* (1983), describes teenage girls as "shattered by the chaos of adolescence":

> The story of Ophelia, from Shakespeare's *Hamlet*, shows the destructive forces that affect young women. As a girl, Ophelia is happy and free, but with adolescence she loses herself. When she falls in love with Hamlet, she lives only for his approval. She has no inner direction; rather she struggles to meet the demands of Hamlet and her father. Her value is determined utterly by their approval. Ophelia is torn apart by her efforts to please. When Hamlet spurns her because she is an obedient daughter, she goes mad with grief. Dressed in elegant clothes that weigh her down, she drowns in a stream filled with flowers.
>   Girls know that they are losing themselves.[16]

The blueprint (or pawprint) for this servile behavior is provided, of course, by Shakespeare himself. "I am your spaniel," announces Helena to a dismayed Demetrius:

> The more you beat me, I will fawn on you.
> Use me but as your spaniel, spurn me, strike me,
> Neglect me, lose me; only give me leave,
> Unworthy as I am, to follow you.
> What worser place can I beg in your love—
> And yet a place of high respect with me—
> Than to be used as you use your dog?
>   (*A Midsummer Night's Dream* 2.1.204–10)

Despite the wisdom of modern-day pop therapists, this is not only female-patterned behavior. Petruchio has a spaniel named Troilus, presumably because he is so pathetically faithful. "Base spaniel fawning" seems to be a specialty of courtiers (*Julius Caesar* 3.1.43; *King Henry VIII* 5.2.160) but also of lovers, male as well as female. Proteus protests that the more he professes his love to Silvia and is rejected, the more he loves her: "spaniel-like, the more she spurns my love, / The more it grows, and fawneth on her still" (*Two Gentlemen of Verona* 4.2.14–15). *Two Gentlemen*, of course, is the play

that features the beguilingly disobedient mongrel Crab, whom Launce is commanded
to give as a present to Silvia. (Actually he is sent to give her a lap dog, Proteus's "little
jewel," but when the jewel is stolen he makes the supreme sacrifice and offers her his
own dog instead. Happily for Launce, the smelly, thieving, imperfectly housebroken
Crab, whom he adores, is rejected by Silvia and returned to the sender.)

But in the theater of the 1990s it is not Crab but Silvia who is the dog, the
adoring, adorable protagonist of A. R. Gurney's surprise hit play *Sylvia*, now on
Broadway. The title role was played to tail-wagging perfection by a human actress,
crimp-haired Sarah Jessica Parker, in ordinary jeans and ragged sweater, a figure whose
entry in full sniff and high-spirited bark ("Hey-hey-hey") was greeted by the audience
with delighted smiles of recognition.

Here's the plot: Sylvia, discovered wandering in Central Park, is brought home
by a man named Greg, who is in the midst of what used to be called a midlife crisis.
But Greg's wife Kate (a good Shakespearean name), who has an exciting new job as
(guess what?) a teacher of Shakespeare, does not want Sylvia moving in. And in a way
she's right—Sylvia has become the other woman. When she returns from the groomer
resplendent in pink leggings and kneepads (for Sylvia's wardrobe is, like Sylvia herself,
drawn from the vocabulary of human rather than canine style), Sylvia is beautiful, in
Greg's eyes. And—best of all—she loves him, loves him uncritically, showing her
gratitude at every turn. How can a wife compete, especially when her own career is
burgeoning and her husband's is apparently at a standstill?

Who is Sylvia, what is she? Shakespeare's Silvia spurned the dog sent by the
inconstant Proteus. In Gurney's play Kate wouldn't have the dog Sylvia as a gift. She
decides that Sylvia should be given away to a nice family in the country so Greg and
Kate can go to England on Kate's academic fellowship (it has not escaped Kate's notice
that English law requires foreign dogs to be quarantined for six months before they
can enter the country). Ultimately, of course, Kate relents and Sylvia stays.

Gurney's play is full of literary canine allusions, from Lassie and Albert Payson
Terhune to *The Odyssey*, but the choice of "Sylvia" for the dog's name seems to me to
be symptomatic. Incorruptible, faithful, fair and kind: these are today the traits of *dogs*.
And not only today.

In a famous court argument in 1870 attorney George Graham Vest, later to
become senator from Missouri, defended the honor and glory of the dog, comparing
his fidelity to man's ingratitude. The case was a suit for damages by the owner of
a dog shot for trespassing, and Vest's moving account and high-flown rhetoric set
the tone for more than a hundred years of sentiment. As you listen to this speech,
which was later repeated on the Senate floor, see if you can hear its Shakespearean
subtext:

Gentlemen of the jury: The best friend a man has in the world may turn against him and become his worst enemy. His son or daughter that he has reared with loving care may prove ungrateful. Those who are nearest and dearest to us, those whom we trust with our happiness and our good name, may become traitors to their faith. . . . The one absolutely unselfish friend that a man can have in this selfish world, the one that never deserts him and the one that never proves ungrateful or treacherous is his dog. A man's dog stands by him in prosperity and poverty, in health and sickness. He will sleep on the cold ground, when the wintry winds blow and the snow drives fiercely, if only he can be near his master's side. He will kiss the hand that has no food to offer, he will lick the wounds and sores that come in encounter with the roughness of the world. He guards the sleep of a pauper as if he were a prince. . . .

If fortune drives the master forth an outcast in the world, friendless and homeless, the faithful dog asks no higher privilege than that of accompanying him to guard against danger, to fight against his enemies, and when the last scene of all comes, and death takes the master in its embrace and his body is laid away in the cold ground, no matter if all other friends pursue their way, there by his graveside will the noble dog be found, his head between his paws, his eyes sad but open in alert watchfulness, faithful and true even to death.[17]

Here the fragility of human loyalty to human beings (friends, relatives, business associates) is unfavorably contrasted with the unconditional love and loyalty of the dog. The echoes of Shakespeare's *King Lear*, the quintessential play of human ungratefulness, are probably not accidental: the ungrateful children, the wintry winds tormenting the outcast, the willingness to kiss the hand that has no food to offer. Shakespeare's loyal earl of Gloucester, encountering the mad king on the heath, exclaims, "O, let me kiss that hand," and Lear replies, "Let me wipe it first, it smells of mortality." Decrying the cruelty of his daughters Lear exclaims,

> filial ingratitude.
> Is it not as this mouth should tear this hand
> For lifting food to't?

"Mine enemy's dog," laments the true daughter, Cordelia, "Though he had bit me should have stood that night / Against my fire."[18]

The mad Lear on the heath imagines the ultimate sign of household rejection in unmistakable terms.

> The little dogs and all,
> Trey, Blanch, and Sweetheart, see, they bark at me.
> (3.6.60–1)

Trey, Blanch, and Sweetheart are probably lap dogs or toy spaniels, then very much in fashion. But Lear's Fool has earlier alluded to the role of outdoor dogs in the Lear economy, as well. "Truth's a dog that must to kennel; he must be whipped out, when the Lady Brach may stand by the fire and stink" (1.4.109–11). In this case the servile spaniel Lady is allowed indoors, while the truth-telling (male?) dog is thrust out of the house, like the Fool and Kent. "Brach" is a now obsolete term for a bitch hound—Sir Thomas More apparently thought it was a genteel euphemism, since he notes in his *Comfort Against Tribulation* (1573), "I am so cunning that I cannot tell whether among them a bitch be a bitch, but as I remember she is no bitch, but a brach."[19] This may be a wry commentary on the just published *De Canibus Britannicis*, where Caius explains that, despite popular usage, "brache" does not mean "scenthound" but "female": bloodhounds are "in English . . . called *Brache*, in Scottishe *Rache*, the cause hereof resteth in the shee sexe and not in the generall kind."[20]

"Lady" appears to be a popular name for bitches in the period—you'll recall that Hotspur's "brach" was also a "Lady"—proof (perhaps) that we are still living in a Shakespearean universe, since "Lady" remains (according to the makers of Purina Dog Chow) one of the most popular dog names today. But among the top five dog names nationally are "Duke" and "Shadow": evidence, perhaps, that if we do live in a Shakespearean universe, we have adjusted it to meet our own necessities. The unquestioning fidelity of the duke of Kent, the loyalty of the Fool ("Lear's shadow") are today canine qualities, qualities we have come to expect from animal companions rather than human ones.

It may also be worth noting that "Caius" is the pseudonym Kent chooses for himself when he goes underground to follow Lear. Since (as we have noticed) John Caius (physician and cofounder of Cambridge's Gonville and Caius College) was the author of the celebrated Renaissance treatise on English dogs, the name here functions as a kind of metonymy for "dog": the disguised Kent reproaches Regan with "if I were your father's dog / You should not use me so" (2.2.133–4). As for Lear, his declension in social status is marked by the revised valuation he himself puts on dogs: Oswald is a "mongrel," a "cur," a "whoreson dog" (1.4.48; 78–9).

In the late twentieth century the fidelity Senator Vest found a century ago only in the dog has become even more explicitly a sign of pathos, that quintessential "human" (and humanist) emotion. And here too, unsurprisingly, one favored intertext is *King Lear*. (In *Endgame*, for example, Samuel Beckett's Hamm enjoys the unswerving fidelity of a stuffed dog.) Perhaps the most moving single scene in Milan Kundera's *The Unbearable Lightness of Being* is the death of a dog. When Tomas and Tereza's beloved dog Karenin becomes seriously and painfully ill with cancer, Tomas, a doctor, decides to give the dog a fatal injection.[21] Karenin's death scene echoes, I assume consciously, that of King Lear's daughter Cordelia, in a play that we have already seen to present persistent and powerful analogies between dog and human love. Tereza "found a mirror in her bag and held it to his mouth. The mirror was so smudged she thought she saw drops on it, drops caused by his breath. 'Tomas! He's alive!' she cried," but Tomas shakes his head.[22] "Lend me a looking-glass," cries the distraught Lear. "If that her breath will mist or stain the stone, / Why then she lives."

> Why should a dog, a horse, a rat have life
> And thou no breath at all? . . .
>   Look on her: look, her lips,
> Look there, look there![23]

It is not, after all, a farfetched analogy. Cordelia too was an emblem of unconditional—and silent—love.

But if Shakespeare's dogs are the markers of humanity, they are also—as Macbeth and Lear both suggest—indexes of inhumanity, of the borderline between the human and the animal. Othello kills a Turk he calls a "circumcised dog." Richard III is called a dog several times by Queen Margaret, and once by the unlovable Richmond ("the day is ours; the bloody dog is dead" [5.5.2]). These are not complimentary comparisons.

For a modern example with unexpected Shakespearen resonance consider the case—which would ordinarily be simply amusing—of a tax-dodging English sheepdog with the appropriate name of "William"—a tale that might be called "Where There's a 'Will'."

In England in 1985 tax accountants advised Mr. Robert Beckman, an investment analyst, that William, an Old English sheepdog, was not liable to pay taxes. The matter came up because William had apparently done so well in the stock market over the period of eleven years with Mr. Beckman's investment advice that he was worth some one hundred thousand pounds. Both Beckman and William's owner, who was Beckman's former assistant, insisted that the money was all William's, and that therefore no capital gains tax was owing, since William was not a "legal entity." A commentator in a tax journal took up the challenge, arguing that the law prohibited a dog from owning property, and citing case precedents. If William was not a "legal entity," nor yet a "person," according to the law, it might well be that William was not liable to tax. But in that case, neither could he own money. And since by their own insistence neither his investment counselor nor his owner had any rights to the money, it was clear, argued the commentator, that the money—all of it, not just the tax—belonged to the Crown.[24]

The headline accompanying the story of William the sheepdog in the British journal *Taxation* bore a Shakespearean tag: "Hath a dog money? Is it possible / A cur can lend three thousand ducats?" This must have seemed drolly apposite to the editors as they flipped through the pages of *Bartlett's Familiar Quotations*. (Indeed the hoist-on-your-own-petard legal reasoning here a little bit resembles Portia's courtroom strategy.) But in giving the source—"(*The Merchant of Venice* 1.3)" was parenthetically noted in the headline, for the benefit of any Shakespeare-deprived tax accountant— they might have taken a moment to consider the context. For the speaker, of course, is the aggrieved Jew, Shylock, reviled by the Christian Antonio for lending money at interest, and the term of revilement Antonio has chosen is "dog":

> You call me misbeliever, cut-throat dog,
> And spet upon my Jewish gaberdine,
> [. . .]
> And foot me as you spurn a stranger cur
> Over your threshold,
> [. . .]
> You call'd me dog.

"I am as like to call thee so again, / To spet on thee again, to spurn thee too," replies Antonio (1.3.106–23).

Manifestly, neither Jews nor dogs are well-treated in this figure of speech, which stresses the "inhuman" image of the Jew. Words like "stranger" and "cur," here used to typify the dog as a homeless mongrel stray, resonate with the equally typical period accounts of Jews as homeless and stateless, of "mongrel" race and "cut-throat" tendency. The association of Jews with dogs not only was popular invective in the period, but also found itself in some aspects of the law. Sixteenth-century Flemish jurist Joost de Damhoudere declared in his legal handbook that coitus between a Christian and a Jew was sodomy, and "a certain Jean Alard, who lived in Paris with a Jewess and had a number of children with her, was condemned for sodomy and burnt at the stake together with his girlfriend, 'since coitus with a Jewess is exactly the same as if a man were to copulate with a dog.'"[25] And this brings us back to the question of identities and histories that it seemed that the "dog" as universal signifier might be seeking to finesse.

Since, as we have noted, Shakespeare is amply capable of presenting quite clear images of dogs, from cherished pets (*Two Gentlemen of Verona*; *King Henry IV, Part 1*; *The Taming of the Shrew*; *King Lear*) to hunting dogs (*A Midsummer Night's Dream*) to "fawning greyhounds" (*King Henry IV, Part 1*; *Coriolanus*) and "dogs of war" (*Julius Caesar*), the use of "dog" in this stigmatizing context in *The Merchant of Venice* is not merely an index of early modern cruelty to animals, but rather a way of construing dog society, once more, as a model of human society. ("Ay, in the catalogue ye go for men.")

None of this has anything to do with the comic tale of William the investing sheepdog. But it has a good deal to do with how the literal and the figurative intersect with each other to make what we call "culture"—and thus not a little, or at least one would hope, to do with the nature and purpose of law. Kent—also known as Caius—the faithful follower, is a good dog. Shylock is a bad dog, a "stranger cur," a stray.

The narrative of the homeless or stateless Jew, the "stranger cur," may lead us, finally, to one of the greatest exponents of Shakespeare's universal humanism, and one of this century's most affectionate dog owners: Sigmund Freud. (This is the man who turned an essay on the three caskets in *The Merchant of Venice* into a story about King Lear and his three daughters, and thus rewrote the particularist story of the Jew into the universal tale of humankind.)[26]

In his final years the aging Freud became a passionate dog lover. Not only did he keep and cherish his own beloved chows (one of whom lay at the foot of the famous couch during the analytic hour), he also collaborated with his daughter Anna on a translation of Marie Bonaparte's book about her own treasured chow, whose name was Topsy. Bonaparte, the French psychoanalyst who would be instrumental in getting Freud and his family safely out of Nazi-occupied Vienna, chronicled the story of Topsy's illness and recovery; for Topsy, it developed, suffered from cancer of the oral cavity, just like Freud. But unlike Freud, Topsy was healed. Topsy lives; Freud, the beloved "master," will die. Perhaps inevitably, one of the key chapters in Bonaparte's book is called—with no sense of bathos—"Topsy and Shakespeare." What is the point of mere literary immortality? asks Bonaparte. "Of what importance to-day to Caesar, to Shakespeare, are their names, their works. . . . [W]ho will read Homer or Shakespeare when there are no more human eyes? . . . That is why Topsy, whose happiness is confined to the narrow limits of each day, is wiser than I." Topsy lives each day to the fullest; Bonaparte merely writes, "striv[ing] laboriously to trace vain signs on this paper." Topsy, in short, is *better* than Shakespeare.

Freud's essays and case studies speak eloquently about Lear, and the Macbeths, and Richard III (all Shakespearean figures, incidentally, who are compared to dogs). But the Shakespeare play of most decisive importance for Freud, of course, was *Hamlet*, often construed (and not only by Freud) as the ultimate Shakespearean repository of humanist values for our time. (*Hamlet*, of course, was a particular interest of Fredson Bowers.) It will not come as a surprise, then, to find that some of Shakespeare's dogs are Hamlets. Sir Walter Scott's black greyhound was called Hamlet. A British murder mystery I read not too long ago featured a huge Great Dane known affectionately to his owner as "Hammy." (It took me a moment to get the joke.)

Hamlet's quotation of an old Tilley proverb, "The cat will mew and dog will have his day," has been cleverly rewritten by a *New Yorker* cartoonist. Three dogs chatting under a tree commiserate about thoughtless human clichés: "Speaking personally," says one, "I haven't had my day, and I've never met any dog who has."[27] But it is the great melancholy Dane—or the mourning-and-melancholy Great Dane—who seems, and seems always to have seemed, to capture the modern imagination. Shakespearean Harry Levin had a dog—a golden retriever, not a Great Dane—whose name was Yorick. Inevitably, he came in for more than his share of "alases." And though *Hamlet* strives mightily, in some ways, to distinguish man from beast, it is striking that in our time it is the conjunction of the two that is sometimes most moving.

I want therefore to end today with two images that, I hope, will help to make this clear. The first is a remarkable self-portrait of photographer Robert Mapplethorpe, who would shortly die of AIDS. In this, one of many Mapplethorpe self-portraits, the black-clad artist leans upon a stick that is topped with a death's-head. The two heads look uncannily alike. As in the well-known engraving of the skeleton philosophically contemplating a skull, the story of Hamlet and humanism, the nobility and pathos of human life and death, is here writ both poignantly and large. "What a piece of work is a man." "And yet to me what is this quintessence of dust?" This is a portrait of a gay man in the late twentieth century, both intensely particular and, arguably, "universal." Compare Mapplethorpe's to another modern, or rather, postmodern, double portrait, this one by photographer William Wegman. This is "Man Ray Contemplating Man Ray." Man, as he was affectionately known, was Wegman's first Weimaraner model (named, of course, after the surrealist). So in Wegman parlance we should probably say that in this portrait Man contemplates Man.

That this, too, is a portrait of Hamlet seems to me to be unquestionable. "Look here upon this picture, and on this." But this is no mere counterfeit presentment of two brothers. Nor is the Wegman a parody or a sendup. It is a meditation on meditation. On consciousness and the borderline—if it is a borderline—between the human animal and others. Between these two portraits, it might almost be said, we may find the new place (which is to say, the old place, the place in the heart) of "Shakespeare and the Twentieth Century." As Launce the clown puts it, with perfect clarity, in *The Two Gentlemen of Verona*, "I am the dog. No, the dog is himself, and I am the dog. O, the dog is me, and I am myself. Ay, so, so" (2.3.21–3).

Shakespeare's Laundry List

10

> The unhistorical and the historical are necessary in equal measure for the health of an individual, of a people and of a culture.
>
> **Friedrich Nietzsche, "On the Uses and Disadvantages of History for Life"**

> —What useful discovery did Socrates learn from Xanthippe?
> —Dialectic, Stephen answered.
>
> **James Joyce, *Ulysses***

I

We who profess literary studies have been living through a time of infatuation with history. This is not the first such crush, to be sure, but it is a heady one. And like all infatuations, it carries with it a certain overestimation of the object. History seems to know everything that we want to know, and to offer "answers" to knotty textual questions: questions of context, interpretation, and indeed meaning.

Earlier in this century articles and footnotes about Macbeth lay emphasis on the facts of the Gunpowder Plot and the lineage of James I. An entire mini-industry in what might be called "Essex Studies" grew up around the Earl of Essex, his marital connection to the Sidney circle, and his ill-fated rebellion—all in service of readings, not only of Shakespeare's history plays, but also of his tragedies, comedies, and romances. Readings of *The Merchant of Venice* still routinely incorporate the unhappy story of Queen Elizabeth's Jewish doctor, Roderigo Lopez, and, informed by a growing interest in race, analyses of *Othello* detail the numbers and social occupations of Moors and Africans in sixteenth-century London.

But where these inquiries focused on political history, today's scholars of early modern literature and culture are more likely to turn to conduct books, mothers' manuals, and medical and rhetorical treatises. We have seen in recent years an intense interest in court culture, literacy and reading practices, the printing house, sexuality and the stage, witchcraft and colonial encounters, all "grounded in material and social determinants."[1] This is the counterpart of the earlier infatuation on the part of historians for literary theory, the so-called "linguistic turn"—a passion now strenuously disavowed, like so many love-affairs-gone-wrong. Whereas historians were once struck by the non-transparency of their medium and the need to study it rather than simply to look at the past through it, today's literary scholars are fascinated by the task of reconstructing "the real" that must lie behind any of its representations.

Indeed, recent critiques of the literary-critical genre known as New Historicism have taken it to task for not being historical enough: too anecdotal, not sufficiently rigorous, "evas[ive] when it comes to causal argument," tending "to adduce a Zeitgeist from an accident," in the phrase of one friendly critic.[2] In other words, precisely what distinguishes "new historicism" from history, its interest in "the literary," has seemed to some scholars—both historians and literary scholars—to be its weakness rather than its strength. Itself spawned by postmodernism, New Historicism had tried to avoid or complicate causality: it preferred words like resonance, circulation, and poetics to the term causation. But New Historicism's nuanced and sophisticated avoidance has returned with a vengeance. In effect New Historicism has whetted the appetite for causation through its very avoidances. New Historicism began by reading history as a text, but it created a desire for history as a ground. As a result, causality (the priority of history; history as what Fredric Jameson calls "absent cause") cried out to be made present. For the scholar of literature—and here I want to emphasize that I am speaking about literary scholars, not about historians—history as cause is the unfulfilled desire, the projected and introjected fantasy, the prohibited wish.

II

It occurs to me that you might imagine my title to refer to the need for "historical correctness," as implied by a headline in *The New York Times*: "We Happy Many, Playing Fast and Loose with History." The point of the accompanying article was that although Shakespeare, like many modern artists and writers, did manipulate history, he had a more nuanced, complex, and learned way of doing so than, for example, director Oliver Stone, or actor-director Tim Robbins. "Shakespeare approached history with depth and integrity," insists the *Times* reviewer. "The contract that he made with his viewers was that they were witnessing an interpretation of history, not an exact reproduction of events. Most historical movies, by contrast, not only reduce history to a simple situation but also strive to give the impression that they are reconstructing what really happened."[3]

Whatever the truth value of this distinction—and it does become muddier as time goes on, when Shakespeare's plays are all that many modern non-historians know about English or even Roman history—it is not in fact precisely what I mean by "historical correctness." For as you've surely guessed, I want here to invoke the cognate phrase "political correctness," one of the most denigrated and vilified imperatives in contemporary journalistic and academic life.

Political correctness in popular parlance these days is understood to mean an insensitive attack on insensitivity. With its roots in old-style totalitarian discourse (as early as 1947 Vladimir Nabokov could mock it in his novel *Bend Sinister*[4]), the phrase was used in the 1970s with heavy self-irony by the left as a kind of amused reality-check on its own excesses, and often abbreviated by its initials as a sign of this ruefully affectionate self-estrangement (as in, "oh, don't be so P.C.!"). Perhaps inevitably, the term was picked up by the right, denuded of any soupcon of irony, and used as a club to beat those very persons who had ironized it to begin with.[5] "Political correctness" is rather old and rather tired news in the U.S., where it tends to be employed principally by diehard cultural conservatives and the authors of novels and plays about academic life. A review of *The Winter's Tale* at the American Repertory Theatre took the director to task for adding "a politically correct ending," noting that "it is political correctness to disallow Shakespeare's forgiveness."[6]

European commentators often consider political correctness a symptom of both American Puritanism and feminist excess. Thus a French book on the history of flirting deplores the "return to puritanism" and the rise of sexual harassment laws, insisting that "there is nothing politically incorrect in a little ambiguous banter between men and women."[7] In Britain "political correctness" has been decried in the press as having "some of the characteristics of a religious sect." When a popular judge at the Old Bailey stepped down from the bench he did so in a highly publicized speech that inveighed against a new conduct book for judges on how to avoid the perception of racial bias and against "political correctness in all its horrid forms."[8] Horrid or not, political correctness has been regarded as a kind of overly rigid form taken by oppositional thinking, a tendency to turn critique into a new orthodoxy or orthopedic thinking, framing and shaping what can be thought and said.

What, then, is "historical correctness"? We might say that it is the suggestion, either implied or explicit, on the part of literary scholars, that history grounds and tells the truth about literature. The point is superbly well made by Walter Benjamin's remark at the end of an essay called "Literary History and the Study of Literature":

> What is at stake is not to portray literary works in the context of their age, but to represent the age that perceives them—our age—in the age during which they arose. It is this that makes literature into an organon of history; and to achieve this, and not to reduce literature to the material of history, is the task of the literary historian.[9]

III

The most specifically *literary* charge offered against those who do not read historically or who deliberately and joyously flout chronology and sequence is the charge of anachronism—in effect, historical *in*correctness. Anachronism, from the Greek for "back" and "time," has itself had a checkered history. As the neglect or falsification of chronological relation, whether intentional or not, it is often regarded merely as a vulgar error. A clock strikes in the Rome of Shakespeare's *Julius Caesar*. An attendant to the Pharaoh in Cecil B. DeMille's *The Ten Commandments* appears in tennis shoes. In the canonical history of art and literature anachronisms are frequent, and some have been naturalized over the years in the service of "timeless" art or the double time of revealed truth. The *sacra conversazione* of Renaissance religious paint-ing brings together Madonna, Christ Child, angels, saints, and contemporary donors from the artist's time in a single transhistorical space. In Northern European art you may encounter Joseph hard at work in a fifteenth-century shop, or the Virgin Mary as a Netherlandish burger's daughter. In Florence or in Naples she is an Italian peasant girl. The Belgian painter James Ensor depicts, in 1880, Christ's Entry into Brussels.

In literature we find similar "errors," often deliberately contrived for effect. Dido and Aeneas are made contemporaries by Virgil, when they lived 300 years apart. Shakespeare famously alters history from time to time. He depicts King Duncan of Scotland as an elderly and beloved monarch, rather than the younger and feebler ruler described in Holinshed's *Chronicles*. He makes his two Harrys, Harry Percy and Harry Monmouth, age-mates rather than a generation apart. He describes the historical Cleopatra, a mere twenty-nine years old when his play opens, as "wrinkled deep in time." In *Titus Andronicus* a Goth from the time of the Roman Empire pauses "to gaze upon a ruinous monastery" (5.1.21), thus invoking the Reformation context and Henry VIII's dissolution of the monasteries.[10] Mark Twain places a Connecticut Yankee in King Arthur's court. Thornton Wilder moves a single set of characters through a variety of geological and historical periods from paleolithic to modern in his play *The Skin of Our Teeth* (1942). In each of these cases a point is being made about the present day.

Yet often artists and writers are taken to task for their anachronisms, like the Gothic novelist Ann Radcliffe or the Roman historian Sallust. In these instances "anachronism" becomes conflated with sloppiness or ignorance rather than aesthetic, political, or satirical effect. The Hollywood specialty known as "continuity" is meant to clean up such inadvertent errors. Forgeries in films are often detected, or detectable, by unwitting anachronisms: too many stars on the U.S. flag, the wrong period fashion in dress or hair, a telephone in the "old west" saloon, a piece of advanced technology out of its time and place. The two faces of anachronism (deliberate juxtaposition to make a clever point; awkward and revealing error of fact) are often held to be different in kind as well as degree. It is the bugbear of "intentionality" again: a knowing error is a cleverness, an unknowing error is a bêtise. But it is sometimes hard to tell the difference. DeMille's film of the *Ten Commandments* stages a Passover celebration that vastly postdates the time of the Biblical event, presenting a modern-looking rabbinic seder rather than a lamb sacrifice. The Joseph L. Mankiewicz film of Shakespeare's *Julius Caesar* (1953) featured portrait busts that closely resembled the Emperor Hadrian, who was born about a century and a half later. Joseph von Sternberg's 1934 film, *The Scarlet Empress*, offered Marlene Dietrich in the role of Catherine the Great. The soundtrack of this film about eighteenth-century Russia included the music of Mendelssohn, Tchaikovsky, Rimsky-Korsakov, the 1812 Overture and Wagner's "Ride of the Valkyries."[11] Such anachronisms could be inadvertent or deliberate: whether intended or not, they tell us something about the moment of production and consumption. Anachronism in this sense is another term for bricolage.

Kathleen Coleman, a professor of Latin and an expert on Roman games, was hired as a consultant to the film *Gladiator* (2000), and found it "an interesting but ultimately disillusioning experience." No sooner did she set the historical record straight, she noted, than "a whole range of fresh inaccuracies and anachronisms" crept in, and were immortalized on film, including made-up inscriptions in bad Latin engraved upon the public buildings. Misunderstanding Juvenal's phrase "bread and circuses," the placating of the hungry and discontented masses with public spectacles like chariot races, the filmmakers invented a slew of imperial caterers tossing bread into the stadium stands.[12]

"*Gladiator* ain't history," wrote Philip Howard jauntily in *The Times*. "Its account of Roman politics is nonsense. Marcus Aurelius never dreamt of restoring power to the people. . . . The heroic general Maximus with republican dreams in the film is John Wayne fantasy. The Senate gave up any republican inclinations long before." Howard found "the anachronism [he] most enjoyed" was Maximus praying to the shade of his murdered son, and advising him to keep his heels down when riding. "Since the Roman had not yet cribbed the stirrup from the Goths, this was seriously foolish advice." And modern culture, it seems, has the thumbs up / thumbs down gesture backward. "When the crowd in the Colosseum wanted a popular gladiator to be spared they turned their thumbs down into their fists. Thumbs up meant 'Cut his throat,'" Howard explained.

Readers seeking corroboration for this point might consult Montaigne's essay "Of Thumbs":

> It was a sign of favor in Rome to close in and hold down the thumbs—
> Your partisan with both his thumbs will praise your game
>
> Horace
>
> —and of disfavor to raise them and turn them outward:
> When the people's thumb turns up.
> They kill their man to please them.
>
> Juvenal[13]

Nonetheless Howard liked the film, which he thought embodied modern as well as ancient tastes for blood sports, from boxing to professional football. "We continually reinvent the past to match our present concerns, causes and totems," he observed.[14]

Nor is the allure of anachronism a new development, a mere artifact of modern or postmodern life. The fashion for dialogues with the dead, modeled after Lucian, provided the opportunity for explicitly anachronistic interchange: Fontanelle's *New Dialogues of the Dead* (*Nouveaux Dialogues des Morts*, 1683, 1684) offered dialogues between Socrates and Montaigne, Seneca and Scarron. Fénelon's *Dialogues des morts* (1700–18) followed the same pattern, as did English writers like Walter Savage Landor, whose *Imaginary Conversations* (1824) included colloquies between Achilles and Helen, Galileo and Milton, Essex and Spenser, Joan of Arc and Agnes Sorel (all invented, of course, by Landor).

The most memorable recent instance of this once-popular genre is probably comedian Steve Allen's television show "Meeting of Minds," which ran for four years on the Public Broadcasting System (PBS-TV), and presented dramatic confrontations of four "talking heads" from the past. On one occasion Aristotle, Sun Yat-Sen, Machiavelli, and Elizabeth Barrett Browning debated; on another, a lively argument developed among Teddy Roosevelt, Thomas Aquinas, Cleopatra, and Thomas Paine; a third panel featured Florence Nightingale, Plato, Voltaire, and Martin Luther; a fourth, Attila the Hun, Emily Dickinson, Galileo, and Charles Darwin. (Steve Allen to Galileo: "You know, it's most interesting. You sir, Miss Dickinson, and Dr. Darwin all had difficulty with domineering fathers." Attila: "My father, too, was no bargain." Or this, from a panel discussion involving Ulysses S. Grant, Marie Antoinette, Thomas More, and Karl Marx: Marx to Marie Antoinette: "did it ever enter your mind, Your Majesty, that . . . empty rituals and customs would in time destroy the people's respect for the monarchy? Marie: "Nonsense, Dr. Marx, the people adored the rituals and customs!" Thomas More: "Yes, Dr. Marx, . . . rituals and manners aided the people to express their respect for royalty. I understand that in today's Marxist nations there is still room for pomp and circumstance."[15]) These were not séances; actors played the parts. Allen's wife Jayne Meadows performed almost all the female roles.[16]

The pleasure opened up by these deliberate violations of history seems somehow old-fashioned today. But why should that be? What was being disregarded then—or now? Are we simply too conscious of history to be playful in this way? Is there something about the interest in history and politics that gives anachronism a bad name? Or is anachronism simply returning in a new form? There is a useful analogue to this problem in the current "antichronology" debates among art historians, curators, and art critics—debates inflamed by the thematic, non-chronological installations at such high-profile museums as the Tate Modern, the Tate Britain, the Museum of Modern Art, and the Brooklyn Museum. As art historian Linda Nochlin noted, "there is a tendency to use chronology as teleology." A "nonchronological hang," she suggested, can "break up the idea of an uninterrupted flow." But many other critics objected, seeing the loss of chronology as a loss of coherence. Thus for example British art critic David Sylvester thought the Tate Modern's decision to follow themes rather than periods was a mistake; chronology, he argued, was "an objective reality, built into the fabric of the work," not "a tool of art-historical interpretation which can be used at one moment and discarded at another."[17]

What was at stake here? Chronology implied evolution and a certain kind of progress narrative, privileging some works and movements above others. History was a history of aesthetic forms: their development and evolution was the ground of meaningful art history. Antichronology (dismissed in some quarters as "political correctness" because it shifted the focus away from "masterpieces") drew attention to merely looking. It invited pleasure and irresponsibility, not the accuracy of any story. Antichronology, then, is both old and new: both a resistance to an older notion of historical sequence and development (like MOMA founder Alfred Barr's influential 1936 diagram on the evolution of modern art, a chart that traced the line from Neo-Impressionism and Cubism to Abstract Art), and a rediscovery of familiar categories like genre, theme, and structure. These categories were not simply resurrected; they were substantially altered, as for example in the notion of many alternative modernisms rather than one.[18] But their chief effect was to open up some kinds of interpretation that might have been closed off by chronology. Placing a Rembrandt next to a Rothko or a Rockwell raises issues of similarity and difference, form and mood, which neither chronology nor historical context will address or ground.

This brings me to another sense in which the word "anachronism" has been used to criticize and control a development in literary studies: the "anachronism" not within the text itself but within the framework used to read it. In some ways, of course, the question of history's value for literature is an old and familiar debate. In a 1910 essay called "Anachronism in Shakespeare Criticism," the literary scholar Elmer Edgar Stoll lamented that "Criticism forgets that Shakespeare wrote in the sixteenth century," turning him instead into a "twentieth-century symbolist." (The tension here was partly one between "scholars" and "critics," the latter excoriated as "poets, essayists, gentlemen of taste and leisure, not to mention a horde of the tasteless and leisureless—propagandists and blatherskites.") Stoll's chief culprit was character criticism and psychology, which he thought wildly off-target for Elizabethan literature. The issue, in short, was one of what I have called respect: respect for sixteenth-century ideas about the preeminence of story and plot, as against "our modern ideas" of character and social problems.

It was anachronistic, Stoll said, to regard Shakespeare as having any interest in "the newer psychology concerning subconscious states, racial distinctions, criminal and morbid types." Ghosts and witches were signs of superstition, not "personifications of conscience." Nor should Shakespeare be read as having any relevance to politics. The English history plays and the Roman plays "are political plays with the politics left out." Here was a gauntlet thrown down on behalf of historical correctness. "Ours is the day of the historical method," Stoll declared. "Fetichism [sic; what he called the "cult" of Shakespeare] is all that stands in the way."[19]

More recently, when Terry Eagleton's book on Shakespeare was published in 1986, reviewers zeroed in on what they called its "anachronisms." "Mr. Eagleton does in print what directors regularly do on stage," said *The New York Times*, "change the century, stitch up new costumes, but preserve the story-line and language." Herbert Mitgang found Eagleton "bold" and "courageous" but also sometimes "maddening." "Rather ingeniously, Mr. Eagleton united Freud and Marx in discussing *The Merchant of Venice*," he notes, although by 1986 this had become a fairly common starting point for discussions of the play. "Inevitably, Mr. Eagleton turns to Lady Macbeth to interpret militant feminists," he observes, adding that "it is doubtful if present-day women's organizations . . . would accept Lady Macbeth as a role model. The parallel is too narrow and strained." (Little did he know what a goldmine Hillary Clinton was going to be for Lady Macbeth-hunters in the daily press. The comparison between these two politicians' wives became a standard trope of journalism in the 1990s.)

When Eagleton alleges slyly that "Though conclusive evidence is hard to come by, it is difficult to read Shakespeare without feeling that he was almost certainly familiar with the writings of Hegel, Marx, Nietzsche, Freud, Wittgenstein and Derrida," Mitgang regards this as more playful than persuasive. There seems to be something exciting about anachronism, then, and at the same time something illicit. What does this have to do with the relations between history and literature?

IV

Let me offer an example of the seductiveness of history for me that also rang some alarm bells, reminding me of where my own resistances and textual predilections lay. A brilliant young teacher of colonial American literature and culture recently explained a technique he had developed for teaching the seventeenth-century American poet Anne Bradstreet, whose work, he suspected, might seem temporally distant to his presentist young students. The poem he wanted to discuss was Bradstreet's "The Author to Her Book." Bradstreet wrote it after her brother-in-law, without her knowledge, brought a manuscript of her verses to London and had them published under the title *The Tenth Muse, Lately Sprung Up in America*. Let me read you the beginning of the poem, in which Bradstreet addresses her pirated works, describing them as, in effect, the victims of a kidnapping:

> Thou ill-formed offspring of my feeble brain,
> Who after birth didst by my side remain,
> Till snatched from thence by friends, less wise than true,
> Who thee abroad, exposed to public view,
> Made thee in rags, halting to th' press to trudge,
> Where errors were not lessened (all may judge).
> At thy return my blushing was not small,
> My rambling brat (in print) should mother call,
> I cast thee by as one unfit for light,
> Thy visage was so irksome in my sight:
> Yet being mine own, at length affection would
> Thy blemishes amend, if so I could:
> I washed thy face, but more defects I saw,
> And rubbing off a spot still made a flaw,
> I stretched thy joints to make thee even feet,
> Yet still thou run'st more hobbling than is meet. . . .[20]

The poem is, as you can see, clearly imagined in the genre of the title, "the author to her work." The phrase "even feet" means "regular metrics," the "rags" suggest rag paper, and so forth.

My acquaintance, a scholar of Puritan America, knowing the social and medical history of the period, and mindful of another poem by Bradstreet, "Before the Birth of One of Her Children," in which the poet anticipated the possibility of dying in childbirth, handed out to his students, as a way of making Bradstreet's words vivid and her historical predicament clear, photocopies of early seventeenth-century articles and woodcuts of deformed children and monstrous births, a familiar preoccupation of recent early modern scholarship. When his students had sufficiently put themselves in the place of a mother contemplating anxieties attendant upon childbirth in a med-ically rudimentary context, he gave them another historical grid to defamiliarize their own sense of corporeal vulnerability. In Puritan America, deformed children were a sign that the mother had consorted with the devil. Thus the fear and fascination was itself a sign of religious, not just medical history. For this literary scholar—and here is my point—the cause or ground of interpretation was the historical situation—the historical fact and the historical framework through which it was viewed. Bradstreet's references to the "ill-formed offspring" were troped on a mother's hopes and fears.[21]

But Anne Bradstreet, who wrote in the mid-seventeenth century, was well-read in sixteenth- and early seventeenth-century English literature, including the works of Raleigh, Camden, Sidney, and Sylvester's Du Bartas.[22] What if, instead of contem-plating the fate of deformed children in the colonies, we were to juxtapose to her poem "The Author to Her Book" the following passage:

> It had been a thing, we confesse, worthie to haue bene wished, that the Author himselfe had liv'd to haue set forth, and ouerseen his owne writings; But since it hath bin ordain'd otherwise, and he by death departed from that right, we pray you do not envie his Friends, the office of their care, and paine, to haue collected & publish'd them; and so to have publish'd them, as where (before) you were abus'd with diuerse stolne, and surreptitious copies, maimed, and deformed by the frauds and stealthes of iniurious impostors, that expos'd them: euen those, are now offer'd to your view cur'd, and perfect of their limbes; and all the rest, absolute in their numbers, as he conceived them.[23]

This is John Heminge's and Henry Condell's letter "To the great Variety of Readers" affixed to the First Folio of Shakespeare's plays. The similarities are so striking as to be obvious: the parent who was unable to oversee the publication of his writings, the (consequent) maiming and deformation of the text, the need in particular to regularize the meter (Bradstreet's "even feet," Heminge's and Condell's "absolute . . . num-bers") and so on. It will not escape your attention that this text, too, is from the past—that is, embedded in the history of the period. It is not a late twentieth-century product, juxtaposed to the seventeenth century. I would be quite willing to defend and indeed promote the use of anachronism for reading. But for now I want only to point out a difference between what might be called the vehicle and the tenor of historical literary scholarship. To illuminate Anne Bradstreet's poem "to her book" by framing it with images of "real" deformed children and information about death in childbirth is one kind of reading. To examine the same poem by considering it to be, itself, a legitimate or illegitimate offspring of a famous textual passage and a familiar figure of speech is another. The "Author" referred to in the First Folio's prefatory letter is also (like the speaker in Bradstreet's poem) said to have "conceived" his writings, which were "expos'd" by thieves just as Bradstreet's works were "snatched" and "exposed to public view."

Which is the "ground" here? Literary trope or social condition? Text or life? Figure of speech or historical fact? Every piece of writing inhabits these various worlds, and every text offers a dilemma, or an opportunity, in terms of its frames of reference. We have perhaps over-corrected earlier literary histories that confined texts within a world of other texts. But mightn't the intertextual references have shaped this poem as much as the medical realities? It seems that that question is all the more urgent in the case of a woman poet. Why are anxieties about reproduction seen as more real or more literal here than anxieties about authorship? Are women more naturally literal—less involved with literary history—than men? And could it be that in this case the desire to have a more complete picture of history impedes, rather than brings out, the female poet in whose name it is often undertaken? It is not necessary to my argument for Bradstreet actually to be referring to, or remembering, or even half-remembering the Folio letter. If she were, we could perhaps allege that her modest demurral was in fact a bold claim in disguise: Bradstreet as successor to Shakespeare. But I do not care, at least right now, whether this is the (historical) case. And I do not want, either, to dismiss or impugn the usefulness of historical context and the power of contemporary images of childhood and deformity. This is not an either-or issue. It is, instead, a question of the goals sought by a discipline, or the practitioners of that discipline. Why do we read literature? Why do we teach it? What do we teach?

V

Perhaps anachronism—playing fast and loose with history—is not just something that sometimes happens to literature, but is connected to it in a more profound way. Suppose we return for a moment to Shakespeare's *Julius Caesar*, not by accident the locus classicus of some favorite literary anachronisms. That striking clock, for instance. Arden Shakespeare editor David Daniell reminds us—citing Sigurd Buckhardt's important essay on the topic—that the warring systems of the calendars were very much an issue of contention in late sixteenth-century Europe, and that Julius Caesar had himself sorted out an earlier set of calendrical discrepancies. The Julian calendar, named in his honor, was the official calendar of Protestant England, while the "New Style" Gregorian calendar, named after the Pope, reigned throughout Catholic Europe. The striking clock, which, as Daniell notes, "amused and irritated eighteenth- and nineteenth-century commentators for its anachronistic ignorance"[24] was in fact a powerful sign. Caesar had not only set the date with his reforms of the calendar, but also "set the clocks of Rome," and his *Commentaries* are full of his concern for time-keeping. The clock and its striking are thus reminders within the play-text of Caesar's power over and against Brutus'.

Julius Caesar contains a number of other celebrated anachronistic references, some of them sartorial: a reference to "hats," for example, describing the conspirators before the murder: "their hats are plucked about their ears / And half their faces buried in their cloaks" (2.1.73–4). Alexander Pope found this so unhistorical that he printed the line "their—are pluckt about their ears"—"as if the word were some obscenity," observes Daniell, who adds "Quite apart from the fine dramatic furtiveness of Shakespeare's image, the Romans did wear headgear," and sends the reader to the previous Arden edition, where we are told the particulars of that headgear: "the petasus, a broad-brimmed traveling hat or cap, the pilleus, a close-fitting, brimless hat or cap, worn at entertainments and festivals, and the cucullus, a cap or hood fastened to a garment." We also learn that Pope was "similarly unwilling to accept *hat*" in *Coriolanus*, where he emends the word to *cap* (2.3.95;164).[25]

The same criticism might be made of the reference to the turned-down "leaf" in Brutus' book (4.3.271–2: "is not the leaf turned down / Where I left reading?"). Living in ancient Rome, Brutus would properly be reading from a scroll, not a codex, a book with leaves. The sleeping Imogen in another of Shakespeare's Roman plays, *Cymbeline*, also folds down the leaf of a book as she falls asleep (2.2.4). But of course by the time we get to *Cymbeline* ancient Britain, Rome, modern Italy, and rural Wales are all nicely mingled in a transhistorical stew. This is not a mistake; it is a point.

Whether such temporal dissonances are admired or scorned, anachronisms in literature have their purposes and their effects. We see this very clearly and obviously as well in the history of performance, where the tension between so-called "modernization" and equally so-called "period costume" (also known as "museum Shakespeare") is the frequent target of theatrical reviews. Thus the director JoAnne Akalaitis, often criticized (or lauded) for the chances she takes with Shakespeare, is described in a review of her production of *King Henry IV* (Parts 1 and 2) as surprisingly conventional: "performed in predominantly period costumes . . . the production has only occasional anachronisms—a TV or telephone thrown in to drive home a motivation."[26] Peter Sellars has staged *Antony and Cleopatra* in a swimming pool and put King Lear in a "kingmobile" (aka a Lincoln Continental). The scheming villain Aaron in Julie Taymor's *Titus* (a film version of *Titus Andronicus*, set in ancient Rome) seals Titus' hand in a zip-lock plastic bag.

Charles Spencer, assessing the Michael Boyd RSC production of *Troilus and Cressida* in 1998, began by declaring that he was "not one of those arch conservatives who believes that Shakespeare should always be staged in period costume," but went on to speculate about the setting: the scene opened with sepia photographs that seemed to evoke the Western Front during the First World War, but many characters had Irish accents, and it eventually became clear that while the Trojans were Irish, the Greeks were British. "Why then," he wondered, "does Achilles look like a present-day Serbian war-crimes thug, and Ajax resemble a particularly dim heavy metal rock star?" Spencer admired the production, with reservations, and offered his own interpretation: "What Boyd is presumably trying to suggest is any modern, war-torn territory in which fine words cover vile actions."[27]

Some people love this stuff, and others hate it. Opinion was divided on the Baz Lurhmann film of *Romeo + Juliet* with its black drag queen Mercutio and its CNN talking-head prologues. In Michael Almereyda's film of *Hamlet* (2000), starring Ethan Hawke, letters are delivered by fax machine; Ophelia wears a wire(tap) to entrap Hamlet in the lobby scene; Rosencrantz and Guildenstern are heard on the speakerphone in Gertrude's bedroom; the prayer scene happens in a limousine (Hamlet substitutes for the driver), and a young slacker Hamlet makes an indie video film of "The Mousetrap" to catch the conscience of the king. (Elsinore is a hotel. Denmark is a corporation. Claudius is a CEO. So runs the world away.) But these uses of anachronism, however startling, function by destabilizing juxtaposition: bringing a metaphor to devastatingly literal life, or striving, like the Boyd *Troilus*, for the postmodern version of timelessness, that is, multi-timeliness. Some productions do this via costume, mingling classical dress, Nazi uniforms, seventies punk and thirties gangster-wear. Others do it through cross-casting, mixing nations, races, genders, and accents.

Whether or not we like it, we have become accustomed to this kind of theatrical anachronism, as we have to its more moderate and "straight" avatars, modern dress and rehearsal clothes. Indeed even if we cherish the old ways, and hang an engraving of Mrs. Siddons as Lady Macbeth on the wall, we will have to acknowledge that she too is in "modern dress," and not in authentic "period costume"—whatever that would be. Authentic Jacobean costume—or authentic medieval Scottish garb? As Eric Hobsbawn and others have argued about "the invention of tradition," authenticity is itself a cultural effect.

There is a difference, of course, between using historical data anachronistically and the anachronistic use of theoretical ideas. But the reviewer who accused Terry

Eagleton of anachronism seems himself to have conflicting notions of history and chronology as they affect literary interpretation. He subscribes to two inconsistent, but widely held, fantasies: the fantasy of historical determination, and the fantasy of universality. Thus he can say both that Eagleton's "strongest arguments are backed by history"—for example, the information "that inflation in the 1590's led to debased coinage and speculation" and also that political analysis of the plays is misguided: "Is not the range of [Shakespeare's] characters neither conservative nor even neoconservative but universal?"[28] I want here to contest both of these views—that history is data and that "universality" is something different from the theories it opposes, rather than being yet another theory.

There is a great deal—a very great deal—that history can do for literary study, and for the study of Shakespeare and his contemporaries. I am not urging a return to the old days of timeless transcendence, against which I have myself written and spoken passionately in both academic and public venues. The criterion for "timelessness" is the most historically time-bound thing of all, since there is no real evidence for it other than consensus. The timeless is what has stopped being considered a theory and has passed into stereotype. But there are some things history cannot do, and those things are—I want to suggest and in fact to insist—at the core of the literary enterprise.

VI

I will illustrate this claim, if I may, in my own anachronistic and unhistorical fashion, by citing a well-known passage of literary criticism that addresses not a Renaissance text but a nineteenth-century one. The writer is discussing a particular kind of "research," the kind called a "search." (The two words search and research are versions of the same). Here he discusses a search of the premises undertaken by detectives:

> We are spared nothing concerning the procedures used in searching the area submitted to their investigation: from the division of that space into compartments from which the slightest bulk could not escape detection, to needles probing upholstery, and, in the impossibility of sounding wood with a tap, to a microscope exposing the waste of any drilling at the surface of its hollow, indeed the infinitesimal gaping of the slightest abyss. As the network tightens to the point that, not satisfied with shaking the pages of books, the police take to counting them, do we not see space itself shed its leaves like a letter?
>
> But the detectives have so immutable a notion of the real that they fail to notice that their search tends to transform it into its object. A trait by which they would be able to distinguish that object from all others.

This would no doubt be too much to ask them, not because of their lack of insight but rather because of ours. For their imbecility is neither of the individual nor of the corporative variety; its source is subjective. It is the realist's imbecility, which does not pause to observe that . . . what is hidden is never but what is missing from its place, as the call slip puts it when speaking of a volume lost in a library. And even if the book be on an adjacent shelf or in the next slot, it would be hidden there, however visibly it may appear. For it can literally be said that something is missing from its place only of what can change it: the symbolic. For the real, whatever upheaval we subject it to, is always in its place; it carries it glued to its heel, ignorant of what might exile it from it.[29]

The real is what the realist doesn't find. The belief that the real can be exhaustively measured and mapped is a form of blindness. The real is what escapes that mapping. The real is what literature, not "the world," is hiding.

The passage I have just quoted is taken from Jacques Lacan's reading of Edgar Allan Poe's "The Purloined Letter," and it is conceivable that Lacan's view of Poe may seem far removed from the study of either Shakespeare or history. So let me place next to this an uncannily similar passage from the works of Ralph Waldo Emerson in his essay on "Shakespeare; Or, The Poet." In that essay, published in the 1850 volume *Representative Men*, Emerson had this to say about "the researches of antiquaries, and the Shakespeare Society":

> [T]hey have left no book-stall unsearched, no chest in a garret unopened, no file of old yellow accounts to decompose in damp and worms, so keen was the hope to discover whether the boy Shakespeare poached or not, whether he held horses at the theatre door, whether he kept school, and why he left in his will only his second-best bed to Ann Hathaway, his wife . . .
>
>   The Shakespeare Society have inquired in all directions, advertised the missing facts, offered money for any information that will lead to proof; and with what result? . . . they have gleaned a few facts touching the property, and dealings in regard to property, of the poet. It appears that, from year to year, he owned a larger share in the Blackfriars' Theatre . . . that he bought an estate in his native village . . . that he lived in the best house in Stratford; was intrusted by his neighbors with their commissions in London, as of borrowing money, and the like. . . . About the time when he was writing *Macbeth*, he sues Philip Rogers, in the borough-court of Stratford, for thirty-five shillings, ten pence, for corn delivered to him. . . . I admit the importance of this information. It was well worth the pains that have been taken to procure it.

For Emerson "we are very clumsy writers of history." The questions we ask are the wrong questions, our real is the wrong real. Emerson feels so strongly about this that he claims to prefer knowing nothing of the specifically historical as it affects the case of Shakespeare, lest it impinge upon imagination and poetic genius.

> . . . Can any biography [he asks] shed light on the localities into which the *Midsummer Night's Dream* admits me? Did Shakespeare confide to any notary or parish recorder, sacristan, or surrogate, in Stratford, the genesis of that delicate creation? The forest of Arden, the noble air of Scone Castle, the moonlight of Portia's villa, "the antres vast and desarts idle" of Othello's

> captivity—where is the third cousin, or grand-nephew, the chancellor's file of accounts, or private letter, that has kept one word of those transcendent secrets? . . .

Thus he offers his famous and paradoxical assertions: that "Shakspeare is the only biographer of Shakspeare," and that "So far from Shakspeare's being the least known to us, he is the one person, in all modern history, known to us."[30] Not having his history is what gives Emerson his Shakespeare.

This rhetorically framed either / or choice, between the historical-archival and the imaginative-poetic ("Can any biography shed light on the localities into which the *Midsummer Night's Dream* admits me? . . . where is the third cousin . . . or private letter, that has kept one word of those transcendent secrets?") is just what has been debunked and analyzed in late twentieth-century literary scholarship. To contemporary scholars there is no methodological contradiction, no doubt that historical research can and does illuminate imaginative writing, enriching rather than impoverishing aesthetic response. It is no longer a question of finding answers to questions that don't matter: it is a matter of discovering questions one never thought to ask. History has defamiliarized literary study in such a way that no one feels sure any longer of the location of the forest of Arden.

As a result, far from supplying a text's ground, historical study can unground it in a new way. Productions of *The Merchant of Venice* have been used both to inflame feelings of antisemitism and to critique them, depending upon the director's and actor's interpretation and (always historicize) the culture and circumstances of production. Notice that the word "production" here has two equal and adjacent meanings. But as the example of *Merchant* suggests, once they are written plays and poems and novels take on a life of their own, and even an "intention" or intentionality of their own—what is sometimes called the unconscious of the text. Their history starts with their writing and reading, and is never completed, and can never be completely known.

It is worth remembering that the history of literary analysis has itself been dialectical. Thus in the course of the past century of literary study philology and editing have given way to literary history, and then to "character criticism" and psychology, and then to close reading and the pursuit of images and themes, and then to archetypal criticism, and then to philosophical and psychoanalytic theory, and then to historicism and an emphasis on socially and culturally produced categories like race, class, gender, and sexuality, and now once again to philology and editing (and "the history of the book") as well as to appreciation (also known as "aesthetics") and value (also known as "ethics"). The return of these last two categories, aesthetics and ethics, was in retrospect virtually guaranteed by their previous abjection, just as that abjection was virtually guaranteed by their enormous earlier success and prestige.

The critique of what is often called "presentism" by scholars of early modern literature and culture has been a necessary corrective for a failure of historical specificity that can obscure what is most striking and powerful about a literary text.[31] The days of Jan Kott's frisky *Shakespeare Our Contemporary* have to a certain extent given way to the rigors, and longeurs, of Shakespeare Not Our Contemporary. But it seems equally crucial to acknowledge that some kinds of literary questions—questions about "what repeats"—cannot be posed through a predominantly historical approach.

Furthermore, there is yet another pertinent paradox for us to note, and it is this: What the best literary historicists look for is not the moments when the author is consciously historical but when he or she is unconsciously historical. Anachronism or fantasy, which seems to escape historical determination, is intimately connected to it in ways that escape the author's conscious perception. Thus, in neglecting the ahistorical, literal-minded literary historicists are in reality neglecting the historical. And it is the analysis of the historicity of the present that prevents "presentism."

VII

"The injunction to practise intellectual honesty usually amounts to sabotage of thought," writes Theodor Adorno with characteristic acerbity.

> The writer is urged to show explicitly all the steps that have led him to his conclusion, so enabling every reader to follow the process through and, where possible—in the academic industry—to duplicate it. This demand not only invokes the liberal fiction of the universal communicability of each and every thought . . . but is also wrong in itself as a principle of representation. For the value of a thought is measured by its distance from the continuity of the familiar. . . . Texts which anxiously undertake to record every step without omission inevitably succumb to banality, and to a monotony related not only to the tension induced in the reader, but to their own substance.[32]

In Adorno's critique of demands for intellectual honesty, we can dimly make out what we are asking literature to do. Literature, in fact, is the discourse in which the knowledge of the discontinuity of thought is made fleetingly available.

"The demand for intellectual honesty is itself dishonest," writes Adorno, since it ignores or rejects the messier ways in which knowledge is actually acquired, "through a network of prejudices, opinions, innervations, self-corrections, presuppositions and exaggerations." If "honest ideas" always manifest themselves as "mere repetition, whether of what was there before or of categorical forms," something crucial is missing in intellectual life. To illustrate this naivete, he adduces an image of a man dying satisfied that his life has all added up. It is, as it happens, an image that carries a strong, though indirect, whiff of Shakespeare:

> Anyone who dies old and in the consciousness of seemingly blameless success, would secretly be the model schoolboy who reels off all life's stages without gaps or omissions, an invisible satchel on his back.

At first recollection, of course, Shakespeare's school-boy in *As You Like It* is scarcely a model, that "whining school-boy with his satchel / And shining morning face, creeping like snail / Unwillingly to school."[33] Why then associate this passage with Shakespeare at all? Why not think instead only of the modern German gymnasium student seemingly directly evoked by Adorno? For two reasons: first, because the indirect line of associative thinking is the one Adorno himself recommends in this passage ("a wavering, deviating line"; a kind of thought "which, for the sake of its relation to its object, forgoes the full transparency of its logical genesis"). And second, because the "mere repetition" of "categorical forms" is in fact present, in extreme form, in the passage where Shakespeare's schoolboy makes his appearance— Jaques' famous, or infamous, "Seven Ages of Man." It is Jaques who, to cite Adorno's phrase again, "reels off all life's stages without gaps or omissions, an invisible satchel on his back." It is Jaques, the "melancholy Jaques," who is the model schoolboy, showing off—here in parodic fashion—the well-worn "knowledge" which had by Shakespeare's time become a cliché:

> All the world's a stage,
> And all the men and women merely players.
> They have their exits and their entrances,
> And one man in his time plays many parts,
> His acts being seven ages. (2.7.139–43)

Instead of the diligent schoolboy, Adorno recommends the model of the slugabed and the truant:

> Every thought which is not idle . . . bears branded on it the impossibility of its full legitimation, as we know in dreams that there are mathematics lessons, missed for the sake of a blissful morning in bed, which can never be made up. Thought waits to be woken one day by the memory of what has been missed, and to be transformed into teaching.

Teaching—like thought—depends upon what has been missed. Upon the gaps in knowledge, the resistance to the idea of a citation of facts, a "discursive progression from stage to stage," the recording of every step without omission. It is in order to resist the inevitability of such a progression that I want to point toward the usefulness of anachronism, play, and all the other ways in which literature shocks us into awareness, and preserves something that can't be reduced to a ground. Whatever modes of reading are on the way, I hope that they and their practitioners will dare—at least from time to time—to be historically incorrect.

Shakespeare's Faces

11

Painting in England was not any *great shakes* at this time.
Catherine Johnston, Curator of European and American art at the
National Gallery of Canada, speaking of the "Sanders portrait"

Was this face the face . . .?
Shakespeare, *King Richard II* 4.1.281

"What a striking face! Do tell me who he is," says the narrator of Henry James' tour de force of a novella, *The Aspern Papers*, as he fondles a small oval portrait with "fingers of which I could only hope that they didn't betray the intensity of their clutch." He is determined not to mention the name of the portrait's subject, the romantic poet, Jeffrey Aspern, although he longs to acquire the poet's unpublished letters. His interlocutor, the niece of Aspern's former mistress, replies that, "critic and historian though you are," it is possible he will not recognize the name, since "the world goes fast and one generation forgets another," and all the while the narrator is afraid she will name a price that is too high. "The face comes back to me, it torments me," he remarks, with all the casualness he can summon. "You expressed doubt of this generation's having heard of the gentleman, but he strikes me for all the world as a celebrity. Now who is he? I can't put my finger on him—I can't give him a label. Wasn't he a writer? Surely he's a poet."[1]

James' story is loosely based on the life of Lord Byron, not of Shakespeare, but the same burning gaze is always directed toward what purports to be Shakespeare's face. At a time when the discovery of a "new Shakespeare portrait" has intrigued both critics and historians and the general public, it is worth remembering those earlier moments of literary lionization, and the way they have tended to turn on images and relics. Of course the use of portraits as evidence of character, personality, honor, and sympathy—not to mention Shakespeare's vaunted "genius"—has a history as long as Shakespeare himself. What *is* it, though, that we seek in a face, whether it is the face of Shakespeare or another? What counts as evidence—and, most importantly, what might it be evidence *of*?

There is, of course, no point in gazing at Shakespeare's face with deep interrogation if his portrait turns out to be a forgery. Hence, a great deal of effort goes into the available modes of authentication. What counts as evidence in that process is capable of a certain objective verification: dates, watermarks, carbon, uninterrupted provenance. But while authentication can eliminate anachronism and forgery, can it give us the "authentic" Shakespeare? Can there be evidence of real historical existence to ground an individual in certainty, in the absence of any reliable point of comparison? What can tell us—beyond a reasonable doubt—that this is the real historical Shakespeare? And even if we knew for sure that this was what a certain man from Stratford really looked like, on a certain day in a certain year, do we have any way of verifying that this man is the author of the plays and sonnets that are, after all, the real objects of our investment?

In "Shakespeare's Ghost Writers" I looked at the so-called "Shakespeare authorship controversy" as a cultural symptom, noting that writers, in particular, have preferred the mystery about the author of the plays to any "answer" that would locate Shakespearean genius in a mere mortal, with personal quirks, a family history, a set of ambitions and wishes and failings—and a face. The less clear we are about "who wrote Shakespeare," the more "Shakespeare" can be idealized, and indeed idolized. "Shakespeare is the only biographer of Shakespeare," wrote Ralph Waldo Emerson, and Charles Dickens summed up the views of many when he wrote, "the life of Shakespeare is a fine mystery, and I tremble every day lest something should turn up." Those who have actively, even aggressively, sought to identify the author of the plays, and especially to identify him / her as someone *other* than William Shakespeare of Stratford, have also been motivated by a strong set of personal concerns, ranging from something like cultural *Schadenfreude* to concerns of status and class, to more pragmatic issues having to do with the huge economic investment in the Shakespeare business—from publishing to tourism to T-shirts—and the sheer pleasure of investigative reporting against the grain. Just as "man bites dog" is a more eye-catching headline than "dog bites man," so "Oxford is Shakespeare" makes a better story than "Shakespeare is Shakespeare"—at least in some quarters. The brouhaha about any portrait is beside the point if the subject of the portrait didn't write the plays. The "historical Shakespeare" has all the fascination and power of the "historical Jesus"—in fact, as we shall see, looking "too Jewish" haunts them both.

The philosopher and cultural critic Michel Foucault set down some precepts for what he called the "author-function" in his influential essay called "What Is an Author?" The historical concept of the author was an instrumental one, Foucault argued: it permitted a way of organizing and categorizing texts, of ascribing a certain coherence to a body of work and a literary style, and of according prestige. Noting that "authors" were not particularly important, valued, or even known, in Western literature before 1500, when anonymous texts were the norm, Foucault explored the role the "author" had played in the recent past, and might play in the future. The "author-function" was distinct from the romantic humanization of a supposedly historical figure. Rather than beginning with the "originating subject" (in the case of Shakespeare, the "author" of the plays and poems published under that name), the author-function described the way literary reputation was conveyed, and the backstory that could be told about the "author" by and through a historical consideration of "his" (or "her") works.

I want now to propose a variation on Foucault's provocative title question and equally provocative phrase, in order to speak directly to our present concerns. Suppose that we asked the question, "What is a portrait?" And that we tried to elaborate a theory of the "portrait-function," both for Shakespeare's time, and for our own?

It may be interesting on the occasion of the discovery of the Sanders portrait to recall some of the history of the portraits that have gone before, and the way they have been received. The nineteenth and twentieth centuries produced a myriad of works on this fascinating topic, from *Shakespeare's Portraits Phrenologically Considered* (1875)[2] to *A New Portrait of Shakespeare: The Case of the Ely Palace Painting as against that of the so-called Droeshout Original* (1903),[3] to Leslie Hotson's *Shakespeare by Hilliard: A Portrait Deciphered* (1977)[4]—which begins, "Consider for a moment the opening of a hunt in real life for a Wanted Man"—to *Changing the Face of Shakespeare* (1996),[5] a posthumous, privately-printed monograph by an American schoolteacher who had worked as a cryptographer in the Second World War and helped to break the Japanese code. In many if not most of these accounts the attempt is to read the man in the portrait, and, not infrequently, to read the man *into* the portrait, or, conversely, to cast doubt on the authenticity of the portrait because it does not seem to match the Man.

Thus, for example, the author of *The Droeshout Portrait of William Shakespeare, An Experiment in Identification* (1911) demonstrates to his own satisfaction that the portrait is in fact that of Francis Bacon, whose authorship of the plays he had shown, "in two books [which have been] in some quarters misunderstood, and consequently misrepresented and ridiculed, but which neither ha[ve] been nor can be refuted."[6] In his previous books he had detected Bacon's signatures cunningly hidden in the "Shakespeare" text, some in acrostics. Using a method of identification he compares to fingerprinting or to the Bertillon measurements used in the identification of criminals, he finds that "the portrait of the poet, used as a frontispiece to the plays in which Bacon's structural signature is found, is anatomically identical with the portrait of the man bearing the name so signed."[7]

Likewise, the author of a book called *The Bacon-Shakespearean Mystery*, which had claimed to prove that Anthony Bacon, Francis' brother, was the real author of the plays, weighed in six years later with *The Shakespearean Portraits and Other Addenda* (1964, revised 1966), in which she disclosed that Anthony Bacon's initials could be read on the collar of the Droeshout engraving (she was able to discern this, she said, by putting a piece of tracing paper over a copy of the Kökeritz facsimile of the Yale University First Folio).[8]

But even when the object is not to prove that someone else wrote the "Shakespeare" plays, the degree of critical energy and ingenuity applied to the portraits cannot really be disentangled from cultural fantasy. *A New Portrait of Shakespeare* (1903) makes a claim for the authenticity of the so-called Ely Palace portrait, which came into the possession of the Bishop of Ely in 1846, having previously languished in "an obscure broker's shop." Cleaning of the portrait disclosed the words "Aet. 39, 1603," the supposed age of Shakespeare in that year. The author is especially impressed with the suitability of the portrait's image: "It gives the impression of representing a real person, a sentient human being. . . . The eyes, in spite of the error in drawing, have a very distinct and interesting expression—a disquiet vacancy that often denotes a deeply troubled mind. The mouth is both sensuous and sensitive, and the seriousness of the lower part of the face indicates dignity, even elevation of character." Since the supposed date of the portrait, 1603, was the very time in Shakespeare's life which "critics have generally taken as marking some sudden change in the underlying mood of Shakespeare's mind," leading to the writing of *Measure for Measure* and the great tragedies, the portrait supports the theory of a crisis in spiritual development. "If now the Ely Palace portrait may be taken as authentic, it distinctly confirms the theory. The expression of the disquiet, indwelling eyes, and the dignified, serious face, is what one would naturally expect at the period of *Hamlet*."[9] Thus assumptions or projections about Shakespeare's spiritual life and his character are brought to bear upon the question of authenticity; although visual evidence and issues of provenance are part of the argument, the clincher is that this portrait looks like Shakespeare. Or at least like the Shakespeare that critics were thinking and writing about at the time.

If psychology, emotion, and affect were not convincing, there was science to be consulted. As Dickens wrote of Shakespeare, "If he had had a Boswell, society wouldn't have respected his grave, but would calmly have had his skull in the phrenological shop-windows."[10] Thus the questions raised by *Shakespeare's Portraits Phrenologically Considered* are those of what was regarded as a certain kind of cutting-edge science. Only "within the present century," writes the author, has the discovery been made that "special characteristics are connected with particular portions of the head, and that mental greatness mainly depends on the size, form and condition of the brain."[11] The head of a "mere mathematician" will differ from that of a musician, and both from the linguist, "while the universal genius must possess a well-balanced and finely constituted nervous organization." The Stratford bust fails the universal genius test. It "presents the appearance of a stout unintellectual figure." Admittedly "it has a jovial, cheerful, life-like look," but "the features are not those indicative of sensibility and refinement." Especially disturbing to the phrenologist is the fact that the head is broadest at its base, evidence of "destructiveness, secretiveness, alimentiveness, and acquisitiveness," while "ideality and wit are scarcely indicated." This, in short, cannot be Shakespeare. "I have examined many thousands of heads, and never met with such a heavy-looking figure associated with a man of capacity, culture, and mental power." What is likely is that the image is just a monumental effigy, and not an exact likeness, and that the "tombmaker" Gerard Johnson "left details to be executed by his assistants."[12] The Droeshout engraving comes out better; from the shape of the head it seems that "there is an ample endowment of the higher sentiments. The imaginative and imitative faculties are represented as very large," as are "ideality, wonder, wit, imitation [again], benevolence, and veneration." This is a much more appropriate phrenology for Shakespeare: "his large benevolence, veneration and ideality, and his small destructiveness and acquisitiveness leading to his control over his feelings and generous sympathy with others." All this can be read in the Droeshout portrait. It is worth noting that the phrenologist is not daunted by the wide variety of representations in the "various portraits" of Shakespeare: if they are all to be believed, his eyes "must have been at the same time black, brown, and blue," the nose "at once Roman, Grecian, aquiline and snub," and so on. But what emerges, nonetheless, is a clear sense of Shakespeare's "temperament, which was evidently a combination of the mental, the nervous, and sanguine, imparting great susceptibility, activity, quickness and love of action."[13] "Evidently." From the evidence of the portraits and the shape of the skull.

So strong, in fact, was this interest in Shakespeare's skull, that J. Parker Norris, an American keenly interested in Shakespeare portraits, initiated the idea of disinterring the body. "If we could even get a photograph of Shakespeare's skull, it would be a great thing, and would help us to make a better portrait of him than we now possess."[14] As Norris observes serenely, "It is strange how differently people look at the same object." Thus, for example, nineteenth-century opinions on the Stratford bust varied from J. O. Halliwell-Phillipps' assessment, that "to those who can bring themselves to believe that, notwithstanding his unrivaled genius, Shakespeare was a realization of existence, and, in his daily career, much as other men were, the bust at Stratford will convey very nearly all that is desirable to know of his outward form,"[15] to the very different ideas of the distinguished lawyer and Shakespearean C. M. Ingleby. To Ingleby, the Stratford bust was "coarse and clownish, suggesting to the beholder a countryman crunching a sour apple or struck with amazement at some unpleasant spectacle."[16] The portrait painter Abraham Wivell, author of yet another study, *An Inquiry into the History, Authenticity, and Characteristics of the Shakespeare Portraits,*[17] admires the bust's nose and forehead, and thinks that if the space between the nose and mouth were just a little shorter "the face would be remarkably handsome." He also thinks this portrait "has much less the look of a Jew than most of them," since the beard is fashionably trimmed. A century later, Sam Schoenbaum added his own judiciously acerbic commentary: "Can this be a true likeness of the Bard? Surely not—this must be some affluent burgher of Stratford confronting us with his sleek, well-fed, middle-aged prosperity. . . . Supposedly we are to conceive of the poet as declaiming verses he has just composed, but he appears for all the world to be struggling with indigestion."[18]

Coarse and clownish, dyspeptic, remarkably handsome, not very intellectual, not like a Jew. A similarly Rashomon-like panoply of views can be marshaled for virtually any of the Shakespeare portraits, as well as for works once described as portraits of Shakespeare and now fallen out of favor. On the Droeshout engraving in the First Folio, for example, the editor George Steevens says Ben Jonson probably lacked acquaintance with the graphic arts, otherwise he would not have permitted his memorial verses to be printed in conjunction with it.[19] Ingleby, who does not doubt its authenticity, though he thinks it is copied from another sketch or painting, regards it as "such a monstrosity that I, for one, do not believe that it had any trustworthy exemplar."[20] On the other hand, James Boaden, yet another scholar of the portraits, thinks this one "exhibits an aspect of calm benevolence and tender thought; great comprehension, and a kind of mixt feeling, as when melancholy yields to the suggestions of fancy."[21]

In point of fact, though, no one has much wanted Shakespeare—their Shakespeare—to look like either the Stratford bust or the Droeshout engraving. In the late 1880s, when J. Parker Norris was writing in the journal *Shakesperiana*, the Chandos portrait, with its pointed beard, lace collar, and earring, was "the most familiar to the large mass of people,"[22] and the "popularly accepted representation of Shakespeare." Here, even at the risk of digression, I cannot resist quoting the epigraph to this interesting journal, in which the editor performs a superb re-gendering of Enobarbus' praise of Cleopatra. Under the large-print title *Shakespeariana*, and above the date and the portrait image, runs the line

"Age cannot wither nor custom stale his infinite variety."—ANT. & CLEO.

Through the blithe replacement of one possessive adjective with another, *her infinite variety* becomes *his*, and the quotation-out-of-context praises Shakespeare's art rather than Cleopatra's erotic power.

In any case, the Chandos portrait, of much more doubtful "authenticity" than the bust or the engraving, excited a good deal of commentary, pro and con. For one thing, it was too "Jewish." The eighteenth-century editor George Steevens disputed its authority, announcing that "our author exhibits the complexion of a Jew, or rather of a chimney-sweeper in the jaundice."[23] A mid-century Victorian, J. Hain Friswell, found it disappointing at first glance, because the person depicted looked foreign, and—again— too much like a Jew: "One cannot readily imagine our essentially English Shakespeare to have been a dark, heavy man, with a foreign expression, of a decidedly Jewish physiognomy, thin curly hair, a somewhat lubricious mouth, red-edged eyes, wanton lips, with a coarse expression, and his ears tricked out with ear-rings."[24] J. Parker Norris agreed: "very Jewish," "foreign," "most disappointing." Though some Englishmen did wear earrings in Shakespeare's day, the rings, he thought, contributed to the "foreign look." (Critics today who cast doubt on Chandos because of its un-English appearance tend to call this look "Italianate"[25] rather than "Jewish.") The lack of similarity between this portrait and the more fully authorized versions, the bust and the Droeshout engraving, led some scholars to dispute its genuineness (the irrepressible Steevens, noting the many hands through which it had passed, called it the "Davenantico-Bettertono-Barryan-Keckian-Nicolsian-Chandosan" portrait) but the real issue remained cultural, political, and aesthetic: Was this the way Shakespeare, our Shakespeare, *should* look?

We could make our way, one by one, through the succession of proposed "portraits" and likenesses of Shakespeare that have attracted attention over the years, and, should we do so, we would be able to notice the same pattern again and again. Assessment of the portrait appears to depend on technical questions like the age of the wood and the paint, the provenance and history of ownership, the clothing and hair styles, and so on, but what is really at stake is the question of whether the image fits the man. If not, the fault may be said to lie in the artist (too unskilled for his task), the medium (intractable stone, clumsy engraving tools), or the occasion (funerary moments all looked alike); alternatively, a competing aesthetic could be called into play, discovering that what one beholder found stolid, or vapid, or monstrous, another could find emblematic of wisdom, wide experience, imagination, and sympathy. Here we have a lesson, displayed for all to see, in the limits of both historical and inter-pretative criticism. When read backwards, beginning from a supposed goal (is this really an image of Shakespeare?), these supposedly neutral elements become materials for conscious fiction-making, of however benign or well-intentioned a purpose. Thus—just to emphasize this point—the editor and critic John Dover Wilson chose the so-called "Grafton portrait," an attractive small painting in the style of Holbein or Nicholas Hilliard which had come to light in the early years of the twentieth century, as the frontispiece for his *Essential Shakespeare*, even though it had small claim to authenticity, because he simply liked it better than the "pudding-faced effigy" of the Droeshout engraving, or the "self-satisfied pork-butcher" depicted in the putative "Janssen portrait."

Dover Wilson cites the " learned essay by Mr. M. H. Spielmann" in which the Stratford bust is characterized as having a "wooden appearance and vapid expression," staring eyes "set too close together," a nose "too small for the face." He notes that Spielmann's essay "also draws attention to the extraordinary upper lip, the hanging lower lip, and the general air of stupid and self-complacent prosperity. All this," writes Dover Wilson, "might suit well enough with an affluent and retired butcher, but does gross wrong to the dead poet." In short, "this Shakespeare simply will not do." People don't want their Shakespeare to look like this; in fact Dover Wilson thinks that the bust is largely responsible for "the campaign against 'the man from Stratford' and the attempts to dethrone him in favor of Lord Bacon, the Earl of Derby, the Earl of Oxford, or whatever coroneted pretender may be in vogue at the present moment." His own explanation for the problem is a familiar one: the artist was not up to the task. "The proportions are admirable, and the architectural design, with its pillars and canopy, its mantled shield, and its twin cherubs, is quite beautiful. But one thing was clearly beyond the workman's scope—the human face, the face that happened to be Shakespeare's!"

Ah yes, that elusive "face that happened to be Shakespeare's." For reasons about which he is admirably clear, Dover Wilson prefers a fantasy to the possibly real, but palpably disappointing, historical monument. For him the "beautiful" Grafton portrait, inscribed with a date that shows the sitter was Shakespeare's exact contempo-rary, looks much more the way Shakespeare *should* look, although, as he unblushingly acknowledges, "there is nothing whatever to connect the unknown youth of the wonderful eyes and the oval Shelley-like face with the poet who was also twenty-four years old in 1588." In other words, the Grafton portrait is a screen, a fantasy, a wish fulfillment. Another Shakespeare biographer of the time had "found in it his own idea of the youthful Shakespeare and wished it genuine," and Dover Wilson explains, in direct and explicit terms, why he has selected this image for the frontispiece of his book:

> I do not ask the reader to believe in it, or even to wish to believe in it. All I suggest is that he may find it useful in trying to frame his own image of Shakespeare. It will, at any rate, help him to forget the Stratford bust. Let him take it, if he will, as a painted cloth or arras, drawn in front of that monstrosity, and symbolizing the Essential Poet.[26]

We might draw an analogy here with the modern practice of "profiling" in law enforcement and in media marketing: in so-called "racial profiling," for example, law enforcement officers select their targets for investigation or stronger action on the basis of race, national origin, or ethnicity. The word "profile," which derives from the drawing of the outline of the human face, quickly became a term for a biographical sketch or character study. In effect, what Shakespeare scholars and amateur enthusiasts have engaged in over the years is a form of what might be called "author profiling": developing an ideal image for what the author of the Shakespeare plays *ought* to look like. Indeed, Dover Wilson's word "frame" ("to frame his own image of Shakespeare") also carries an inadvertent second-meaning from the world of criminal investigation. The Shakespeare profiled, and framed, in these accounts of the portrait evidence, is, I want to submit, an idealized and idealizing activity, that owes as much to psychology and projection as it does to provenance and paint.

Trying to frame our own image of Shakespeare has become, in these post-*Shakespeare in Love* days, an increasingly respectable activity. The alleged new portrait of Shakespeare discovered in Canada, whether it is ultimately determined to be real or fake, fits into this strong history of "counterfeiting" Shakespeare perfectly well: preparing a face to meet the faces that we meet. If the culture correspondent for the *Los Angeles Times* was moved to say, on behalf of the Hollywood film industry, that the Shakespeare of the portrait looks a lot like Joseph Fiennes, the eponymous hero of *Shakespeare in Love*, are we at risk of revaluing our portraits—and our Shakespeares—yet again, to fit this year's fashions? If so, we can at least take comfort in the fact that this way of reading portraits as if they told us something about character and genius rather than about art and counterfeiting is part of a tradition as old as Shakespeare, and his plays.

A commentator in the *Courier Mail* makes the point without undue emphasis, once past the tendentious claim that this might be "the real face of William Shakespeare." The new portrait "conflicts with the traditional image of Shakespeare having a bald head, thin brows, and humourless countenance. Instead, it suggests he was a mischievous-looking chap with fluffy red hair and blue-green eyes."[27] Verlyn Klinkenborg editorialized in *The New York Times* that "if this is Shakespeare, it is a younger and more roguish Shakespeare than we have ever seen," and went on to argue, in a way that many literary critics have as well, that "the resemblance we see in this portrait is not a resemblance to Shakespeare," but rather "a resemblance to what we would like to imagine that Shakespeare looked like."[28] Tim Rutten in the *Los Angeles Times* was even blunter: what is "troubling to many, is how the balding, stiff, dour old man the engraving and bust portray could have created the world's most enduring body of dramatic and poetic art. It is precisely that reservation that has churned the enthusiasm for the new portrait."[29]

The authors of modern detective stories have long known about this device, of making the artist look like his or her work. Robert Barnard's mystery *The Cherry Blossom Corpse* features the murder, at a romance writers convention, of the woman who apotheosizes everything a writer of romance novels should look like—and who turns out to be an actress hired to put a glamorous face on books ghost-written by drabber women, and men, behind the scenes. In Ngaio Marsh's *Final Curtain* a famous actor owes his celebrity to his superbly theatrical head, which is as outsized as his ego. Despite her forebodings the detective's wife, herself a notable painter, cannot resist the invitation to do his portrait. Both stories, it is worth noting, end in the tragic deaths of the actor-author-artist. "Looking the part" has its dangers as well as its pleasures.

There is a superb fictional analysis of the "portrait-function" in Josephine Tey's classic murder mystery, *The Daughter of Time*, which turns on a portrait of Richard III. Inspector Alan Grant of Scotland Yard, hospitalized with a broken leg, is entertained by an actress friend who, knowing his "passion for faces," brings him an array of portrait-images. Thumbing through images of Lucrezia Borgia, Louis XVII, and the Earl of Leicester, each labeled only on the back of the sheet, Grant tries to read the story behind the face. When he encounters the portrait that will engage him for the rest of the novel, and that has continued to engage scholars and amateur history buffs through the years since Tey's story was first published—the portrait of a man dressed in "the velvet cap and slashed doublet of the late fifteenth century," a man about 35 years of age, lean, clean-shaven, wearing a rich jeweled collar and caught in the act of putting a ring on his finger, he tries to speculate about the man and his character. "A judge? A soldier? A prince? Someone used to great responsibility, and responsible in his authority. Someone too conscientious. A worrier; perhaps a perfectionist. A man at ease in a large design, but anxious over details." When he turns the picture over and reads the caption he finds printed there the following words: "Richard the Third. From the portrait in the National Portrait Gallery. Artist Unknown."[30] The rest of the plot consists of the Inspector's quest to read the face against the reputation of the man, and, ultimately, to exonerate the portrait sitter from the calumny of having murdered the princes in the tower. The man with the "interesting face" and the "haunted eyes" could not be a destroyer of innocence, a "synonym for villainy," so the remainder of the novel puts the case, in terms at once artful and engrossing, for Henry VII, the Earl of Richmond (and Queen Elizabeth's grandfather) as the true author of the crime.

So successful was Tey in putting the case for Richard that her novel has become a key piece of "evidence" for members of the Richard III Society, an international organization dedicated to restoring Richard's reputation. The function of portrait-evidence as a guarantor of character carries over even into the Society's web pages. Thus the American branch of the Society, pinpointing the true villain according to its lights (and Tey's) offers a feature called "rearranging Henry Tudor's face," in which Ricardians are presented with a period portrait of the man who would become Henry VII and asked to "click and drag on Henry's face to reveal his true character" (http://www.r3.org/alexwarp/henry7.html).

But what, we might ask again, are we looking for in a portrait—and especially in a new portrait of Shakespeare? Can the "true character" be read in the painted face, whether or not it is "rearranged" by the viewer? What was Shakespeare himself (whoever he was) looking for when he addressed the face of his male beloved, "A woman's face, with Nature's own hand painted, / Hast thou, the Master Mistress of my passion" (Sonnet 20.1–2)? Aren't all those obsessed with Shakespeare portraits looking for a face that objectively portrays their own passion for the beloved author? Might the passion be such that it cannot be contained in mere reality? Yet what we are asking from the face is precisely the image of that excess.

Oscar Wilde writes about the kind of love that exceeds historical accuracy in his fictionalized work of critical theory and literary detection about the object of Shakespeare's passion, *The Portrait of Mr. W. H.* The form of the essay is familiar: a dialogue between two men of wealth and taste, sitting in a house on Birdcage Walk over their coffee and cigarettes, discussing the truth of artistic forgery, and the powerful literary hoaxes of "Macpherson, Ireland, and Chatterton." Ireland, of course, is the celebrated Shakespeare forger, and Chatterton the "marvelous boy" who took his own life at the age of seventeen. Both will cast shadows on the story to come.

The narrator of *The Portrait*, who is a stand-in for Wilde, offers the opinion that "so-called forgeries were merely the result of an artistic desire for perfect representation," and that "all Art being to a certain degree a mode of acting, an attempt to

realize one's own personality on some imaginative plane out of reach of the tram-
meling accidents and limitations of real life, to censure an artist for a forgery was to
confuse an ethical with an aesthetical problem."[31] His companion asks him what he
would think about "a young man who had a strange theory about a certain work of
art, believed in his theory, and committed a forgery in order to prove it."[32] The test
case is the portrait of Mr. W. H., the dedicatee of Shakespeare's sonnets, now in the
possession of the host: a "full-length portrait of a young man in late sixteenth-century
costume, standing by a table, with his right hand resting on a book. He seemed about
seventeen years of age, and was of quite extraordinary beauty." The portrait, it turns
out, is itself a forgery, created by the young man with the "strange theory" to
demonstrate that "W. H." was not an aristocratic patron of Shakespeare's but "the
boy-actor for whom he created Viola and Imogen, Juliet and Rosalind, Portia and
Desdemona, and Cleopatra herself."[33] When the forger was confronted with his act,
he explained that he had done it to make a point. "You would not be convinced any
other way. It does not affect the truth of the theory." Told that the fact of the forgery
in fact invalidated his argument, he committed suicide, leaving behind a letter
enjoining his friend to present the theory to the world, and "unlock the secret of
Shakespeare's heart."[34]

So what's in a face? Wilde's observation that a forged portrait of a true idea confuses
an ethical with an aesthetic problem brings to mind what the contemporary
philosopher Emmanuel Levinas has to say about "the face":

> I think rather that access to the face is straightaway ethical. You turn yourself toward the Other
> as toward an object when you see a nose, eyes, a forehead, a chin, and you can describe them.
> The best way of encountering the Other is not even to notice the color of his eyes! When one
> observes the color of the eyes one is not in social relationship with the Other. The relation with
> the face can surely be dominated by perception, but what is specifically the face is what cannot
> be reduced to that.[35]

The capital-O "Other" employed by Levinas designates a particular and idealized one-
to-one relationship. This Other differs from all "others." And in the numinous world
of literary-biographical fantasy Shakespeare is clearly the Other rather than one of the
"others," for his critics, readers, and admirers. Matthew Arnold's famous sonnet
of 1844 entitled "Shakespeare" begins with this same comparison, in the form of
an address to its subject: "Others abide our question. Thou art free. / We ask and
ask—Thou smilest and art still, / Out-topping knowledge." Where "others" have
biographical stories that explain them (they "abide our question"), Shakespeare is, for
Arnold, unique, and the mystery of his identity is preferred to any solution. Arnold's

poem ends, significantly, with an unmistakable glance at the portraits, and specifically at the high forehead of the Stratford bust and the Droeshout engraving:

> All pains the immortal spirit must endure,
> All weakness which impairs, all griefs which bow,
> Find their sole speech in that victorious brow.

Here is another evidence of the portrait-function, a speaking picture. The "victorious brow" (later to be described by Dover Wilson as a "great forehead") speaks volumes about human pain, grief, and weakness, while the enigmatic Shakespeare, Mona-Lisa-like, smiles and is still, refusing to explain the source of his wisdom.

Those who gaze in fascination, and recognition, at the Sanders portrait will not find wisdom writ large on the somewhat foxy face, even though the "great forehead" (a.k.a. receding hairline) is again present to the view. Arnold's sonorous verses may sound dated to us, but the wish they express continues to be felt. Our own celebrity-culture, though, pries into every personal detail, unsatisfied with mystery and with silence. When asked about the interest provoked by the Sanders portrait, Toronto Shakespeare scholar Alexander Leggatt nicely voiced the general dissatisfaction with the traditional authenticated images, "the engraving and the sort of lumpy statue," which "have a kind of inexpressive quality that is frustrating."[36] "Inexpressive" is the key word here, I think. These portraits do not speak to us, whereas the male minx in the Sanders image, with his darting eyes and flirtatious, up-curved mouth, seems about to burst into words—words as witty and perhaps as improper as our current taste will permit. This is not Arnold's Victorian Shakespeare. If this Shakespeare looks more like Benedick than like King Lear (or Polonius), that, too, seems to suit the temper of our time. *Shakespeare in Love* fantasizes about the secret life, the personal life, the private life of the world's most celebrated and venerated author, trying to explain the inexplicable, which is how he came to write those astonishing plays, those luminous sonnets. For Stoppard, it was the fictional Viola de Lesseps (or the actress who played her, Gwyneth Paltrow). For Oscar Wilde, in a playful work of literary detection called *The Portrait of Mr. W. H.*, it was the imaginary Willie Hughes, "the boy-actor for whom he created Viola and Imogen, Juliet and Rosalind, Portia and Desdemona, and Cleopatra herself."[37] This is a distinction without a difference. We will not find "genius," whatever it is, in any biographical detail, or in any portrait. What we will find, when we look at the portrait of Shakespeare, as Richard II did when he called for a looking glass, and as Jaques in *As You Like It* did when he gazed into the brook, was an image of ourselves.

Is the Sanders portrait an "authentic" portrait of Shakespeare, the "real" Shakespeare? Why not think so, if you like? Every age invents its own Shakespeare, as

Coleridge found "a smack of Hamlet" in himself, and Goethe, too, and Freud, and just about every scholar and artist and actor who has spent time reading and performing Shakespeare's plays. The portrait-function is a reflection-effect, holding, in the case of this author above all others, the mirror up to Shakespeare, showing the very age and body of the time his form and pressure. Dover Wilson sought his "essential Shakespeare," and we seek ours. In an era where "rearranging [the] face" is as easy as dragging a cursor or turning to Photoshop, the portrait, and the portrait-function, will inevitably read very differently from the way they read in Shakespeare's time, or in the lively Shakespeare-portrait debates of a century ago.

One thing is almost sure, though. If this portrait is judged to be genuine, or catches the media's fancy, its cultural effect will be felt in fashion circles before it is adopted by the history of literature. The Shakespeare collar and the Shakespeare doublet—maybe even the new Shakespeare beard, in a hue dubbed "Bard-red,"—will appear on the runways and in the fashion magazines. It is no accident, believe me, that the first full-page reproduction of the Sanders portrait in a major periodical could be found in the December 2001 issue of *Vanity Fair*, with a bare-chested Brad Pitt on the cover, and the legend, "All-American Heartthrob," emblazoned there, right below the "van" of Vanity. This is the new mode of *vanitas* painting, replacing Holbein's sixteenth-century *Ambassadors*: Sanders-Shakespeare / Brad Pitt as two sides of the same, All-(North) American coin.

McGuffin
Shakespeare 12

I had my father's signet in my purse,
Which was the model of that Danish seal,
Folded the writ up in the form of th'other,
Subscrib'd it, gav't th'impression, plac'd it safely,
The changeling never known.

Hamlet 5.2.49–53

"But what purpose had you," I asked, "in replacing the letter by a *fascimile*? Would it not have been better, at the first visit, to have seized it openly, and departed?"

Poe, "The Purloined Letter"

Recent Shakespearean scholarship has been much preoccupied with the fascinating business of editing. Once famously dismissed by Alexander Pope, the "dull duty of an editor" has become among the liveliest scenes in early modern studies, bringing together a social and material interest in what is called "print culture" (from printing houses to title pages to the London book trade) and the history of the book, with a persistent interest in "textuality," the language of the plays. New or renewed emphasis has been placed upon collaboration in writing and staging, and on the role of the theatrical company and the audience in shaping and reshaping play texts.

I am not an editor, nor was meant to be. Although I have learned enormously from these recent explorations, what I want to focus on here is a slightly different phenomenon: the production, from within Shakespeare studies itself, of textual problems—problems about ambiguities of sense and meaning—that are generated by the ingenious speculation of editors and critics. The production, in other words, of what might be called ghosts in the machine. Editors from the eighteenth century on have called this "conjectural criticism" or "conjectural emendation." I am going to call it— for reasons I will disclose in a moment—"McGuffin Shakespeare."

I

In his response to Pope's "dull duty" phrase, already notorious in the eighteenth century, Doctor Johnson had offered an amplification and a correction. Pope, he suggested, "understood but half his undertaking:

> The duty of a collator is indeed dull, yet, like other tedious tasks, is very necessary; but an emendatory critic would ill discharge his duty, without qualities very different from dullness. . . . Out of many readings possible, he must be able to select that which best suits with the state, opinion, and modes of language prevailing in every age, and with his author's particular cast of thought, and turn of expression. Such must be his knowledge, and such his taste. Conjectural criticism demands more than humanity possesses, and he that exercises it with most praise has very frequent need of indulgence. Let us now be told no more of the dull duty of an editor.[1]

Johnson has a good deal to say about "conjectural criticism," which he finds both daunting and unavoidable: "The collator's province is safe and easy, the conjecturer's perilous and difficult"; "As I practiced conjecture more, I learned to trust it less"; "Conjecture has all the joy and all the pride of invention, and he that has once started a happy change, is too much delighted to consider what objections may rise against it"; "Yet conjectural criticism has been of great use in the learned world; nor is it my intention to depreciate a study, that has exercised so many mighty minds."[2]

Many of the mighty minds of recent years have spoken out against conjectural criticism, or at least against conjectural emendation, urging instead the "unediting" of Shakespeare's texts. Nor is this resistance—or rather this impulse to leave things alone—a concept of modern manufacture. Almost a century and a half ago C. M. Ingleby warned against "a destruction now in progress . . . latent, insidious, slow, and sure," in the "constant and unstaying process of supplantation and substitution" that had overtaken the editing of the plays. "The innocent-looking little modifications which we now introduce into Shakespeare on the plea of textual misprinting will sooner or later themselves require modernizing." For Ingleby the saving technology was photography, which had enabled the "multiplication of copies" from the folio of 1623, and thus preserved the text against well-meaning learned corruption.[3] Later critics would praise their own technological advances, from collating machines to digitization.

But a relatively short time ago a textual scholar like Fredson Bowers could defend, with pleasure and excitement, the uses of conjecture—at least in the past. Bowers and his fellow New Bibliographers had set as their goal the rediscovery of the original, or rather, the ideal of that original, dedicating their labors "to approach as nearly as may be to the ideal of the authorial fair copy by whatever necessary process of recovery, independent emendation, or conflation of the authorities."[4] This process was especially exciting, it is fair to say, when the author to be approached and summoned from the past was William Shakespeare. "Sometimes an inspired guess gives us with absolute conviction of rightness what Shakespeare must have written, even though we rely on faith and not on concrete evidence," writes Bowers. He points to "the old critic Theobald" and his emendation of the "nonsense" phrase "A Table of green fields," in the story of Falstaff's death in *King Henry V*, to "a babbl'd of green fields." Here, says Bowers, Theobald had "what was surely a real meeting of minds with Shakespeare."[5]

"Admittedly, if we follow one editor's version of *Hamlet* rather than another's, we shall not discover Claudius emerging as the hero, nor will Hamlet suddenly be exposed as a woman in disguise." So says Bowers, setting aside what he jovially calls "these scary possibilities" for the relative comfort zone of editorial decision-making: "whether Hamlet's father's bones were *interred* or *enurned*; whether the *safety*, *sanity*, or the *sanctity* of the Danish state is involved; or indeed, whether Hamlet's flesh, he regrets, is *too, too solid* or *too, too sullied*."[6] The folly of such a view must have been much on Bowers' mind, since he repeats it later in the same book: " No blinding new revelations about plot or character are to be anticipated [by advances in editing techniques]. Hamlet will not be revealed as a woman in disguise, nor will Lear save Cordelia from hanging."[7] Some of the "scary possibilities" Bowers discounts—Claudius as hero, Hamlet as woman—have in fact been urged by one or another critic over the years, from E. P. Vining's *The Mystery of Hamlet* to John Updike's *Gertrude and Claudius*. But Bowers is concerned to decide "what Shakespeare must have written."

I want to turn our attention, for a moment, away from "what Shakespeare wrote," that fatal Cleopatra of textual studies, and toward the dangerous pleasures of conjecture, on the part of editors, readers, and stagers of the Shakespearean text. I am interested, in particular, in textual problems and traces that have been brought to light, and to life, by the exertions of editors and lay scholars, and which remain, like unlaid ghosts, hovering about the page and the stage. This is what I call "McGuffin Shakespeare."

II

"Mac" means "son of" in Gaelic, and these spin-off problems—which have engaged some of the finest minds in the field—are in a sense "sons of," or offspring of, or artifacts of, the critical and editorial process. They stem, many of them, as you'll see, from a certain fantasy of what Shakespeare was like, or what he had in mind, or what his characters have in mind. For as will quickly become clear, the quest for "what Shakespeare wrote," and even more tellingly, for "a real meeting of minds with Shakespeare," always returns, even if the editorial permutations have led us, apparently, far afield.

I take the term "McGuffin," of course, from the film director Alfred Hitchcock. The McGuffin (also spelled MacGuffin and Maguffin) was Alfred Hitchcock's term for the missing thing that everybody wants, the "plot pretext,"[8] the "deliberately mysterious plot objective—the non-point."[9] The secret plans, the radioactive isotope, the photographic negatives, the cipher or code. Uranium 235 in Hitchcock's thriller *Notorious*. The "project" in David Mamet's *Spanish Prisoner*. The "proof" in playwright David Auburn's recent play of that name—a play that the author said could have taken off from "any number of Maguffins."[10]

The foundation-narrative for the term, its supposed source, is an anecdote told by Hitchcock's old friend, the film editor Angus MacPhail. Two men were traveling to Scotland on a train from London, when one of them noticed that the other had an odd-looking parcel stowed in the luggage rack:

> "What have you there?" asked one of the men.
> "Oh, that's a McGuffin," replied his companion.
> "What's a McGuffin?"
> "It's a device for trapping lions in the Scottish Highlands!"
> "But there aren't any lions in the Scottish Highlands!"
> "Well, then, I guess that's no McGuffin!"

This is a famous story, frequently retold, and the "moral" seems to vary with the teller. Hitchcock's biographer Donald Spoto says "the point is that a McGuffin is neither relevant, important, nor, finally, any of one's business. It simply gets the story going."[11] Thus for example in Hitchcock's film *The 39 Steps* the McGuffin is a secret formula. But, as Spoto writes, "it is to *prevent* the secret from being known—rather than to reveal it—that the adventure-chase is precipitated; thus the formula, which at first seems crucial, is immediately reduced in significance."[12]

Hitchcock himself was constantly asked—by journalists, film students, colleagues, and biographers—to describe his concept (in one interview he called it simply "my own term for the key element in any suspense story"[13]) and, inevitably, the McGuffin became itself a McGuffin, its meaning endlessly pursued, and always just out of reach.

Literary critics will immediately spot the similarity to Poe's "Purloined Letter." In his essay on Poe's famous story, Jacques Lacan notes that it is a "signifier nothing but whose obverse anyone except the Queen has been able to read." Furthermore, the letter is "destined by nature to signify the annulment of what it signifies."[14] The letter's contents are kept from the reader; we guess at its import and purport by the effects it has on characters in the story.

It's not surprising, then, to find the McGuffin appropriated by a cultural theorist like Slavoj Žižek and mapped onto the psychoanalytic work of Jacques Lacan. The McGuffin was, in Žižek's terms,

> "nothing at all," an empty place, a pure pretext whose sole role is to set the story in motion: the formula of the warplane engines in *The Thirty-Nine Steps*, the secret clause of the naval treaty in *The Foreign Correspondent*, the coded melody in *The Lady Vanishes*, the uranium bottles in *Notorious*, and so on. It is a pure semblance: in itself it is totally indifferent and, by structural necessity, absent; its signification is purely auto-reflexive, it consists in the fact that it has some signification for others, for the principal characters of the story, that it is of vital importance to them.

The McGuffin thus accorded, said Žižek, with Lacan's "*objet petit a*, a gap in the centre of the symbolic order—the lack, the void of the Real setting in motion the symbolic movement of interpretation, a pure semblance of the Mystery to be explained, interpreted."[15] With or without the analogy to Lacan, this perception is a useful one. Especially, as we'll see, when it comes to trying to pluck out the heart of a mystery.

One of the curious attributions of Hitchcock's McGuffin was what might be called its recursive nature, its tendency to double back upon itself and become true after the fact. Take the notorious case of the bottles of uranium in *Notorious*. Hitchcock often claimed—as he did, for example, to fellow director François Truffaut—that the choice of uranium was an uncanny accident. The plot of the film was to involve a woman working as a government agent who is told "to sleep with a certain spy to get some secret information." What was the information? It didn't much matter. But they needed to make something up.

"Gradually, we develop the story," Hitchcock told Truffaut, "and now I introduce the McGuffin: four or five samples of uranium concealed in wine bottles." The film's producer wanted to know what the uranium was, and what it was for, and Hitchcock told him that it was for the making of an atom bomb. The year was 1944, a year before Hiroshima, and the idea seemed far-fetched. Hitchcock offered to change the McGuffin to industrial diamonds—the atom bomb "wasn't the basis for our story, but only the McGuffin and . . . there was no need to attach too much importance to it"—

but the studio remained unconvinced. ("We turned it down because it was such a goddamn foolish thing to base a movie on," they recalled.) A few weeks later the whole project was sold to RKO, where it turned a huge profit.

Meantime Hitchcock's nosy questions about the atom bomb, which he had first heard about through a friend, landed him on the FBI surveillance list for three months.[16] Or so he said. Spoto, the biographer, contests this account, chalking it up to embellishment and Hitchcock's great "sense of publicity." FBI files reveal no evidence of "surveillance." In fact, claims Spoto, by the time the film was actually in production Japan had been bombed, and Hitchcock had made the acquaintance of several famous German emigré scientists who would finally be cast in the film, and who presumably told him about uranium. But producer David O. Selznick, warned by the FBI that any representation of American intelligence officers would have to get State Department clearance, advised Hitchcock, we're told, "that the McGuffin of spies and intelligence activities should remain just that—a McGuffin, entirely subordinate to the romance that Hitchcock had always wanted to emphasize in any case."[17]

In this case, again, the McGuffin was itself a McGuffin: that is to say, the fiction that Hitchcock was an uncanny prophet—always something easier to accomplish after the fact, as several Shakespearean prophecies make clear—was itself a plot device to forward the Hitchcock myth.

But how does the McGuffin function in Shakespeare?

III

I want to suggest that "McGuffin Shakespeare" is an effect that springs to life as the result of an interaction between text and reader, and especially between the text and a certain kind of reader: not the naif, but the learned close reader, the critic and the editor. It is the result, not of careless inattention but of hyper-vigilant attention. In describing this effect, and its uncanny production of textual ghosts, I will focus my attention on *Hamlet*, which for a variety of reasons has become the McGuffin of McGuffins for Shakespeare critics over the years. First, however, let me offer one example of a McGuffin from another play, just to demonstrate what I mean about the creative energy of editors bent on doing their jobs.

I choose this particular example among a myriad of possibilities because the heated tone of the editorial contestants is so revealing, the textual suggestions so divergent, and the passage itself so pertinent. Again the critic doing the adjudication is the nineteenth-century amateur of Shakespeare, C. M. Ingelby, trained as a lawyer, whom we will encounter a number of times, as it happens, in our quest for the

Shakespearean McGuffin. The passage in question is from the opening scene of *Timon of Athens*, where the characters called the Poet and the Painter are discussing their respective arts and the role of the patron. In the First Folio, the only surviving text, the Poet asserts

> Our Poesie is as a Gowne, which uses
> From whence 'tis nourisht. (1.1.21–2)

The line seemed to make no sense as it stood, and it was conjecturally emended by two eminent eighteenth-century editors, themselves poets not unfamiliar with the vagaries of patronage:

> Our Poesie is as a Gumme (Pope) which oozes (Johnson).

These emendations, we might note, are still accepted by modern editors; the Norton edition uses them without comment, though the Riverside puts them in square brackets. The Arden editor remarks that "this generally accepted emendation seems probable," and adds his own gloss: "The basic idea is of poetry, like gum, flowing steadily."[18] Here is the Victorian C. M. Ingleby's rather overwrought summary of the controversy, which will focus, at least in part, on the view of the German romantic writer and critic (Johann) Ludwig Tieck, himself a translator of Shakespeare.

> Shakespeare undoubtedly wrote,
>   Our poesie is as a gumme which oozes,
>   From whence 'tis nourisht.
> But in the edition of 1623, the passage was, as we have seen misprinted
>   Our Poesie is as a Gowne which uses
>   From whenc 'tis nourisht.
> And Tieck, who set himself up as a critic on Shakespeare and other English Dramatists, defended the nonsense, under the impression, perhaps, that Shakespeare meant to compare poetry to a worn-out robe!
>   Unhappy passage! In a letter on "The influences of Newspapers on Education," written by Mr. Blanchard Jerrold, in the *Daily News*, he had intended to quote the amended version; but to his horror it appeared in a totally new form,
>
>   Our poesy is as a queen that dozeth;
>
> And it now remains for some conceited foreigner of the future to contend that the bard meant to signalize the drowsiness of our poetry, by comparing it to a queen, who despite the calls of her high station, falls asleep on the throne![19]

The sideswipe against "some conceited foreigner of the future" is of course meant for Tieck and other German critics of Shakespeare, but its interest for us may rest more in the awareness of criticism as a slippery business. Once a textual variant is printed, however unreliable the source, it becomes a possible target for analysis, explanation, and adoption. What "the bard meant" can be extrapolated from almost any piece of "evidence," and then read backward into the text. That poetry should be a sleeping (or dreaming?) queen may not, at least to a modern reader, seem any odder than that it should be an oozing gum, or a worn gown.

IV

Of all Shakespeare's plays, it is not surprisingly *Hamlet* that seems to have provoked the most eager and earnest McGuffinism. I say "not surprisingly" because the themes of *Hamlet* are so relevant to this quest for source and certainty. Haunted by ghostly traces, itself a Hitchcockian thriller before the letter, *Hamlet* is also, perhaps most pertinently, a play about homology, about kin and kind, and about communication. The brilliance of the new Michael Almereyda film (in which Ophelia wears a wiretap, Rosencrantz and Guildenstern are heard over a speakerphone, Hamlet edits videos, the "sealed commission" commanding his death is found on a laptop, and the Player King's lines "our thoughts are ours" are read by real-life news anchor Robert McNeill from a scrolling teleprompter) stems in part from his perception that Shakespeare's *Hamlet* reflects a similar concern with technologies of performance and reproduction: the players, their acting styles, the "town crier" who mouths for the general populace, the letter, the signet-ring as stamp or signature, the ghost's injunction to remember, Hamlet's real or mimed note-taking ("my tables, meet it is I set it down"). Himself an inveterate punster, Hamlet stars in a play in which double meanings abound, and have made their way into the textual apparatus.

Let us consider a couple of brief examples before coming to the most obvious and fascinating McGuffin of them all.

Like the peacock, for instance. You may—or may not—remember him. His cameo appearance takes place in Act 3 scene 2, right after the play-within-the-play, when Hamlet is quoting, or rather misquoting, to Horatio a verse about the old king and the new king:

> For thou doest know, O Damon dear,
>   The realm dismantled was
> Of Jove himself, and now reigns here
>   A very, very—pajock. (3.2.275–8)

"This creature, otherwise unknown," writes Arden editor Harold Jenkins dryly, "first appears in this guise in F2 through what is presumably a modernized form of *paiocke* (Q2, F). It is usually taken to be a peacock." Editors have conjectured the omission of the missing letter *c*, and have urged the case of the peacock on substantive grounds: "The peacock's gross and lecherous reputation is held to make it an apt symbol for Claudius; it was said to break its mate's eggs and to swallow its own dung," and so forth.[20] Jenkins is dubious ("one may question whether so splendid a creature is altogether suitable for an antithesis to Jove and for the degree of disgust implied here") and notes, following the *Oxford English Dictionary*, that the word "peacock" is spelled correctly (no missing *c*) the five other times it appears in Shakespearean texts.

According to the indefatigable Ingleby, the nineteenth-century writer "Eden Warwick," (the pseudonym of George Jabet, the editor of *The Poet's Pleasaunce*, 1847, and of a volume called *Nasology:, or Hints Toward a Classification of Noses*, 1848), "proposed to substitute for Hamlet's *pajock* or *paiocke* the strange word *patokie*, a word he had coined expressly for the occasion, as a possible derivative of *patocco* or *patokoi*."[21]

It has been claimed that *paiocke* derives from an "alleged northern Scottish" form, *pea-jock*, meaning peacock. But "there seems no reason," says the *OED*, reasonably enough, "why Hamlet should here use a stray dialect word." Editor Jenkins therefore prefers *patchock*, "a contemptuous diminutive of *patch*," meaning clown, linking it to similar uses in Spenser, and also to Hamlet's later comment about "A king of shreds and patches" (3.4.103; it is Shakespeare, not W. S. Gilbert, who coins this phrase.)

Exit peacock. Except that, having been conjured up, it is hard to banish from our minds completely. Indeed productions that make Claudius into something of a popinjay may have the strutting peacock somewhere in mind.

As with the reigning "peacock," so with the notorious "sledded Polacks" or "sleaded pollax." Here the phrase is Horatio's, at the very beginning of the play, remembering—apparently from legend—Old Hamlet's warlike air:

> So frown'd he once, when in an angry parle
> He smote the sledded Polacks on the ice. (1.1.65–6)

The word is "pollax" in both the Quartos and the Folio, and is amended to "Poleaxe" in the Fourth Folio, "Pole-axe" by Nicholas Rowe, "Polack" by Pope, and "Polacks" by Edmund Malone.

Does the phrase refer to "inhabitants of Poland riding in sleds," or to a heavy weighted or studded weapon wielded by King Hamlet? Jenkins prefers the Polish invaders to the weapon. Why would Old Hamlet smite an axe on the ice if there were no threat: "if no Polanders and no sledges, why ice?" Poland and its king are mentioned elsewhere in the play (2.2.63; 75; 4.4.23) and the name of "Polonius" is in Jenkins' mind obliquely connected to this theme. But above all he finds the first scenario more stirring than the second: "what, along with the natural sense of *sledded*, gives the preference overwhelmingly to Poles in sleds as the object of [King Hamlet's] smiting is their power to stir the imagination, which a pole-axe so signally lacks."[22]

Leaving aside the comparative capacity of Poles and axes to stir the imagination, this seems reasonable enough. But having misconceived the travelling foes as a mighty weapon and thus conjured up the pole-axe, it is hard for some critics to give that weapon up completely: After all, axes, also known as "battle-axes" and "polaxes," were used by heroes in what *OED* calls "olden warfare." The word began as "poleaxe" (one word) and began to be spelled as two ("pole-axe") in the sixteenth century; by 1625 pole-ax was the usual spelling. (*OED* pole-axe, poleax.) And while "sleaded" does indeed mean "on sleds," or "sledges," there was also the "sledge," or sledge-hammer, which was wielded by both hands. Those who struck with sledge-hammers could be said to be of a different social class from King Hamlet (blacksmiths are often cited), but, for what it's worth, *sledge*, from *slegge*, *slaegge*, is derived from an old Danish word. Thus some critics have compared King Hamlet's ancient and primordial ax with the more sporting rapier of the civilized courtier sons, Laertes and young Hamlet.

The McGuffin effect here is a kind of mental fetish ("I know . . . but still . . ."). If we believe in the Poles on sleds, do we have to give up the battle axe or sledge-hammer as a regal accessory? Once this crux arises, it may be resolved, but not forgotten.

The Shakespearean texts are full of such cruxes, some famous, some infamous, and others oddly neglected. Consider for example, as a McGuffin not taken, the fascinating choice between a "pelican" and a "politician" in Act 4, scene 5 of *Hamlet*. Laertes has returned to Denmark, enraged at the murder of Polonius, and Claudius asks artfully whether in seeking vengeance for his father's death Laertes will distinguish between friends and foes. "To his good friends thus wide I'll ope my arms," replies Laertes,

> And, like the kind life-rend'ring pelican,
> Repast them with my blood. (4.5.146–7)

A modern editor (Jenkins) comments on the "pelican" image, a traditional figure: "the pelican feeds its young from its own breast, in some versions reviving them from seeming death," and notes that "the extravagance of the image here is no doubt meant to characterize Laertes's 'emphasis' and 'rant.'"[23] But in the Folio text the line reads

> To his good Friends, thus wide Ile ope my Armes:
> And like the kinde Life-rend'ring Politician,
> Repast them with my blood.

It has been conjectured that the compositor set *Policion*, which was then misidentified as a misprint and "corrected" to *Politician*.[24] The idea of a politician as self-sacrificing and life-rendering, then or now, has a certain counterintuitive charm, but there have been few if any champions of the Folio reading, although a "politician," or at least the rotted skull of one, does appear in the play in Act 5 scene 1.

V

Of all the editorial McGuffins in Shakespeare's most celebrated play, however, the most ardently sought in the last century of criticism have been the "dozen or sixteen lines" that Hamlet asks the players to insert in "The Murder of Gonzago"— his Mousetrap play.

> You could for a need study a speech of some dozen or sixteen lines, which I would set down and insert in't, could you not? (2.2.534–6)

The dozen or sixteen lines are a kind of model or template for McGuffin Shakespeare. Harold Jenkins observes in his Arden edition that "The voluminous attempts to locate the speech in the Gonzago play are only a degree less absurd than speculations about how the players came to have this play at all."[25] And it is also worth noting that, since the audience is unfamiliar with the text of *Gonzago*, neither they nor we can hear the crucial shift of tone that this supposed insert would supply. But this has not kept scholars and passionately motivated amateurs from trying to find them.

Indeed, needless to say, they have scoured the text of the play-within-the-play for the identity of these lines. The most recent to have "found" them is Harold Bloom, who, perhaps following his self-identification as Falstaff, discovers that the twelve or sixteen have become twenty-six, much as eleven buckram men grew out of two (Falstaff's buckram men are Shakespearean McGuffins, in fact). Here is Bloom's account:

> With a cunning subtler than any other dramatists before or since, Shakespeare does not let us be certain as to just which lines Hamlet himself has inserted in order to revise *The Murder of Gonzago* into *The Mousetrap*. Hamlet speaks of writing some twelve or sixteen lines, but we come to suspect that there are rather more, and that they include the extraordinary speech in which the Player King tells us that ethos is not the daemon, that character is not fate but accident, and that eros is the purest accident.

Bloom goes on to hypothesize that Shakespeare himself might have played not only the part of the Ghost but also that of the Player King: "There would be a marvelous twist to Shakespeare himself intoning lines that his Hamlet can be expected to have written."[26]

This is first-class McGuffinism: the missing lines are not only found but also connected, by an astounding feat of logic, to the double-presence of the playwright as author and actor. As if the conjecture about Shakespeare as Player King were further "proof" of the identification of the dozen or sixteen lines.

The phrase "dozen or sixteen" indicates that Hamlet is making an approximation; the word *dozen* is often used colloquially in the period to mean "a moderately large number." But critics and editors have tended to fixate on the numbers, whether or not they can actually locate them in the text. A. C. Bradley is so sure of the identity of the interpolated lines that he can tell us "only six are delivered." Thus he writes of

the "dozen or sixteen lines" with which Hamlet has furnished the player, and of which only six are delivered, because the King . . . rushes from the room.

And again

When only six of the "dozen or sixteen lines" have been spoken [the King] starts to his feet and rushes from the hall, followed by the whole dismayed Court.[27]

The speech to which he points is thus that of Lucianus, the murderer, who utters six portentous lines, in rhyming couplets, before [but in the Folio stage direction only] he "*pours the poison in the sleeper's ears*":

Thoughts black, hands apt, drugs fit, and time agreeing,
Confederate season, else no creature seeing,
Thou mixture rank, of midnight weeds collected,
With Hecate's ban thrice blasted, thrice infected,
Thy natural magic and dire property
On wholesome life usurps immediately.

John Dover Wilson notes "the vexed problem of the identification of Hamlet's inserted speech, over which much paper and ink have been expended." He too is quite sure he has identified the lines, and they are the same lines to which Bradley points:

The speech, as we have seen, was one of passion. . . . Moreover, it is the words of the murderer which cause Claudius to blanch, and there is therefore a strong presumption that they were Hamlet's contribution. . . . Last, they are the only words in the interlude which point directly at the crime of Claudius.

But in what sense have we "seen" that the speech was one of passion? We have seen it because Dover Wilson insists that Hamlet's advice to the players at the very beginning of this scene ("Speak the speech, I pray you, as I pronounced it to you, trippingly on the tongue . . ." [3.2.1–2]) was in fact about *this* speech, the interpolated dozen or sixteen lines added by Hamlet, lines that are given to the First Player and that Hamlet is eager for him not to overdramatize ("if you mouth it as many of your players do, I had as lief the town-crier spoke my lines"). Dover Wilson dismisses Granville-Barker's report that by theatrical tradition the First Player is given the part of the Player King, not that of the murderer Lucianus. "Hamlet expressly asks the First Player . . . to 'study' his inserted speech, which must, as I show, be the Lucianus speech."[28]

Dover Wilson calls the matter of the dozen or sixteen lines a "vexed problem"; Bradley had addressed himself to the task of identification as an important critical issue. And yet before the middle of the nineteenth century apparently no one worried much about this question at all.

It was the German critic E. H. (Eduard Wilhelm) Sievers, editing the play in 1851, who identified the lines in question for perhaps the first time, choosing the speech of Lucianus. Among English critics, the first to address the problem in print were the editors of the Cassell's Shakespeare (1864–68), Charles and Mary Cowden Clarke, who locate the passage added by Hamlet in the Player King's speech, at the point when the King responds to the Player Queen's vow that she will never remarry:

> I do believe you think what now you speak;
> But what we do determine, oft we break.
> Purpose is but the slave to memory,
> Of violent birth but poor validity,
> Which now, the fruit unripe, sticks on the tree,
> But fall unshaken when they mellow be.
> Most necessary 'tis that we forget
> To pay ourselves what to ourselves is debt.
> What to ourselves in passion we propose,
> The passion ending, doth the purpose lose.
> The violence of either grief or joy
> Their own enactures with themselves destroy.
> Where joy most revels grief doth most lament;
> Grief joys, joy grieves, on slender accident.
> This world is not for aye, nor 'tis not strange
> That even our loves should with our fortunes change,
> For 'tis a question left us yet to prove,
> Whether love lead fortune or else fortune love.
> The great man down, you mark his favorite flies;
> The poor advanc'd makes friends of enemies;
> And hitherto doth love on fortune tend;
> For who not needs shall never lack a friend,
> And who in want a hollow friend doth try
> Directly seasons him his enemy.
> But orderly to end where I begun,

> Our wills and fates do so contrary run
> That our devices still are overthrown:
> Our thoughts are ours, their ends none of our own.
> So think thou wilt no second husband wed,
> But die thy thoughts when thy first lord is dead.

The Clarkes believe that the added lines are those that go from the phrase "Purpose is but a slave to memory" to "Our thoughts are ours, their ends none of our own." This is a passage of some twenty-five lines—plainly they did not feel bound by a strict construction of "a dozen lines, or sixteen lines." And what is their reasoning in singling out this passage? The speech can be readily cut without disturbing the flow of the scene; without it the Player King says merely

> I do believe you think what now you speak;
> But what we do determine, oft we break. . . .
> So think thou wilt no second husband wed,
> But die thy thoughts when thy first lord is dead.

Thus offering a much briefer reply to his Queen, and one far more to the point.

Furthermore they say that the speech sounds like Hamlet, not like the rest of the play-within-a-play ("it is signally like Hamlet's own argumentative mode"). And why does he want this particular passage inserted—a passage that reflects on the changeableness of the world and of love, on the fickleness of fortune, and on the difficulty of fulfilling one's own purposes? Here is what the Clarkes have to say:

> "His motive in writing these additional lines for insertion, and getting the player to deliver them, we take to be *a desire that they shall serve to divert attention from the special passages directed at the king, and to make these latter seem less pointed.*[29] [emphasis added]

Thus the "dozen or sixteen lines" are a decoy, not a smoking gun; it is their innocuousness, not their pointedness, which singles them out as the intruders. Without them *The Murder of Gonzago* already points sufficiently at Claudius' guilt. Hamlet did not need to add anything to indicate the identity of the murderer, but rather needed to lull the King into a false sense of confidence and safety. This is subtle indeed. It is based upon a desire to find Hamlet himself—his consciousness, his thinking style, his "self"—even in the place where it might seem to be most unlikely, the voice of a Player King speaking in rhymed couplets in the play-within-the-play.

The Clarkes are not alone in this conjecture. In a lively interchange published by the New Shakespere Society in the year of its founding, 1874, two scholars debated the question, which had stirred up considerable interest among the members. History professor J. R. Seeley of Cambridge University, noting that "here is a Shakesperian problem which has been overlooked, that Shakespere evidently meant us to ask which the '12 or 16 lines' were, and that apparently no one (except Mr. and Mrs. C. Clarke) has thought of doing so," directed attention to the one speech in the play longer than twelve lines, the speech of the Player King, the only speech from which lines could be cut (and therefore the only speech into which lines might have been inserted). Like the Clarkes, he maintained that this speech "suits Hamlet's general character," and, more importantly, reflects his preoccupation with his mother ("it is this which really fills his mind"), but Seeley's central argument was that no other speech could satisfy the necessary conditions (be longer than twelve lines; be able to be cut without damage to the action). "No other such passage can be found in the sub-play," Seeley says with serene logic. "Those who reject this passage are driven to the shift of supposing that Shakespere after promising us such a passage and leading us to expect it has not given it."[30]

W. T. Malleson of University College London, in reply, insists that Hamlet's advice to the players—"speak *the speech*, I pray you, *as I pronounced it to you*"—leads one to expect that his interpolated lines will exhibit "the torrent, tempest, and whirlwind of passion," and asks, with incredulity, whether the reader can find "anything of passion, with which 'to split the ears of the groundlings,'" in the measured and philosophic lines of the Player King. No. For Malleson, as for others, the only speech that will do is the speech of the murderer, Lucianus. Indeed Malleson finds the parallel between the plot of *The Murder of Gonzago* and the death of old Hamlet so uncanny that he suspects "that Hamlet altered the manner of the murder in the old play to make it tally precisely with the awful secret fact. If not, it is strange that so odd, if not impossible a way of committing murder should have occurred in both the plays."[31]

On the objection raised by Seeley, that the speech of a dozen or sixteen lines described by Hamlet "must consist of some 12 or 16 lines," and that it must be enclosed in a speech even longer than that in order to be "inserted" as promised, Malleson dismisses this as "somewhat strained":

> Hamlet never says he *has written* a passage of so many lines and inserted it. If he had said so the matter would be simpler. We only know that he *intended to write* and insert some lines of the number of which he was not himself certain, "12 or 16." When he sat down with the play before him he may have written 20 or 26. . . .

And would they really have to have been plugged into a longer speech?

> may not Hamlet have inserted his lines in substitution for others which he struck out?[32]

asks Malleson rhetorically—a conjecture that Seeley, in rebuttal, calls "an unnatural interpretation of the words." Seeley's own interpretation is preoccupied with Hamlet's state of mind. He thinks *The Murder of Gonzago* probably needed no insertion to catch the conscience of the king—"the play did its own work." But as for Hamlet, the composition of additional lines is cathartic: Hamlet "thinks with great delight of the opportunity [the play] affords him of relieving himself of the weight of feeling that has been oppressing him so long by putting it into verse. He will write a poem on his mother, and insert it in the play. It may not have much effect upon her when she hears it; indeed, he probably knows too well already how unimpressionable she is; but his object will be gained if he only writes it, for it will be a relief to his feelings."[33]

I have been describing this debate as if it had only two participants, Mr. Malleson and Dr. Seeley, both, we might say, interested amateurs. But the protocols of the New Shakspere Society meant that the exchange was triangulated, in its published form, via the distinguished English scholar F. J. [Frederick James] Furnivall, the Society's founder and chair. Malleson read his paper at a meeting of the society; Seeley—whose views had been mentioned and refuted by Malleson—responded in a letter to Furnivall, Malleson offered a "rejoinder," and the whole discussion was published together with a response by Furnivall which, while printed in smaller type and single spaced as if to underscore its relative unimportance, in fact pulled rank, easily trumping the views of both the lay participants.

Furnivall felt that Seeley's view (the dozen or sixteen lines were part of the Player King's speech) was "technically" strong, but weak "on the merits." He was inclined to agree with Malleson that the lines Hamlet inserted were the ones he described to Horatio in Act 3 scene 2 as the "one speech" that would "unkennel" the King's "occulted guilt." "To me," he writes, "fair criticism requires the identification of the two." Before Malleson can congratulate himself on having won, however, Furnivall immediately proceeds to demolish his claim:

> But I hold very strongly that Lucianus's speech, "thoughts black," &c., is not this speech; and that, in fact, the speech is not in the printed play.

Why not? It is simply a matter of the playwright having rewritten as he went along.

> The inconsistency of Shakspere's having made Hamlet first talk so much about inserting one speech, and then having afterwards left it out, doesn't trouble me in the least. It's just what one might fairly expect in the recast *Hamlet*.

Perhaps, he says, Shakespeare found as he wrote the scene that the King's conscience was more quickly stung than Hamlet had anticipated, so that the written scene was never needed, or that Hamlet changed his plan, "and put his 'dozen or sixteen lines' into action instead of words." The fact that the play so exactly resembled the circumstances of the murder, rather than being, as Hamlet had at first said, "*something like* the murder of my father," meant that the lines would be superfluous. This inconsistency seems minor, thinks Furnivall, in comparison with the "really startling" inconsistencies on other matters, like Hamlet's age and Ophelia's suicide. And even about these, Furnivall is serene. On the question of Hamlet's age, the first and second halves of the play "*are* inconsistent," with a youthful Hamlet-as-lover at the beginning and a mature Hamlet-as-philosopher / mourner at the end.

"What matter? Who wants 'em made consistent by the modification of either part?" asked Furnivall briskly. "The 'thirty' is not in the first Quarto; yet no one wants to go back to that." (As I write this, many scholars and actors are in fact "going back" to the First Quarto as a lively, playable text with a legitimate claim to be Shakespeare's.) As for the dozen or sixteen lines, "what can it matter whether an actual speech of a dozen or sixteen lines, though often announct, is really in the play or not? The comparative insignificance of the point is shown by no one having noted it in print before Mr. and Mrs. Cowden Clarke."[34] Other members of the Shakespeare Society seemed to agree: "I think that there is no warrant for assuming that the lines announced by Hamlet are to be supposed to exist in the sub-play at all," wrote one, pointing out appositely that in other Elizabethan plays-within-the-play, like that in *A Midsummer Night's Dream*, there is no connection between the scene rehearsed (in Act 3 scene 1) and the play as ultimately performed. Likewise with *Histriomastix*, where the play of the *Prodigal Son* is read to the actors in an early scene, and is acted toward the end. "Not a passage in these two presentations of the same piece agrees." Thus the writer concluded, "I don't believe that the poet ever meant us to pick out a bit, and say, This is the plum contributed by Hamlet himself."[35] In fact this very modern-sounding solution, the idea that there were no dozen or sixteen lines to find, was one of the earliest conjectures put forward in the nineteenth century. "I do not see symptoms of the lines which Hamlet was to insert," comments Charles Bathurst in 1857.[36]

Indeed, yet another Victorian critic, entering into the debate, vehemently discounts the whole idea that there was any addition to be found. "Hamlet writes no speech at all, whether of six, twelve, or sixteen lines, nor recites such a speech; Shakespeare simply wrote the entire play, *not* writing any additions *in persona Hamleti*, still less writing an addition to a play which he had previously written in the character of the author of an Italian morality." So H. H. Furness summarizes the views of "my friend Dr. Ingleby."

Ingleby is that same C. M. Ingelby whom we have already encountered as a critic sometimes skeptical of "conjectural emendation" and at other times certain of what "Shakespeare undoubtedly wrote." Clement Mansfield Ingleby, the author of such works as *Shakespeare the Man and the Book*, *Shakespeare's Bones: The Proposal to Disinter*

Them, and *The Shakespeare Fabrications*, was a lawyer who had quit the law to give over his life to Shakespeare and philosophy.

According to Ingleby, Shakespeare had quite a different goal in mind from merely giving Hamlet opportunity to catch the conscience of the king by adding a few lines to *The Murder of Gonzago*. His purpose, in fact, had nothing to do with revenge. It was rather to make the play "a vehicle for the highest possible instruction in the art of elocution." He would "make Hamlet instruct the Player, and through him all players, how to act." But since it would hardly be plausible for Hamlet to tell the Player how to perform roles or scenes that were already part of his professional repertory (roles and scenes the Player would know far better than would Hamlet), Shakespeare invents the idea of the Prince writing "a speech of his own composition," about which he would be entitled to give instructions. The device of the "dozen or sixteen lines" was merely a pretext, in order to enable Shakespeare to achieve "his own object (kept wholly out of view)"—that is, "to prepare the audience for his own lesson (*voce Hamleti*) on elocution." As for the seemingly specific "dozen or sixteen," Furness insisted, it "does not mean what it says; it is even more indefinite than 'ten or a dozen' or 'a dozen or fourteen,' which Mrs. Quickly uses in *Henry V* II, I; the prefix 'some' adds vagueness to what was vague before. These lines, by the very nature of the case, can never have been in *Hamlet*."[37]

'Tis here. 'Tis here. 'Tis gone. From this perspective, the "dozen or sixteen lines" (or, according to the second Quarto, "*some* dozen lines or sixteen lines") are very like Poe's purloined letter: we can only see the outside, the fact of their supposed existence, not the interior, the actual and particular text. And they are also very like Žižek's understanding of the McGuffin: "'nothing at all,' an empty place, a pure pretext whose sole role is to set the story in motion."

VI

One of the most intriguing secondary issues attending upon this editorial scavenger hunt for the dozen or sixteen lines is what the quest does to Hamlet's famous advice to the players. As several scholars point out, the instruction that begins Act 3 scene 1,

Speak the speech, I pray you, as I pronounced it to you,

draws the actors—and the audience's—attention to *one speech*, as will Hamlet's later aside to Horatio ("If his occulted guilt / Do not itself unkennel in *one speech*" [3.1.80–1], emphasis added). Instructing the players, Hamlet emphasizes his own authorship: "if you mouth it as many of your players do, I had as lief the town-crier spoke *my lines*" (3.2.2.4). Thus this celebrated passage, the locus classicus of a doctrine of "natural" acting and of holding "the mirror up to nature," begins not as a piece of transcendent philosophy about theater's relationship to life, but as a highly particular piece of coached performance: "speak 'my lines,' the ones that I have written and inserted, the way I pronounced them to you when I read you the script." As Martin Dodsworth points out, "It is easy to stretch Hamlet's first-person in 'my lines' to include his author speaking through him." But this is to miss some of the crucial particularity of the scene. For Dodsworth the "immediate business of the episode" is to mark the difference between Hamlet and the actors, a difference of class: the aristocrat addressing his inferiors.[38] For other readers, especially those concerned or obsessed with the "dozen or sixteen lines," Hamlet's storied "advice" is actually pragmatic and instrumental: not pride of authorship or abstract theorizing, but the effectiveness of one key dramatic moment, is what is at stake.

The difference between a philosophical observation on verisimilitude in art and life, on the one hand, and a stratagem for putting across an interpolated set of lines, on the other, makes the "speak the speech" speech a performative crux. Is Hamlet functioning here as "Shakespeare" or as Hitchcock?

Insertions and enlargements of the text are, of course, the common practice of early modern dramaturgy. "The text in Q1," notes R. A. Foakes, "includes two comic additions, one in Hamlet's advice to the players and a second in mockery of Osric's perfume, that are not in Q2 or F, and presumably these were inserted for or by the players. . . . Playhouse interpolations, in the form of improvised jokes, dying O's, or whatever, deserve more consideration than to be simply dismissed as corruptions." But in the nature of things the acting version is often cut down, rather than enlarged, for reasons of time; it is the second Quarto, a "text for reading," that announces itself as "Newly imprinted and enlarged to almost as much again as it was, according to the true and perfect Coppie."[39] Recent attention to stage directions, extant or imputed, and speculation about the improvisation of pieces of stage business (from Kemp's jig to Hamlet's leaping in the grave) that subsequently became a conventional part of the play, have likewise emphasized the fact that there is always something "missing" and something "added" in the playtexts as we have them, something that escapes being pinned down and enshrined.

VII

Perhaps no version of the "dozen or sixteen lines" story is as uncannily revealing as the story of John Payne Collier, antiquarian, Shakespeare editor and bibliographer, and co-founder of the Shakespeare Society. Collier, who gained early fame with his *History of English Dramatic Poetry to the Time of Shakespeare* (1831), was an acquaintance of Keats, Coleridge, Hazlitt, and Lamb. He dedicated his *History* to the Duke of Devonshire, and was soon asked to look after the library at Devonshire House. Shortly after he was also welcomed by the Earl of Ellesmere to Bridgewater House, where a rich trove of Elizabethan manuscripts was to be found, many of them previously unexplored.

The diligent Collier explored them, to remarkable effect. He found previously undiscovered letters and other documents with new and sometimes startling information about Shakespeare's life. In his *New Facts Regarding the Life of Shakespeare* (1835), he thanks the noble Earl for letting him view the manuscripts: "if the example were followed by others possessed of similar relics, literary and historical information of great novelty and of high value might in many cases be obtained." Although he occasionally detected—and scrupulously corrected—some factual errors in these new documents, Collier's discoveries significantly enlarged, and changed, what was known about Shakespeare's life. In subsequent publications he was able to do the same for the works, discovering key if questionable information about previously unsuspected performances (a performance of *Othello* in 1602, for example, when the play is dated by scholars 1603–04), and previously unknown sources for the plays.

Collier's reputation blossomed. He became one of the best-known and most highly regarded Shakespeare editors of his time. With some scholarly friends he founded the Shakespeare Society in 1840. His biography of Shakespeare, published in 1844, explained the importance of the new factual and textual discoveries he had made. Then, in 1852, he announced an even more breathtaking discovery: a copy of the 1632 Second Folio of Shakespeare, inscribed with the name of one "Tho. Perkins," presumably the owner, which was full of marginal and textual annotations—thousands of them, in a handwriting dating to the 1630s.

How had the author of the annotations, who became known as the Old Corrector, come by his corrections? Collier speculated in print about whether it was from better manuscript sources, or from oral evidence—speeches heard in performance. In any case, this was fresh evidence that the Shakespeare text needed careful emendation to restore it to its original state. Moreover, it turned out that many of the suggestions that Collier as editor had proposed in his Shakespeare edition were confirmed and corroborated by the handwritten insertion of the Old Corrector in the

Perkins Folio. Collier himself marveled that in the volume he so fortuitously discovered many of "the conjectures of Pope, Theobald, Warburton and Hanmer are
remarkably confirmed." (He does not mention his own, which are conveniently proved
accurate by the same discovery.) In 1853 he published his *Notes and Emendations to
the Text of Shakespeare's Plays, from Early Manuscript Corrections in a Copy of the Folio,
1632.*

The problem was that Collier had apparently himself inserted these corrections,
just as he had forged the newly "discovered" documents in Bridgewater House. As
one critic later acerbically noted, there was an " extraordinary sympathy" between the
"Old Corrector" and Collier.[40] What Collier treats as "*coincident anticipations,*" wrote
Samuel Weller Singer, were in fact his own belated grafting: "it is not within the
doctrine of probabilities that two writers, at distant periods, without any communication or knowledge of each other, should in *hundreds of instances* coincide so exactly
as we find the major part of the corrections in Mr. Collier's volume do with the later
emendations, slowly elaborated by a succession of commentators, and many of them
far from obvious."[41]

Collier fought back. When he was attacked in a pamphlet called *Literary Cookery*
in 1855 he sued the author for libel, and swore in an affidavit that "I have not . . . to
the best of my knowledge and belief, inserted a single word, stop, sign, note, correction, alteration or emendation of the said original text of Shakespeare, which is not
a faithful copy of the said original manuscript, and which I do not believe to have been
written, as aforesaid, not long after the publication of the said folio copy of the year
1632."[42]

Meantime the Perkins Folio was itself proving elusive to scholars and literary
detectives; Collier put it in the library of the Duke of Devonshire, and for some time
it could not be produced to be examined by experts. Among other advantages, this
meant that he alone could publish the "emendations," and thus out-point his rival
editors at a time when there was a fierce contest among scholars to publish new
editions of Shakespeare. The arrangement was beneficial to both Collier's bank
account and his reputation.

But ultimately the Perkins Folio was shown to the Keeper of Manuscripts at the
British Museum, Sir Frederick Madden, who, troubled in mind, confided his doubts
to his private *Journal.* The ink corrections, it seemed, were retracings of insertions
initially made in pencil, and the "ink" was actually a kind of watercolor made to
resemble old writing. As Madden wrote in his diary, "These corrections are *most
certainly* in a modern hand, and from the extraordinary resemblance of the writing to
Mr. Collier's own hand (which I am well acquainted with) I am really fearful that I must
come to the astounding conclusion that Mr. C. is himself the fabricator of the notes!"[43]

One of Madden's assistants, Nicolas S. E. A. Hamilton, wrote to *The Times* on July 2, 1859, to declare the Perkins Folio a fraud: "I consider it positively established that the emendations, as they are called, of this folio copy of *Shakespeare* have been made within the present century." Collier's reputation plummeted. Other forgeries and fabrications in his publications were quickly alleged: he had invented "historical" documents and inserted them into the record.

And the chief agent in exposing the Shakespeare forgeries of John Payne Collier—which we have seen to be a much more extended version of the inserted "dozen or sixteen lines"—was none other than C. M. Ingleby, whose 1861 investigation, *A Complete View of the Shakespere Controversy, Concerning the Authenticity and Genuineness of the Manuscript Matter Affecting the Works and Biography of Shakspere, Published by Mr. J. Payne Collier as the Fruits of his Researches*,[44] was published with a facsimile frontispiece from Act 1 scene 4 of *Hamlet* taken from the Perkins Folio (Hamlet's apostrophe to the ghost on rewriting the "Table of [his] Memory," with the interjection "Oh Villaine, Villaine, smiling damned Villaine!") and an epigraph from De Quincey:

> Now, Reader, a falsehood *is* a falsehood, though uttered under circumstances of hurry and sudden trepidation; but certainly it becomes, though not more a falsehood, yet more criminally and hatefully a falsehood, when prepared from afar, and elaborately supported by fraud, and dovetailing into fraud, and having no palliation from pressure and haste.

Ingleby begins his examination of Collier by explaining, for members of the lay public, the state of the Shakespeare text: "Shakespere wrote for the boards, and not for the table. The Globe Theatre was his book; and his admirers used their ears and eyes conjointly in the perusal of his immortal dramas. He died, and made no sign indicative of a care for the preservation of his works as classics for posterity." Thus "we possess no authoritative text at all," and "the door is open to legitimate conjecture as to the readings to be adopted." Because of the corrupt state of the text, editors and conjectural critics "fell into the extreme of loose conjecture; they were more anxious to reform, than to understand."[45]

After some three hundred pages of specific textual and documentary evidence, lawyer Ingleby is ready to sum up his argument for the public, to whom he entrusts "the task of returning a verdict":

> Here then we have a case in which 30,000 manuscript notes, written on the vacant spaces of a copy of the second folio of Shakespere, are simulations of handwritings of the seventeenth century, and written sometimes on the top, sometimes by the side of half obliterated pencil marks and words—such pencillings being in almost every case instructions for the superposed, or at least after-written, ink corrections.

Moreover, the pencillings in "Mr. Collier's 'plain round English hand'" were the same as those on a number of supposedly genuine documents also supposedly discovered by Collier, and having a bearing "on the life and character of Shakspere."[46]

And this is what concerns Ingleby so deeply. "Shame to the perpetrator of that foul libel on the pure genius of Shakspere!" he writes about the fabrication of the Perkins notes. He deplores the incursions on the native tongue of "Gallicisms" and "(still worse) American slang, and the cant and shibboleth of professions and sects."

> The texts of Shakspere and of the English Bible have been justly regarded as the two river-heads of our vernacular English. . . . To the texts of Shakspere and of our Bible we must cleave, if we would save our language from deterioration. Yet it is one of these texts that a tasteless and incompetent peddler has attempted to corrupt throughout its wide and fertile extent.[47]

To reinforce his point Ingleby has recourse once again to a literary text, citing, in quotation marks but without attribution, some lines from Samuel Butler's satire *Hudibras*. Collier, he notes, had produced a letter supposedly written by the wife of the Elizabethan actor Edward Alleyn to her husband, in which she reports having seen "Mr. Shakespeare of the Globe"—a reference that Ingleby, among others, insists is a falsification. Collier had defended himself against this charge in his *Reply*, where he mentions "the charge that I interpolated a passage not met with in the original."[48] In forging this anecdotal reference to Shakespeare, says Ingleby, Collier "has contrived to

> find void places in the paper
> To steal in something to entrap her—
> or rather to entrap a confiding public in general, and the Shakspere
>   Society in particular."[49]

In fact these two lines from *Hudribras*, which appear in the final pages of Ingleby's *Complete View of the Shakspere Controversy* merely as an elegant embellishment to his lawyerly argument, suggest that somewhere in the back of his mind Ingleby may have himself made the connection with Hamlet's dozen or sixteen lines. For Butler's satirical instructions for ensnaring a wife, when viewed in context, allude glancingly both to the insertion of new text and to the "Mousetrap":

> And if she miss the Mousetrap-Lines,
> They'll serve for other By-Designs:
> And make an Artist understand,
> To Copy out her Seal, or Hand:
> Or find void places in the Paper,
> To steal in something to Intrap her.[50]

VIII

Forgery is on *someone's* mind in *Hamlet*, that's for sure. The elder statesmen of the play are obsessed with it—the word recurs in their speech. Here is the Ghost to Hamlet: "the whole ear of Denmark / Is by a forged process of my death / Rankly abus'd" (1.5.36–8). And Polonius to Reynaldo, about investigating the reputation of his son Laertes in Paris: "put on him / What forgeries you please" (2.1.19–20). And King Claudius on the mysterious and accomplished horseman of Normandy, Lamord: "So far he topp'd my thought / That I in forgery of shapes and tricks / Come short of what he did" (4.7.87–9). As for the forgeries we see, the forgeries of and by Hamlet himself, they become the plot of the "Mousetrap," the plot of political reversal, and the plot of the play. We may think once again of the key moment of forgery and substitution in *Hamlet*:

> I sat me down,
> Devis'd a new commission, wrote it fair—
> I once did hold it, as our statists do,
> A baseness to write fair, and labour'd much
> How to forget that learning, but, sir, now
> It did me yeoman's service. Wilt thou know
> Th'effect of what I wrote? . . .
>
> I had my father's signet in my purse,
> Which was the model of that Danish seal,
> Folded the writ up in the form of th'other,
> Subscrib'd it, gav't th'impression, plac'd it safely,
> The changeling never known. (5.2.31–7; 49–53)

For thirty years after the publication of Ingleby's *Complete View* John Collier lived on in disgrace as the most notorious and self-aggrandizing of Shakespeare forgers, although more than a hundred years later at least one recent biographer has sought to absolve Collier of blame.[51] But what is so curious about his saga is that whatever Collier's motives, of fame, fortune, or grandiosity, his story is a progress of sorts, for as he forges and fabricates, erases and invents, he moves from being an editor of Shakespeare to becoming Shakespeare himself. As he wrote late in life in his unpublished autobiographical memoirs,

> Nobody could deny the excellence of many of [the emendations], they have been gladly adopted since, and they were in fact the foundation of my second edition of 1858. . . . If the proposed emendations are not genuine, then I claim them as mine, and there I intend to leave the question without giving myself further trouble: anybody else is welcome to solve the enigma.—Good or bad, mine or not mine, no edition of Shakespeare, while the world stands,

can now be published without them: I brought them into life and light, and I am quite ready to be answerable for them.[52]

A few pages later he repeats this claim, and here, as one modern critic notes, he "brings himself to speak the forbidden word," although in the third person:

> If the emendations be forgeries how the inventor of them, if alive, must laugh at the ridiculous result of his unrejectable fabrications: they now form an essential part of every new edition of Shakespeare, and never hereafter can be omitted.[53]

The Collier forgeries bespeak a kind of truth. Hamlet is a forger. Collier's forgeries are a textual effect. "If the proposed emendations are not genuine, then I claim them as mine." His additions and emendations change the text to make it into the real thing, into "Shakespeare." Their "authenticity" is the authenticity of McGuffinism. What has been "lost" has been "found."

The quest for the missing—or masquerading—dozen or sixteen lines in *Hamlet*, a *mise en abyme* of textual studies, is, as we have seen, symptomatic both of a pair of linked desires: the desire to "fix" the Shakespearean text, and the desire to experience that "real meeting of minds with Shakespeare" so earnestly sought by readers, actors, and editors. (Recall that the phrase was editorial scholar Fredson Bowers', and was his highest praise for the eighteenth-century editor Lewis Theobald.) Indeed the ultimate "McGuffin" in Shakespeare studies is the Shakespeare authorship contro-versy, the open-ended quest for the "real" author of the plays, a plot pretext that enables us to fashion a Shakespeare in whatever image we desire. A "meeting of minds with Shakespeare" is the missing thing that everybody wants. As I have argued else-where, it is the existence of the authorship controversy that creates Shakespeare's authority.[54] Those who deplore the controversy are those who require it. The act of doubt generates certainty, increases the prestige of the author who needs to be defended against it. And this is also the case with the question of the Shakespeare forgeries. By demonizing the fake, scholars are able to deny, cover up, or repress any doubts about the existence of the real. The forger is in a way necessary in order to enhance the prestige of the authentic.

Fatal Cleopatra 13

Most women have no characters at all.

Alexander Pope, "Epistle to a Lady"

A person whose desires and impulses are his own—are the expression of his own nature, as it has been developed and modified by his own culture—is said to have a character. One whose desires and impulses are not his own, has no character, no more than a steam-engine has a character.

J. S. Mill, "On Liberty"

My topic is the character of Shakespeare's Cleopatra—or Shakespeare's Cleopatra as a character. By "character" here, we might mean dramatic character, or ethical character, or moral character. In the case of Cleopatra in particular but also of character in general, this is a daunting and perhaps even an impossible task.

"Much has been written about the characterization of Cleopatra," writes Frank Kermode. "On the ethical level she is irresponsible in every way—lubricious, cruel, self-regarding; but to ignore the divine attributes of this 'triple-turn'd whore' is to ignore the text." Cleopatra, concludes Kermode, "deserves to be called the greatest of Shakespeare's female characterizations."[1]

What is "character"? And can the study of Shakespeare help us to read it? The word *character*, like all the other treacherous touchstones in that quagmire we call "human nature," has two equal and opposite connotations. We say that a person *has* "character" when we find him, or her, morally admirable; we also say that someone *is* "a character" when he or she is odd, eccentric, or extraordinary.

As literary critics from the Renaissance to the twentieth century have delighted to point out, the etymology of the word *character* in English comes from engraving and handwriting. By the time of Shakespeare the word could mean a brand, a stamp, a graphic sign or symbol, writing and printing in general, the alphabet; or, by an extension in the direction of the figurative, a trait, a distinguishing feature, an essential peculiarity or nature, the face as an index of moral qualities within, and those moral qualities themselves. The use of the term "character" to describe the persons of a play, which we find completely commonplace today (as in "Hamlet is the main character in the play that bears his name") is in fact a mode that comes into practice *after* Shakespeare, and is itself apparently an extension of the idea of moral essence.

In Shakespeare's own time the "speech-prefixes" designating a particular actor's "part" were just that: indications of who was to speak the lines. In a number of cases the printed text gives the name of the *actor* rather than the fictional speaker, what we would call the "character." The line between so-called fiction and so-called reality was blurred. As it was, of course, in the material fact that boys played the parts of women on the English public stage. So the part or character of Cleopatra—to look ahead for a moment—would have been played by a boy: a fact that is famously acknowledged by Cleopatra herself late in the play, in a moment of high metadramatic risk, when she imagines herself brought back to Rome in triumph, where

> I shall see
> Some squeaking Cleopatra boy my greatness
> I'th' posture of a whore. (5.2.218–20)

What the original Shakespearean audience would have seen was some version of this very scenario: a boy actor speaking these lines, the extraordinary and "essential" femininity of Cleopatra, so remarked on by later critics, bodied forth by a young man whose voice had not yet changed, and who performed, onstage, the role of an Egyptian queen wrinkled deep in time, whom age could not wither or custom stale.

In any case, Shakespeare and his contemporaries would not have called such figures "characters" in the plays, but rather "persons," a word that derives, conveniently, from the mask worn by a player (*persona* = mask). The surviving Latin phrase, *dramatis personae*, persons of the drama, is less redundant now than it was then, since the word "person" has drifted in the intervening years from meaning "a character or personage acted" to an agent or a social actor, a human being acting in some capacity, and, in juridical terms, "a being having legal rights." But in Shakespeare we find, for example, an actor in the play-within-the play in *A Midsummer Night's Dream* being introduced as one who "comes . . . to present the person of Moonshine" (3.1.56–7). "Moonshine" is the name of the character (as we would say). But the word "character" itself, just to repeat, is never used by Shakespeare in this sense: *character* in his plays almost always means letters, handwriting, or sign, though the sign could sometimes be an indication of what later ages would come to call "character" ("his nose stands high, a character of honor," we hear of one of the knights in *The Two Noble Kinsmen* [4.2.110]).

When "character" does begin to emerge as a term for a fictive personage in a play, its connotations tend to be linked with distinct personal attributes and qualities. Thus Dryden, for example, repeatedly couples the word "character" to the word "humour" ("He may be allow'd sometimes to Err, who undertakes to move so many Characters and Humours as are requisite in a Play [*Rival Ladies*, Epistle Dedicatory, 1664]; "Besides Morose, there are at least 9 or 10 different Characters and humours in the *Silent Woman*" [*Essay on Dramatic Poesie*, 1668]). A "humor" in this sense was a mental disposition, the term itself traced to the theory of humors from medieval physiology. A character, then, was a type, not an ethical ideal.

The literary *genre* of the "character," which came into vogue in the years following Shakespeare, was that of the set-piece. Thus for example a series of eighty-two witty, satirical prose portraits of Jacobean types were published as *Characters* in a volume attributed to Sir Thomas Overbury, an English poet and essayist. Many of Overbury's "characters" were in fact written by playwrights—like John Webster and Thomas Dekker—and poets like John Donne. These "Characters" were forerunners to the essay, and give a vivid sense of the persons and mores of Jacobean society. Here are some examples of Overburian characters: "An Ignorant Glory-Hunter"; "A Fine Gentleman"; "A Braggadochio Welshman"; "A Roaring Boy"; "A Virtuous Widow"; "An Ordinary Widow." Overbury concludes his collection of "characters" with a short account of "What a Character Is," tracing the word to its Greek origin: "to ingrave, or make a deepe impression." Thus, he says, it was related both to letters of the alphabet and to "an Aegyptian hieroglyphic."[2] To this Aegyptian hieroglyphic, as might be expected, we shall want to return.

In France in the latter part of the seventeenth century Jean de La Bruyère wrote a set of *Characters* modeled after the fourth-century BCE character writer Theophrastus. La Bruyère selected a group of qualities, like dissimulation and flattery, and created a set of character portraits that illustrated those qualities, depicting social types from the Parisian court. The "characters," or "characteristics," of the age were held up for inspection, in portraits that could be aphoristically brief or deftly sketched. Of the first kind, we have, for example, these two aphorisms from his chapter "Of Women": "A handsome woman, who possesses also the qualities of a man of culture, is the most agreeable acquaintance a man can have, for she unites the merits of both sexes." And "We should judge of a woman without taking into account her shoes and headdress, and, almost as we measure a fish, from head to tail." Of the second kind of portrait, the brief narrative sketch, consider these from the chapter called "Of Fashion":

> A certain citizen loves building, and had a mansion erected so handsome, noble and splendid that no one can live in it. The proprietor is ashamed to occupy it, and as he cannot make up his mind to let it to a prince or a man of business, he retires to the garret, where he spends his life, whilst the suite of rooms and the inlaid floors are the prey of traveling Englishmen and Germans. . . . There is a continual knocking going on at these handsome doors, and all visitors ask to see the house, but none the master.

When a certain man tells him "that books are more instructive than travelling,

> and gives me to understand he has a library, I wish to see it. I call on this gentleman, and at the very foot of the stairs I almost faint with the smell of Russian leather bindings of his books. In vain he shouts in my ears, to encourage me, that they are all with gilt edges and hand-tooled, that they are the best editions, and he names some of them one after another, and that his library is full of them, except a few places painted so carefully that everybody takes them for shelves and real books, and is deceived. He also informs me that he never reads nor sets foot in this library, and now only accompanies me to oblige me. I thank him for his politeness, but feel as he does on the subject, and would not like to visit the tan-yard which he calls a library."

Or this:

> Iphis attends church, and sees there a new-fashioned shoe; he looks upon his own with a blush, and no longer believes he is well-dressed. He only comes to mass to show himself, but now he refuses to go out, and keeps his room all day on account of his foot . . . he sometimes rouges his face, but not very often, and does not do so habitually. In truth, he always wears breeches and a hat, but neither earrings nor a pearl necklace; therefore I have not given him a place in my chapter "Of Women."[3]

Although La Bruyère steadfastly denied that any of these composites was an image of a real person, the game of guessing the identities behind these portrait sketches became popular. So popular, and so risky, that it was many years before his friends succeeded in electing La Bruyère to the prestigious French Academy.

More recent examples of this kind of "character sketch" in words would be Baudelaire's dandy, flâneur, military man, and prostitute, from "The Painter of Modern Life,"[4] or even—in a variation that again will demonstrate the dangers and slippages of the word "character"—the "psychological types" of C. G. Jung, including the shadow, anima and animus, child, trickster, and self.[5]

In the modern theater a "character part" is not a redundancy, but a type of role; the ambivalence in which these roles are regarded may be seen in the way "character-acting" is compared to real or "legitimate" acting. "What is known as character acting has definitely established its supremacy in England upon the ruins of tragic art," wrote a contributor to the *Atheneum* in 1878, and a few years later *Stage* defined the terms: "By a 'character actor' is understood one who pourtrays individualities and eccentricities, as opposed to the legitimate actor who . . . endeavours to create the role as limned by the author."[6] Again the distinction is between the idiosyncratic and the ideal.

At about the same time Sigmund Freud developed a theory of "character-traits" and "character-types," for which he actually used some of Shakespeare's dramatic characters as models. This has had a curious effect upon our notion of universal types, since Freud, reading Shakespeare, promulgated some general theories of human character that post-Freudian readers have then identified *as* timeless and universal because they can be found in Shakespeare. To be clear: the normative, typical, and universal instincts on which Freud bases his theories of psychoanalysis are in fact taken from two kinds of case studies: his patients, many of them women, most drawn from the middle- and upper-middle classes in his native Vienna; and the fictional characters he singles out from his reading of literature. Thus Freud's essay "Some Character-Types Met With in Psychoanalytic Work" (1916) featured analyses of Richard III (to illustrate "The 'Exceptions'") and the Macbeths (to illustrate "Those Wrecked by Success"). Other essays featured figures from King Lear to Shylock to Hamlet, each considered as a human type. Theatrical metaphors would continue to be vital to Freud's readings of human character throughout his career. Thus, to give just one example among many, he describes the possible symptoms of neurosis as like the "members of a theatrical company. Each of them is regularly cast for his own stock role—hero, confidant, villain, and so on; but each of them will choose a different piece for his benefit performance."[7]

"Freud has been judged a fatalist about character, and with reason," wrote Philip Rieff in a book called *Freud: The Mind of the Moralist*. "His conception of human sickness *is* dramatic," Rieff writes, "for Freud sought to understand character precisely by the reversals embedded in it. As the greatest dramatists—Sophocles, Shakespeare, Ibsen—have pursued 'the problems of psychological responsibility with unrelenting rigor,'[8] so the great psychologist will pursue unrelentingly a dramatic understanding of character. Freud's dramaturgy is more technical than tragic. By showing that all character develops not in a straight line but through a series of crises by which certain attitudes or roles are exchanged, Freud exhibits at once the commonplace element in tragic character and the tragic element in everyday character."[9]

If we return for a moment to the question of engraving, stamping, or writing, we can locate and pinpoint the dissatisfactions that post-structuralist critics have expressed with the "character criticism" that emerged from nineteenth- and early twentieth-century approaches to Shakespeare. In order to have a stable notion of "character" in this older sense one needed to believe in essence, in depth, and in the unity or coherence of the person, or subject. Hamlet would behave in a certain way; Othello in a certain way. Each would express his character in his language as well as his actions. Thus early editors would, for example, occasionally reassign certain lines in the Shakespearean texts from the speaker indicated by the Folio or the Quarto to a more appropriate speaker, given their estimation of what would be "in character" or "out of character," uncharacteristic, for a given person in the drama. For example, Dr. Johnson suggests, following what he calls the "ingenious" suggestion of a "learned lady," that the line "Oh, horrible! Oh, horrible! most horrible!" in the middle of the Ghost's speech in *Hamlet* "seems to belong" not to the Ghost but to Hamlet himself, "in whose mouth is a proper and natural exclamation."[10] Even more indicatively, many editors have refused to believe that the sweet Miranda of *The Tempest* could be either cruel or vindictive toward Caliban. Not wanting to hear this innocent heroine address the island's native inhabitant in terms like "Abhorred slave, / Which any print of goodness wilt not take," a "savage," "a thing most brutish," or a member of a "vile race" (1.2.354–9), they have reassigned this speech—clearly given to Miranda in the Folio text—to her father, Prospero.[11]

But, recent critics and theorists have wondered, if the person, the subject, was "split," divided, internally *in*coherent or at war within himself or herself—if *this* was what could be called an aspect of "human nature"—was the concept of "character" even thinkable?[12] And if one also bore in mind that literary characters, and particularly dramatic characters, were only marks on paper, traces and clues, indications for the actor to perform (or indeed records of a particular actor's performance in the past), then what happened to the notion of "character"? Did it not become more like the cloud formation so mock-didactically expounded by Hamlet to Polonius ("Do you see yonder cloud that's almost in shape of a camel? . . . Methinks it is like a weasel . . . Or like a whale." "Very like a whale."[13]) Or, even more germanely, like the cloud formation to which Antony compares himself in Shakespeare's *Antony and Cleopatra*:

> Sometimes we see a cloud that's dragonish,
> A vapour sometime like a bear or lion,
> A towered citadel, a pendent rock,
> A forked mountain, or blue promontory
> With trees upon't that nod unto the world
> And mock our eyes with air. . . .
> That which is now a horse, even with a thought
> The rack dislimns and makes it indistinct
> As water is in water . . .

> now thy captain is
> Even such a body. Here I am Antony,
> Yet cannot hold this visible shape.[14]

In a briefer phrase, but one that is equally compelling, Antony also challenges the identity of Cleopatra when he finds himself betrayed by her in war: "What's her name since she was Cleopatra?" he asks bitterly. (She is and is not Cleopatra, just as, for Troilus, his unfaithful lover was, and was not, Cressida.) She is not, we might say, "herself"—at least in Antony's eyes—although to us this changeable creature might be said to be exactly who she "is."

To illustrate the problem further, let me quote an inadvertent gloss on Cleopatra's character, in the form of a malapropism or mis-speaking. The mis-speaker in this case is another dramatic character, in fact the very one who bears the name of mis-speaker, Mrs. Malaprop in Sheridan's play *The Rivals* (1775). Here is Mrs. Malaprop's famous phrase, which in the context of the play she used to describe her rebellious niece:

As headstrong as an allegory on the banks of the Nile.[15]

You can probably see why I would associate this phrase with Cleopatra. She is headstrong, she is on the banks of the Nile, and the malapropism in question—Mrs. Malaprop's substitution of "allegory" for "alligator"—makes it all too clear that Cleopatra herself is the stuff of legend, the repository of what Lucy Hughes-Hallet, in a fine book on the cultural trajectory of Cleopatra through the ages, called "histories, dreams, distortions."[16] In short, Cleopatra herself is an allegory. Not merely, and perhaps not ultimately, a historical personage, or even a dramatic character.

Yet Mrs. Malaprop makes, of course, not one but two mistakes, since if we replace her erroneous term "allegory" with its near-homonym, "alligator," we are still in trouble, geographically speaking. Alligators are found in the southern United States and also in China; a stuffed alligator skin hangs in the apothecary's shop in Shakespeare's *Romeo and Juliet*, where it may be used as a remedy in folk medicine. But the reptile of *Antony and Cleopatra*, the reptile associated with the river Nile and with the goddess Isis, is the crocodile (*crocodilus niloticus*), famous, among other things, for its artful weeping.

The fascinating phenomenon of "crocodile tears" had been described in Hakluyt's *Voyages* of 1565: "[The crocodile's] nature is ever when he would have his prey, to cry and sob like a christian body, to provoke them to come to him, and then he snatcheth at them." Spenser picked up this image and gave the crocodile's tears to the false Duessa (*Faerie Queene* 1.5.18–19):

> As when a wearie traueller that strayes
> By muddy shore of broad seuen-mouthed *Nile*,
> Vnweeting of the perillous wandring wayes,
> Doth meet a cruell craftie Crocodile,
> Which in false griefe hyding his harmfull guile,
> Doth weepe full sore, and sheddeth tender teares; . . .
>
> So wept *Duessa* vntill euentide

Shakespeare endowed the Duke of Gloucester in *King Henry VI, Part 2* with the twin aspects of crocodile and serpent that would surface again in the seductive Cleopatra:

> Gloucester's show
> Beguiles him, as the mournful crocodile
> With sorrow snares relenting passengers,
> Or as the snake, rolled in a flowering bank,
> With shining checkered slough doth sting a child
> That for the beauty thinks it excellent.[17]

In Nahum Tate's libretto for Purcell's *Dido and Aeneas* (1689), an angry Dido accuses her lover of perfidy:

> Thus on the fable banks of Nile
> Weeps the deceitful crocodile.

Since Purcell's opera was written to be performed by a girls' school, Aeneas would have been performed *en travestie*. Male and female, deceitful and crafty, the crocodile—rumored to be hermaphroditic and self-generating—was the perfect emblematic (and allegorical) figure for Cleopatra.

"What manner o' thing is your crocodile?" the drunken Lepidus asks Antony at an Egyptian banquet, and Antony's answer is something between a joke and a riddle:

> It is shaped, sir, like itself, and it is as broad as it hath breadth. It is just so high as it is, and moves with it own organs. It lives by that which nourisheth it, and the elements once out of it, it transmigrates. (2.7.42–6)

We could translate this as tautology or evasion: a crocodile is a crocodile, that is all you need to know. It isn't comparable to anything else. So also with Cleopatra, who "beggars all description," as Enobarbus feelingly announces, and who seems herself to be at once hyperbole and metaphor: "We cannot call her winds and waters sighs and tears; they are greater storms and tempests than almanacs can report."[18] Cleopatra is virtually impossible to describe, from the very beginning of the play. These lines are from Enobarbus' great speech in the second scene. The design of *Antony and Cleopatra* is to offer the audience, repeatedly, a series of set pieces describing the incomparable and indescribable lovers, against which their human (and actorly) avatars must strive to compete, and fail. Octavius testifies to the heroism of the absent Antony, Enobarbus to the inexpressible eroticism of Cleopatra at Cydnus. By the end of the play, of course, Cleopatra herself pronounces her own impossibility:

> I have nothing
> Of woman in me. Now from head to foot
> I am marble-constant. Now the fleeting moon
> No planet is of mine. (5.2.237–40)

"Nothing" and "no" are the key words here, the negation, against all odds, becoming a superlative. The crocodile, "the elements once out of it," transmigrates into allegory, or into an allegory of allegory.

"As headstrong as an allegory on the banks of the Nile." Mrs. Malaprop's famous, or infamous, line was remembered with fondness by, of all people, Louisa May Alcott, who put it into the mind of her alter ego Jo March in *Little Women*. Near the end of the novel Jo is on her own in New York City teaching children for a living and beginning her independent career as a writer. At a New Year's Eve masquerade she "rig[s] up as Mrs. Malaprop, and sailed in with a mask on," surprising the other residents, who did not dream that "the silent, haughty Miss March . . . could dance, and dress, and burst out into a 'nice derangement of epitaphs, like an allegory on the banks of the Nile.'"[19]

At the same party Jo's future husband, the German professor Frederick Bhaer, dresses up as "Nick Bottom," from *A Midsummer Night's Dream*. In fact the courtship of Jo by Professor Bhaer is accomplished to no small degree through the match-making mediation of Shakespeare. On New Year's Day he gives her "a fine Shakespeare," from his own collection, remarking that Shakespeare is the equivalent of an entire library:

> "You say often you wish a library; here I gif you one; for between these two lids (he meant covers) is many books in one. Read him well, and he will help you much; for the study of character in this book will help you to read it in the world, and paint it with your pen."[20]

Jo agrees, writing home to her family: "I thanked him as well as I could, and talk now about 'my library' as if I had a hundred books. I never knew how much there was in Shakespeare before." And here is the assessment of the novel's narrator: "I don't know whether the study of Shakespeare helped her to read character, or the natural instinct of a woman for what was honest, brave and strong; but while endowing her imaginary heroes with every perfection under the sun, Jo was discovering a live hero, who interested in spite of many human imperfections. Mr. Bhaer, in one of their conversations, had advised her to study simple, true, and lovely characters, wherever she found them, as good training for a writer; Jo took him at his word—for she coolly turned round and studied him."[21]

I have thus far been following the itinerary of the question of "character" linguistically and generically through its manifestation in the early modern and modern traditions. But obviously there is a prior, and crucially important, tradition to be reckoned with here, and that is the notion of "character" as it appears in Aristotle and is apprehended—or misapprehended—by his later readers. This is an issue of much dispute and debate, but the general issues for our purpose are fairly straightforward.

In the *Poetics* Aristotle claims that "characterisation" is the second-most important element in drama, after plot. "Character," he says, "is the element which reveals the nature of a moral choice" (Chapter 6).[22] As the translator and commentator Stephen Halliwell explains, "the main challenge for the modern reader is to grasp the great divide between what the *Poetics* understands by the concept [of character] and what we now commonly mean by it." For Aristotle associates character with "ethical purposes and dispositions," and not with "anything like the intricacies of personality or consciousness which more recent traditions of individualism and psychology have associated with the term." Yet, as Halliwell notes, and as we have seen, "character" in English once meant something closer to Aristotle's sense of the term than it does now. "It is interesting, for example, to learn how eighteenth-century Shakespeare criticism moves from a concern with consistency and morality in characterisation (two of Aristotle's own four requirements) to a more psychological approach to character."[23]

The dictum attributed to Heraclitus, "character for man is fate" or "a man's character is his fate" (*ethos anthropo daimon*), is often understood as the central tenet of Aristotelian tragedy. A classic example of this view can be found in Samuel Johnson's celebrated "Preface to Shakespeare," in which Shakespeare's genius is said to lie in his delineation of character:

> Shakespeare is above all writers, at least above all modern writers, the poet of nature; the poet that holds up to his readers a faithful mirrour of manners and of life. His characters are not modified by the customs of particular places, unpractised by the rest of the world; by the peculiarities of studies or professions, which can operate but upon small numbers; or by the accidents of transient fashions or temporary opinions: they are the genuine progeny of common humanity, such as the world will always supply, and observation will always find. His persons act and speak by the influence of those general passions and principles by which all minds are agitated, and the whole system of life is continued in motion. In the writings of other poets a character is too often an individual; in those of Shakespeare it is commonly a species.[24]

Let me repeat this resounding final sentence: "In the writings of other poets a character is too often an individual; in those of Shakespeare it is commonly a species."

This was the sentiment to which William Hazlitt took such exception, labeling Johnson's mode of understanding *didactic* rather than *dramatic*: he "found the general species or *didactic* form in Shakespeare's characters, which was all he sought or cared for; he did not find the individual traits, or the *dramatic* distinctions, which Shakespeare has engrafted on the general nature, because he felt no interest in them."

For Johnson, Shakespearean characters transcend the merely time-bound and the temporary. They are "the genuine progeny of common humanity, such as the world will always supply, and observation will always find." Thus they are exemplary, and, in the profoundest sense, ethical.

What did Johnson think of Shakespeare's Cleopatra, and the play in which she appears? "The play keeps curiosity always busy," he wrote when he edited it, "and the passions always interested." But the best part of the play was the action, he thought: "the power of delighting is derived principally from the frequent changes of the scene: for, except the feminine arts, some of which are too low, which distinguish Cleopatra, no character is very strongly discriminated."[25] So none of the characters of the play is especially striking except for Cleopatra, and she is distinguished particularly for her "low" feminine arts.

As Lucy Hughes-Hallet points out in her cultural history of Cleopatra, Shakespeare's own audience would have regarded the overmastering passion of the two lovers in this play as highly dangerous to political stability and order.[26] The romantic and post-romantic idealization of love and eroticism as the fullest expression of passionate selfhood is highly anachronistic when it comes to early modern England.

Over the years many of the play's detractors—and even many of its admirers—have found Shakespeare's Antony and Cleopatra—the characters, if not the play—immoral. In the preface to his revision, *All for Love, or the World Well Lost* (1678), John Dryden comments on the necessity of bringing the play to a tragic conclusion, citing "the excellency of the moral: for the chief persons represented were famous patterns of unlawful love; and their end accordingly, was unfortunate. . . . The crimes of love, which they both committed, were not occasioned by any necessity, or fatal ignorance, but were wholly voluntary; since our passions are, or ought to be, within our power."[27]

Three hundred years later the critic T. R. Henn noted that the play "raises certain moral issues which I was forced to consider, in a peculiar manner, early in my teaching career." It seems that a certain pupil ("admittedly from overseas") had threatened a lawsuit against those who had put the play on the required reading list, since it "was calculated to corrupt the mind and morals of any student who was forced, under duress of examinations, to read it."[28]

More typically, readers concerned with character have given the Egyptian queen her due as the embodiment of contradiction. Thus William Hazlitt, whose brief essay on *Antony and Cleopatra* in his *Characters of Shakespeare's Plays* focuses almost entirely on Cleopatra, remarks that

> The character of Cleopatra is a masterpiece. . . . She is voluptuous, ostentatious, conscious, boastful of her charms, haughty, tyrannical, fickle. The luxurious pomp and gorgeous extravagance of the Egyptian queen are displayed in all their force and luster. . . . She had great and unpardonable faults, but the grandeur of her death almost redeems them. She learns from the depth of despair the strength of her affections. She keeps her queen-like state in the last disgrace, and her sense of the pleasurable in the last moments of her life. She tastes a luxury in death.[29]

This romantic view of Cleopatra is still very much in force; it is not by accident that Hazlitt's sense of her paradoxical power and of the brilliance of her characterization is shared, as we have noted, by Frank Kermode.

"Many unpleasant things can be said of Cleopatra; and the more that are said, the more wonderful she appears." So declares A. C. Bradley, the great exponent of character criticism, writing—again it is not an accident—in the same years as Sigmund Freud. Bradley goes on to particularize her charms and flaws in a spirit very like that of the reluctantly admiring Enobarbus:

> The exercise of sexual attraction is the element of her life; and she has developed nature into a consummate art. . . . She lives for feeling. . . . Her body is exquisitely sensitive. . . . Some of her feelings are violent, and, unless for a purpose, she does not dream of restraining them. . . . It seems to us perfectly natural, nay, in a sense perfectly right, that her lover should be her slave, that her women should adore her and die with her; that Enobarbus . . . who opposes her wishes and braves her anger, should talk of her with rapture and feel no bitterness toward her. . . . That which makes her wonderful and sovereign laughs at definition.[30]

In a footnote that is significant both as a marker of the taste of his time and as an index of its difference from ours, Bradley compares the superlatively bad Cleopatra to the Shakespearean female character he regards as the best of the "'good' heroines," Imogen in *Cymbeline*, quoting with approval Swinburne's verdict that Imogen is "the woman above all Shakespeare's women"—a view that, as Bradley says, is shared by "so many readers" in his day.

Who in our day, less than a hundred years after this confident assertion, would say that Imogen is the apogee of Shakespearean womanhood? How many of today's readers and theater-goers will even recognize her name? Let this stand for us as a humbling reminder that aesthetic and cultural values are of an age and not for all time. But Cleopatra, the serpent of old Nile, wrinkled deep in time, seems to give this temporal relativism the lie. Swinburne himself had called her "the perfect and everlasting woman," and had described *Antony and Cleopatra* as "the greatest love-poem of all time."[31]

It is highly symptomatic of the problem of Cleopatra's "character" that, faced with the necessity of describing it, many twentieth-century commentators have wound up doing something else. Whenever they think they are talking about character, they are really talking about style.

The Problem of Style was the title that J. M. Murry chose for his lecture series, delivered at Oxford in 1921. "The highest style," he insists, "is that wherein the two current meanings of the word blend: it is a combination of the maximum of personality with the maximum of impersonality; on the one hand it is a concentration of peculiar and personal emotion, on the other it is a complete projection of this personal emotion into the created thing." And what does Murry offer as an example of "the style that is the very pinnacle of the pyramid of art"? The scene of the death of Cleopatra.

> Give me my robe. Put on my crown. I have
> Immortal longings in me. (5.2.279–80)

In four packed pages Murry analyses this scene between the queen and her attendant Charmian, its management of grand style and simple style, simile and metaphor. As he points out, "Cleopatra's [words] are not those of a queen, nor are they, in reality, those of a lover. A dying woman does not use such figures of speech; and at the pinnacle of her complex emotion, a Cleopatra would have no language to express it." And yet "in the death scene of Cleopatra [Shakespeare] achieves the miracle: he makes the language completely adequate to the emotion and yet keeps it simple. The emotion is, to the last drop, *expressed*." The achievement is that of "the highest genius and the finest style."[32]

Murry, the great rival of T. S. Eliot as the premier reviewer and essayist of his day, is pretty clearly thinking of Eliot, both in his remarks on "the maximum of personality" and the "maximum of impersonality," and in his description of the death scene's language as "completely adequate to the emotion," an emotion which is "to the last drop, *expressed*." In contradistinction to Eliot's Hamlet, who "is dominated by an emotion which is inexpressible, because it is in *excess* of the facts as they appear," Murry's Cleopatra finds what Eliot famously called in the "Hamlet" essay an "objective correlative": "a set of objects, a situation, a chain of events which shall be the formula of that *particular* emotion; such that when the external facts, which must terminate in sensory experience, are given, the emotion is immediately evoked."

Murry's word "adequate" (in the death of Cleopatra Shakespeare "makes the language completely adequate to the emotion") is likewise borrowed from Eliot's essay of two years before, the essay in which Eliot boldly declared *Hamlet* (the play) to be an "artistic failure." "The artistic 'inevitability,'" Eliot had written, "lies in this complete adequacy of the external to the emotion." This was, he thought, "what is deficient in *Hamlet*."[33]

By claiming to find this "complete adequacy" (the word "complete," as well as "adequate," taken from Eliot's celebrated formulation) in Cleopatra, where Eliot had found it lacking in Hamlet, Murry trumps his rival while paying him homage. In fact Murry's Cleopatra not only *finds* what Eliot famously called in the "Hamlet" essay an "objective correlative," she *is* for him that objective correlative, emotion perfectly embodied, perfectly simulated, through language.

For the late twentieth-century critic Rosalie Colie, Cleopatra was an aspect of *rhetorical* style. Colie observed that both of the major characters in the play are constantly linked with hyperbole—in fact, with a hyper-hyperbole. They "demand a language for their love which rejects conventional hyperbole and invents and creates new overstatements, new forms of overstatement. . . . Nothing is enough for these two, not even the most extravagant figures of speech." ("Eternity was in our lips, and eyes"; "His legs bestrid the ocean, his rear'd arm / Crested the world"; "Age cannot wither her, nor custom stale / Her infinite variety.") Their style, says Colie, "*must* in honesty be bombastic," testing the boundaries between sublimity and bombast. In the end Shakespeare "manages to show us," through what Colie calls "the *ping* and *pong* of plain and grandiloquent styles," the "problem and the problematics, in moral as in literary terms, at the heart of style."[34]

I want now to introduce into evidence a passage from A. C. Bradley's first lecture on Shakespearean tragedy. Part of my objective in these remarks, and part of my pleasure in working on this topic, has been to bring back into prominence some of these once-central voices in Shakespeare studies, especially those who have fallen out of favor or undergone some critique in the past few decades. So I hope you will forgive me if I quote a longish passage here; it is the rhetorical power as well as the content to which I want to draw your attention. Here Bradley is talking about Shakespeare's creation of character, and especially about his finest achievements in that mode:

> His tragic characters are made of the stuff we find within ourselves and within the persons who surround them. But, by an intensification of the life which they share with others, they are raised above them; and the greatest are raised so far that, if we fully realize all that is implied in their works and actions, we become conscious that in real life we have known scarcely anyone resembling them. Some, like Hamlet and Cleopatra, have genius. . . . In almost all we observe a marked one-sidedness, pre-disposition in some particular direction; a total incapacity, in certain circumstances, of resisting the force which draws in this direction; a fatal tendency to identify the whole being with one interest, object, passion, or habit of mind. This, it would seem, is, for Shakespeare, the fundamental tragic trait . . . It is a fatal gift, but it carries with it a touch of greatness; and when there is joined to it nobility of mind, or genius, or immense force, we realise the full power and reach of the soul, and the conflict which it engages acquires that magnitude which stirs not only sympathy and pity, but admiration, terror, and awe.[35]

There are two things in this passage to which I want to draw your attention: first, that Bradley singles out Cleopatra, alone with Hamlet, as a Shakespearean character who in his view has "genius." Implicitly Middleton Murry did the same, in juxtaposing the "competely adequate" Cleopatra to Eliot's emotionally inadequate Hamlet. G. Wilson Knight would make a similar comparison between these two figures a few years later, calling Cleopatra "Shakespeare's most amazing and dazzling single personification," and claiming that she has "far more than Hamlet, all qualities potential in her." She is not one character but many: "She is at once Rosalind, Beatrice, Ophelia, Gertrude, Cressida, Desdemona, Cordelia, and Lady Macbeth."[36]

The second thing I want to point out in the passage from Bradley is that twice in this passage he has recourse to the word "fatal." "A *fatal* tendency to identify the whole being with one interest, object, passion, or habit of mind." "A *fatal* gift," which yet "carries with it a touch of greatness." *Fatal* here is of course related to the problematic word "fate," to which Bradley will shortly turn, and about which he expresses some fine interpretative doubt that is often ignored by his less careful readers.[37] We have already heard Freud described as a "fatalist" when it comes to character. But this notion of the fatal tendency and the fatal gift, especially in a passage that begins with such high praise of the character of Cleopatra, may lead us back usefully and provocatively to the opinions of Doctor Johnson.

Here then is another, equally famous passage from Samuel Johnson's "Preface to Shakespeare," in which Johnson discusses not Shakespearean character delineation, of which he so profoundly approves, but Shakespearean wordplay, which he deplores:

> A quibble was to Shakespeare, what luminous vapours are to the traveler; he follows it at all adventures, it is sure to lead him out of his way, and sure to engulf him in the mire. It has some malignant power over his mind, and its fascinations are irresistible. Whatever be the dignity or profundity of his disquisition, whether he be enlarging knowledge or exalting affection, whether he be amusing attention with incidents, or enchaining it in suspense, let but a quibble spring up before him, and he leaves his work unfinished. A quibble is the golden apple for which he will always turn aside from his career, or stoop from his elevation. A quibble, poor and barren as it is, gave him such delight, that he was content to purchase it, by the sacrifice of reason, propriety, and truth. A quibble was to him the fatal Cleopatra for which he lost the world, and was content to lose it.[38]

In this celebrated complaint Johnson, the Shakespeare editor, lexicographer, and moralist, performs a striking pair of critical moves. First he evokes for us a vivid portrait of Shakespeare as thinker and writer, distracted from the proper pursuit of his craft by language, and specifically by what he calls a "quibble," and what we would today call a pun, a piece of wordplay, or a double meaning. The quibble is described in turn as a luminous vapour, a golden apple like the ones that distracted Atalanta from her "career," and a "fatal Cleopatra for which he lost the world, and was content to lose it." This last is surely a reference to Antony (both the Antony of Shakespeare's *Antony and Cleopatra*, and the Antony of Dryden's 1678 adaptation, *All For Love, or The World Well Lost*). This is the first move, culminating in the tacit syllogism "a quibble was to Shakespeare as Cleopatra was to Antony." What do these have in common? Both are "fatal"—distracting, delighting, enchanting. They seduce a man away from the proper pursuit of "reason, propriety, and truth."

So what then is the second move? It is what might be termed recursive, turning back upon itself. For Johnson is himself, as I have already noted, a celebrated editor of Shakespeare. The passage appears in his "Preface," where he undertakes to explain and justify his editorial principles and practice.

Let us return for a moment to the mention of the "luminous vapour" that lures the traveler astray. There is a Latin name for this vapor: *ignis fatuus*. A phosphorescent light that is seen to hover or flit over marshy ground, and that often seemed to recede as the traveler approached, or to vanish and reappear in another direction. It was thus believed by some to be the work of a mischievous sprite. Over time *ignis fatuus* came to mean, more generally, a thing—or in rare cases a person—that deludes or misleads, or a false or foolish hope or goal. But it began as something literal, something empirical or "real." In earlier days the *ignis fatuus*, literally "foolish fire" rising from the marshes, was apparently a fairly common phenomenon, which is one reason that it was given folk names as well as its Latin name. Among those names were *Jack-a-lantern* and *Will-o'-the-wisp*.

Will-o'-the-wisp. A name also associated with "Robin Goodfellow," the other name for Shakespeare's Puck. The *Will* in Will-o'-the-wisp is the abbreviation for William, and means "anyone," or "someone," or "some fellow." But in the context of Dr. Johnson's metaphor, Dr. Johnson's figure of speech, this Will-o'-the-wisp, described merely as "luminous vapours" but clearly identical to the *ignis fatuus*, is an alter ego for the playwright Will, who often quibbles on his own name in his sonnets. "A quibble was to Shakespeare, what luminous vapours are to the traveler; he follows it at all adventures, it is sure to lead him out of his way, and sure to engulf him in the mire." In other words, at the core of this figure for Johnson is a buried pun, the pun on Will, as in William Shakespeare, and Will, as in Will-o'-the-wisp.

Johnson is performing the very act he deplores in Shakespeare. He is making a pun, or a quibble, although I think it is almost surely an unconscious one (which does not make it less a quibble . . .). Furthermore, the hidden Will (the Will-o'-the-wisp) in the "luminous vapours" are what is leading *Dr. Johnson* astray, down the path of the quibble: *his* Will-o'-the-wisp, we could say, is Shakespeare.

The fatal Cleopatra for Johnson, in short, is the duplicity of language. Figure itself, the doubleness of meaning. This is not, of course, a bad description of Cleopatra herself, Cleopatra the "character." It is her figural function, her function as a figure of speech, that most accurately describes her "character." Antony calls her a "wrangling queen / Whom everything becomes . . ." (1.1.49–50). Enobarbus reports that "For her own person, / It beggared all description" (2.2.207–8), that "she did make defect perfection" (2.2.241), and that "she makes hungry / Where most she satisfies; for vilest things / Become themselves in her" (2.2.247–9). Cleopatra, in short, is a walking textbook of rhetorical figures, from *occupatio* to *paradox*, from *hyperbole* to *enigma*. Above all, she and Antony constitute a "mutual pair" which, like a similar pair in Shakespeare's lyric poem, "The Phoenix and Turtle," ("co-supremes and stars of love") seem to be emblems of metaphor itself.

> So they loved as love in twain
> Had the essence but in one,
> Two distincts, division none;
> Number there in love was slain.

And again,

> Single nature's double name,
> Neither two nor one was called.[39]

Commenting on the question of stylistic *decorum*, or what he translated into English as "decencie," George Puttenham the great Renaissance compiler and theorist of rhetorical terms, had observed in *The Arte of English Poesie* (1589) that "figures" are "transgressions of our dayly speech," and that "writing is no more than the image or character of speech."[40] "Character" here is used in the sense of transcription, the written version of the spoken word. But of course it is impossible, either in a written text or in a dramatic text intended to be performed, to separate the question of rhetoric or style from the question of character.

If character for mankind is fate, so fatality is in part an artifact of language. The central pun of *Antony and Cleopatra*, the familiar Renaissance pun on death and dying, which meant both to experience sexual climax and to reach the end of life, establishes the notion of the fatal at the heart of the play. Should Cleopatra learn of Antony's plan to leave Egypt, quips Enobarbus to his master in an early scene, she "dies instantly. I have seen her die twenty times upon far poorer moment. I do think there is mettle in death which commits some loving act upon her, she hath such a celerity in dying" (1.2.148–51). Later we will hear Antony call out to her (in her allegorical person as queen), "I am dying, Egypt, dying," as she pulls him up to her monument. "Die when thou has lived; / Quicken with kissing," she implores him (4.15.39–43). By embodying the paradoxes and slippages and transgressions of wordplay, the character of Cleopatra, whom everything becomes, becomes precisely the "fatal Cleopatra" of Johnson's edgy warning. She *is* a living pun. Her decorum lies in her indecorousness, or what Puttenham called "indecency." Not in moral terms, but in the terms of style.

Cleopatra the paradox, who makes hungry where most she satisfies, who is according to Antony "cunning past man's thought," at once a goddess and a "triple-turn'd whore," constantly turning and troping herself into new figures, new characterizations, new "characters." Cleopatra is a figure of speech, a figure *for* speech, a living emblem of the relation between language and character, character and style. Or, to recall that phrase from Thomas Overbury's definition of character, "an Aegyptian hieroglyphic."

If a quibble was to Shakespeare the fatal Cleopatra for which he lost the world, we may think that it was a world well lost. But since the plays are not only sublime pieces of poetry but brilliantly imagined theatrical vehicles, constantly aware of their own mediation between page and stage, perhaps we should remind ourselves of that other piece of wordplay that marked the sign of Shakespeare's own theater, the "Globe" which for him meant both stage and world. In this case the world is not only lost, but also found: made possible by the enchanting infidelity of language, the inevitability of encountering, whether or not you are hunting for one, an allegory on the banks of the Nile.

What Did
Shakespeare Invent? 14

Author's note: A few years ago I was asked by the Shakespeare Association of America to speak on a panel with the provocative title, "What DID Shakespeare Invent?"[1] The remarks below retain the informal presentational tone of that public talk. The title of the panel, which I deliberately adopted (and adapted) for my own purposes, owed a manifest debt to the subtitle of Harold Bloom's book, Shakespeare: The Invention of the Human.[2] *As will be clear, I used the occasion to query not only the symptomatic romance of "Shakespeare" in our time, but also the significance of the contemporary quest for origins. The logic of what follows is that of hysteron proteron, the present producing the past.*

Thou that beget'st him that did thee beget.

Pericles, 5.1

What did Shakespeare invent?

First pass: "Shakespeare." Not only the familiar trajectory from bardolatry to theme park logo and all-purpose secular pundit, but also "Shakespeare" as a set university topic, a canonical place-holder, a way of imagining an entire educational field. Thus,

Second pass: "English studies." The concept of the "major author," the fantasy of literature as the study of other minds. Thus also, incidentally, "the SAA" and other gatherings for which "Shakespeare" is centerpiece, mouthpiece, and piece de resistance. Not incidentally, therefore,

Third pass: "Harold Bloom." The idea of the omniscient literary-critic-thinker-through-literature who is authorized, by his calling, to pronounce likes and dislikes as doxa and doxies. Certainly, therefore,

Fourth pass: "romantic love." Falsely ascribed to the Petrarchists and the Arthurians and others who dally with the possible/impossible obstacles of "she is a virgin," "she is married," "she is dead;" "she is he." Perhaps the key term here should not be "romantic love" but "young love" and "marriage for love." Here I do not mean to appropriate all the "invention of childhood" discourse, but rather to recognize "Romeo-and-Juliet" as a major cultural instantiation. Finally, and most obviously,

Fifth pass: "the movies." Note the ubiquitous claim, since Walter Benjamin, that Shakespeare would have written for the screen rather than the stage if he had been born in the twentieth century (perhaps with *Romeo-and-Juliet* necking in the balcony).

Thus Shakespeare, having invented "Shakespeare" and therefore "English studies" and therefore a critic like Bloom and the notion of doomed adolescent romantic love, winds up inventing *cultural studies*, *new media*, and *interdisciplinarity* —in other words, all the newfangled forms of cultural attention that have posed challenges to the place of English studies, and, perhaps inevitably, to the place of Shakespeare, or, at least, "Shakespeare," in the curriculum of intellectual life.

Shakespeare could also, incidentally, be said to have invented literary jargon. The list of words supposedly "coined by Shakespeare"[3]—including such terms as *watchdog, skim milk, assassination, eyeball* and *birthplace*—not to mention *critic, cold-blooded*, and *undervalue*—are largely changes in linguistic function (the turning of nouns into verbs (*film* as a verb—"skin and *film* the ulcerous place"), verbs into nouns ("if the *assassination* could trammel up the consequence"); names into adjectives and nouns—*Promethean, pander*). Thus Shakespeare could be properly imagined as the precursor of contemporary academic jargon, the foster father of words like *problematize, reference* (as a verb), *agency, subjectivity*, and of course all adjectives based on the names of critics, philosophers and other famous people: *Foucaldian, Deleuzian*, Emersonian, Shakespearean.

All these Shakespearean inventions are, in a way, a sign of Shakespeare under erasure. The crossed-out term, Shakespeare, is an old word put in question: "To make a new word is to run the risk of forgetting the problem or believing it solved."[4] The sign ~~Shakespeare~~ shows "an ineluctable nostalgia for presence" or the "mark of the absence of a presence, . . . the lack at the origin that is the condition of thought and experience."[5] Shakespeare the inventor is an overcompensation for a lack at the origin.

But if everything from romantic love to literary jargon can be said to be invented by something, or someone, we have learned to call "Shakespeare,"

What *didn't* Shakespeare invent?

Here the list is equally easy to generate.

- The "Shakespearean sonnet," three quatrains and a couplet, imported into English verse by Wyatt and Surrey.

- *Shakespearean* as a word of intensification, conferring sublimity at the level of journalism: an event of "Shakespearean proportions." As in this fairly typical example from the daily press: "The long unsolved murder of the Manhattan multimillionaire R. Theodore Ammon has at times been likened to a Shakespearean drama, a five-act tragedy set on Long Island and layered with death, sex, incredible wealth and a purloined urn of human ashes."[6]

- And of course, "the human." That Shakespeare did not invent "the human" was a point strongly argued by various literary critics long before Harold Bloom, or his editor, put that phrase in his book's subtitle. Of course scholars at that time were a little shy of using a phrase so unabashedly humanistic as "the human"—as I've argued in another place, humanists gave up on a term like "human nature," the long-time preoccupation of poetry and philosophy, just as it was becoming a hot topic in evolutionary biology and neuroscience, thus ceding the front-pages (and the best-seller lists) to the likes of Jared Diamond and Stephen Pinker.[7] No, no. Our word for "human" was "subjectivity," a word passed through the alembic of French theory. Initially there was a good reason to make this defamiliarizing shift away from "the human," or the "self," as Barbara Johnson explains:

> The concept of "self" is closely tied to the notion of property. I speak of "my" self. In the English tradition, the notions of "self" and "property" are inseparable from the notion of "rights." . . . The French tradition, derived most importantly from Descartes' "I think therefore I am," centers on the importance of reason or thought as the foundation of the (human) being. Where the "self" as property, resembles a thing, the "subject," as reason, resembles a grammatical function . . . And in the sentence, "I think, *therefore* I am," what is posited is that it is *thinking* that gives the subject being.[8]

But, as Johnson went on to report, Jacques Lacan, following Freud, translated the *cogito* in a way that reflected the *disjunction* between human thinking and human being: "I think where I am not, therefore I am where I do not think . . . I am not wherever I am the plaything of my thought; I think of what I am where I do not think to think."[9] The term "subject" was given further concreteness by Foucault, from whom many contemporary literary critics derive their use of the word, since Foucault's interest in the double notion of "discipline" and disciplinary suggested that—to quote Johnson's typically lucid formulation—"on some level the very definition of the 'human' at any given time is produced by the working of a complex system of 'imprisonments.'" Far from being an autonomous, rational entity who thinks in isolation, the human 'subject' is a function of what a given society defines as thinkable."[10]

Human or subject, Shakespeare did not invent it. There was a time ten and twenty years ago—we could call it BB, "before Bloom"— when it was not uncommon for literary critics to talk about Hamlet, the character and the play, in connection with the supposed "invention of subjectivity"—or, as it was sometimes named, "modernity." Hamlet certainly exemplified Lacan's thought-teaser: "I think where I am not, therefore I am where I do not think....I am not wherever I am the plaything of my thought; I think of what I am where I do not think to think." The idea that Hamlet somehow signaled the founding moment of modernity and subjectivity became the target of powerful, erudite, and often sardonic critiques from medievalists, and, indeed, from scholars of the Greek and Roman classics.

Lee Patterson, in a compelling and astringent account, put in question the work of a number of Renaissance critics who had made claims for an epistemological break between their period and the supposedly "pre-bourgeois" middle ages, citing, among others, Terry Eagleton, who had suggested that "Hamlet represents 'the beginning of the dissolution of the old feudalist subject.'" Patterson noted that the idea that Hamlet "expresses our modernity" was a view also commonly held by A.C. Bradley and T.S. Eliot, and cites the medieval scholar David Aers as proposing—in a book published in 1988—that it was time for "a self denying ordinance on claims about the new 'construction of the subject' and its causes in allegedly new features of the sixteenth century.'"[11] I will just mention in passing that the works of criticism that provoked this response in medievalists—and produced as Patterson intended, a shift in how medieval studies refitted itself for postmodern readers, and repositioned itself within English departments—these works of Renaissance scholarship and theory dated from the 1970s and 1980s. By the time Shakespeare was being proclaimed to have invented the human in bookstores all over America, this proposition—and the historical, cultural, and theoretical assumptions that had generated such a wish for origins—had been pretty fully debated, discussed, embraced and resisted, by scholars across time periods and across the theoretical spectrum.

But this time lag is perhaps symptomatic of a larger problem. It is not only that Bloom firmly decline to read the works of most living Shakespeare scholars (not to mention living medievalists). It is rather that the idea of *invention* is so seductive. We are still stuck on origins, still looking for that eyewitness account, that cultural primal scene, at the same time that we try to disavow it.

"Invention" as a term to describe a conceptual origin and its problems was a byword of the last part of the last century, and the early years of this one. Together with its fraternal twin, "construction," "invention" emerged as a resistance to an older mode of humanistic inquiry, a nod in the direction of postmodernity. It allowed so well for both instantiation and critique, two moves in one.[12]

The very question, "What did Shakespeare invent?"—or, to use the emphasis of the program's typography, "What DID Shakespeare invent?" expresses a cultural transference and a cultural desire. If he didn't invent "the human," he must have invented *something*. If I were to arrive here and, following Rosalind's urgent entreaty to Celia, answer you in one word—and if that word were Cordelia's word, "nothing"—you would, I suspect, be unsatisfied.

The word *invention* from the nineteenth century to the present day has tended to refer to the creation of machines for living. Its preeminent cultural icon was Thomas Alva Edison, whose inventions included an improved telegraph, a telephone, an electric pen, the phonograph and the electric light. Often described as the link between the nineteenth-century "lone inventor" and the twentieth-century industrial researcher, Edison founded, as well, the modern "research park" with its emphasis on collaborative problem-solving and commercial productivity. Certainly to Edison himself "invention" meant objects, machinery, and "work"—sweat equity: he was the very definition of a "workaholic" *avant la lettre.* He spent most of his days and nights in the lab, he nicknamed his first daughter and son Dot and Dash, and he wrote in his notebook a month after his first marriage that "My wife Dearly Beloved Cannot invent work a Damn!"[13] (After his wife's death he proposed to the second Mrs. Edison by tapping out the proposal in Morse code as they traveled together on a group tour of the White Mountains.) To him the phonograph was essentially a business machine, not an artifact for entertainment. And motion pictures, he thought, might make their best contribution as part of the educational system, not as a new mode of leisure or art.

But from the fifteenth through the early nineteenth centuries the word *invention* meant, precisely, a work or writing produced by the exercise of the mind or imagination, a literary composition, or the devising of a subject, idea, or method of treatment for a work of art. No less a personage than Falstaff famously observed that man's brain "is not able to invent anything that intends to laughter more than I invent, or is invented on me; I am not only witty in myself, but the cause that wit is in other men" (*King Henry IV, Part 2* 1.2.6–9) "Laboring in invention" is Shakespear-ese for "trying to write a poem," and Dryden, reaching back to the etymology (from Latin for "find") would write that "The first happiness of the poet's imagination is properly invention, or finding of the thought."[14] Indeed, literary "invention" may be the converse of literary "*con*vention"—a flash of originality that alters and disrupts the accepted, and expected course of things. "Invention" was a word used by all the arts—painting, sculpture, and music as well as poetry.

The cultural "forgetting" of this meaning of the term in the twentieth century is exemplified by a remark made by no less a personage than Edison himself, when, late in life, he recalled an important model for his own creativity: "Ah, Shakespeare!" he exclaimed to an interviewer. "That's where you get the ideas! My but that man did have ideas! He would have been an inventor, a wonderful inventor, if he had turned his mind to it."[15] That Shakespeare *was* an inventor in his own century's primary sense of the term might have surprised the pragmatic machinist Edison, whose own favorite character was Richard III.

This is certainly the case with some of those words "invented by Shakespeare." The special attention paid to Shakespeare as the "origin" of many words derives in part, as Otto Jespersen long ago noted, from the wide availability of Shakespeare Concordances and the *Shakespeare-Lexicon*. "The frequency with which Shakespeare's name is found affixed to the earliest quotation for word or meanings," Jespersen suggested in 1906, comes from the presence of these research tools, "so that his words cannot escape notice, while the same words may occur unnoticed in the pages of many an earlier author."[16] But at the same time this was a desired result. The editorial staff of the *OED*, wishing to fulfill the promise of the Philological Society "to make a Dictionary worthy of the English Language," turned, as it were naturally, to Shakespeare. They found what they sought, in part because they wished to find it. The Philological Society sent their readers to the Shakespeare concordances, even at the acknowledged cost of "fail[ing] to give the earliest use of those few words which . . . were used by some of the earlier writers in the interval between 1526 and Shakespere."[17] Thus, as John Willinsky observes, "In Shakespeare's name" the *OED* "breaks the one-a-century rule for citations; it uses multiple instances from a single author; . . . it offers citations that fail to substantiate definitions." The dictionary organized "on Historical Principles" records "virtually every word Shakespeare is known to have written, attributing 1,904 new coinages" to him.[18] What did Shakespeare invent? Perhaps we should add to our list the *Oxford English Dictionary*. And, thus, the English language.

Of course the idea that Shakespeare was the origin, or originator, was not unattractive. Yet Ralph Waldo Emerson, for one, had disavowed this desire. His essay on Shakespeare begins, "Great men are more distinguished by range and extent, than by originality . . . The greatest genius is the most indebted man." Emerson had looked at Malone's annotated edition, which "hardly leaves a single drama of [Shakespeare's] absolute invention." But he was not fazed by this information. A good poet borrows whenever he can. "Shakespeare knew that tradition supplies a better fable than any invention can . . . , at that day, our petulant demand for originality was not so much pressed."[19]

Emerson thought Shakespeare was the only biographer of Shakespeare. Pericles greets his long-lost daughter with "Thou that beget'st him that did thee beget,"

(5.1.195) a redeemed version of the incest riddle that begins his play, and his quest. ("He's father, son, and husband mild; / I mother, wife, and yet his child: / How they may be, and yet in two, / As you will live, resolve it you" [1.1.69–72]). In *Macbeth* the show of eight kings in the magic glass seems to stretch out to the crack of doom. Tautology, or incest? Incest, or autogenesis?

The phrase *mise en abyme*, a phrase that has come in literary theory to mean something like self-reflection, a hall of mirrors in which the origin is endlessly deferred, is itself—nonetheless—a phrase with an identifiable origin. (That is to say, *mise en abyme* itself is not *en abyme*.) André Gide used it, borrowing the term from heraldry, where it meant an escutcheon that contains, at its center, a smaller version of itself. Gide wrote, "That retroaction of the subject on itself has always tempted me. It is the very mode of the psychological novel." Inevitably, perhaps, one of Gide's examples was the play within the play in Hamlet.[20] *Mise en abyme* has a certain structural similarity to another term, to which it may be indebted, the phrase *mise en scène*, which began as a word from the lexicon of the theater and has now become a term of art in film studies—the arrangement of actors, scenery, and properties, the physical environment in which an event takes place. *Mise en scène* literally means "putting on stage"; *mise en abyme* means "putting into the abyss," although, as I have noted, its local ("material") origin comes from heraldry.

Let me end, then by proposing a new term, one that might well accord with both our cultural transference onto Shakespeare and our interest in his own origins. For Shakespeare, too, has a connection to heraldry. The coat of arms sought by his father, John ("the said John Shakespeare, Gentleman . . . and his children, issue & posterity") appears on William Shakespeare's tomb at Stratford. The term I propose, on the model of *mise en scène* and *mise en abyme*—both of them terms that are important for an understanding of Shakespeare's "invention" in all of that word's rich sense is a coinage, or invention, of my own: *mise en a-bard*. To "put into Shakespeare." He that invents us that did him invent.

Bartlett's Familiar Shakespeare

15

What are Shakespeare's beliefs about love and politics, nature and art, men and women? This remarkable figure, whom Coleridge once called "myriad-minded Shakespeare"—this playwright claimed by nations and individuals around the globe as "our Shakespeare" (*unser Shakespeare*)—what were his real opinions about art and life? What would Shakespeare say about the world we inhabit today? What would Shakespeare *say*—and, to paraphrase another contemporary mantra, what would Shakespeare *do*?

The ardent wish to know Shakespeare has, perhaps paradoxically, never been more vivid than it is right now. Even though a smaller proportion of the population may be *reading* the plays than in the past (when memorizing the English classics was a cornerstone of a liberal arts education) other media—like film, video, television, MTV, advertisements, and popular music—have brought "Shakespeare" as a cultural icon to the insistent attention of global audiences.

My topic here, though, is not the universal popularity of Shakespeare, but a certain aspect of his cultural and ethical authority: the aspect that comes from citing or quoting him and his supposed opinions, as voiced in and through the plays. My claim will be that as much as we long to know what Shakespeare thinks, believes, or even advises, we cannot get to that knowledge by identifying him with one or another remark, or speech, or aphorism spoken by a character in his plays. Remember that "who steals my purse, steals trash," the famous defense of "good name in man and woman" as "the immediate jewel of their souls" is spoken by Iago, Shakespeare's most eloquent and unregenerate hypocrite, who doesn't believe a word of it.

As you will see, I do not regard this quest for Shakespeare's moral authority as a problem, but rather as a commentary on the contemporary longing for disinterested wisdom combined with eloquence—something it is not so easy to come by these days in the ordinary world of politics, ethics, and the public sphere. What I will be suggesting is a return to the plays themselves, and the discovery, there, of a set of dialogues and interchanges that illuminate not only the playwright's brilliant mode of stagecraft, but also the interactive and situational nature of thought itself.

I am going to begin with some recent citations from Shakespeare, all of which originate in some version of contemporary popular culture, by which I mean television and media, on the one hand, and the U.S. Congress on the other. But there is a point to be made here beyond the inadvertent comedy of the moment.

Here is anchor Rick Sanchez, chatting on-air with another CNN reporter about President Bush's possible plans for his second term:

> Going back to Dana Bash now, picking up on some themes that we started to allude to at the beginning. There is word—as you heard the president mention just moments ago—that there would be some cuts in education. When you consider that this president once was running as an education candidate, may this end up being, as I suppose William Shakespeare would say, the unkindest cut of all, Dana?

Here is legal reporter Nancy Grace, on the *Larry King Show*, discussing the trial of Scott Peterson for the murder of his wife, Laci:

> It's my understanding that blood was found in Peterson's car. But it was Peterson's blood, and in fact, he openly volunteered that to witnesses before they even asked him. Oh, yes, they're going to find my blood in my car. Shakespeare says me thinks thou dost protest too much.

And here is a conversation between then-*Today* co-host Katie Couric and John Ramsey, the father of JonBenet Ramsey:

COURIC:	And finally, Mr. Ramsey, despite the fact that these new leads are being investigated, many people still believe that you and your wife, Patsy, are responsible for JonBenet's death. What would you say to them this morning?
MR. RAMSEY:	Well, you know, Katie, two things were taken from us in 1996, our precious child and our family's honor. It's very difficult to—to recover your good name, regardless of what happens after it's taken. And we're struggling with that, and it's—it's a challenge. There's a line in Shakespeare that says, "My life and my honor are intertwined. Take away my honor, and my life is—is done." And that's—it's difficult for us.

The first thing I would say about all of these citations of Shakespeare is that the speaker is reaching for *gravitas*, for some way to signify, and dignify, the seriousness of the topic. In the last two cases, where what is at issue is a murder and a family's grief, the association with Shakespearean tragedy is perfectly understandable. Shakespearean language lends an eloquence that is all too often absent from modern-day public—or private—discourse.

How appropriate are these citations? Well, the "unkindest cut of all" comes from Mark Antony's funeral oration in *Julius Caesar*. His point is that of all the conspirators who gathered to murder Caesar, the most culpable, because he was Caesar's friend, was Marcus Brutus.

> For Brutus, as you know, was Caesar's angel.
> Judge, O you gods, how dearly Caesar loved him.
> This was the most unkindest cut of all. (3.2.179–81)

I leave it to you to judge—O ye gods—whether the use of this phrase, "the unkindest cut of all," is witty or clever when applied to proposed reductions in the national budget for education. On this matter I have, myself, no opinion, or none that matters. What I want to point to here is the authorizing expression, the invocation of Shakespeare's opinion: "as I suppose William Shakespeare would say." This is the phenomenon I call "Bartlett's Familiar Shakespeare." Quoting a passage from the plays as if it were, without question, "Shakespeare's" point of view.

On the second citation, the one from legal analyst Nancy Grace, here too the source is pretty familiar—it's Queen Gertrude, Hamlet's mother, responding to the ardent claim of the Player Queen in the play-within-the play that she'll never take a second husband if she should ever lose her first. (Gertrude, of course, has done just that, and is sitting in the audience with her new husband, King Claudius—the brother, and as it turns out the murderer, of Old Hamlet.)

In the context of the *Larry King* show, Nancy Grace's comment "Shakespeare says me thinks thou dost protest too much" is a familiar, and slight, misquotation—the text of the *Hamlet* Second Quarto says "The lady doth protest too much, methinks." (Incidentally, both the Folio and the First Quarto are less archaic, and have Gertrude saying simply, "The lady protests too much, methinks," without the "doth," but this has clearly not sounded "Shakespearean" enough for those who wish to be understood as really quoting Shakespeare.)

In fact the phrase about protesting too much is so common—and so commonly misapplied—that "doth protest" appears, often ungrammatically, as what I've called, in my introduction to *Shakespeare After All*, a shorthand expression that "implies a generalized doubt about someone's sincerity—not a specific reference to *Hamlet*, Gertrude, or the way a play can catch the conscience of the king (or queen.)"[1]

Again, though, what I want to point out is Shakespeare's authoritative position; the way the "doth protest" phrase is attributed, not to the actual speaker, Hamlet's mother Gertrude (who might conceivably have something of a guilty conscience on this very point), but rather to Shakespeare. Now, neither Nancy Grace nor Larry King presumably believes that Shakespeare, peering through the clouds, has a clear opinion on the guilt or innocence of Scott Peterson. The invocation of "Shakespeare says" in this example is what we loosely call "rhetorical." It is an attempt to raise the cultural stakes. "Shakespeare says" here means something like "as everyone knows" or "it's an admitted fact of human nature" or "we've seen this a thousand times before, haven't we?" But even in context—or, I should perhaps say—especially in context, it isn't "Shakespeare" who says anything about false gestures of protest, but a character in one of his plays, and, indeed, a character whose own false protests—far more unbelievable than those of the Player Queen—put her veracity as the voice of "Shakespeare" in serious question.

Turning to the third example from media culture, we can see a similar dynamic at work. John Ramsey, feeling beleaguered and aggrieved, invokes "a line in Shakespeare" to express the profundity of his distress. It is, indeed, not so easy to figure out precisely which line he is invoking, since what he cites is a kind of amalgam of several passages from different plays. "My life and my honor are intertwined. Take away my honor, and my life is—is done." This is perhaps closest to Hermione in *The Winter's Tale* ("no life, / I prize it not a straw, but for mine honour, / Which I would free" [3.2.109–11])—a very unlikely phrase and speaker for John Ramsey to be recalling—but there is a distinct hint of Cassio on the loss of his "reputation" in *Othello*, of the standard Iago phrase about losing your "good name," and also an echo of Brutus:

> Set honour in one eye, and death i'th other,
> And I will look on both indifferently.
> For let the gods so speed me as I love
> The name of honour more than I fear death. (*Julius Caesar* 1.2.86–9)

The line may be inexact, but the sentiment is appropriate, and Ramsey's paraphrase does less violence to text and context than most evocations of "the lady doth protest too much."

But what is Shakespeare's own view about honor, or about hypocrisy and protestation? Despite these resounding phrases, we simply cannot know. Because in every case there is both a qualifying context and also a dialogic reply.

Remember the game of "Simon Says"? It's a kind of follow-the-leader. Instructions are given by the leader or teacher, who must preface the command with the phrase "Simon says." If that phrase is not spoken, the students / followers are not supposed to obey the order. "Simon says, 'touch the tip of your nose with your finger.'" Or "Touch the tip of your nose with your finger." If you follow the second instruction, you are "out." This habit of quoting Shakespeare is a version of the same game—"Shakespeare Says."

Perhaps unsurprisingly, this is a game frequently played in the halls of the U.S. Congress, where Senators and Congressmen call upon Shakespearean authority to authorize their own statements, whether those statements are actually presented to colleagues (that is, performed on the floor of the House or Senate chamber) or merely read into the record. Such examples are embarrassingly easy to come by, but let me share a couple of them with you.

- This is Representative John Mica (Republican, Florida) a few years ago on the requesting of FBI files by the White House: "Mr. Speaker, Shakespeare said, 'Something is rotten in Denmark.' Mr. Speaker, I say something is rotten in the White House."[2]
- And this is Representative Sheila Jackson-Lee (Democrat, Texas), speaking—in the mid-1990s—on behalf of funding for the National Endowment for the Arts despite the political objections that had been raised about some contemporary artists. "Mr. Speaker. . . . Let us be instructed wisely. Shakespeare said the first thing we should do is kill all the lawyers. Some would say, as a trained lawyer, I would want to burn that and not want to hear the play that offered those words. But I think in the spirit of art, certainly, there are limitations, but it is important to have that kind of diversity, that kind of contradiction and conflict, but as well, the opportunity for artists to express themselves."[3]

Shakespeare said, "Something is rotten in Denmark." Well, almost. The phrase is from *Hamlet*, of course, and is in blank verse, iambic pentameter: "Something is rotten in the state of Denmark." But who said it? "Shakespeare"? "Hamlet"? Actually, the speaker is Marcellus, a member of the King's guard, present on the battlements with Hamlet and Horatio when the Ghost appears. Marcellus is right (methinks), since Denmark as unfolded in the play is indeed morally, socially, and politically corrupt. But it's only his opinion. Nonetheless, had Representative Mica reminded the House that "Marcellus" thought something was rotten in Denmark, the implied universality of the comment would almost surely have been lost.

As for that famous quote about killing the lawyers, available on T-shirts across the nation, the speaker—in *King Henry VI, Part 2*, one of the earliest and least read of the history plays—is a minor character called Dick the Butcher, a henchman of the rebel leader Jack Cade, whose insurrectionary rhetoric and far-fetched claim to be the true king of England are deliberately juxtaposed in the play to the more plausible claims of the Lancaster King, Henry VI, and his rival, Richard, Duke of York. Modern-day lawyers, law students, and plaintiffs have tended to debate whether Shakespeare did or did not mean to speak ill of the legal profession. But in context this remark—which may have elicited general laughter in the Elizabethan playhouse, as it often does in the theater today—addresses a whole range of topics, from law to literacy, that are central to the design of the play. The dramatist's choice here is to emphasize Cade's contempt for lawyers. Shakespeare may have written the phrase "First thing let's do, let's kill all the lawyers" for his rebellious butcher to proclaim. But that's a different thing from saying that "Shakespeare said . . . we should . . . kill all the lawyers."

The dean of Shakespearean quotation in the Congress these days is Senator Robert Byrd of West Virginia, whose mellifluous speeches often stand in contrast to the more prosaic and businesslike language of his colleagues. Admittedly, Byrd's use of Shakespeare is idiosyncratic. He often cites from little-known plays, or with doubtful relevance to the context. But whatever else one can say about Byrd, he is a consummate player of the game of "Shakespeare says." Here then is Senator Byrd on the declining standards of education in America:

> Bad music overwhelms good music. Bad taste destroys good taste. Bad literature drives out good literature. And, I might add, apparently ignorance often displaces fact. Shakespeare said, "Ignorance is the curse of God, knowledge the wing wherewith we fly to heaven." As a case in point [this is still Senator Byrd talking], I cite the February 7, 1994 issue of *People* magazine."[4]

"Shakespeare said, 'Ignorance is the curse of God, knowledge the wing wherewith we fly to heaven.'" The speaker of "Shakespeare says" here is (perhaps somewhat uncannily) an English nobleman named Lord Saye, a minor character, again from *King Henry VI, Part 2*, known in history for his reputation for extortion, but presented in Shakespeare's play, according to a modern editor, as "a vulnerable victim, pathetic, sick, and frightened."[5] By ignoring the fact that the line has a speaker, and that the speaker has a character and a dramatic situation (he's facing imminent death at the hands of a mob, and has his head cut off shortly after he says these words), Senator Byrd does what he clearly intends: he takes Shakespeare's text, all of it, as a coherent philosophy traceable to the playwright's own views. "Shakespeare says."

Here, likewise, is Senator Byrd's praise of his then-colleague, Senator Daniel Patrick Moynihan (Democrat, New York), on the occasion of Moynihan's retirement: "Of whom I shall say—not in the past tense—as Shakespeare said it; He [is] a scholar, and a ripe, and good one, exceeding wise, fair-spoken, and persuading."[6] In this case the Shakespeare play is the very late *Henry VIII*, the speaker a servant of the Dowager Queen Katherine of Aragon, and the subject of conversation, very much in the past tense, the recently deceased and previously disgraced Cardinal Wolsey. ("He was a scholar, and a ripe and good one . . ." *King Henry VIII* 4.2.51). In the immediately preceding speech the Queen has accused the Cardinal of graft, high-handedness, and lying to authority. So maybe this is not in fact the unstinting praise that Senator Byrd intends to bestow upon his esteemed colleague Daniel Moynihan, whether in the past tense or in the present. "As Shakespeare said it."

"Shakespeare says." Newspaper headline writers likewise capitalize on the high recognition-factor of half-remembered lines from Shakespeare. (One of my recent favorites, from the sports pages of the *New York Times*, involved the football running back Ron Dayne, whose play had improved dramatically after he was traded from one team to another. The headline read simply—and brilliantly—"Melancholy No More, Dayne runs Wild."[7]) An article on the business page of the *Times* likewise took a knowledge of *Hamlet* for granted, reporting a link between the sleeping pill Ambien and "unconscious food forays" into the kitchen and refrigerator: "To Sleep, Perchance to Eat. Is it the Pill?"[8] (In case you're wondering, the article did not invoke the name of Lady Macbeth in its account of binging sleepwalkers.) For a more typical case, though, consider the familiar phrase from *The Tempest*, "What's past is prologue" (2.1.253). In the context of the play, this is an injunction to usurpation and murder. Sebastian, the brother of the King of Naples, is being urged by his confederate, Antonio, to kill the sleeping King, and seize the crown for himself:

> perform an act
> Whereof what's past is prologue, what to come
> In yours and my discharge! (2.1.252–4)

Under the nimble imaginative manipulation of modern headline writers, this flexible phrase has turned up on the arts pages ("A Choreographer Employs Past Ballets as Prologue," *New York Times*, June 16, 2005), the political pages ("In the Confirmation Dance, the Past but Rarely the Prologue," *New York Times*, July 24, 2005), the sports pages ("Past is Prologue as Piazza Rediscovers the Sweet Spot," *New York Times*, July 25, 2005), and the automobile pages (a trip in a stylish new sports car through an area of southern California devastated by a forest fire: "What's Past is Prologue: Emerging from the Ashes," *San Diego Union*, May 28, 2005). Clearly in these cases there was no attempt, and no intention, to refer to the conspiracy scene in *The Tempest*. The "Shakespearean" phrase merely floated free, a mildly recognizable, nicely paradoxical, conveniently alliterative macro. (When director Oliver Stone used the same phrase in his film *JFK*, he cleaned it up, improved it, banishing the apostrophe and the contraction so as to produce the film's final epigraph in stark letters on a black background: "What Is Past Is Prologue.") Shakespeare, a figure of

high seriousness, is apparently not supposed to speak in something as undignified—
or as supposedly modern—as a contraction. The same decision seems to have been
made by the designers of the National Archives in Washington D.C., where—on the
plinth of a statue on the Pennsylvania Avenue side of the building—is inscribed the
motto: "What Is Past is Prologue." Perhaps this is where Stone, a *quondam*
Washington habitué, got the idea.

It is too easy, you may think, just to trace down these apparently free-floating
quotations and tether them to the plays and to the context. Isn't the very point about
Shakespeare that he transcends these petty considerations, and that his magnificent
language—not of an age, but for all time—can in fact be turned to almost any (good)
use? Well yes, in a way. This is one of the effects of Shakespeare as omniscient Wise
Person—what I've elsewhere termed "the Shakespeare effect." Any good phrase can
be recycled—ask the solons of modern advertising, many of them former English
majors. But quoting—or misquoting—Shakespeare's words is not the same as
quoting "Shakespeare."

The hopeful, romantic, and ultimately delusory belief that we can in fact intuit
what is in Shakespeare's mind by reading his words, making a direct connection
between writer and reader ("Shakespeare" speaks to "me"), has been fostered in part
by the very structure of books of quotations, which remove the speech-prefix, or name
of the fictional speaker (Lady Macbeth, Iago, Prospero, Richard III) when citing a line
or speech from the plays. If you go to your personal copy of *Bartlett's*, or of any other
quotation index, in print or on-line, you will find such sentiments as "Good coun-
selors lack no clients," and "Liberty plucks justice by the nose" and "The miserable
have no medicine / But only hope" and "Death is a great disguiser" all attributed to
"Shakespeare," without any indication that they are spoken, in context, by dramatic
characters. All of these quotations are from a single play, *Measure for Measure*.

There is some evidence that early modern playwrights, Shakespeare included, did
not originally write lines for specific speakers. Thus for example, the passages of the
play called *Sir Thomas More* that are usually attributed by editors to Shakespeare
include some named speakers (Lincoln, Serjeant) but also lines assigned to "Other,"
"Some," "Another," and "All." Since actors at the time received their lines in literal
"parts," cut-up pieces of text containing only their lines and the cues to them rather
than an entire playscript, the assignment of these lines to particular actor-speakers
seems to have been part of the production process rather than the writing process.[9]
Nonetheless, by the time the plays were printed, speech prefixes, however consistent
or inconsistent, were part of the apparatus. To a large extent our sense of dramatic
"character" derives from these speech attributions, and secure notions of character
can be destabilized by changes in the speaker. In the two versions we have of *King*

Lear, the 1608 Quarto (*The History of King Lear*) and the 1623 Folio (*The Tragedy of King Lear*) lines attributed to one character in the Quarto are not-infrequently given to a different character in the Folio. The famous final lines, for example,

> The weight of this sad time we must obey,
> Speak what we feel, not what we ought to say.
> The oldest hath borne most; we that are young
> Shall never see so much, nor live so long. (5.3.321–5)

are given to Albany in the Quarto, to Edgar in the Folio. Plainly it makes a difference to the play's tone whether it is the son-in-law of Lear, or the surviving son of Gloucester, who pronounces this somber benediction. Nonetheless, despite this variability, so disconcerting to modern notions of "character," the plays have come down to us with speakers and speech-prefixes, whether they are traceable to the author, the acting company, the printer, the editor, or any other set of mediating factors. Our ideas of Edgar, or Albany, or Rosalind, or Hamlet, are formed by our sense that they are what they speak. By the same token, of course, we have formed our idea of "Shakespeare" from the belief—or perhaps the wish or fantasy—that the words a playwright puts in the mouths of his dramatic characters are *his* opinions. And this wish was given a local habitation and a name by the mid-nineteenth century interest in books of familiar quotations.

The design and intention of John Bartlett's *Familiar Quotations* was, from the beginning to collect the proverbial, or—as his title directly proclaimed—the already "familiar." "The object of this work," he wrote in the preface to the first edition in 1855, "is to show, to some extent, the obligations our language owes to various authors for numerous phrases and familiar quotations which have become 'household words.'"[10]

Within his book of quotations, Bartlett listed the authors chronologically. But he did not give speech prefixes to the passages he quoted from Shakespeare (or from other dramatists). The simple but in some ways cataclysmic result of these two facts— that he wanted to cite quotations that had already become household words, and that he deliberately omitted the names of the speakers within the plays, was to present the familiar quotations as quotations from "Shakespeare." From "Sell when you can, you are not for all markets" to "Man delights not me; no, nor woman, neither" to "Be absolute for death," they are all "Shakespeare." (We can guess that this is the kind of source that modern politicians, or their speechwriters, will consult when they quote "Shakespeare.")

John Bartlett himself was an intriguing figure. Employed at age sixteen by the Harvard bookstore, he immersed himself in books, becoming so knowledgeable that the phrase "Ask John Bartlett" itself became proverbial on the Harvard campus. The first edition of his *Quotations* was based on a notebook he kept beneath the counter to assist his customers. He rose to become the owner of the store, and, ultimately, the senior partner of the publishing firm Little, Brown, and Company, which still publishes *Bartlett's Familiar Quotations*, now in its seventeenth edition. John Bartlett never attended college, but he received an honorary degree from Harvard in 1871, and was a fellow of the American Academy of Arts and Sciences. His wife was the daughter of a Harvard professor of Hebrew, and the granddaughter of a former president of Harvard College, Joseph Willard.

In some ways a classic nineteenth-century autodidact, Bartlett was also a serious Shakespeare buff. In addition to the *Concordance* he published an earlier *Shakespeare Phrase Book* (1881), remarking that the plan of the book was "to take every sentence from his dramatic works which contains an important thought, with so much of the context as preserves the sense, and to put each sentence under its principal words, arranged in alphabetical order."[11] The idea that these "important thought(s)" have speakers who might inflect their meanings was occluded, completely, since no speakers were indicated, only plays. (So, for example, our proof text, "Good name in man and woman, dear my lord / Is the immediate jewel of their souls" is attributed to *Othello* [the play], 3.3.159–60, not to Iago, the speaker.) Thus, making the already "familiar" quotations or "important" thoughts easily accessible to readers meant dislocating them from their dramatic situations. Bartlett's phrase "so much of the context as preserves the sense" was addressed only to syntax, and not to tone, inflection, irony, or anything else that might alter the *contextual* sense of the phrase in question.

The phrase "household words" itself is taken from Shakespeare, from Henry V's exhortation to the troops on the eve of the battle of Agincourt (the famous "Crispin Crispian" speech). The King is imagining a time after the battle when those who fought there will be famous (as, indeed, Shakespeare's play will make them)—old men recalling the battle will retell the story, and celebrate the heroes: "then shall our names, / Familiar in his mouth as household words. . . . Be in their flowing cups freshly remembered" (*King Henry V* 4.3.51–5). As Michael Hancher points out, the use of this phrase to describe a new book of quotations listed by the name of the *author*—rather than the topic—originated in fact with the compiler of a book published two years before Bartlett's, and to which he seems to have been considerably indebted for both the format and some of the citations: the *Handbook of Familiar Quotations from English Authors*, published in 1853 in England by John Murray, and compiled by an editor who used the initials I. R. P.—Isabella Rushton Preston. It is perhaps of more than passing interest—and some little irony—that John Bartlett was himself greatly assisted by other American scholars who did not get co-billing on the final title page—notably Henry W. Haynes, who worked closely with Bartlett on collecting the quotations—and on the borrowings from Preston's book— and was the author of the original preface.[12]

Remember that it was the *names* of the heroes of Agincourt ("Harry the King, Bedford and Exeter, / Warwick and Talbot, Salisbury and Gloucester") that were to become "familiar . . . as household words." Basically what Bartlett (and Haynes, and Preston) did, was to foreground the apparent sentiments expressed in the plays and present them as positive utterances, devoid of dramatic "spin," attaching them to the name of the author, "Shakespeare," rather than, as had been the case with previous quotation books, arranging them alphabetically by topic. Earlier collections, like John T. Watson's *Poetical Quotations* (1847), were—like Bartlett's own *Shakespeare Concordance*—"*Arranged Under Appropriate Heads*" for the ready use of the "editor, the author, and the public speaker."[13] The quotations were there to be *appropriated*. The writer was less important than the content. But when the "household words" and "familiar quotations" were returned to the authority of the author by the new system of indexing and attribution adopted by Bartlett (and *Bartlett's*), it was a natural assumption on the part of the reader that what "Shakespeare" said was something "Shakespeare" believed.

This practice of quoting "Shakespeare" as if what is uttered in the plays represents the opinion of the playwright is, of course, much older than *Bartlett's Familiar Quotations* itself. It is directly related, for example, to the so-called commonplace-book, a book in which commonplaces or memorable passages were collected, often under general headings like loyalty, decadence, friendship, and so on. Popular in the English and European Renaissance and through to the time of Washington and Jefferson, these commonplace books helped students and scholars to amass personal collections of wise sayings (before the advent of the public library, the paperback book, or the Internet), and were, from the beginning, used as sources for speech-writing as well as for composition. When Hamlet calls for his "tables," or writing tablet, to transcribe a particularly poignant piece of information imparted by the Ghost: "My tables. Meet it is I set it down / That one may smile, and smile, and be a villain" (1.5.107–8)—he is writing his observations on a portable, erasable, note-taking device, prior to inserting these words into his commonplace book under a general heading like "hypocrisy."[14]

As with the individual commonplace book, so also, increasingly, with the pub-lished plays—there too the quotable phrase was already being lifted out of context. The poet Alexander Pope, in his edition of Shakespeare's plays (1725) marked "some of the most shining passages" with printed commas in the margin, and explained to his readers that "where the beauty lay not in particulars but in the whole a star is prefix'd to the scene."[15] So if you wanted to find the "good parts," you needed only to skim the text, looking for clues in the margin: follow the commas, or the stars.

By 1752, less than a century and a half after Shakespeare's death, the Reverend William Dodd had published a book with a thoroughly explanatory title: *The beauties of Shakespear, regularly selected from each play: with a general index, digesting them under proper heads: illustrated with explanatory notes, and similar passages from ancient and modern authors.* A reader in search of wise words about grief, politics, fatherhood, women, or any other conventional topic could consult Mr. Dodd's book with profit, since Dodd selected out, from each play, what he considered the most important passages, and gave them each a heading: from *The Tempest* we find "A Guilty Conscience," "Continence Before Marriage," "Compassion and Clemency superior to Revenge," as well as highlighted passages on sleep and music.[16]

This eighteenth-century practice of singling out the "beauties" of the plays, first by marking them—as Pope did—in the text, and then (a logical, though fatal, next step) by removing them from the plays and putting them in topical lists, saved the quoter in quest of the perfect Shakespearean tag the unnecessary labor of actually reading the plays themselves in their entirety. In the same spirit the famous Shakespeare Jubilee staged by the actor David Garrick in 1769 established Shakespeare as the "national poet" and Stratford-upon-Avon as a tourist site. On that occasion, we might note, no work of Shakespeare was performed. The Jubilee was a kind of Shakespearean theme park, with horse races, dancing, an ox-roast, odes to Shakespeare, champagne toasts, and a song written for the occasion with the refrain "The lad of all lads was / A Warwickshire lad." Shakespeare had already become an event and a cultural hero, rather than (merely) a playwright. Garrick himself, the most famous Shakespearean actor and theater manager of his day, had a "Temple to Shakespeare" in his garden; he himself posed for the statue of Shakespeare within it, which ultimately combined Garrick's own features with Shakespeare's.

The term "bardolatry" (worship of Shakespeare) was coined by George Bernard Shaw at the beginning of the twentieth century,[17] although the practice was much older. Some modes of quotation and citation today do seem rather a lot like "channeling" Shakespeare (to use the language of transcendental meditation), or like trying to find your "inner Shakespeare" (to echo the Jungian concept of the inner child) or, indeed, your "personal Shakespeare" (to adapt the popular evangelical phrase). In effect, *Shakespeare* has become a commonplace book for *us*.

In fact, the very purpose, as well as the effect, of quoting or citing Shakespeare has changed over time. There was a period in the early- to mid-twentieth century when such a quotation was almost like a social password or club handshake, signifying the speaker's confidence that his or her listener was also comfortably

Shakespeare-literate—indeed so comfortably so that the listener could be counted upon to recognize both the quotation and its context. Educated urbanity was once the stock-in-trade of the noble amateur sleuth. Thus, for example, confronted with an awkward domestic situation, Lord Peter Wimsey, Dorothy L. Sayers' detective-hero can cite a line from Benedick in *Much Ado About Nothing*, "This looks not like a nuptial," and his lady, the equally well-educated Harriet Vane (herself a detective novelist), without missing a beat, responds with the play's next line, "True, o god." It is only when a country policeman turns up on the scene that surprise is evinced (and quickly suppressed) at his facility with quoting, and identifying, Shakespeare.[18] It's the same impulse, if not exactly the same readership or audience, that led William Faulkner to title a novel *The Sound and the Fury* (1929), or Aldous Huxley in 1932 to use the phrase *Brave New World* as a title for his novel—or, in more recent days, led a mathematician to call his book on zero *Signifying Nothing*.[19]

But perhaps significantly, the most insistent quoters and citers of Shakespeare these days are not professors, novelists, directors, or sports writers. Nor are they politicians. Instead they are motivational speakers and, specifically, specialists in business communication. Here are the titles of some recent books on the topic: *Shakespeare in Charge: The Bard's Guide to Leading and Succeeding on the Business Stage* (1999); *Shakespeare on Management* (1999); *Power Plays: Shakespeare's Lessons in Leadership and Management* (2000); *Inspirational Leadership: Henry V and the Muse of Fire—Timeless Insights from Shakespeare's Greatest Leader* (2001).

And, even more directly pertinent to our fantasy game of "Shakespeare says," a book called *Say It Like Shakespeare: How to Give a Speech Like Hamlet, Persuade Like Henry V, and Other Secrets from the World's Greatest Communicator* (2001). The phrase "world's greatest communicator" is in capital letters, and the cover image shows a man in a modern business suit, but with an Elizabethan ruff and a high-forehead page-boy hairdo, earnestly addressing a table of male and female executives, one of whom is transcribing his words on a laptop. What would Shakespeare say?

The inspirational quotations in *Say It Like Shakespeare* are sometimes quite out of kilter with their original Shakespearean contexts. Lady Macbeth urging Macbeth to screw his courage to the sticking-place, and "we'll not fail" is included in a section about the fear of failure and the importance of preparation; no one bothers to recall that Lady Macbeth is trying to persuade her husband to kill the king. Again, Shakespeare functions as a kind of commonplace book, this time for business professionals.

At this point, it will be useful to turn to a few classic Shakespeare set-pieces, and try to see both why they are regarded as "the voice of Shakespeare," and what the problem is in trying to find the psyche or philosophy of Shakespeare behind the voice.

Polonius' long speech of advice to his son Laertes at the beginning of *Hamlet*, for example, is studded with "wisdom" often quoted as Shakespearean. "Neither a borrower nor a lender be." "Be thou familiar, but by no means vulgar." "The apparel oft proclaims the man." "This above all, to thine own self be true." But none of these is Shakespeare's original idea, needless to say. Polonius himself is a kind of caricature, a walking commonplace book. Such bromides were commonplaces of the period, and the genre of "advices of fathers to sons" was at least as prevalent in "life" as in "literature," especially among the nobility. So it is not necessary to see Polonius as a buffoon when he makes these remarks, although a great deal of his language throughout the play is clearly presented as being quoted, or slightly misquoted, from other people's remarks that he has sometimes not wholly understood. Our modern day statesmen have a penchant for emulating Polonius, or at least for citing him. "To thine own self be true" is a perennial favorite.[20] As the critic E. M. W. Tillyard once observed, "Shakespeare's [remarks] on the state of man seem to be utterly [his] own, as if compounded of [his] very life-blood; divested of their literary form they are the common property of every thirdrate mind of the age."[21]

But to an audience watching *Hamlet* what is striking and disconcerting, given this glut of good advice to his son, is to find Polonius a few scenes after this touching interchange with Laertes, in close conversation with his man Reynaldo, coaching him about how to elicit discreditable information about Laertes from third parties. Reynaldo is to "by indirections find directions out"—to suggest that Laertes may be given to drinking, drabbing [whoring], and gambling—and see who confirms these suspicions. Needless to say, this advice about spying on your son, which might be regarded as domestic Machiavellianism or household surveillance, does not make it into the canon of Shakespearean wisdom. Yet it is the juxtaposition of these two scenes that puts Polonius, and his holier-than-thou advice, into context.

The same kind of ironic dramaturgy is at work in the placement of another classic Shakespearean set-piece, Jaques' oft-quoted speech about the seven ages of man from *As You Like It*—a speech which begins with one of Shakespeare's most famous lines:

> All the world's a stage,
> And all the men and women merely players.
> They have their exits and their entrances,
> And each man in his time plays many parts,
> His acts being seven ages.

Jaques goes on, of course, to list the ages: the infant, the school-boy, the lover, the soldier, the justice ("full of wise saws, and modern instances"), the pantaloon, or foolish old man of stock comedy, and finally the

> Last scene of all,
> That ends this strange eventful history,
> Is second childishness and mere oblivion,
> Sans teeth, sans eyes, sans taste, sans everything. (2.7.139–66)

In this speech, and especially in its celebrated opening lines, we would seem to have a prime example of Shakespeare's philosophy. The key phrase—"all the world's a stage"—has itself been so unproblematically associated with Shakespeare, and therefore with common shared wisdom, that it is used by NASA for a website about the migration of dust clouds ("All the World's a Stage . . . for Dust"), and has been cited in testimony before the House International Relations Committee ("Shakespeare would say: 'All the world's a stage, and all the men and women merely players.' In today's global and interdependent economy, this phrase takes on a whole new connotation . . . whereby one could readily say, 'the world is one market and we are all but investors or economic indicators.'")[22] My personal favorite among the many citations of this phrase—"all the world's a stage"—is its appearance in a song sung by Elvis Presley. The song is his early classic, "Are You Lonesome Tonight?"[23] Here is the spoken passage that comes after the opening verse, murmured in the inimitable style of the young Elvis:

> You know someone said that the world's a stage
> And each must play a part.
> Fate had me playing in love with you as my sweetheart.
> Act one was when we met . . .

Notice that we are told "someone" said that the world's a stage. The song makes no explicit mention of Shakespeare (although "Shakespeare" would fit the scansion as well as "someone"). The source of the quotation has become proverbial, disseminated, neither highbrow nor middlebrow, but timeless. Indeed it's a little hard to imagine Elvis citing Shakespeare. But in fact he, or his song, is "right" to attribute this saying to "someone," since the concept—if not the exact phrase—is in fact much older than Shakespeare or *As You Like It*.

The motto of the Globe Theatre, which opened in 1599, and for which *As You Like It* seems to have been written, was *Totus mundus agit historionem* (the whole world is a stage), a phrase derived from a twelfth-century treatise on politics and diplomacy. Jaques in effect gestures at the theater in which he is performing, or cites its motto as a kind of self-referential advertisement, as he begins his speech. Whoever coined the phrase, it was certainly not Shakespeare. The quotability of Jaques' "All the world's a stage" is put in double quotation marks; it is an internal quotation of a long-overused phrase, the motto of the playhouse in which he is performing.

And in theatrical terms, the issue of dramatic irony, the clichés or social truisms spoken by a self-important speaker and then undercut by dramatic events in the play, operates here as it did in the example of Polonius.[24] From a production point of view, as any director will see, the lengthy seven ages speech is inserted in the play to cover a piece of offstage action, as Orlando has gone off to rescue his faithful old retainer, Old Adam. When Orlando returns with Adam, the physical presence of the old man onstage—loyal, dignified, and loving—gives the lie to the cynical devolution of "man" into a foolish, toothless caricature, "sans teeth, sans eyes, sans taste, sans everything."[25]

I want to underscore the fact that this device—a piece of quotable and quoted Shakespearean wisdom being immediately contradicted by (a far less quoted) piece of Shakespearean practice (as we saw with Polonius coaching his spy Reynaldo, and Jaques' dismissal of old age as "second childishness" followed by the onstage arrival of the dignified Old Adam)—is in fact one of the central techniques of Shakespearean dramaturgy. The plays are brilliantly designed with this kind of counterpoint in mind. Another good and symptomatic example would be that of Ulysses in *Troilus and Cressida*, who after his great and famous speech on "degree," articulating the idea that there is both a divine and a human hierarchy in which everyone has a fixed place, deliberately violates his own precept, suggesting that the Greeks reserve their great champion, Achilles, and send out "the dull brainless Ajax" instead to meet the challenge of the Trojan hero Hector. Why should they send out their best man first? "Let us, like merchants, show our foulest wares, / And think perchance they'll sell."

Ulysses' speech on degree was a centerpiece of mid-twentieth century arguments about "the Elizabethan world picture."[26] As many commentators have noted, the speech deliberately echoes two Elizabethan homilies read out in the churches.[27] Is it Shakespeare's *own* political view, and voice? Maybe so. Certainly it is eloquent enough, and it does fit neatly in with the prevailing fears of popular uprisings. But we might just notice that—as with Polonius—no sooner does Ulysses speak this speech of excellent, and moving, political advice, than he proceeds to do just the opposite of what he advises.

Of course in many ways it doesn't matter what Shakespeare's opinion was, on this or many other topics. In fact it only matters what Shakespeare "really thought" about one or another of these questions if we want to take Shakespeare as a moral guide, rather than as a clever and brilliant and sometimes quirky playwright.

It is often observed that we live today in a "celebrity culture," a culture of public "confession," of "talking heads" and of "public intellectuals." The fantasy of putting Shakespeare on Charlie Rose—or on the analyst's couch—lies very close to the surface of our preoccupation with his elusive authority. And that authority, like the authority of all celebrities, is two-sided; we want Shakespeare's aura, and we also want his vulnerability.

This is one reason for the persistence of the idea that Shakespeare used one of his most authoritative dramatic characters to confess his own feeling about leaving the world of the theater, an event usually described, in defiance of history, as his "farewell to the stage." I am speaking, of course, about the figure of Prospero in *The Tempest*.

The Tempest is the site of one of the most quoted of all of Shakespeare's gorgeous set pieces, a gorgeous set piece about a gorgeous set piece, the speech that begins "Our revels now are ended:"

> Our revels now are ended. These our actors,
> As I foretold you, were all spirits and
> Are melted into air, into thin air;
> And—like the baseless fabric of this vision—
> The cloud-capped towers, the gorgeous palaces,
> The solemn temples, the great globe itself,
> Yea, all which it inherit, shall dissolve,
> And like this insubstantial pageant faded,
> Leave not a rack behind. We are such stuff
> As dreams are made on, and our little life
> Is rounded with a sleep. (4.1.148–58)

This is one of the passages in Shakespeare that I find real difficulty in reading aloud without a noticeable catch in my throat. It is written, we might say, to produce that effect. Written by a playwright still at the height of his powers. The pathos it induces is a stage effect, and—as a stage effect—it is very real.

But what this passage certainly is not, is "Shakespeare's farewell to the stage." The imagined social pathos of his departure from London—which would not come for more than a year after *The Tempest*, and after he had written at least one more play, *King Henry VIII, or All Is True*, and possibly parts of some others—is something some readers and commentators have wanted to elicit from these words, for a variety of reasonable reasons. So far from being "Shakespeare's farewell," it is not even, in the play, "Prospero's farewell," since it takes place in Act 4 of a five-act play.

Prospero is not dying. He is furious. And worried. Caliban and the other low conspirators are still out there, plotting against his life, and "the minute of their plot is almost come" (4.1.141–2). And this play within a play, the masque of Juno and Ceres, takes place in the fourth act. It is not until the end of the fifth act, of course, that Prospero releases Ariel, marking the end of his magic ("Be free, and fare thee well") and speaks his Epilogue. In Patrick Stewart's performance of the part in the mid-1990s, Stewart, classically trained with the Royal Shakespeare Company but perhaps best known for his detour into *Star Trek*, relinquished the microphone-amplification that he had used throughout the rest of the play. His voice was suddenly, and only, that of a man, not a magician—or a demigod.

So why do we persist in calling the "revels now are ended" speech Shakespeare's farewell? (*Ok, it is not his literal farewell, but it is a* kind *of farewell, right*?) Freud had a name for this: disavowal. The refusal to believe something we really, really do not want to believe—or rather, in the case of Freud's patient, and in our case as readers of Shakespeare, the wish not to give up believing something we really, really, want to believe. The desire, in this case, for Shakespeare to be talking to *us*, confessing his vulnerability to *us*. But like all overmastering desires, this one—the desire to know what is in Shakespeare's mind—cannot ever be wholly gratified, or satisfied. There is a filter between Shakespeare's opinions and us, and that filter, or curtain, or scrim, is not the 400-plus years between his time and ours. It is the genre of his work: the fact that they are plays.

Ralph Waldo Emerson was sure he could locate Shakespeare's opinions in the plays, and his testimony on this point is eloquent:

> We have his recorded convictions on those questions which knock for answer at every heart,— on life and death, on love, on wealth and poverty, on the prizes of life . . . on the characters of men, and the influences, occult and open, which affect their fortunes. . . . What point of morals, of manners, of economy, of philosophy, of religion, of taste, of the conduct of life, has he not settled? What mystery has he not signified his knowledge of? What office, or function, or district of man's work, has he not remembered? What king has he not taught state . . .? What maiden has not found him finer than her delicacy? What lover has he not outloved? What sage has he not outseen?[28]

There is much here with which I would agree; certainly the plays of Shakespeare contain an astounding amount of information and insight about kingship, and love, and even sagacity. But that information is dispersed, and it is, so to speak, reliably unreliable. A villain can speak truths about the human condition, as Iago does, as Richard III does. A fool, a clown, a knave, a coward—Bottom, Costard, Lucio, Thersites—these are often the wisest speakers in the plays. Taken as bromides their utterances are doxa, of a sort, wise saws and modern instances (to quote Jaques on the clichés dispensed by the well-fed, self-satisfied middle-aged judge[29]). But are these, in fact, Shakespeare's "recorded convictions," as Emerson would have it?

It is very hard to tell. Especially because, in addition to the commonplace book and its packaging of familiar quotations, there was another important element of early modern educational practice that also had a bearing upon the matter of Shakespeare's opinions and whether we can guess at them from reading and quoting the plays. What I have in mind here is what is sometimes called a disputation, or a prolusion, or a *question*, in the formal sense of a topic posed for argument, whether in the schools or in the law courts. (Which is better, night or day? The joyful man or the pensive man? Both of these were used by the poet John Milton.) The most famous Shakespearean appearance of this technical term from academic disputation comes in a context in which we no longer even hear it as a technical term—and therefore mistake the nature of the utterance. Here it is:

> To be, or not to be; that is the question.

The speaker, of course, is Hamlet, and the occasion, too many people have thought, is his deliberation about whether he should take his own life. "To be or not to be." But in early modern education this phrase, "to be or not to be" was a *question*, that is, a traditional topic for debate, about which young scholars of the period were trained in rhetorical argument: "is it better to be unhappy, or not to be at all?" This very famous question was debated in writings by St. Augustine, by Montaigne, and by a host of classical authors. The point was to be able to argue capably on either side of the question, not according to one's own private views, but rather as a rhetorical exercise—good practice for lawyers and statesmen. Hamlet, as a student at Wittenberg, had surely learned this technique (as did those other celebrated Wittenberg scholars, Martin Luther and Dr. Faustus). The art here is rhetoric, not philosophy. The point is to do justice to both sides, not to allow one to "win."

Shakespeare's plays are chock-full of such debates, sometimes serious, sometimes comic, often a little of each. And he will in each case give the debate a dramaturgical twist, just as we have seen him do with "familiar quotations," moving them from the banal and proverbial to the ironic and unexpected. What is often called loosely "*dramatic irony*" is, in this case, precisely apt. Let me mention some famous examples:

- The debate between King Polixenes and the shepherdess Perdita in Act 4 of *The Winter's Tale* on which is better, Nature or Art.
- The debate between Touchstone the clown (or fool) and the shepherd Corin in *As You Like It* on which is better, the city or the country.
- The debate between Troilus and Hector in *Troilus and Cressida* on whether things have intrinsic value or only get their value from the marketplace ("What's aught but as 'tis valued? But value lies not in particular will").
- The debate between Prince Hal and Falstaff on the nature of kingship, held in the tavern at Eastcheap: each playing, in turn, the part of the stern father (King Henry) and the errant son (Prince Hal).

Every one of these Shakespearean debates, and many others I could name, have a particular "Shakespearean" double-cross built into them, because the speaker is very often arguing passionately in rhetorical terms about something that is against his or her personal interest: thus for example the shepherdess Perdita in *The Winter's Tale* is vehemently opposed to the kind of gardening that she considers to be "art," rather than "nature," that is, to grafting one variety of plant onto another—even though she herself is a shepherdess hoping to marry a king's son, and Polixenes likewise argues against his own interest (gardens get better if you mix your plants, high and low: "the art itself is nature"). (Luckily for them both, Perdita turns out to be a princess in disguise, so that neither their horticultural nor their genealogical prejudices are ultimately put to the test.)

Although Western literary theory begins with Aristotle's reading of tragedies like Sophocles' *Oedipus*, the theory revolution of the mid-to-late twentieth century was notoriously silent about drama as a genre. At the same time, paradoxically, theorists made rich use of performance-based terms like *heteroglossia, carnivalization*, the split subject and the "other scene" of the unconscious to talk about other literary genres, like fiction and lyric. Philosopher J. L. Austin coined the term "performative" to describe a certain kind of utterance—but pointedly excluded drama from his list of examples. Mikhail Bakhtin's heteroglossia—literally, "othervoicedness," which he located in novels as contrasted with epics—is quite literally performed on the stage. Julia Kristeva called a similar linguistic split "*polylogue*," manyvoicedness (as contrasted with "dialogue"). Sigmund Freud's notion of the unconscious as the "other scene," taken up by Jacques Lacan, was meant initially as a metaphor, but many of Freud's own most persuasive theories about human consciousness and psychic motivation are based upon his readings of plays—and especially the plays of Shakespeare. The idea of the "Oedipus complex" was predicated in part upon a reading of Sophocles' play, but even more centrally on a reading of *Hamlet*. Famously, Freud saw the dividedness of Hamlet's character, his refusal or inability to do what Oedipus did (kill the father and marry the mother), as evidence of the "secular advance of repression in the emotional life of mankind." Repression grounds civilization, and produces both neurosis and drama. Hamlet thinks, and desires, but does not act upon his desires. At least according to Freud. The subject is split. And the perfect theatrical embodiment of that split is the soliloquy, a dialogue within the self, performed on the *other* "other scene," the stage.

Where Freud thought that only neurotics exhibited this kind of split or divided behavior, whereas healthy people did not, Jacques Lacan, reading both Freud and Shakespeare, developed the idea into a general concept of *Spaltung*, or splitting, "a general characteristic of subjectivity itself."[30] The subject undergoes this split "by virtue of being a subject only insofar as he speaks."[31] The need to speak, to communicate one's desires and thoughts, is itself evidence of the fact that we are not magically understood by others. Here the most obvious example from Shakespeare would be the catastrophic silence of Cordelia, who refuses to answer her father, King Lear ("nothing, my lord"; "nothing will come from nothing, speak again") or the enforced and imprisoning silence of Lavinia in *Titus Andronicus*, whose tongue has been cut out so that she cannot speak and name her attackers. These disempowered non-speakers are an index of a larger phenomenon, the fact that humanity is measured in terms of language, of speech and silence.

I will risk one more citation from Lacan to try to make clear how fundamentally theatrical and performative is this notion of the split subject. In discussing Freud's notion of the "other scene" (*ein andere Schauplatz*), which is what Freud calls the place of the unconscious and of dreams, Lacan observes that "*It* speaks in the Other." *It* is the ideas, desires, fantasies we do not know we have; the Other is the social world demarcated by speech. We find our secret thoughts in interaction with language, and with the world beyond the "self" as we think we know it. *It* speaks in the Other. This is a perfect and succinct description of drama as a genre.

The device of the soliloquy, literally, "talking alone," or "talking to oneself" (a term coined by St. Augustine), took on new and subversive power when it was presented, in the English Renaissance, not on the page but on the stage. In point of fact, drama is always the most subversive of genres, at the same time that it masquerades as the most compliant. The "first person" is always asserted and never fully present: whether the "I" is Richard III, or Hamlet, or Portia, or Caesar, the doubt is as powerful as the certainty: "For always I am Caesar." "This is I, Hamlet the Dane." The quest for "Shakespeare" is in this context a quest for a kind of imagined stability on the level of theory and genre, cognate to, but on a different critical plane from, the quest for the moral authority of an omniscient author "out-topping knowledge," in the terms of Matthew Arnold's famous sonnet about Shakespeare:

> Others abide our question. Thou art free.
> We ask and ask: Thou smilest and art still,
> Out-topping knowledge.
> Arnold, "Shakespeare" (1849)

"We ask and ask: Thou smilest and art still." A great deal of emotional effort, and a great deal of what used to be called "identification," goes into trying to winkle out the inner truth of Shakespeare's own cultural, political, and humane beliefs. But the plays are brilliantly designed to outwit this emotional detection.

What we should be discussing, far more than Shakespeare's opinions or Shakespeare's politics or Shakespeare's ethics, is what might be termed "contrapuntal Shakespeare," the way in which Shakespeare as a dramatist stages rhetorical confrontations, presenting the dazzling play of disparate, sometimes warring ideas *across* voices and speakers, or *within* them.

The contrapuntal devices in Shakespeare's dramaturgy are readily listed. In addition to staging debates between two characters, he sometimes—as we have seen—stages an internal debate within one speaker. Here the innovation of the soliloquy allows for the performance of a conflicted mind. Hamlet on mortality. Macbeth on regicide. Richard III, sleepless at Bosworth Field, on his own guilt: "Is there a murderer here? No? Yes. I am. Fool, of thyself speak well; fool, do not flatter." It is these internal debates that give the sense of "roundness" to a character; paradoxically, the fact that they are split or divided against themselves makes them seem "real," three-dimensional, or whole.

The plays also use a contrapuntal structure of repetition. This is one of Shakespeare's favorite dramatic tricks: he has a character do the same thing twice, but under such different conditions that the audience's estimate of the action changes radically. A good example can be found in *Richard III*. In any early scene the Duke of Gloucester, later to be Richard III, woos the Lady Anne and convinces her to marry him against all logic and reason, although he has killed her father-in-law and her husband. "Was ever woman in this humor wooed? Was ever woman in this humor won? I'll have her, but I will not keep her long." Richard's success here is a startling index of his rhetorical power and will. But when Richard tries the same trick again, later in the play, trying to convince his brother Edward's widow, Queen Elizabeth, to let him marry her daughter, his advances fail: "Relenting fool, and shallow, changing woman," he says dismissively when she leaves the stage, but the mistake is his, not hers, this time, and his fall can be charted. The two twinned scenes act as a counterpoint to one another: contrapuntal Shakespeare.

Sometimes the playwright performs the same kind of dramaturgical trick, not in *time* but in *space*, creating two characters rather than one, and playing them off against one another. This is especially true in the various love comedies that involve pairs of women (Katherina and Bianca in *The Taming of the Shrew*, Hermia and Helena in *A Midsummer Night's Dream*, Adriana and Luciana in *The Comedy of Errors*, Rosalind and Celia in *As You Like It*, Beatrice and Hero in *Much Ado About Nothing*, and so on). In these cases the women are often, deliberately, contrasted with one another: one outspoken, the other reticent, one compliant to authority, the other resistant to it, and so on. This is not always a comic device: Desdemona and Emilia, in one of Shakespeare's most unrelenting tragedies (*Othello*) play out the same two roles. You can see that this is in fact a variation on the split within a character; instead of heroic, loyal Macbeth and ambitious, disloyal Macbeth, we have a pair of characters personating loyalty and disloyalty (like, let us say, the Gloucester brothers, Edmund and

Edgar, in *King Lear*, or the constant comparison between Hal and Hotspur, Harry Monmouth and Harry Percy, in *King Henry IV, Part 1*). A complex version of this characterological counterpoint can be seen in *Hamlet*, that great play about foils and rapiers, in which Hamlet himself is measured, sequentially, against a series of very different dramatic foils: from Horatio to Laertes to Rosencrantz and Guildenstern to the First Player in the acting troupe to Fortinbras—not to mention the Ghost of his father. Again, the drama proceeds by counterpoint, as Hamlet compares himself to each of these, in turn.

Such contrapuntal structures elude the question of "what does Shakespeare believe," or "think." Instead of "siding" with one character, or voice, or opinion, the dramatic form enables the multiplication of speakers, and of authorities. It is only *we* who, with our modern prejudices developed from the novel, demand a "point of view" and an "authorial voice." It is not that "Shakespeare," whoever he was, didn't have such opinions. It is that we flatten the plays if we use them as source material for trying to figure out what his opinions might be. Time after time, reading after reading, production after production, the plays outsmart the critical detectives who are looking for the truth about Shakespeare. What we find is something else. If it is the truth about anything, it is the truth about drama. As for Shakespeare and his opinions—to quote the play of *Hamlet* once more— "'Tis here." "'Tis here." "'Tis gone."

Consider, if you will, the following passage:

> [He] is recognized as a master of the dialogue form and as one of the great . . . stylists of the . . . language. His published writings . . . consist of . . . dramatic dialogues on philosophical and related themes. The central problematic posed by this form is that it becomes virtually impossible to attribute any statement directly to [him]. . . . For the most part, [he] places his arguments in the mouths of characters who may or may not be based on historical persons. The speakers can never be assumed to be voicing [his] own views or the views of those whose names they bear. . . . These complications, which thwart efforts to fix [his] thought within a series of propositional statements, have attracted much attention . . .,

This could readily be a description of the frustration, or "problematic," faced by readers of Shakespeare. As it happens, it is not. It is the headnote to the entry on Plato from the *Norton Anthology of Theory and Criticism*. Plato is as elusive as Shakespeare, perhaps more so in some ways. But the Platonic dialogues contain a continuing figure—let's call him, for a moment, a dramatic character—in the enigmatic person of Socrates. For Shakespeare, despite the periodic appearance of essays like "Hamlet: The Prince or the Poem," or attempts to read the sonnets as a map of the playwright's emotional life, there is no figure, continuing or episodic, whether under one name or under many pseudonyms, who speaks for Shakespeare, who tells us what Shakespeare thinks and believes. Hamlet does not speak for Shakespeare. Falstaff does not speak for Shakespeare. Rosalind does not speak for Shakespeare. Prospero does not speak for Shakespeare.

If we are actually interested in Shakespeare's own observations about what is so often, so easily, and so transhistorically labeled "human nature," we have a much better chance of approaching his views by looking at the complex interplay of voices in his plays than by appropriating any one voice, or any particularly resounding utterance, and calling it "Shakespeare." Shakespeare the playwright is behind Iago, Roderigo, Othello, Desdemona, Emilia, Cassio, and Brabantio, but each of these characters has a distinct and different point of view about human cupidity, love, loss, war, and reputation.

It is predictable—we might indeed say that it is "natural" (by which we mean that it is structurally compelled and emotionally compelling) that audiences and readers should want to penetrate this mystery. But the mystery is itself the most compelling of dramatic illusions. Behind the characters there is no unitary "truth," in the form of a settled set of beliefs. To seek such a false "reality" is to fail to trust the plays as plays. All the justly famous remarks about Shakespearean dispersal, from Dryden's assertion that Shakespeare was "the man who of all modern, and perhaps ancient, poets, had the largest and most comprehensive soul" to Coleridge's "myriad-minded Shakespeare" and Keats' claim that "Shakespeare led a life of Allegory; his works are the comments on it" and indeed his celebrated notion of "Negative Capability"—all these are poetic and philosophical attempts to come to terms with a formal and structural barrier of resistance. These are plays. Their illusion of depth is just that, the most extraordinary and effective of dramatic illusions, the illusion wrought by a master, who has made himself disappear.

Let me close by saying, as I hope is clear, that I am not here advocating the position either of a purist or of an "expert" or the guardian of scholarly turf. As far as I am concerned, the more quotation—and cheerful, unapologetic misquotation—of "Shakespeare" the better. No headline, no politician's speech, no movie, no T-shirt slogan can harm these remarkable plays. The more we read, interpret, produce, discuss, and argue over Shakespeare, the better place this Globe we live in is likely to be. But in order to know Shakespeare's mind, and to divine, or guess at, his opinions, we will need—happily, and always—to return to the plays, and to the dramatic form in which he has so brilliantly wrought them, and not merely to excerpts or sound bites, however appealing. We can be both borrowers and lenders of his words, but the pleasure and the value of Shakespeare to our culture, and to any culture, is in the art he practiced, and not in the raw material that he crafted, not in what he thinks, but in what makes his plays and his characters say.

Notes

Chapter 1

1 See *The Riverside Shakespeare*, ed. G. Blakemore Evans (Boston: Houghton Mifflin, 1974), p. 1684.
2 James G. McManaway, *The Authorship of Shakespeare* (Washington, DC: Folger Shakespeare Library, 1962), p. 12.
3 ibid., pp. 12–13.
4 ibid., p. 29.
5 ibid., p. 19.
6 Charlton Ogburn, Jr., *The Mysterious William Shakespeare: The Myth and the Reality* (New York: Dodd, Mead, 1984), p. 145.
7 William F. and Elizabeth S. Friedman, *The Shakespearean Ciphers Examined* (Cambridge: Cambridge University Press, 1957), pp. 7; 181.
8 ibid., p. 1
9 ibid., p. 5.
10 Michel Foucault, *Language, Counter-Memory, Practice*, ed. and trans. Donald F. Bouchard (Ithaca: Cornell University Press, 1977), p. 125.
11 Frank W. Wadsworth, *The Poacher from Stratford* (Berkeley and Los Angeles: University of California Press, 1958), p. 52. Wadsworth's book gives a good overview of the controversy.
12 ibid., p. 45.
13 *Harvard Magazine*, 77 (January 1975).
14 ibid., 77 (April 1975).
15 ibid.
16 John H. Stotsenburg, *An Impartial Study of the Shakespeare Title* (Louisville, Kentucky: J. P. Morton, 1904), p. 174.
17 S. Schoenbaum, *Shakespeare's Lives* (Oxford: Clarendon Press, 1970), p. 612.
18 Georg Brandes, *William Shakespeare: A Critical Study* (New York: Macmillan, 1909), p. 87. Cited in Ogburn, p. 153.
19 Wadsworth, p. 89.
20 Mark Twain, "Is Shakespeare Dead?" in *What is Man? And Other Essays* (New York and London: Harper Brothers, 1917), p. 324.
21 Ralph Waldo Emerson to William Emerson, 29 May 1849, in *The Letters of Ralph Waldo Emerson*, ed. Ralph L. Rusk (New York: Columbia University Press, 1939), 4, p. 149.

22 Horace Traubel, *Walt Whitman in Camden* (Boston: Small, Maynard, 1906), p. 136.

23 Walt Whitman, "November Boughs," in *Complete Poetry and Prose of Walt Whitman, as Prepared by Him for the Death Bed Edition* (New York: Pelligrini & Cudahy, 1948), 2, p. 404.

24 Sir Charles Spencer Chaplin, *My Autobiography* (New York: Simon & Schuster, 1964), p. 364. Ogburn, p. 260.

25 Ralph Waldo Emerson, "Shakespeare, or, The Poet," *Representative Men* in *Ralph Waldo Emerson: Essays and Lectures* (New York: Library of America, 1983), p. 720.

26 Henry James, Letter to Violet Hunt, 26 August 1903, in *The Letters of Henry James*, ed. Percy Lubbock (New York: Scribner, 1920), 1, p. 424.

27 Henry James, "The Birthplace," in *Selected Short Stories* (New York: Rinehart, 1955), pp. 246–47.

28 ibid., p. 238.

29 ibid., p. 256.

30 Twain, p. 372.

31 Ralph Waldo Emerson, *The Journals and Miscellaneous Notebooks of Ralph Waldo Emerson*, ed. Ralph H. Orth and Alfred R. Ferguson (Cambridge, Mass.: Harvard University Press, 1971), 9, p. 184.

32 Charles Dickens, Letter to William Sandys, 13 June 1847, in *Complete Writings of Charles Dickens*, ed. "by his sister-in-law" (Boston, Mass.: Charles E. Lauriat, 1923), 37, p. 206.

33 Samuel Taylor Coleridge, *Biographia Literaria* (1817), Chapter 15.

34 John Keats to George and Thomas Keats, 21 December 1817, in *The Selected Letters of John Keats*, ed. Lionel Trilling (Garden City, NJ: Doubleday Anchor Books, 1956), p. 103.

35 Keats to George and Georgiana Keats, 14 February–3 May 1819, *Selected Letters*, p. 229.

36 John Dryden, "An Essay on Dramatic Poesy," *The Works of John Dryden*, Notes and Life by Sir Walter Scott; revised by George Saintsbury. (Edinburgh: William Patterson, 1882–83), 15, p. 344.

37 Foucault, p. 130.

38 Matthew Arnold, "Shakespeare," in *The Poems of Matthew Arnold*, ed. Kenneth Allott (London: Longmans, Green & Co., 1965), pp. 48–50, ll. 1–3.

39 Foucault, p. 166.

40 ibid., p. 117.

41 Nicholas Rowe, "Some Account of the Life, & c., of Mr. William Shakespeare," in *The Works of Mr. William Shakespeare, in Six Volumes* (London: Jacob Tonson, 1709), 1; p. vi.

42 William Oldys (ca.1743–61), quoted by E.K. Chambers, *William Shakespeare: A Study of Facts and Problems* (Oxford: Clarendon Press, 1930), 3, p. 278.

43 Sigmund Freud, *Beyond the Pleasure Principle*, 1; italics Freud's.

44 ibid., p. 37.

45 ibid., p. 45.

46 See Jacques Derrida, *Of Grammatology*, trans. G. C. Spivak (Baltimore: Johns Hopkins University Press, 1974), pp. 141–64.

47 Barbara Johnson, unpublished manuscript.

48 See J. H. Pafford, ed., *The Winters Tale*, The Arden Shakespeare (London: Methuen, 1963), p. 139n. Pafford cites Harold Brooks's observation that "with this clue one can see that Paulina's comparison of the first wife with any second has resemblance with Hamlet's indignant comparison of Gertrude's first husband with her second." For Gertrude's ears, see *Hamlet* 3.4.95.

49 Sigmund Freud, "The Uncanny," in *Studies in Parapsychology*, ed. Philip Rieff (New York: Macmillan, 1963), p. 40.

50 See Walter Benjamin, *Illuminations*, ed. Hannah Arendt, trans. Harry Zohn (New York: Schocken Books, 1969), p. 76.

51 ibid., p. 71.

52 ibid., p. 220.

53 ibid., p. 221.

54 ibid., p. 224.

55 Robert Lowell, "Epilogue," in *Day by Day* (New York: Farrar, Strauss & Giroux, 1977), p. 127.

56 Abel Gance, "Le Temps de l'image est venu," *l'Art cinématographique* (Paris: Gance, 1927) 2: 94F. Cited in Benjamin, "The Work of Art in the Age," *Illuminations*, pp. 221–2.
57 A concept is said to be "under erasure" when it is put in question or under critique. This signifying practice, employed by Martin Heidegger and, after him, by Jacques Derrida and other deconstructive critics, is described by Gayatri Spivak as "to write a word, cross it out, and then print both word and deletion. (Since the word is inaccurate, it is crossed out. Since it is necessary, it remains legible.)" (in Jacques Derrida, *Of Grammatology* (Baltimore: Johns Hopkins University Press, 1974), translator's preface, p. xiv). Thus Heidegger, in *The Question of Being*, writes that "Man in his essence is the memory [or memorial, *Gedächtnis*] not of Being, but of ~~Being~~. This means that the essence of man is a part of that which in the crossed intersected lines of Being puts thinking under the claim of a more originary command [*anfänglichere Geheiss*]." (*The Question of Being*, tr. William Kluback and Jean T. Wilde, bilingual edition (New York: Twayne Publishers 1958), cited by Spivak, p. xv). Spivak comments that "Heidegger is work-ing with the resources of the old language, the language we already possess. To make a new word is to run the risk of forgetting the problem or believing it solved" (Spivak, p. xv). But, she remarks, it is important to distinguish between what Heidegger puts under erasure and what Derrida does. Heidegger critiques the master-word, "Being," a transcendental signifier. Derrida, while he does not reject this idea, is concerned with the "trace," "a word that cannot be a master-word, that presents itself as the mark of an anterior presence, origin, master" (*Of Grammatology*, p. xv). Spivak's example from Derrida is this: ". . . the sign ~~is~~ that ill-named ~~thing~~ . . . which escapes the instituting question of philosophy . . ." (*Of Grammatology*, p. 19). The nostalgia for a lost presence, a lost originary moment, that animates the writings of Heidegger is specifically absent from Derrida. "Derrida's ~~trace~~ is the mark of the absence of a presence, an always already absent present, of the lack at the origin that is the condition of thought and experience" (Spivak, xvii). It is this specifically Derridean inflection of "under erasure," "*sous rature*," that so uncannily resembles a ghost—resembles, in fact, the ~~Being~~ of a ghost. "There are more ~~things~~ in heaven and earth. Horatio, / than are dreamt of in your philosophy" (*Hamlet* 1.5.166–67).
58 Jacques Derrida, "Signature, Event, Context," in *Margins of Philosophy*, trans. Alan Bass (Chicago: University of Chicago Press, 1982), p. 328.
59 T. S. Eliot, "Shakespeare and the Stoicism of Seneca," *Selected Essays* (New York: Harcourt, Brace & World, 1960), p. 67; M.C. Bradbrook, *Shakespeare and Elizabethan Poetry* (Harmondsworth: Penguin, 1964), p. 96; E. M. W. Tillyard, *Shakespeare's History Plays* (New York: Collier Books, 1962), p. 160. In a lecture on *Titus Andronicus* delivered at the Stratford (Ontario) Shakespeare Festival some years ago, Richard Wheeler alluded to this peculiar tendency in *Titus* criticism.
60 J. C. Maxwell, ed., *Titus Andronicus*, The Arden Shakespeare (London: Methuen, 1968), p. xxiv.
61 John Bulwer, *Chironomia* (London, 1644), p. 16. Cited in B. L. Joseph, *Elizabethan Acting* (London: 1951), p. 39. See Maxwell, ed., pp. 109–10.
62 Elaine Showalter, "Representing Ophelia: Women, Madness, and the Responsibilities of Feminist Criticism," in Patricia Parker and Geoffrey Hartman, eds., *Shakespeare and the Question of Theory* (New York: Methuen, 1985), p. 80.

Chapter 2

1 Sigmund Freud letter, 15 October 1897, in *The Complete Letters of Sigmund Freud to Wilhelm Fliess, 1887–1904*, ed. and trans. Jeffrey Moussaieff Masson (Cambridge, Mass.: Harvard University Press, 1985), pp. 272–3.
2 ibid., 21 September 1897, p. 264.
3 ibid.
4 ibid., p. 265.
5 ibid.
6 ibid.

7 ibid.

8 ibid., pp. 265–6.

9 Masson, ed., p. 266.

10 Sigmund Freud, "The Uncanny," in *Studies in Parapsychology*, ed. Philip Rieff (New York: Collier Books, 1963), p. 43.

11 ibid.

12 Sigmund Freud, *The Interpretation of Dreams*, ed. and trans. James Strachey (New York: Avon Books, 1965), pp. 480–1.

13 Freud, "The Uncanny," p. 30.

14 ibid., p. 37.

15 ibid., p. 33.

16 ibid., p. 35.

17 ibid., p. 55.

18 ibid., p. 56.

19 ibid., p. 44.

20 Norman N. Holland, *Psychoanalysis and Shakespeare* (New York: Octagon Books, rpt 1976), p. 165.

21 Frank Kermode, *Forms of Attention* (Chicago: University of Chicago Press, 1985), p. 49. See his whole argument, "Cornelius and Voltimand: Doubles in *Hamlet*," pp. 35–63.

22 Jacques Lacan, *The Four Fundamental Concepts of Psycho-Analysis*, ed. Jacques-Alain Miller, trans. Alan Sheridan (New York: W.W. Norton, 1981), p. 38.

23 Jacques Lacan, "Desire and the Interpretation of Desire in *Hamlet*," ed. Jacques-Alain Miller, trans. James Hulbert, in *Literature and Psychoanalysis*, ed. Shoshana Felman (Baltimore: Johns Hopkins University Press, 1982), p. 50.

24 Sigmund Freud, "The Passing of the Oedipus Complex," in *Sexuality and the Psychology of Love*, ed. Philip Rieff (New York: Macmillan, 1963), p. 179.

25 Lacan, *The Four Fundamental Concepts*, pp. 34–5.

26 ibid., p. 35.

27 Jacques Lacan, *Écrits: A Selection*, trans. Alan Sheridan (New York: W.W. Norton, 1977), p. 215.

28 ibid., p. 219.

29 ibid., p. 218.

30 ibid., pp. 218–19.

31 Lacan, *The Four Fundamental Concepts*, p. 35.

32 Lacan, "Desire," p. 12.

33 Lacan, *The Four Fundamental Concepts*, p. 88.

34 Lacan, "Desire," p. 30.

35 Lacan, *The Four Fundamental Concepts*, p. 89.

36 ibid.

37 ibid.

38 ibid., p. 92.

39 ibid., pp. 88–9.

40 See Francis Barker, *The Tremulous Private Body: Essays on Subjection* (London: Methuen, 1984), pp. 25–40, for a compelling treatment of this question. The "modern subject" constituted here, of course, is male. Indeed, the centrality of *Hamlet* to the emergence of the "modern subject" seems connected to its *lack* of a powerful (or rather, an empowered) female presence. The play takes place entirely within the male unconscious, and its battleground is the conflict, quite specifically, of fathers and sons. Women are protected (the Ghost repeatedly tells Hamlet not to punish his mother) or dismissed ("get thee to a nunnery"; "Marry, I will teach you"). Yet the play uncannily includes the two female figures that have most preoccupied the modern feminist imagination—the Madwoman and the Mother.

41 Lacan, *The Four Fundamental Concepts*, pp. 87–8.

42 ibid., p. 235.

43 Paul de Man, "Autobiography as De-Facement," in *The Rhetoric of Romanticism* (New York: Columbia University Press, 1984), pp. 75–6.

44 ibid., p. 78.

45 Merritt Y. Hughes, ed., *John Milton, Complete Poems and Major Prose* (New York: Odyssey Press, 1957), p. 63.

46 Michael Riffaterre, "Prosopopeia," in *The Lesson of Paul de Man*, Yale French Studies 69 (1985): 112.

47 Freud, "The Uncanny," p. 35.

48 Molière, *The Miser and Other Plays*, trans. John Wood (Harmondsworth: Penguin, 1953).

49 Julian Rushton, *W.A. Mozart, Don Giovanni* (Cambridge: Cambridge University Press, 1981).

50 Stanley Cavell, *The Claim of Reason* (Oxford: Oxford University Press, 1979), p. 492.

51 Letter to Leopold Mozart, 29 November 1780. In Emily Anderson, ed., *The Letters of Mozart and His Family* (New York: W.W. Norton, 1985), p. 674.

52 "Dramaturgische Blätter," Frankfurt am Main, 1789, cited in Otto Erich Deutsch, *Mozart, A Documentary Biography*, trans. Eric Blom, Peter Branscome, and Jeremy Noble (Stanford: Stanford University Press, 1965), p. 341.

53 William Gresser, "The Meaning of 'due della notte' in *Don Giovanni*," *Mozart Jahrbuch* (1971–2): 244.

54 Peter Shaffer, *Amadeus* (New York: Signet, 1984), p. 108.

55 ibid., p. 110.

56 ibid., p. 137.

57 ibid., pp. xi–xii.

58 Freud, *Interpretation of Dreams*, p. 299.

59 James Joyce, *Ulysses* (New York: Random House, 1986), p. 175.

60 Cavell, pp. 481–2.

61 Francis Grose, *A Provincial Glossary*; Brand, *Popular Antiquities*, ed. Hazlitt; cited in Harold Jenkins, ed., *Hamlet*, The Arden Shakespeare (New York: Methuen, 1982), p. 424.

62 de Man, p. 77.

63 ibid., pp. 75–6.

64 ibid., p. 76.

65 For a full discussion of these distinctions, and of the history of the controversy, see Eleanor Prosser, *Hamlet and Revenge*, 2nd edn (Stanford: Stanford University Press, 1971).

66 de Man, p. 78.

67 Jonathan Culler, "Apostrophe," in *The Pursuit of Signs* (Ithaca: Cornell University Press, 1981), p. 148.

68 Paul de Man, *Allegories of Reading* (New Haven: Yale University Press, 1979), p. 29. See also Cynthia Chase, *Decomposing Figures* (Baltimore: Johns Hopkins University Press, 1986), pp. 82–112.

69 Culler, p. 148.

70 ibid., p. 152.

71 ibid., p. 153.

72 Rosalie Colie, *Shakespeare's Living Art* (Princeton: Princeton University Press, 1974), p. 11.

73 de Man, "Autobiography," p. 78.

74 "'For O, for O, the hobby-horse is forgot' was the refrain of a popular song. . . . From its frequent use we seem to have an instance of a catchphrase continuing in popularity after the original point of it had been lost. What is certain is that the hobby-horse, while very much remembered, became a byword for being forgotten and as such the occasion for numerous jokes in Elizabethan plays" (Jenkins, ed., 1982), pp. 500–1.

75 Paul de Man, "Sign and Symbol in Hegel's *Aesthetics*," *Critical Inquiry* 8 (Summer 1982): 761–75.

76 See Chase, pp. 113–26.

77 de Man, "Sign and Symbol," p. 771.

78 ibid., p. 772.

79 Sigmund Freud, "Mourning and Melancholia" (1917), in *General Psychological Theory*, ed. Philip Rieff (New York: Macmillan, 1963), pp. 164–79.
80 See Freud, "A Note upon the 'Mystic Writing-Pad'" (1925), in Philip Rieff, ed., *General Psychological Theory* (New York: Macmillan, 1963), pp. 207–12; Jacques Derrida, "Freud and the Scene of Writing," in *Writing and Difference*, trans. Alan Bass (Chicago: University of Chicago Press, 1978), pp. 196–231.
81 See Jonathan Goldberg, *Voice Terminal Echo* (New York: Methuen, 1986), p. 99.
82 Janet Adelman's fine essay, "'Anger's My Meat': Feeding, Dependency, and Aggression in *Coriolanus*," in *Representing Shakespeare*, ed. Murray M. Schwartz and Coppélia Kahn (Baltimore: Johns Hopkins University Press, 1981), pp. 129–49, while it does not mention *Hamlet*, is in many ways relevant to Hamlet's situation as son and speaker, and to Gertrude's lack of nurturing qualities.
83 Shoshana Felman, *The Literary Speech Act*, trans. Catherine Porter (Ithaca: Cornell University Press, 1983), p. 55.
84 Jacques Derrida, *Mémoires: for Paul de Man*, trans. Cecile Lindsay, Jonathan Culler, and Eduardo Cadava (New York: Columbia University Press, 1986), p. 56.
85 ibid., pp. 58–9.
86 Stéphane Mallarmé, *Oeuvres Complètes* (Paris: Éditions Gallimard, 1945), p. 299.
87 ibid. Translation Barbara Johnson.
88 The Ghost of *Hamlet* indeed turns up in some unlikely places. For Marx, the Ghost is a figure for the revolution:

> But the revolution is thoroughgoing. It is still journeying through purgatory. It does its work methodically. By December 2, 1851, it had completed one half of its preparatory work; it is now completing the other half. First it perfected the parliamentary power, in order to be able to overthrow it. Now that it has attained this, it perfects the *executive power*, reduces it to its purest expression, isolates it, sets it up against itself as the sole target, in order to concentrate all its forces of destruction against it. And when it has done this second half of its preliminary work, Europe will leap from its seat and exultantly exclaim: Well grubbed, old mole!

> Karl Marx, *The Eighteenth Brumaire of Louis Bonaparte*, in Karl Marx and Friedrich Engels, *Selected Works* (New York: International Publishers, 1968), p. 170.

In Whitehead, it is a figure for mathematics:

> The study of mathematics is apt to commence in disappointment . . . We are told that by its aid the stars are weighed and the billions of molecules in a drop of water are counted. Yet, like the ghost of Hamlet's father, this great science eludes the efforts of our mental weapons to grasp it.—'Tis here, 'tis here, 'tis gone'—and what we do see does not suggest the same excuse for illusiveness as sufficed the ghost, that it is too noble for our gross methods.

> Alfred North Whitehead, *An Introduction to Mathematics* (New York: Henry Holt, 1911), p. 7.

89 See Goldberg, *Voice Terminal Echo*, p. 99.
90 J. Hillis Miller, *Fiction and Repetition: Seven English Novels* (Cambridge, Mass.: Harvard University Press, 1982), p. 6.
91 ibid., p. 9.
92 Walter Benjamin, "The Image of Proust," in *Illuminations*, trans. Harry Zohn (New York: Schocken Books, 1969), p. 202. De Man, too, turns to Proust as a test case for his two types of memory, pointing indirectly (via the *madeleine*) to the eating imagery behind the term *Erinnerung*: "Proust struggles with the distinction in his attempts to distinguish between *mémoire volontaire*—which is like *Gedächtnis*—and *mémoire involontaire*, which is rather like *Erinnerung*" ("Sign and Symbol in Hegel's *Aesthetics*," p. 772).

93 Friedrich Nietzsche, "The Use and Abuse of History," *Untimely Meditations*, trans. R.J. Hollingdale (Cambridge: Cambridge University Press, 1983), p. 62. Emphasis added.

94 ibid.

95 Jenkins, ed., p. 554.

96 See Marjorie Garber, "'Remember Me': *Memento Mori* Figures in Shakespeare's Plays," *Renaissance Drama* 12 (1981): 15–17.

97 Nietzsche, p. 59. Emphasis added.

98 ibid.

99 ibid., p. 60.

100 ibid., p. 61. Emphasis added.

101 See Margaret W. Ferguson, "*Hamlet*: Letters and Spirits," in *Shakespeare and the Question of Theory*, ed. Patricia Parker and Geoffrey Hartman (New York: Methuen, 1985), p. 302.

102 Freud, *Interpretation of Dreams*, p. 143n.

103 ibid., p. 564.

104 Terry Eagleton, *William Shakespeare* (Oxford: Basil Blackwell, 1986), p. 72.

105 Goldberg, p. 99.

106 Sigmund Freud, "Further Recommendations in the Technique of Psychoanalysis: Recollection, Repetition and Working Through" (1914), in *Therapy and Technique*, ed. Philip Rieff (New York: Macmillan, 1963), p. 160–1.

107 ibid., p. 161.

108 ibid., p. 164.

109 ibid., p. 165.

110 Sigmund Freud, *Beyond the Pleasure Principle*, trans. James Strachey (New York: Bantam Books, 1959), p. 41.

111 ibid., p. 37.

112 ibid., p. 44.

113 ibid., p. 65.

114 ibid., p. 67.

115 Sigmund Freud, "Further Recommendations in the Technique of Psychoanalysis: Observations on Transference-Love" (1915), in *Therapy and Technique*, ed. Philip Rieff (New York: Macmillan, 1963), p. 172. Emphasis added.

116 Lacan, *The Four Fundamental Concepts*, p. 232.

117 ibid.

118 ibid.

119 ibid., 234.

120 Lacan, *Ecrits*, p. 199.

121 Georg Brandes, *William Shakespeare: A Critical Study* (New York: Macmillan, 1909).

122 Freud, *Interpretation of Dreams*, p. 299.

123 ibid., p. xxvi.

124 See, for example, the title and argument of Jeffrey Moussaieff Masson, *The Assault on Truth: Freud's Suppression of the Seduction Theory* (New York: Penguin, 1985).

125 Marianne Krüll, *Freud and His Father*, trans. Arnold J. Pomerans (New York: W.W. Norton, 1986), p. 63.

126 ibid., pp. 124–5; cf. Ernest Jones, *The Life and Work of Sigmund Freud* (New York: Basic Books, 1953), 1, pp. 10ff.

127 Krüll, p. 180.

128 John Gross, review of Krüll's *Freud and his Father*, in *The New York Times* (August 15, 1986): C25.

129 Masson, ed., 2 November 1896, p. 202; Freud, *Interpretation of Dreams*, pp. 352–3.

130 ibid., p. 353.

131 Krüll, p. 63.

132 Freud, *Interpretation of Dreams*, p. 352. Emphasis added.

133 Masson, ed., p. 202.

134 Sigmund Freud, *The Origins of Psychoanalysis. Letters to Wilhelm Fliess*, ed. Marie Bonaparte, Anna Freud, and Ernst Kris, trans. Eric Mosbacher and James Strachey (New York: Basic Books, 1954).

135 ibid., pp. xi–xii.

136 Freud, *Interpretation of Dreams*, p. 298.

137 ibid.

138 Freud, "Mourning and Melancholia," p. 169.

139 ibid.

140 ibid., p. 172.

141 ibid., p. 173. Emphasis added.

142 ibid., Emphasis added.

143 ibid., pp. 173–4.

144 ibid., p. 179.

145 ibid., pp. 167–8.

146 Shoshana Felman, "To Open the Question," in *Literature and Psychoanalysis*, ed. Felman (Baltimore: Johns Hopkins University Press, 1982), p. 9.

147 Lacan, *The Four Fundamental Concepts*, pp. 149, 203.

148 Felman, p. 10.

149 Krüll, p. 208.

150 Sigmund Freud, letter to J. Thomas Looney, June 1938, in Looney, *Shakespeare Identified as Edward de Vere, the 17th Earl of Oxford*, 3rd edn, ed. and augmented by Ruth Loyd Miller (Port Washington, NY: Kennikat Press, 1975), 3, p. 273.

151 Letter 344 J, 6 January 1913, *The Freud / Jung Letters*, ed. William McGuire (Princeton, NJ: Princeton University Press, 1974), p. 540.

152 Shoshana Felman, *Writing and Madness* (Ithaca: Cornell University Press, 1985), p. 50.

153 Thomas Lodge, *Wit's Misery*, 1596, p. 56. Harold Jenkins notes that "'Hamlet, revenge,' became a byword" citing Dekker, *Satiromastix*, 4.1.121; and Rowlands, *The Night-Raven*, 1620, sig. D2. See Jenkins, ed, p. 83.

154 See n 66.

155 Prosser, p. 246.

156 ibid., p. 247.

157 ibid.

158 ibid., p. 256.

159 ibid.

160 Prosser cites "a few ambiguous hints" in G. Wilson Knight's *The Wheel of Fire*, but more especially Harold Goddard, *The Meaning of Shakespeare* (Chicago, 1951); Roy Walker, *The Time is Out of Joint* (London, 1948); John Vyvyan, *The Shakespearean Ethic* (London, 1959); and L.C. Knights, *An Approach to "Hamlet"* (Stanford, Calif.: 1961). Since the publication of her book a number of other critics have argued this point as well.

161 *Alternative Shakespeares*, ed. John Drakakis (London: Methuen, 1985); *Political Shakespeare*, ed. Jonathan Dollimore and Alan Sinfield (Ithaca: Cornell University Press, 1985); *Shakespeare and the Question of Theory*, ed. Patricia Parker and Geoffrey Hartman (New York: Methuen, 1985).

162 J. Hillis Miller, "Ariachne's Broken Woof," *The Georgia Review* 31 (Spring 1977): 44–63.

163 Elaine Showalter, "Representing Ophelia: Women, Madness, and the Responsibilities of Feminist Criticism," in *Shakespeare and the Question of Theory*, ed. Patricia Parker and Geoffrey Hartman, pp. 77–94.

164 Paul de Man, "Literary History and Literary Modernity," in *Blindness and Insight* (Minneapolis: University of Minnesota Press, 1983), p. 157.

Chapter 3

1 For this and subsequent information about *Macbeth* and theatrical superstition I am indebted to
   Richard Huggett, *Supernatural On Stage: Ghosts and Superstitions of the Theater* (New York:
   Taplinger Publishing Company, 1975), pp. 153–211. I was witness to the Stratford, Ontario
   incident (July 1980).
2 Huggett, pp. 162–3.
3 Sigmund Freud, "The Uncanny," in *Studies in Parapsychology*, ed. Philip Rieff, trans. Alix Strachey
   (New York: Macmillan, 1963), p. 57.
4 Stéphane Mallarmé, *La Fausse Entrée Des Sorcières dans Macbeth*, in *Crayonné au théâtre, Oeuvres
   Completes* (Paris: Pléiade, 1945), p. 348. I am indebted to Barbara Johnson for calling this essay
   to my attention, and for the translation.
5 Huston Diehl, in "Horrid Image, Sorry Sight, Fatal Vision: The Visual Rhetoric of *Macbeth*,"
   Shakespeare Studies 16 (1983): 191–203, comments on the problematics of reading the play,
   contrasting Macduff's ethical reading of the dead body of Duncan with Macbeth's rejection of
   the spiritual and ethical, and noting the audience's participation in the act of seeing and
   interpreting.
6 H.J. Rose, *A Handbook of Greek Mythology* (New York: E.P. Dutton, 1959), pp. 29–30.
7 What is the relationship between anxiety of gender and the anxiety generated by an application
   of Freud's theory? Is the Medusa head like a King Charles head for modern critical theory,
   a whimsical obsession, always turning up where least wanted and expected? Or is it, in fact, a
   radical of this play's dramatic subtext, everywhere present because everywhere absent,
   something we fall in love with because we fear to look on it? Medusa, after all, was a figure of
   surpassing beauty—it is for this reason, according to some versions of the story, that Athena had
   her killed, and annexed (while disabling) her beauty by depicting the head on her shield.
8 Jane Ellen Harrison, *Prolegomena to the Study of Greek Religion* (Cambridge: Cambridge University
   Press, 1922; rpt New York: Meridian Books, 1955), p. 187.
9 Caesare Ripa, *Iconologia* (Florence, 1613), p. 182.
10 Walter Friedländer, *Carvaggio Studies* (Princeton, N.J.: Princeton University Press, 1955), p. 88.
11 Francis Bacon, *The Wisedome of the Ancients*, trans. Arthur Gorges (London, 1619), p. 41.
12 ibid., p. 43.
13 ibid., p. 44.
14 Richard Hosley, ed., *Shakespeare's Holinshed* (New York: G.P. Putnam, 1968), p. 17. An excerpt
   from Holinshed's *Chronicles of Scotland* appears in Kenneth Muir, ed., *Macbeth*, The Arden
   Shakespeare (London: Methuen, 1962), pp. 170–88.
15 Alexander Ross, *Mystogogus Poeticus* (London, 1647), p. 103.
16 ibid., p. 213.
17 *The Political Works of James I, reprinted from the Edition of 1616*, ed. Charles Howard McHwain
   (Cambridge, Mass.: Harvard University Press, 1918), p. 29.
18 ibid., p. 272.
19 ibid., p. 65.
20 ibid., p. 43.
21 ibid., p. 6.
22 ibid., p. 21.
23 ibid., p. xxviii.
24 ibid., pp. 18ff.
25 J.M.C. Toynbee, *Art in Britain Under the Romans* (Oxford: Clarendon Press, 1964), *passim*.
26 ibid., p. 136.
27 ibid., p. 32.
28 J.M.C. Toynbee, *Art in Roman Britain* (London: Phaidon Press, 1962), p. 163.
29 Nelson Glueck, *Deities and Dolphins: The Story of the Nabataeans* (New York: Farrar, Straus &
   Giroux, 1965), pp. 80–4.
30 Kathleen Basford, *The Green Man* (Ipswich, Suffolk: D.S. Brewer, 1978), pp. 9–22.

31 Karl Otfried Müller, *Introduction to a Scientific Study of Mythology*, trans. Leitch (London, 1844). Cited in Burton Feldman and Robert D. Richardson, Jr., *The Rise of Modern Mythology* (Bloomington: Indiana University Press, 1972), p. 420.

32 Freud, "The Uncanny," p. 47.

33 The "omnipotence of thoughts" ascribed to witches could be a self-elected characteristic, concomitant to certain modern mental disorders like schizophrenia—or a more ordinary outgrowth of loneliness and superstition. Thus Reginald Scot in his *Discovery of Witchcraft* (1584) describes them: "One sort of such as are said to be witches are women which be commonly old, lame, blear-eyed, pale, foul, and full of wrinkles; poor, sullen, superstitious, and papists; or such as know no religion: in whose drowsy minds the Devil hath gotten a fine seat; so as, what mischief, mischance, calamity, or slaughter is brought to pass, they are easily persuaded the same is done by themselves, imprinting in their minds an earnest and constant imagination thereof.
. . .

The witch . . . expecting her neighbors' mischances, and seeing things sometimes come to pass according to her wishes, curses, and incantations . . . being called before a Justice, by due examination of the circumstances is driven to see her imprecations and desires and her neighbors' harms and losses to concur, and as it were to take effect: and so confesseth that she (as a goddess) hath brought such things to pass." Cited in G.B. Harrison, ed., *Shakespeare: The Complete Works* (New York: Harcourt, Brace & World, 1952), pp. 1644–5.

34 Freud, "The Uncanny," p. 46.

35 ibid., p. 397.

36 ibid., p. 40.

37 ibid., p. 51.

38 Sigmund Freud, "Medusa's Head," in *Sexuality and the Psychology of Love*, ed. Philip Rieff (New York: Macmillan, 1963), p. 212.

39 See Neil Hertz, *The End of the Line* (New York: Columbia University Press, 1985), pp. 161–215.

40 Freud, "Medusa's Head," pp. 212–13.

41 ibid., p. 20.

42 ibid., pp. 31–2.

43 ibid., p. 35.

44 ibid., p. 57.

45 ibid., p. 47.

46 ibid.

47 ibid., p. 49.

48 For a useful and persuasive discussion of the consanguinities of Shakespearean and Freudian models of psychic representation in *Macbeth*, see David Willbern, "Phantasmagoric *Macbeth*" *ELR* 16 (1986): 520–49. Willbern deals succinctly with the problem of Shakespeare's uncanny prefiguration of Freud: "In brief," he writes, "Shakespeare dramatizes what psychoanalysis theorizes" (p. 544), and again, "Shakespeare prefigures Freud: drama enacts what theory affirms" (p. 545).

49 For another discussion of *Macbeth*, gender anxiety, and androgyny, see Robert Kimbrough, "Macbeth: The Prisoner of Gender," *Shakespeare Studies* 16 (1983): 175–90.

50 For a strong and appealing presentation of this case, see Janet Adelman, "'Born of Woman': Fantasies of Maternal Power in *Macbeth*," in *Cannibals, Witches, and Divorce: Estranging the Renaissance*, ed. Marjorie Garber (Baltimore: Johns Hopkins University Press, 1986), pp. 90–121. Though I admire Adelman's essay, I differ with her conclusion, which maintains that "Macbeth is a recuperative consolidation of male power" (p. 111). Another thoughtful recent reading of the play is offered by Jonathan Goldberg in "Speculations: *Macbeth* and Source," *Post-Structuralist Readings of English Poetry*, ed. Richard Machin and Christopher Norris (Cambridge: Cambridge University Press, 1987). "The hypermasculine world of *Macbeth* is haunted," writes Goldberg, "by the power represented by the witches; masculinity in the play is directed as an assaultive attempt to secure power, to maintain success and succession, at the expense of women" (p. 52). Yet Goldberg too reads the witches, and Mary Queen of Scots, "the figure that

haunts the patriarchal claims of the *Basilikon Doron*" (p. 53), as woman, as female, rather than as the emblems of a disquieting gender undecidability (bearded women; woman as head of state).

51 Muir, ed., p. 12.

52 In his notes on Shakespeare's sonnet 116, coincidentally another poetic narrative of marriage, a tempest, and a "wandering bark," Stephen Booth remarks that "many of the metaphors and ideas of this sonnet seem just on the point of veering off toward puerile joking about temporary abatement of female sexual desire." Booth situates the "puerile joking" and "preposterous teasing" (392) in the confident tone of the lover-poet; in *Macbeth* the tone is of course malevolent rather than erotic; dismissive, vengeful and vituperative rather than indulgent and affectionate— but the trope is a similar one. See also Booth's note on the word *bark* in Sonnet 80, line 7. *Shakespeare's Sonnets* (New Haven: Yale University Press, 1977), pp. 391–2.

53 Quoted in Frank Kermode, ed., *Four Centuries of Shakespearean Criticism*. (New York: Avon Books, 1965), p. 537. From a report of a lecture given in Bristol in 1813.

54 Robert Watson describes the actions of several Shakespearean protagonists, Macbeth among them, as "enforcing their own rebirths by a sort of Caesarean section, carving out the opening through which the ambitious new identity appears" (*Shakespeare and the Hazards of Ambition*, p. 19). If recognized as a Caesarean operation, however, Macbeth's offstage action before the play begins encodes his own dramatic teleology, and thus insures the uncanny appropriateness of Macduff as the man who beheads him, also offstage, at the play's close.

55 *Political Works*, p. 325.

56 Paul Johnson, *Elizabeth I: A Study in Power and Intellect* (London: Weidenfeld & Nicolson, 1974), p. 320.

57 Louis Montrose, "Shaping Fantasies: Figurations of Gender and Power in Elizabethan Culture," *Representations* 1 (Spring, 1983): 77.

> Queen Elizabeth was a cultural anomaly; and this anomalousness—at once divine and monstrous—made her powerful, and dangerous. By the skillful deployment of images that were at once awesome and familiar, this perplexing creature tried to mollify her subjects while enhancing her authority over them (p. 78).

58 Sir Robert Cecil to Sir John Harington, 29 May 1603, printed in John Harington, *Nugae Antiquae*, 3 vols (1779, rpt Hildesheim, 1968), 3, p. 264, quoted in Montrose, p. 78. Elizabeth, who had costumed herself as an Amazon queen, might well be represented as a Medusa, "at once divine and monstrous," by the generation after her death.

59 Lawrence Stone, *The Causes of the English Revolution, 1529–1642* (London: Routledge & Kegan Paul. New York: Harper and Row, 1972), p. 89. Stone cites a number of further references, and remarks about "the widespread gossip about James's sexual tastes" that "the importance of these stories lies in the fact of their existence, not in their truth" (p. 158, n.112).

60 Jonathan Goldberg, *James I and the Politics of Literature* (Baltimore: Johns Hopkins University Press, 1983), pp. 142–6; 269, n. 29.

61 Francis Osborne, *Some Traditional Memorialls on the Raigne of King James I*, in *Secret History of the Court of James I*, ed. W. Scott (Edinburgh, 1811), 1, pp. 274–6.

62 John Freccero, "Medusa: The Letter and the Spirit," in *Dante: The Poetics of Conversion*, ed. and intro. by Rachel Jacoff (Cambridge, Mass.: Harvard University Press, 1986), p. 126.

63 ibid., p. 130.

64 ibid., p. 131.

65 Francesco Petrarca, *Rime Sparse*, 366.

66 Ludwig Goldscheider, *Leonardo da Vinci, Life and Work, Paintings and Drawings, with the Leonardo Biography by Vasari 1568* (London: Phaidon Press, 1964), pp. 13–14.

67 Sigmund Freud, *Leonardo da Vinci and a Memory of His Childhood*, trans. Alan Tyson (New York: W.W. Norton, 1964), p. 23.

68 ibid., p. 30.

69 ibid., p. 46.
70 ibid., p. 45.
71 Friedländer, pp. 87–9.
72 Joyce Carol Oates, "The Unique Universal in Fiction," in *Woman as Writer*, ed. Jeannette L. Webber and Joan Grumman (Boston: Houghton Mifflin, 1978), p. 174.

Chapter 4

1 Stephen Greenblatt, *Shakespearean Negotiations* (Berkeley: University of California Press, 1988), pp. 1–2.
2 ibid., p. 20.
3 Stephen Greenblatt, *Renaissance Self-Fashioning: From More to Shakespeare* (Chicago: University of Chicago Press, 1980), p. 255.
4 Henry M. Stanley, *Through the Dark Continent*, 2 vols. (New York: Harper and Brothers, 1878), vol. 2, pp. 384–86. Cited in Greenblatt, *Shakespearean Negotiations*, p. 162.
5 ibid., p. 198n.
6 Sigmund Freud, "Fetishism," trans. Joan Riviere, in *The Standard Edition of the Complete Psychological Works of Sigmund Freud*, ed. James Strachey (London: The Hogarth Press and The Institute of Psycho-Analysis, 1961), vol. 21, p. 153.
7 *The Boston Globe*, May 29, 1989, p. 25.
8 *The Boston Globe*, July 15, 1989, p. 17.
9 *Time* (July 24, 1989), p. 52.
10 Michael Billington, "Lasciviously Pleasing," in Garry O'Connor, *Olivier: In Celebration* (New York: Dodd, Mead, 1987), p. 71.
11 Anthony Holden, *Laurence Olivier* (New York: Atheneum, 1988), pp. 234–35. "Definitive" is the verdict of Hugo Vickers, *The Times* (London), cited on the dustjacket.
12 Billington, p. 72.
13 ibid., p. 73.
14 ibid.
15 ibid., p. 75.
16 ibid.
17 Donald Spoto, *Laurence Olivier: A Biography* (New York: HarperCollins, 1992). For a more extended discussion of Olivier's bisexuality, see Marjorie Garber, *Vice Versa: Bisexuality and the Eroticism of Everyday Life* (New York: Simon and Schuster, 1995), pp. 136–37.
18 On the subject of transvestism and culture, see Marjorie Garber, *Vested Interests: Cross-Dressing and Cultural Anxiety* (New York: Routledge, 1992).
19 Cheney, *Humanities in America*, p. 14.
20 ibid.
21 Maya Angelou, "Journey to the Heartland" (Address delivered at the 1985 National Assembly of Local Arts Agencies, Cedar Rapids, Iowa, June 12, 1985). Cited in Cheney, p. 15.
22 Greenblatt, *Shakespearean Negotiations*, p. 93.

Chapter 5

1 Senator Alan Simpson. Hearing of the Senate Judiciary Committee on the Thomas Supreme Court Nomination, Saturday, October 12, 1991 (Washington: Federal News Service, Federal Information Systems Corporation [computer disc record]). On the subject of the Senate Committee deliberations, see a witty one-page commentary in *The New Republic* by Barry G. Edelstein that also notes the incongruity of the Shakespeare quotations used in the hearing ("Macbluff," November 11, 1991, p. 13). I am sure that many others at the time likewise noted these references with mingled amusement and dismay.

2   Senator Joseph Biden. Hearing of the Senate Judiciary Committee on the Thomas Supreme Court Nomination, Sunday, October 13, 1991.

3   Biden, October 13, 1991.

4   "Great genial power, one would almost say, consists in not being original at all." The great man "steals by this apology—that what he takes has no worth where he finds it, and the greatest where he leaves it. It has come to be practically a sort of rule in literature, that a man having once shown himself capable of original writing, is entitled thenceforth to steal from the writings of others at discretion. Thought is the property of him who can entertain it and of him who can adequately place it. A certain awkwardness marks the use of borrowed thoughts; but as soon as we have learned what to do with them they become our own. Thus all originality is relative."
      Ralph Waldo Emerson, "Shakespeare," in *Representative Men* (Boston: Houghton Mifflin 1903), pp. 191, 198.

5   William Congreve, *The Mourning Bride*, 3.1.457–58. *The Complete Plays of William Congreve*, ed. Herbert Davis (Chicago: University of Chicago Press, 1967).

6   Lynne V. Cheney, *Humanities in America: A Report to the President, the Congress, and the American People* (Washington, DC: National Endowment for the Humanities, 1988).

7   Emerson, p. 204.

8   ibid., pp. 210–11.

9   Thomas Carlyle, *On Heroes, Hero-Worship, and the Heroic in History* (1840), ed. Carl Niemeyer (Lincoln, Nebraska: University of Nebraska Press, 1966), p. 114.

10 Senator Alan Simpson. Hearing of the Senate Judiciary Committee, October 12, 1991. For an acute media analysis of Simpson on "this sexual harassment crap," see Anna Quindlen, "The Perfect Victim." *The New York Times*, October 16, 1991, p. A25.

11 Senator Patrick Leahy. *Congressional Record*: Proceedings and Debates of the 102nd Congress, First Session, Washington. Tuesday, October 15, 1991. Vol. 137, No. 147, p. S14650.

12 J.C. Alvarez. Hearing of the Senate Judiciary Committee on the Thomas Supreme Court Nomination, October 13, 1991.

13 Marjorie Garber, "A Rome of One's Own," *Shakespeare's Ghost Writers* (London and New York: Routledge, 1987), p. 55.

14 Emerson p. 204.

15 ibid., p. 207.

16 "Excerpt from Senate's Hearings in the Thomas Nomination." *The New York Times*, October 13, 1991, p. 31.

17 "Excerpt from a Statement by Senator Kennedy." *The New York Times*, October 14, 1991, p. A13.

18 Thomas C. Reeves, *A Question of Character: A Life of John F. Kennedy* (New York: The Free Press, 1991).

19 Barbara Garson, *MacBird* (Berkeley: Grassy Knoll Press, 1966).

20 Shakespeare, *As You Like It*, 3.3.58.

21 Robert Sam Anson, "The Shooting of JFK." *Esquire* (November 1991), p. 102.

22 Quoted by Bernard Weinraub, "Hollywood Wonders if Warner Brothers let 'J.F.K.' Go Too Far." *The New York Times*, December 24, 1991, p. C12.

23 *Newsweek* (December 23, 1991).

24 Vincent Canby, *The New York Times*, December 20, 1991.

25 *The New York Times* editorial notebook, December 20, 1991.

26 *The New York Times*, December 20, 1991.

27 *The New York Times*, December 23, 1991, p. 1.

28 "A Troublemaker for Our Times," *Newsweek* (December 23, 1991), p. 50.

29 David Hume, *The Natural History of Religion* (1757), Section VI, "Various Forms of Polytheism: Allegory, Hero-Worship," in *The Philosophical Works*, ed. T.H. Green and T.H. Grose (London, 1882), vol. 4, p. 328. "The same principles [on which human beings create divinities] naturally deify mortals, superior in power, courage, or understanding, and produce hero-worship, in all its wild and unaccountable forms."

30 Carlyle, pp. 108–9.
31 ibid., p. 112.

Chapter 6

I thank David Hillman, Carla Mazzio, and Katherine Rowe (separately and jointly) for their encouragement and their wisdom in matters of the early modern body.

1 Peter Elbow, *What is English?* (New York: Modern Language Association, 1990), p. 136.
2 Ca'da Mosto, *The Voyages of Ca'da Mosto and Other Documents on West Africa in the Second Half of the Fifteenth Century* (London: Hakluyt Society, 1937), p. 46. Joan Barclay Lloyd, *African Animals in Renaissance Literature and Art* (Oxford: Clarendon Press, 1971) p. 117.
3 André Thevet, *Cosmographie de Levant*, 1554, pp. 69–73. Cited in Lloyd, p. 116.
4 *The Works of Sir Thomas Browne*, vol. II, *Pseudodoxia Epidemica*, Books I–VII, ed. Geoffrey Keynes (London: Faber & Faber, 1964), p. 157.
5 Browne, p. 160.
6 Women, of course, also kneel frequently in the dramatic literature of the period (as well as in court). Volumnia and Valeria kneel to Coriolanus, Isabella kneels in petition to Angelo ("sweet Isabel, take my part; Lend me your knees," Mariana implores her (See *Measure for Measure* 5.1.428–9).
7 David Bevington, *Action is Eloquence: Shakespeare's Language of Gesture* (Cambridge, MA and London: Harvard University Press, 1984), p. 164. Bevington's book offers a helpful discussion of "the visual significance" of kneeling "at moments of conflicting loyalty," with reference to plays from *Richard II* to *Measure for Measure*, *Coriolanus* and *King Lear*.
8 Bevington, ibid.
9 Excellent readings of this scene are given by Sheldon P. Zitner, "Aumerle's Conspiracy," *Studies in English Literature* 14 (1974): 239–57, and Leonard Barka, "The Theatrical Consistency of *Richard II*," *Shakespeare Quarterly* 29 (1978): 5–19.
10 Dover Wilson aptly compared this passage to More's lines to the rebellious commons in the Shakespearean additions to the play of *Sir Thomas More*: "your unreverent knees / Make them your feet" (2.4.134–5).
11 The spectacle, at once comic and oddly moving, of a noblewoman past her youth kneeling in passionate suit to an obdurate monarch would be repeated in Shakespeare's *Coriolanus*, where Volumnia kneels to her son and pleads for Rome (5.3). Cleopatra kneels to Caesar and is told to "Arise! You shall not kneel" (*Antony and Cleopatra* 5.2.113). Elsewhere an appalled Cordelia pleads with her father to rise. Brutus tells Portia not to kneel to him (*Julius Caesar* 2.1.278). Meantime, in *Hamlet*, Claudius invokes by his own (counter-) example old York's notion of "true joints," discovering that his "stubborn knees" are reluctant to kneel in penitent prayer (3.3.70).
12 E. R. Curtius, *European Literature of the Latin Middle Ages*, trans. Willard Trask (New York: Harper and Row, 1963), pp.137–8; F. X. Funk, *Patres apostolici*, I (1901), p. 172. The phrase "knees of the heart" is found in the *postcommunio* of the mass *pro reddendis gratiis*.
13 Heinrich von Kleist to Johann Wolfgang von Goethe, January 24, 1808. In *An Abyss Deep Enough: Letters of Heinrich von Kleist*, ed. and trans. Philip B. Miller (New York: Dutton, 1982), pp. 178–9. *Penthesilea*, l.2800.
14 Rainer Maria Rilke, letter to his mother (Phia Rilke), December 17, 1920. I am indebted to David Hillman for this reference.
15 In Fletcher's *Loyal Subject* (1618) a soldier's song anticipates the loss of virginity: "If her foot slip, an down fall she, And break her leg 'bove the knee" (3.5) and in the same playwright's *Wild Goose Chase* (1621) we hear that "She slip'd / And broke her leg about the knee." (4.1). In Heath's *Clarastella* (1650) it is the elbow, not the knee: "And so she broke her elbow 'gainst the bed."(2) By what is presumably a similar logic, Francis Grose's late eighteenth-century *Glossary*

of Provincial and Local Words Used in England 1785 rpt. (London: John Russell Smith, 1839) notes that "a girl who is got with child, is said to have sprained her ankle," and G. W. Matsell's nineteenth-century *Rogue's Lexicon* (New York: G. W. Matsell, 1859) defines both the possessor of a "broken leg" and a "sprained ankle" as "A woman that has had a child out of marriage."

16 Morris Palmer Tilley, *A Dictionary of the Proverbs in England in The Sixteenth and Seventeenth Centuries: A Collection of the Proverbs Found in English Literature and the Dictionaries of the Period* (Ann Arbor: University of Michigan Press, 1950), p. 184.

17 Joaneath Spicer, "The Renaissance Elbow," in *A Cultural History of Gesture*, ed. Jan Bremmer and Herman Roodenburg (Ithaca: Cornell University Press, 1992), p. 95.

18 Erasmus, *De civilitate morum puerilium* (1532), trans. as *A Lytell Booke of Good Maners for Chyldren* by Robert Whitinton. Spicer, p. 95.

19 John Bulwer, *Chirologia: or the Naturall Language of the Hand . . . Whereunto is added Chironomia: or the Arte of Manual Rhetoricke* (two volumes, London 1644), chapter on "Certain prevarications against the rule of rhetorical decorum . . ." section 9. Spicer, 95.

20 The immobility of the elbow, of course, also has the potential to be parodied. In Shakespeare, the pretentious warrior with arms akimbo mocked by Erasmus makes his appearance in *Love's Labour's Lost* in the braggart soldier Don Armado, only to be taught that "folded arms" (3.1.176), "wreathed arms" (4.3.132), or "arms crossed on [the] doublet like a rabbit on a spit" (3.1.17–18) with the elbows in marked the true posture of a lover. The same stereotypical postures appear in *The Two Gentlemen of Verona*, in *The Tempest*, and in *Hamlet*.

21 Jenkins cites a similar lament from Jerome Horsey's late sixteenth-century *Travels in Russia*, "This turbulent time . . . all out of joint, not likely to be reduced a long time to any good form of peaceable government" (in Edward Bond's *Russia at the Close of the Sixteenth Century* [London: Hakluyt Society, 1927], p. 262) and compares Hamlet's remark to Claudius' suggestion, in the play's second scene, that Fortinbras dared to threaten Denmark because he regarded "our state" as "disjoint and out of frame" after the death of the former king.

22 Grafton's *Chronicle at large and meere history of the affayres of England* (1568) finds Thomas More concerned lest (in a phrase that might well have been on Claudius'—or Shakespeare's— mind), "They might peradventure bring the matter so farre out of joynt, that it should never be brought in frame againe." In Hoccleve's *To Sir John Oldcastle* (1415) the roistering knight is told "Thow has been out of joynt al to longe."

23 Jacques Derrida, *Specters of Marx*, trans. Peggy Kamuf (New York: Routledge, 1994), p. 19. The *Hamlet* translations in question are: Yves Bonnefoy (Paris: Gallimard, Folio, 1992); Jean Malaplate (Paris: Corti, 1991); Jules Derocquigny (Paris: Les Belles Lettres, 1989), and André Gide (Paris: Gallimard, Bibliothèque de la Pleiade, 1959). Derrida understands the phrase as describing "Not a time whose joinings are negated, broken, mistreated, dysfunctional, disadjusted . . . but a time without *certain* joining or determinable conjunction" (p. 18). In this discussion Derrida does not express an interest in the anatomical referent; "time," rather than "joint," is his principal concern: the "disjointure of the very presence of the present," the "noncontemporaneity of present time with itself" (p. 25).

24 Slavoj Žižek, *The Indivisible Remainder: An Essay on Schelling and Related Matters* (London and New York: Verso, 1996), pp. 42–3.

25 ibid, p. 73.

26 Slavoj Žižek, *Tarrying with the Negative: Kant, Hegel, and the Critique of Ideology* (Durham: Duke University Press, 1993), p. 12.

27 *The Revenger's Tragedy*, ed. Brian Gibbons (London: A. C. Black, 1990), Act 2 scene 3, lines 44–6 and note. Gibbons, probably influenced by "noon" and "midnight," imagines the phrase to describe a torch out of a wall-socket, or what he calls "a submerged link" with the play's images of skull and eye-socket.

28 John Heminge and Henrie Condell, "To the Great Variety of Readers" (prefatory letter to the First Folio of Shakespeare's Plays, 1623).

29 Morris Palmer Tilley, *A Dictionary of the Proverbs in England in the Sixteenth and Seventeenth Centurys* (Ann Arbor: University of Michigan Press, 1950).

30 Partridge, *Shakespeare's Bawdy*, p. 159. In general, Partridge is on the alert for these anatomical double meanings. Citing Lady Percy's mock threat to Hotspur to "break [his] little finger," he advises the reader that little finger for "penis" is "Still current, among women, as a euphemism" (Partridge, p. 145; *King Henry IV, Part 1*, 2.3.84). "Still current" presumably means in 1948, when the book was first published—or perhaps even in 1960, when the paperback edition appeared.

31 A famous Fats Waller recording of 1937, "The Joint Is Jumpin'" (with lyrics by Andy Rozaf and J. C. Johnson) described Harlem rent-parties at their most raucous and lively: "The roof is rockin' / The neighbors are knockin' / We're all bums when the wagon comes / I'll say the joint is jumpin'." Across the Atlantic in the same years other joints were literally jumping, as the popular Cockney song "Knees-up, Mother Brown!" (1939) produced the slang term "knees-up" for a party or lively celebration.

    To be "in the joint"is to be in prison: "it's the black men who go to the joint, by and large," comments a *Boston Globe* column on prison reform. David Nyhan, "Bumper-Sticker Prison Reform," *Boston Globe* December 6, 1995, p. 23.

32 *Brewer's Dictionary of Twentieth-Century Phrase and Fable.*

33 In Chapman's *All Fools* (1599–1604) a doctor assures his patient that he can cure venereal disease "without perishing of any joint," and is told, anxiously, "'tis a joint I would be loath to lose for the best joint of mutton in Italy" (3.1.394). See Gordon Williams, *Dictionary*, p. 745.

34 John Donne, Sermon 5, *Sermons*, Vol. IX, eds. Evelyn Simpson and George Potter (Berkeley: University of California Press, 1958), p. 135.

35 Aristotle, *Movement of Animals*, trans. A. S. L. Farquarson, in *The Complete Works of Aristotle*, ed. Jonathan Barnes (Princeton: Bollingen, 1984), Vol. I, p. 1087.

36 Helkiah Crooke, *Microkosmographia, A Description of the Body of Man*, 2nd ed. (London: M. Sparke, 1631), p. 930.

37 Crooke, p. 595.

38 John Edwards, *A Demonstration of the Existence and Providence of God* (1690), II, 124.

39 *The Merry Wives of Windsor* 3.5.102 (sword); *Hamlet* 5.2.6 (fetters).

40 Ferdinand de Saussure, *Course in General Linguistics*, eds. Charles Bally and Albert Sechehaye, trans. Wade Baskin (New York: McGraw-Hill, 1966), pp. 112–13.

41 Saussure, pp. 10–11.

42 Heinrich von Kleist, *An Abyss Deep Enough: Letters of Heinrich von Kleist, with a Selection of Essays and Anecdotes*, ed. and trans. Philip B. Miller (New York: Dutton, 1982), p. 211.

43 Scott Cutler Shershow, *Puppets and "Popular" Culture* (Ithaca and London: Cornell University Press, 1995), p. 184. Shershow's book is an illuminating account of the role of puppets and puppetry from Plato to the present.

44 William Butler Yeats, *The Autobiography of William Butler Yeats* (New York: Collier, 1965), p. 233. Cited by Shershow, p. 188.

45 Žižek, *Tarrying with the Negative*, p. 12.

46 For example, in *Bartholomew Fair* 5.3.

47 Ben Jonson, *Epicoene*, 3.4.36–8. In Ben Jonson, eds. C.H. Hereford and Percy Simpson, 11 volumes (Oxford: Clarendon Press, 1925–63).

48 Shershow, *Puppets and "Popular" Culture*, p. 75. Shershow suggests that in *Religio Medici* Sir Thomas Browne is "almost making a pun" when he says that he loves "to use the civility of my knee, my hat, and hand, with all those outward and sensible motions which may express or promote my invisible devotion." Thomas Browne, *Religio Medicie*, pt. 1. sec. 3 (emphasis added), in *The Works of Sir Thomas Browne*, ed. Geoffrey Keynes, 6 volumes (1928–31; rpt. Chicago: University of Chicago Press, 1964), 1:12–13.

49 George Speaight, *The History of the English Puppet Theatre* (London: Harrap, 1955), p. 36.

50 Sigmund Freud, "The Uncanny" (1919), in *The Standard Edition of The Complete Psychological Works of Sigmund Freud*, ed. James Strachey (London: Hogart Press and Institute of Psychoanalysis, 1955; reprint 1986), pp. 17: 266, 244.

51 Beaumont and Fletcher, *The Woman Hater* (c.1606), 3.1.

52 "A Note on the Chester Plays," by Robert Rogerrs, 1609 (Harl. MS 1944), quoted in *The Digby Plays*, Early English Text Society, Extra Series LXX (1896), cited by Speaight, p. 279.

53 Theater historian George Speaight suggests that "a glove puppet, of which the arms are merely the fingers and thumb of the manipulator, does just exactly give the effect of having "half arms" sticking—as if from the elbows—out of its costume." Speaight, p. 65.

54 Stephen Kinzer, "Shakespeare, Icon in Germany," *New York Times*, December 30, 1995, p. 11. Shakespeare's plays had been performed by marionettes in London in the eighteenth century—in a theater run by the cross-dressing actress Charlotte Charke—and in the symbolist theater of Paris in the 1880s. See Shershow, pp. 156, 189, and Max von Boehn, *Dolls and Puppets*, trans. Josephine Nicoll (New York: Copper Square, 1966), p. 346.

55 Sigmund Freud, "The 'Uncanny'" (1919), *The Standard Edition of the Complete Psychological Works of Sigmund Freud*, ed. James Strachey (London: The Hogarth Press and the Institute of Psycho-analysis, 1955; rpt. 1986), Vol. 17, pp. 226, 244.

56 Stilts and stilt walkers date in Europe from the middle ages, when stilts were used not for theatrical purposes but for walking over marshes and streams. They could be strapped to the legs, or fastened beneath the feet, or held by the arms and hands. (The governor of the Belgian city of Namur in 1600 promised the archduke Albert a company of soldiers that would neither ride nor walk, and sent him stilt walkers; the city was rewarded by a pleased archduke with a perpetual exemption from the beer tax.)

57 William Makepeace Thackeray, *The History of Henry Esmond* (1852), Introduction, 1.

58 Jacques Lacan, "The mirror stage as formative of the function of the I as revealed in psychoanalytic experience" (1949), in *Ecrits: A Selection*, trans. Alan Sheridan (New York: W. W. Norton, 1977), p. 4.

59 Within the realm of the jointed body politic, "Continuity" needs "Contiguity" for success and succession, a little more than kin and less than kind. Claudius calls Gertrude "the imperial jointress" of his "warlike state," but the joint there is fragile indeed: "our sometime sister, now our queen" (*Hamlet* 1.2.8). Lear, unwisely investing his sons-in-law Cornwall and Albany "jointly with my power" (*King Lear* 1.1.131) loses both his power and his sanity, railing at a piece of household furniture as if it were his unkind daughter Goneril. "Cry you mercy, I took you for a joint-stool," (3.6.51) quips the fool with mordant wit. A cliché of disparagement in the period, this proverbial phrase ("Cry you mercy, I took you for a joint-stool") is both literalized and banalized in the mad scene on the heath. (For other characteristic uses of the phrase, see for example John Withals' *A short dictionary for yonge begynners* [1553] and John Lyly's *Mother Bombie* [1594] 4.2.) Catachresis (e.g., the "leg" of a chair) becomes catastrophe: what was a jocular insult in the court becomes a hallucinatory delusion not altogether foolish. That the "joiner" was a carpenter did not make it less likely that his work would be "anatomized." For an excellent treatment of carpentry, "artisinal 'joinery'" and joinings in discourse and marriage, see Patricia Parker, "'Rude Mechanicals,'" in *Subject and Object in Renaissance Culture*, ed. Margreta De Grazia, Maureen Quilligan, and Peter Stallybrass (Cambridge: Cambridge University Press, 1996), esp. pp. 48–51.

60 Paul de Man, *The Rhetoric of Romanticism* (New York: Columbia University Press, 1984), p. 287.

61 De Man, pp. 285–6.

62 De Man, p. 287.

63 De Man, p. 288.

64 *Hamlet* 3.2.241–2. Interpreters, somewhat like their twentieth-century puppet-show counterparts (e.g., Fran Allison of "Kukla, Fran and Ollie," "Buffalo Bob" Smith of "Howdy Doody") spoke to and about the puppets, explaining the action, something especially necessary when the show itself was in a foreign tongue. The interaction of human and puppet also produced an odd, metatheatrical atmosphere, the puppets conventionally exhibiting "human" foibles that the interpreters had both to explain and, however futilely, try to control.

65 Paul De Man, "Aesthetic Formalization: Kleist's *Über das Marionettentheater*," in *The Rhetoric of Romanticism* (New York: Columbia University Press, 1984), p. 264–5.

66 The reappropriation of this trope back into the realm of theatrical performance can be seen in a film like Stanley Kubrick's *Dr. Strangelove or: How I Learned to Stop Worrying and Love the Bomb* (1964), in which a fanatical German refugee scientist, the brains of the American nuclear bomb team, is unable to keep his gloved hand and crippled arm from suddenly extending in an apparently unwilled Nazi salute. (Here we might recall once more Žižek's evocation of the Evil Genius, the prototype of the Scientist-Maker, who "pulls the strings of what I experience as 'reality'.") Clearly indebted to *Dr. Strangelove* is Ian McKellen's Richard III, played in a 1995 film version (with a screenplay adapted from Shakespeare by McKellen and director Richard Loncraine) as a self-enthralled fascist in the England of the 1930s. Richard's "deformity" in the film consists largely of stiffness, the inability to bend: his arm is thrust rigidly into his coat pocket, his stiff leg lags. The rhetoric of bodily organic form, as scholars of the play have often observed, leads to the phenomenon of Shakespeare's twisted Richard. But in this production it is not because his body fails to conform to "nature," but rather that it aspires to the condition of a machine.

In the McKellen-Loncraine *Richard III* the society band that plays at the film's outset (while a female singer jauntily warbles, to fox-trot rhythm, Marlowe's "Come Live With Me and Be My Love") offers another, debased, version of Schiller's "English dance," itself once patterned on the heavenly music of the spheres. The dance-band's music stands display the entwined initials "WS."

67 William L. Shirer, *The Rise and Fall of the Third Reich* (New York: Fawcett Crest, 1960), p. 318.

68 De Man, p. 289.

69 Andrew Parker and Eve Kosofsky Sedgwick, eds., *Performativity and Performance* (New York: Routledge, 1995), p. 2.

70 Parker and Sedgwick, ibid, 3.

71 *The Plays of Christopher Marlowe*, ed. Roma Gill (London: Oxford University Press, 1971).

Chapter 7

1 David Owen, *The Walls Around Us: The Thinking Person's Guide to How a House Works* (New York: Vintage, 1992), p. 85.

2 Paul McPharlin, *Roman Numerals, Typographical Leaves and Pointing Hands: Some Notes on Their Origin, History and Contemporary Use* (New York: The Typophiles, Mcmxlii [1942]), pp. 3–5.

3 ibid.

4 Georges Ifrah, *From One to Zero: A Universal History of Numbers*, trans. Lowell Bair (New York: Viking, 1985), p. 131. Originally published as *Historie Universelle des Chiffres* (Paris: Editions Seghers, Paris, 1981).

5 Except in one case in the list of Actors Names for *The Life of Henry the Fift* where the King's title, appearing at the end of a line, is abbreviated as *Henry 5*, with an Arabic numeral (not, please note, a Roman numeral) instead of the word "Fift."

6 Francis Meres, *Palladis Tamia* (New York: Scholars' Facsimile Edition, 1938), ed. Don Cameron Allen, p. 282. Reproduced in S. Schoenbaum, *William Shakespeare: A Documentary Life* (New York: Oxford University Press, 1975), p. 140. Bacon's *Essays* likewise use the ordinal: "K. Henry the 7. of England, K. Henry the 4. of France" (Essay LVm "Of Honour and Reputation." Michael Kiernan, *Sir Francis Bacon: The Essaies or Counsels, Civill and Morall*. Cambridge, MA: Harvard University Press, 1985, p. 164).

7 Helge Kokeritz's 1954 facsimile of the First Folio included a "reference number to the last line of each right-hand column" in Arabic numerals at the foot of the page, so that—for example—the notation on the bottom of the first page of the first play, *The Tempest*, reads 1.2.6 for "Act I, Scene 2, line 6." But Charlton Hinman's 1968 facsimile marked the pages in Roman numerals (the same page in Hinman is labeled I.i.1–I.ii.6).

8 "General Editors' Preface" to the third series of the Arden Shakespeare. In John Wilders, ed., *Antony and Cleopatra* (London and New York: Routledge, 1995), p. xi.
9 Karl Menninger, *Number Words and Number Symbols: A Cultural History of Numbers*, trans. Paul Broneer (Cambridge, MA: The MIT Press, 1969). p. 241.
10 See not only Menninger, but also, for example, Melius de Villiers, *The Numeral-Words: Their Origin, Meaning, History and Lesson* (London: H. F. & G. Witherby, 1923), p. 61.
11 Johanna Drucker, *The Alphabetic Labyrinth* (London: Thames and Hudson, 1995), p. 71.
12 ibid., pp. 70–71.
13 Menninger, p. 281.
14 Jacob Kobel, *Short Book of Arithmetic* (1514), cited in Menninger, p. 286.
15 Menninger, p. 242.
16 ibid., pp. 281–83.
17 "Scientific proof that Barney is Satan." www.mwm.org/barney.html.
18 James Hayes, *The Roman Letter* (Chicago: R. R. Donnelly and Sons, 1951), pp. 37–38.
19 Drucker, p. 162.
20 Elizabeth L. Eisenstein, *The Printing Press as an Agent of Change*, 2 volumes (Cambridge: Cambridge University Press, 1979), vol. 2, p. 532.
21 R. A. Foakes and R. T. Rickert, *Henslowe's Diary* (Cambridge: Cambridge University Press, 1961), p. 319.
22 McPharlin, p. 21.
23 David Eugene Smith and Jekuthiel Ginsburg, *Numbers and Numerals* (New York: Columbia Teachers College Bureau of Publications, 1937), pp. 17–18.
24 Brian Rotman, *Signifying Nothing: The Semiotics of Zero* (Stanford: Stanford University Press, 1987), pp. 9–10.
25 Eisenstein, vol. 1, p. 193.
26 Eisenstein, vol. 2, p. 531.
27 G. F. Hill, *The Development of Arabic Numerals in Europe* (Oxford: Clarendon Press, 1915).
28 "Four" on clock faces is almost always IIII, not IV—a preference ascribed variously to aesthetic symmetry (the IIII balances VIII on the other side) or to a whim of Louis XIV. See Willis Milhamn, *Time and Timekeepers* (New York: Macmillan, 1923), pp. 195–96.

   Today's quartz clocks, which have no works, weights, or pendulum, also often have no dial in the traditional sense, but rather a cathode-ray tube screen. The famous "Movado" watch has no numerals at all. In short, as "analogue" has been replaced by "digital" in the world of computers and clocks, we have moved, or returned, to the world of numbers theorized by Leibniz, who invented the binary code, and for whom 1 symbolized God, and 0 the void.

   The weight-driven clock arrived in England from Italy in "about 1368" (Kenneth Ullyett, *British Clocks and Clockmakers* [London: Collins, MCMXLVII]). Clocks and watches were valued by Renaissance royals: Henry VIII, "a pioneer among English chamber clock owners" had a Bavarian "deviser of the King's horologues," and an Englishman, Bartholomew Newsam, to make his table clocks. (He gave one to Anne Boleyn as a token of his timeless love.) Domestic clocks were a prized new item, and Newsam became clockmaker to Queen Elizabeth at the behest of Sir Philip Sidney (Ullyett, p. 16). Portable timepieces—British pocket "horologues" or watches were obtainable for £20 (upwards of £500 today) in 1600, and when James I came to the throne he sent for the Scotsman David Ramsay, then in France, to be Keeper of his Majesty's Clocks and Watches (Ullyett, p. 17). In 1612 the Keeper of the Privy Purse recorded "Watches, three, bought of Mr. Ramsay the Clockmaker lx li [i.e., £60]." The notation of this transaction is itself of some small interest, because it is a sign of how confusing the use of the letters used for Roman numerals could be for the uninitiated. "lx" is sixty, and "li" a standard abbreviation for "pound" (from Latin *libra*, "pound," balance).

   Theodore Komisarjefsky's famous production of *The Comedy of Errors* at Stratford in 1938 was dominated by a large onstage clock whose hands moved, underscoring the passage of time toward the fateful hour of five. The numbers on the clock were Roman numerals, which might at first be presumed to mark and underscore the "classical" locale. But photographs of the production show no attempt at Roman costume. The effect is rather a hodgepodge of "museum Shakespeare" and Keystone cops. This "Roman" clock, then, is not—except very elusively—a sign of Rome.

29 If we turn from Henslowe to his twentieth-century editors, we can see another set of practices in flux. W. W. Greg's edition (1904–8) of *Henslowe's Diary* is in two (Roman numeraled) volumes, and contains an introduction paginated in minuscule Roman numerals. The second volume has five Roman numeraled chapters, several of which are broken down into sections, each also indicated by a majuscule or capital Roman numeral. Foakes and Rickert's edition, more than fifty years later (1961), still uses minuscule Roman numerals for the Preface and Introduction, but marks its chapters and the page numbers of the book proper in Hindu-Arabic numerals and its Plates in Roman majuscules.

30 Eisenstein, vol. 2, p. 532.

31 Rotman, p. 14.

32 Since Harriot did not publish his findings, the credit for the positional number system has tended to go to the philosopher Gottfried Leibniz (1646–1716), who developed the same ideas independently.

33 Robert K. Logan, *The Alphabet Effect* (New York: William Morrow, 1986), p. 157.

34 Mona Ozouf, *Festivals and the French Revolution*, trans. Alan Sheridan. (Cambridge, MA: Harvard University Press, 1988), p. 93.

35 ibid., p. xvii.

36 Lynn Hunt, *Politics, Culture, and Class in the French Revolution* (London: Methuen, 1986), p. 28. Originally published in 1984 by the University of California Press.

37 ibid., p. 27.

38 Roland Barthes, *Mythologies*, trans. Annette Lavers (New York: Hill and Wang, 1972), p. 26; French edition (Paris: Editions de Seuil, 1957).

39 *Time* (September 4, 1978), p. 60.

40 *The New Catholic Encyclopedia*, 18 volumes (New York: Catholic University of America and McGraw-Hill, 1967), vol. 11, pp. 576–77.

41 In some cases, the numbering system is inconsistent: *Friday the 13th* had a Part 2 and a Part 3, a Final Chapter (which was not, as it turned out, final), and then, in a burst of classicizing fervor, a Part V, Part VI, Part VII, and Part VIII.

42 Anthony Lane, "Power Mad," *The New Yorker*; vol. 70, no. 45 (January 16, 1995), p. 86.

43 Russell Baker, "Supernumerary," *New York Times*, January 31, 1988, Section 6, page 12 (or section VI, p. xii).

44 "Super Bowl is a roman numeral kind of event," Scripps Howard News Service, January 25, 1996. (National Football League Features Page / The National Football League Page / The Football Server.)

45 Mary McGrory, "In a State of Distraction." *The Boston Globe*, February 8, 1997, p. A11.

46 Jan Hoffman, "Tried and Tried Again, With a Vengeance," *New York Times*, February 9, 1997, p. D1.

47 Menninger, p. 245.

Chapter 8

1 S. Schoenbaum, *William Shakespeare: A Documentary Life* (New York: Oxford University Press, 1975), p. 247.

2 Jane Cox, cited in a 1997 book supporting the claim that the Earl of Oxford wrote Shakespeare's plays. Joseph Sobran, *Alias Shakespeare: Solving the Greatest Literary Mystery of All Time* (New York: Free Press, 1997), p. 27.

3 John Ward, *Diary of the Rev. John Ward*, arranged by Charles Severn (London: Colburn, 1839), pp. 56–8.

4 Marchette Chute, *Shakespeare of London* (New York: Dutton, 1949), p. 320.

5 Gerald Eades Bentley, *Shakespeare: A Biographical Handbook* (New Haven: Yale University Press, 1961), p. 63.
6 Sir Edmund K. Chambers, *William Shakespeare: A Study of Facts and Problems* (Oxford: Clarendon Press, 1930), vol. 2, p. 173.
7 Edmond Malone, ed., *Supplement to the Edition of Shakespeare's Plays Published in 1778 by Samuel Johnson and George Steevens* (1780), vol. 1, p. 653.
8 James Walter, *Shakespeare's True Life* (London: Longmans, Green, 1890), p. 386.
9 Joseph William Gray, *Shakespeare's Marriage: His Departure from Stratford and Other Incidents in His Life* (London: Chapman & Hall, 1905), pp. 140–1.
10 John Dowdall, *Traditional Anecdotes of Shakespeare, Collected in Warwickshire in the Year 1693* (London: Thomas Rodd, Great Newport Street, 1838).
11 C[harlotte]. C[armichael]. Stopes, *Shakespeare's Environment* (London: G. Bell, 1918), p. 6.
12 H. Snowden Ward and Catharine Weed Ward, *Shakespeare's Town and Times* (London: Dawbarn and Ward), p. 137.
13 A. L. Rowse and John Hedgecoe, *Shakespeare's Land: A Journey Through the Landscape of Elizabethan England* (San Francisco: Chronicle Books, 1987), p. 190.
14 James Joyce, *Ulysses*, ed. Hans Walter Gabler (New York: Vintage Books, 1986), pp. 166–9.
15 Samuel Neil and F. W. Fairholt, *The Home of Shakespeare* (London: Chapman & Hall, 1847), pp. 22–3.
16 Mark Eccles, *Shakespeare in Warwickshire* (Madison: University of Wisconsin Press, 1961), pp. 164–5.
17 Schoenbaum, p. 247.
18 Frederick George Emmison, *Elizabethan Life: Morals and the Church Courts* (Chelmsford: Essex County Council, 1973), p. 31.
19 E. Vine Hall, *Testamentary Papers II: Wills from Shakespeare's Town and Time*, 2nd series (London: Mitchell Hughes and Clarke, 1933). Cited in Joyce Rogers, *The Second Best Bed: Shakespeare's Will in a New Light* (Westport, CT: Greenwood Press, 1993), p. 77.
20 James O. Halliwell-Phillipps, *Outlines of the Life of Shakespeare*, 10th ed. (London, New York, Bombay: Longmans, Green, 1898), vol. 1, p. 259. Cited in Rogers, p. 77.
21 Cited by Schoenbaum, pp. 302–3, who in turn cites G. R. Potter, "Shakespeare's Will and Raleigh's Instructions to his Son," *Notes and Queries* (1930), p. 364. The passage, as Schoenbaum notes, appears in Raleigh's posthumous "Remains."
22 Sir William Blackstone, *Commentaries on the Laws of England: A Facsimile of the First Edition of 1765–1769*. Vol. II: *Of the Rights of Things* (1766), Introd. by A. W. Brian Simpson (Chicago and London: University of Chicago Press, 1979), pp. 492–3.
23 Blackstone, p. 425.
24 Rogers, p. xvii.
25 Robert Nye, *Mrs. Shakespeare, The Complete Works* (London: Sinclair-Stevenson, 1993), p. 212.
26 Caryl Brahms and S. J. Simon, *No Bed for Bacon* (New York: Thomas Y. Crowell, 1941; 1950), p. 24.
27 Reginald Reynolds, *Beds* (London: Andre Deutsch, 1952), p. 142.
28 *Pillow Talk*, 1959. A film called *Twin Beds*, a comedy about a neighbor constantly interrupting a married couple, appeared in 1942.
29 Alecia Beldegreen, *The Bed* (New York: Stewart, Tabori & Chang, 1991), p. 36.
30 Paul Popenoe, cited in Reynolds, p. 139.
31 Reginald Sharpe, K.C. *Evening Standard*, December 13, 1950. Quoted in Reynolds, p. 141.
32 Groucho [Julius H.] Marx, *Beds* (Indianapolis and New York: Bobbs Merrill, 1930), p. 26.
33 Parker Tyler, *A Pictorial History of Sex in Films* (Secaucus, NJ: Citadel Press, 1974), p. 61.
34 Howard Fineman and Michael Isikoff, "Strange Bedfellows." *Newsweek* (March 10, 1997), pp. 22–8.
35 Richard Lacayo, "Step Right Up." *Time* (March 1997), p. 34.
36 "Still Around: Ghosts of Lincoln and His Era," *The New York Times*, February 13, 1987, p. A18.

37 Plato, *Republic* X. trans. Benjamin Jowett, in David H. Richter, *The Critical Tradition: Classic Texts and Contemporary Trends* (New York: St. Martin's, 1989), pp. 22–3.

38 Jacques Lacan, *The Seminar: Book II. The Ego in Freud's Theory and in the Technique of Psychoanalysis, 1954–55,* trans. Sylvana Tomaselli, notes by John Forrester (New York: Norton; Cambridge: Cambridge University Press, 1988), p. 164.

39 *Republic,* trans. Paul Shorey, in *Plato, The Collected Dialogues,* ed. Edith Hamilton and Huntington Cairns (Princeton University Press, Bollingen Series LXXI), p. 821.

40 From Marie Bonaparte's notes, cited by Peter Gay: "Madame Freud informed me that the analytic couch (which Freud would import to London) was given to him by a grateful patient, Madame Benvenisti, around 1890." Peter Gay, *Freud: A Life for Our Time* (New York and London: Norton, 1988), p. 103.

41 Gay, p. 171.

42 ibid., p. 427.

43 ibid., p. 635.

44 Diana Fuss and Joel Sanders, "Berggasse 19: Inside Freud's Office," in *Stud,* ed. Joel Sanders (Princeton: Princeton Architectural Press, 1996). See also Sigmund Freud, "Papers on Technique," in James Strachey, ed. *The Standard Edition of the Complete Psychological Works of Sigmund Freud* (London: The Hogarth Press and the Institute for Psycho-Analysis, 1953), vol. 12, p. 139.

45 Freud, "Papers," p. 133. Fuss and Sanders, p. 129.

46 Fuss and Sanders, book proposal for the MIT Press: *Berggasse 19: Inside Freud's Office.*

47 Henry James, "The Birthplace," *The Jolly Corner and Other Tales* (London: Penguin, 1990), p. 122.

48 See, for example, Samuel Neil, *The Home of Shakespeare* (Warwick: Henry T. Cooke and Son, 1888), p. 19. Neil quotes Douglas Jerrold, from, James O. Halliwell-Phillipps, *The Life of William Shakespeare* (London: J. R. Smith, 1848), p. 39.

49 Gary Taylor, *Reinventing Shakespeare* (New York: Weidenfeld and Nicolson, 1989), pp. 261–2. A 1927 Prague production had presented a "prominent bed" and Gertrude in her nightgown.

50 This view is put forward by Otto Rank, *Das Inzest-Motiv in Dichtung und Sage* (Leipzig, Wein: Franz Denticke, 1912).

51 Freud, *The Interpretation of Dreams,* in *Standard Edition,* vol. 4, p. 266.

52 Stephen Daedalus makes the same biographical assumptions: "Is it possible that the player Shakespeare, a ghost by absence, and in the vesture of buried Denmark, a ghost by death, speaking his own words to his own son's name (had Hamnet Shakespeare lived he would have been prince Hamlet's twin), is it possible, I want to know, or probable that he did not draw or foresee the logical conclusion of those premises: you are the dispossessed son: I am the murdered father: your mother is the guilty queen. Ann Shakespeare, born Hathaway?" *Ulysses,* p. 155.

53 Ernest Jones, *Hamlet and Oedipus,* 1910 (Rev. ed. New York and London: W. W. Norton, 1949), p. 121.

54 Freud, *Interpretation of Dreams,* p. 266n.

55 Sigmund Freud, *An Autobiographical Study* (1925), in *Standard Edition,* vol. 20, pp. 63–4n.

56 Garber, *Shakespeare's Ghost Writers* (London and New York: Routledge, 1987).

57 Freud, *Autobiographical Study,* p. 34.

58 "I was the first," Freud insists, asserting his own primacy over Adler and Jung, "to recognize both the part played by phantasies in symptom-formation and also the 'retrospective phantasying' of late impressions into childhood and their sexualization after the event." Sigmund Freud, "From the History of an Infantile Neurosis," *Standard Edition,* vol. 17, p. 103n.

59 Freud, "The Goethe Prize" (1930). Trans. Angela Richards, *Standard Edition* vol. 21, p. 211.

60 Letter from Freud to John Looney, June 1938, in J. Thomas Looney, *"Shakespeare" Identified as Edward de Vere the 27th Earl of Oxford,* 3rd rev. ed., ed. and augmented by Ruth Loyd Miller (Port Washington, NY: Kennikat Press, 1975), vol 2, p. 273.

Chapter 9

1 David L. Vander Meulen, foreword to G. Thomas Tanselle, *The Life and Work of Fredson Bowers* (Charlottesville: The Bibliographical Society of the University of Virginia, 1993), viii.
2 Fredson T. Bowers, *The American Kennel Gazette*, March 1934. Quoted in Tanselle, *Life and Work*, 15.
3 Alfred Harbage, in *Modern Language Notes* 59 (1944): 130. Quoted in Tanselle, *Life and Work*, 29.
4 Bowers, *Dog Owner's Handbook* (Boston: Houghton Mifflin, 1936), 10–11.
5 Tanselle, *Life and Work*, 126–7.
6 ibid., 21.
7 "English Notes and Comments," *The Irish Wolfhound Club of America . . . Annual Reports* [for 1934 and 1935] (Battle Creek, MI, 1936), 72–77.
8 John Caius, whose name is also spelled Kees, Keys, Kay or Kaye, was born October 6, 1510 and died July 19, 1573. He was a prominent humanist and physician, the author of a classic account of the English sweating sickness. His description of English dogs was written for Konrad von Gesner, a sixteenth-century naturalist.
9 Abraham Fleming, "To the Reader."
10 Leon Rooke, *Shakespeare's Dog* (New York: Alfred A. Knopf, 1983), 3–7.
11 ibid., 137.
12 Elizabeth Marshall Thomas, *The Hidden Life of Dogs* (Boston: Houghton Mifflin, 1993), 57.
13 "Triumph, the First Choice of Millions of Pets!" and "Triumph Super Savings Coupon Booklet," distributed by Triumph Pet Industries, Inc., 7 Lake Station Road, Warwick, N.Y. 1990.
14 Paul Monette, *Lost Watch of the Night: Essays Too Personal and Otherwise* (New York: Harcourt Brace and Co., 1994), 28.
15 George Sand, *Indiana*, trans. Eleanor Hochman (New York: Signet Classic, 1993), 34–5, 180–1, 226–7.
16 Mary Pipher, *Reviving Ophelia: Saving the Lives of Adolescent Girls* (New York: Ballatine, 1994), 20.
17 George Graham Vest, *Charles Burden, Respondent v. Leonidas Hornsby, Appellant* (1870), quoted in Mary Randolph, *Dog Law*, 9 / 26–7.
18 *King Lear* 4.6.128–9; 3.4.14–16; 4.7.36–8.
19 *King Lear*, ed. Kenneth Muir, The Arden Shakespeare (London: Methuen, 1964), 1.4.118n.
20 Caius, *Of English Dogges*, 7.
21 Milan Kundera, *The Unbearable Lightness of Being*, trans. Michael Henry Heim (New York: Harper & Row, 1984), 300.
22 ibid., 302.
23 *King Lear* 5.3.260–1; 305–10.
24 J. Leigh Mellor, "Hath a Dog Money?" *Taxation*, February 16, 1985, 357.
25 Midas Dekkers, *Dearest Pet*, trans. Paul Vincent (London and New York: Verso, 1994), 118.
26 See my essay "Freud's Choice," in *Shakespeare's Ghost Writers: Literature as Uncanny Causality* (New York: Routledge, 1989), 74–86.
27 James Stevenson cartoon, *The New Yorker Book of Dog Cartoons* (New York: Knopf, 1992), 99.

Chapter 10

This essay was originally published as "Historical Correctness" in *Quotation Marks* (New York: Routledge, 2003) and in *A Manifesto for Literary Studies* (Seattle: Walter Chapin Simpson Center for the Humanities: Distributed in the U.S.A. by the University of Washington Press, 2003).

1 Claire McEachern, "Introduction" to *Religion and Culture in Renaissance England*, eds. Claire McEachern and Debora Shuger (Cambridge: Cambridge University Press, 1997), p. 2.
2 ibid.

3 Richard Bernstein, "We Happy Many, Playing Fast and Loose With History," *New York Times* January 18, 2000, pp. B1–2.

4 Nabokov offers this piece of mindless and fictive "Ekwilist doctrine": "It is better for a man to have belonged to a politically incorrect organization than not to have belonged to any organization at all." Vladimir Nabokov, *Bend Sinister*, 1947 (New York: Vintage Books, 1990), p. 158.

5 Maurice Isserman recalls that among young people on the so-called New Left "it was always used in a tone mocking the pieties of our own insular political counterculture." Maurice Isserman, "Travels with Dinesh," *Tikkun*, vol. 6, no. 5, p. 82.

6 Ed Siegel, "Hazy Shade of 'Winter' at ART," *Boston Globe* May 19, 2000, p. D1.

7 Fabienne Casta-Rosaz, L'Histoire du Flirt," in Charles Bremner, "Sex-Sated French Revive Romantic Art of Flirtation," *The Times* (London) May 11, 2000, p. 16.

8 Clifford Longley, "Sacred and Profane: Labour and the Fall of Political Correctness," *Daily Telegraph*, November 26, 1999, p. 31. A recent publication by the British Institute of Economic Affairs, entitled "Political Correctness and Social Work," insisted that "anti-oppressive practice" was itself oppressive as well as practically ineffectual. "Social Workers Reject Political Correctness," *The Times* Home news, November 22, 1999 (np). Sue Clough, "Judge Attacks Irvine's Politically Correct Rules on Race," *Daily Telegraph*, October 1, 1999, p. 1.

9 Walter Benjamin, "Literary History and the Study of Literature," in *Selected Writings* vol. 2, (1927–34) (Cambridge, MA: Harvard University Press, 1999), p. 464.

10 See Samuel Kliger, *The Goths in England* (Cambridge, MA: Harvard University Press, 1952), cited in Jonathan Bate, ed. *Titus Andronicus*, The Arden Shakespeare (Walton-on-Thames: Thomas Nelson, 1997), pp. 19–20.

11 Alan F. Segal, "The Ten Commandments"; Michael Grant, "Julius Caesar"; Carolly Erickson, "The Scarlet Empress," all in Mark C. Carnes, ed., *Past Imperfect: History According to the Movies* (New York: Henry Holt, 1995), pp. 38, 44, 88.

12 Peter Desmond, "The Roman Theater of Cruelty," *Harvard Magazine* September / October 2000, p. 22.

13 Michel de Montaigne, "Of Thumbs," in *The Complete Essays of Montaigne*, trans. Donald M. Frame (Stanford: Stanford University Press, 1958), p. 523.

14 Philip Howard, "Blood and Circuses," *The Times* (London), May 17, 2000, Section 2, pp. 3–4.

15 Steve Allen, *Meeting of Minds* (Buffalo, NY: Prometheus Books, 1989), pp. 161, 82.

16 Don Freeman, "Scripts Made a Meeting of the Minds," *San Diego Union-Tribune*, December 24, 1989, Entertainment section, p. 6.

17 Sarah Boxer, "Snubbing Chronology as a Guiding Force in Art," *New York Times*, September 2, 2000, pp. A19–21. Boxer cites British art critic David Sylvester in *The London Review of Books* and Jed Perl in *The New Republic*.

18 Iwana Blazwick, quoted in Boxer, p. A21.

19 Elmer Edgar Stoll, "Anachronism in Shakespeare Criticism," *Modern Philology* 7 (April 1910), pp. 1, 5, 7, 8, 12, 19.

20 Anne Bradstreet, "The Author to Her Book," in *The Works of Anne Bradstreet*, ed. Jeannine Hensley (Cambridge and London: Belknap Press of Harvard University Press, 1967), p. 221.

21 The editor of Bradstreet's works makes a similar claim: "In 'The Author to Her Book,' the metaphor of the book as a child expresses how the poet felt when she saw her work in print. It was her own child, even if she was ashamed of its errors. . . ." Jeannine Hensley, Introduction to *The Works of Anne Bradstreet* (Cambridge: Harvard University Press, 1967), p. xxxi. The "new historicist" twist not present in this sixties' reading is the presentation of period images, from authors like Ambroise Paré.

22 Adrienne Rich, "Anne Bradstreet and Her Poetry," in Hensley, ed., *The Works of Anne Bradstreet*, p. x.

23 John Heminge and Henrie Condell, "to the great Variety of Readers." Prefatory letter to the First Folio of Shakespeare. *The Norton Facsimile, The First Folio of Shakespeare*, prepared by Charlton Hinman, (New York: W. W. Norton, 1968), p. 7.

24 David Daniell, Introduction, *Julius Caesar*. The Arden Shakespeare, Third Series (Walton-on-Thames: Thomas Nelson, 1998), pp. 17–22.

25 Alexander Pope, ed., *The Works of Shakespeare* (London, 1725, 1728). There is also in *Julius Caesar* the matter of "sleeves." "As they pass by, pluck Caska by the sleeve" Cassius instructs Brutus (1.2.178). "Togas had no sleeves," corrects John Dover Wilson in his Cambridge edition of the play. Once again the redoubtable Daniell comes to the rescue, suggesting that nearby references to cloak (214) and doublet (264) are clues that "Shakespeare also had London in mind," and reading the combination of pluck plus sleeve as, again, "almost furtive." These anachronistic references to clothing are, in other words, both functional and double-coded: their out-of-place-ness is a theatrical and interpretative marker, reminding the audience that the play is about "now" as well as "then" (Shakespeare's London as well as Caesar's Rome), while also drawing attention to a particular kind of affect (here "furtiveness").

26 David Patrick Stearns, "Akalaitis' Henry IV Conforms," *Gannet News Service*, March 19, 1991 (np).

27 Charles Spencer, "The Arts: Shakespeare Meets Le Carre," *Daily Telegraph*, November 9, 1998, p. 19.

28 Herbert Mitgang, "Books of the Times," *New York Times*, April 18, 1986, p. C31.

29 Jacques Lacan, "Seminar on 'The Purloined Letter'," trans. Jeffrey Mahlman, in *The Purloined Poe*, ed. John P. Muller and William J. Richardson (Baltimore and London: Johns Hopkins University Press, 1988), pp. 39–40.

30 Ralph Waldo Emerson, "Shakspeare: Or, the Poet," in *Representative Men: Essays and Lectures* (New York: The Library of America, 1983), pp. 716–21.

31 Lisa Jardine has argued that the task of literary studies is "to bring historical studies and text studies into constructive tension with one another," suggesting that "what we should be looking at is the converging practices of social historians, intellectual and cultural historians, text critics and social anthropologists, as they move together towards a more sensitive integration of past and present cultural products." She closes her book in the same bi-temporal spirit: "To read Shakespeare historically is to undertake a dialogue with these culturally freighted residues of our own past in order more clearly to illuminate the culture we currently inhabit." What is stressed here, crucially, is dialogue, and, by implication, dialectic. Reading historically means reading the present as well as the past, reading the past as that which produces the present but also the present as that which produces the past (by reading, by analysis, by the very protocols of scholarship). Lisa Jardine, *Reading Shakespeare Historically* (London and New York: Routledge, 1996), pp. 35–6; 148.

32 Theodor Adorno, "Gaps," in *Minima Moralia*, trans. E. F. N. Jephcott (London and New York: Verso, 1978), p. 80.

33 William Shakespeare, *As You Like It* 2.7.145–7.

Chapter 11

This essay was originally published as "Looking the Part" in *Shakespeare's Face* (Nolen, Stephanie, et al. Toronto: Alfred A. Knopf Canada, 2002).

1 Henry James, *The Aspern Papers and The Turn of the Screw* (London and New York: Penguin, 1984), pp. 108–9.

2 E. T. Craig, *Shakespeare's Portraits Phrenologically Considered* (Philadelphia: Printed for private circulation by J. Parker Norris), 1875.

3 John Corbin, *A New Portrait of Shakespeare: The Case of the Ely Palace Painting as against that of the so-called Droeshout Original* (London and New York: John Lane, Bodley Head), 1903.

4 Leslie Hotson, *Shakespeare by Hilliard* (Berkeley and Los Angeles: University of California Press, 1977), p. 9.

5 Marjorie Weeden Champlin, *Changing the Face of Shakespeare* (privately printed, 1996).

6 William Stone Booth, *The Droeshout Portrait of William Shakespeare, An Experiment in Identification* (Boston: W. A. Butterfield, 1911), p. 2.

7 ibid., p. 5.

8 Olive Wagner Driver, *The Shakespearean Portraits and Other Addenda* (Northampton, MA: Metcalf Printing and Publishing, 1966), p. 13.

9 John Corbin, p. 95.

10 Charles Dickens, *Letters*, eds. G. Howarth and M. Dickens (London and New York, 1893), p. 173. Cited in S. Schoenbaum, *Shakespeare's Lives* (Oxford: Clarendon Press; New York: Oxford University Press, 1970), p. 470.

11 E. T. Craig, p. 1.

12 ibid, pp. 2–3.

13 ibid, p. 6.

14 J. Parker Norris, "Shaksperian Gossip," in *American Bibliopolist* 8 (1876): 40.

15 J. O. Halliwell-Philipps, *Folio Edition of Shakespeare* (London, 1853), 1: 230. J. Parker Norris, "The Portraits of Shakespeare," *Shakespeariana* (Philadelphia: Leonard Scott, 1883–84), pp. 4–5.

16 C. M. Ingleby, "The Portraiture of Shakespeare," in *Shakespeare, the Man and the Book* (London, 1877).

17 Abraham Wivell, *An Inquiry into the History, Authenticity, and Characteristics of the Shakespeare Portraits* (London, 1827), p. 140.

18 Schoenbaum, *Shakespeare's Lives*, pp. 6–7.

19 Norris, "Portraits," p. 36.

20 Ingleby, p. 81.

21 James Boaden, *Inquiry into Various Pictures, Prints, etc.* (London, 1824), p. 17.

22 J. A. Norris, *Shakespeariana* 1.3 (1884): 65.

23 George Steevens, quoted in Schoenbaum, *Shakespeare's Lives*, p. 282.

24 J. Hain Friswell, *Life Portraits of William Shakespeare* (London, 1864), p. 31.

25 "Many other scholars are skeptical, in part because [the Chandos portrait] shows a swarthy, 'Italianate' Shakespeare who does not much resemble the bust or the Droeshout." Stephanie Nolen, "Is This the Face of Genius?, *Toronto Globe and Mail* May 11, 2001.

26 John Dover Wilson, *The Essential Shakespeare* (Cambridge: Cambridge University Press, 1932, reprinted 1960), pp. 5–8.

27 [No author], "The Merry Bard Himself," *Courier Mail*, May 14, 2001, p. 3.

28 Verlyn Klinkenborg, Editorial Notebook: "A Knowing Smile on an Unknown Face," *New York Times*, May 27, 2001, Section 4, p. 8.

29 Tim Rutten, "The New Face of Shakespeare," *Los Angeles Times*, June 1, 2001, Part 5, p. 1.

30 Josephine Tey, *The Daughter of Time* 1951 (New York: Scribner, 1995), pp. 29–30.

31 Wilde, *Complete Works*, p. 1150.

32 ibid.

33 ibid., p. 1156.

34 ibid., p. 1160.

35 Emmanuel Levinas, *Ethics and Infinity*, conversations with Philippe Nemo, Trans. Richard A. Cohen (Pittsburgh: Duquesne University Press, 1985), pp. 85–6.

36 Alexander Leggatt, quoted in Stephanie Nolen, "Is This the Face of Genius?", *Toronto Globe and Mail*, May 11, 2001.

37 Wilde, *Complete Works*, p. 1156.

Chapter 12

1 Samuel Johnson, "Preface to Shakespeare" (1765), in Arthur Sherbo, ed., *Johnson on Shakespeare* (New Haven and London: Yale University Press, 1968), pp. 94–5.

2 Johnson, "Preface," pp. 105, 108, 109.

3 C. M. Ingleby, *The Still Lion: An Essay Towards the Restoration of Shakespeare's Text* (London: Trübner and Co., 1874), p. ix.

4 Fredson Bowers, *Textual and Literary Criticism* (Cambridge, 1959), p. 120.

5 Fredson Bowers, *On Editing Shakespeare* (Charlottesville: University of Virginia Press, 1966), p. 116.

6 Bowers, pp. 104–5.

7 Bowers, p. 177.

8 Donald Spoto, *The Dark Side of Genius: The Life of Alfred Hitchcock* (New York: Da Capo Press, 1983; 1999), p. 278.

9 Spoto, p. 145.

10 Mel Gussow, "With Math, a Playwright Explores a Family in Stress" (review of David Auburn, *Proof*), *New York Times*, May 29, 2000, p. B1.

11 Spoto, 145.

12 ibid.

13 "Master of Suspense: Being a Self-Analysis by Alfred Hitchcock," *New York Times*, June 4, 1950, section 2, p. 4. Reprinted in *Hitchcock on Hitchcock*, ed. Sidney Gottlieb (Berkeley: University of California Press, 1995), p. 124.

14 Jacques Lacan, "Seminar on 'The Purloined Letter,'" in John P. Muller and William J. Richardson, *The Purloined Poe: Lacan, Derrida, and Psychoanalytic Reading* (Baltimore and London: Johns Hopkins University Press, 1988), p. 46.

15 Slavoj Žižek, "Introduction," *Everything You Always Wanted to Know About Lacan (But Were Afraid to Ask Hitchcock)*, ed. Žižek (London and New York: Verso, 1992), pp. 6, 8.

16 François Truffaut, *Hitchcock* (New York: Simon and Schuster, 1985), pp. 168–269.

17 Spoto, p. 286.

18 H. J. Oliver, The Arden edition of *Timon of Athens* (London: Methuen, 1959), p. 5.

19 C. M. Ingleby, *The Still Lion*, pp. 111–12.

20 Jenkins, p. 510.

21 Ingleby, *The Still Lion*, p. 120.

22 Jenkins, p. 426.

23 ibid., p. 357.

24 "If . . . we had but the first folio, we should be called upon to explain or amend the following passage in Hamlet:

> To his good Friends, thus wide Ile ope my Armes:
> And like the kinde Life-rend'ring Politician,
> Repast them with my blood.

Such a crux as 'Life-rend'ring Politician' would have been . . . appetising and entertaining [to the critical taste] . . . and the game would naturally have been quickend by the fact, that when Hamlet was first indited Politician, occuring once, however, in this play ('the Pate of a Politician,' iv.[sic] 1) was an insolens verbum, which we now believe to have been first used by George Puttenham in 1589 [in the Arte of English Poesie]. The misprint in an unusual expansion of the original word. It is most unlikely that Pelican (the word of the quarto editions) was (as some have asserted) a difficulty with the old compositor: on the contrary, we may be pretty sure that he set up Polician, and that a pedantic 'read' of the house improved upon this, converting it into Politician." Ingleby, *Still Lion*, p. 113.

25 Jenkins, p. 481.

26 Harold Bloom, *Shakespeare: The Invention of the Human* (New York: Riverhead, 1998), p. 424.

27 A. C. Bradley, *Shakespearean Tragedy* 1904 (London: Penguin, 1991), pp. 99, 131.

28 John Dover Wilson, *What Happens in Hamlet?* 1935 (Cambridge: Cambridge University Press, 1970), p. 162.

29 Charles and Mary Cowden Clarke, *Cassell's Illustrated Shakespeare* (London: Cassell, 1864–68) vol. III, p. 415.

30 W. T. Malleson and J. R. Seeley, *Which are Hamlet's "Dozen or Sixteen Lines"?* (London: New Shakspere Society, 1874), p. 481.

31 ibid., p. 471.

32 ibid., p. 482.

33 ibid., pp. 490–1.

34 F. J. Furnivall, in Malleson and Seeley, pp. 494–5.

35 Richard Simpson, in Malleson and Seeley, pp. 496.

36 Charles Bathurst, *Remarks on the Differences in Shakespeare's Versification in Different Periods of His Life* (London: John W. Parker and Son, 1857), p. 70.

37 Horace H. Furness, ed., *New Variorum Hamlet* orig. pub. 1877 (New York: Dover, 1963), Vol 1, pp. 250–1. Summary of a paper by Dr. Ingleby, to be read at the New Shakspere Society, February 9, 1877.

38 Martin Dodsworth, *Hamlet Closely Observed* (London: Athlone Press, 1985), pp. 153–4.

39 R. A. Foakes, *Hamlet Versus Lear* (Cambridge: Cambridge University Press, 1993), pp. 86–7.

40 Samuel Weller Singer, *The Text of Shakespeare Vindicated from the Interpolations and Corruptions Advocated by John Payne Collier in His Notes and Emendations* (London: William Pickering, 1853), p. x.

41 ibid., p. x.

42 Affidavit of John Payne Collier, concerning his book *Notes and Emendations to the Text of Shakespeare's Plays, from Early Manuscript Corrections in a Copy of the Folio, 1632, in the Possession of J. Payne Collier* (1832), sworn to in the Court of Queen's Bench, 1856. Quoted in N. E. S. A. Hamilton, *An Inquiry into the Genuineness of the Manuscript Corrections in Mr. J. Payne Collier's Annotated Shakespere, Folio, 1632* (London: Richard Bentley, 1860), pp. 16–17.

43 Sir Frederick Madden, Keeper of Manuscripts at the British Museum, private *Journal*, quoted in S. Schoenbaum, *Shakespeare's Lives*, p. 355.

44 Ingelby's own autobiographical writings suggest that he saw himself in the same critical spirit as the Hamlet of Act 3 ("I am very proud, revengeful, ambitious, with more offenses at my beck than I have thoughts to put them in . . ." [3.1.124–6]: "I am morally weak in many respects. In some matters I have been systematically deceptive, & occasionally cowardly & treacherous. I am passionately fond of personal beauty; but, on the whole, I dislike my kind, & my natural affections are weak." Manuscript in Folger Shakespeare Library, quoted by S. Schoenbaum, *Shakespeare's Lives* (New York: Oxford University Press, 1970), p. 357.

45 C. M. Ingleby, *A Complete View of the Shakspere Controversy, Concerning the Authenticity and Genuineness of the Manuscript Matter Affecting the Works and Biography of Shakspere, Published by Mr. J. Payne Collier as the Fruits of his Researches* (London: Nattali and Bond, 1861; reprint, New York: AMS Press, 1973), pp. 14, 19, 21.

46 ibid., p. 323.

47 ibid., pp. 324–5.

48 John Collier, *Reply to Mr. N. E. S. A. Hamilton's "Inquiry" into the imputed Shakespeare Forgeries* (1860), pp. 47–50.

49 Ingleby, *Complete View*, pp. 323–4.

50 Samuell Butler, *Hudribras*, The Third and Last Part, Canto III, ll. 759–64.

51 Dewey Ganzel, *Fortune and Men's Eyes: The Career of John Payne Collier* (Oxford and New York: Oxford University Press, 1982).

52 John Payne Collier, *Autobiography*, Folger Shakespeare Library MS. M.a.230, pp. 146–7. Quoted in Schoenbaum, *Shakespeare's Lives*, p. 360.

53 ibid., p. 148. The comment is Schoenbaum's.

54 Marjorie Garber, *Shakespeare's Ghost Writers: Literature as Uncanny Causality* (New York and London: Methuen 1987). "As They Like It," *Harper's Magazine*, April 1999, pp. 44–6.

Chapter 13

1   Frank Kermode, "Introduction" to *Antony and Cleopatra, The Riverside Shakespeare*, ed. G. Blakemore Evans, second edition (Boston and New York: Houghton Mifflin, 1997), p. 1394.
2   Thomas Overbury, *The Miscellaneous Works in Prose and Verse*, ed. Edward F. Rimbault (London: John Russell Smith, 1856), p. 168.
3   La Bruyère, *Characters*, trans. Henri van Laun (London: Oxford University Press, 1963), pp. 35; 37; 248–9; 254.
4   Charles Baudelaire, "The Painter of Modern Life," in *The Painter of Modern Life and Other Essays*, trans. Jonathan Mayne (London: Phaidon, 1964, 1995), pp. 1–41.
5   C. G. Jung, *Psychological Types*, 1923. Jung believed that individuals have four modes of apprehending the world: thinking / feeling and intuition / sensation. The first two are "rational" functions and the second two "irrational" functions. Each person is born with one of these modes "superior" or predominating, with two more "accessible," and with the fourth "inferior" and difficult to access. In addition, Jung posited two attitudes: extraversion and introversion (taking one's bearing from an object or person in the world; taking one's bearing from within oneself). This typological model of the psyche was central to his theories of personal development, and is not unlike a modern theory of humors.
6   J. Knight in *Atheneum*, March 16, 1978; *Stage*, November 9, 1883. Both cited in *OED*, character 19.
7   Sigmund Freud, "General Theory of the Neuroses," in *The Standard Edition of the Complete Psychological Works of Sigmund Freud*, ed. James Strachey (London: Hogarth Press, 1963), 16: 381.
8   Freud, "Those Wrecked by Success," (*Standard Edition*, 14: 324), quoted here by Philip Rieff, *Freud: The Mind of the Moralist* (Chicago: Chicago University Press, 1979), p. 130.
9   Reiff, p. 131.
10 Samuel Johnson, notes to *Hamlet*, in *Johnson on Shakespeare*, ed. Arthur Sherbo, *The Yale Edition of the Works of Samuel Johnson* (New Haven and London: Yale University Press, 1968), 8: 971.
11 Again Johnson is a good barometer. "This speech, which the former edition give[s] to Miranda, is very judiciously bestowed by Mr. Theobald on Prospero," Notes to *The Tempest*, in Sherbo 7: 124.
12 See, for a good example of this argument, Jacques Lacan, "The Signification of the Phallus":

> The phenomenology that emerges from analytic experience is certainly of a kind to demonstrate in desire the paradoxical, deviant, erratic, eccentric, even scandalous character by which it is distinguished from need. This fact has been too often affirmed not to have been always obvious to moralists worthy of the name. . . . In any case, man cannot aim at being whole (the "total personality" is another of the deviant premises of modern psychotherapy), while ever the play of displacement and condensation to which he is doomed in the exercise of his functions marks his relation as a subject to the signifier.

Ecrits: A Selection trans. Alan Sheridan (New York: W. W. Norton, 1977), pp. 286–7.
13 *Hamlet* 3.2.367–73.
14 *Antony and Cleopatra* 4.14.2–14 (Arden).
15 Richard Brinsley Sheridan, *The Rivals*, 1775 (Boston: Houghton Mifflin, 1910), 3.4.230.
16 Lucy Hughes-Hallet, *Cleopatra: Histories, Dreams, Distortions* (New York: Harper & Row, 1990).
17 *King Henry VI, Part 2* 3.1.225–30.
18 *Antony and Cleopatra* 1.2.154–6.
19 Louisa May Alcott, *Little Women* (Oxford: Oxford University Press, 1994), p. 331.
20 ibid, p. 330.
21 ibid, pp. 336–7.
22 Aristotle, *The Poetics*, trans. Stephen Halliwell (Chapel Hill: University of North Carolina Press, 1987), pp. 38, 47.

notes

(a) first and foremost, that the characters be good. Characterisation will arise . . . where speech or action exhibits the nature of an ethical choice; and the character will be good when the choice is good. But this depends on each class of person: there can be a good woman and a good slave, even though perhaps the former is an inferior type, and the latter a wholly base one.

(b) that the characters be appropriate. For it is possible to have a woman manly in character, but it is not appropriate for a woman to be so manly or clever.

(c) likeness of character—for this is independent of making character good and appropriate, as described.

Consistency of character. For even where an inconsistent person is portrayed, and such a character is presupposed, there should still be consistency in the inconsistency.

23 Aristotle, *The Poetics*, pp. 139, 139n. Halliwell cites Brian Vickers, "The Emergence of Character Criticism," in Stanley Wells, ed., *Shakespeare Survey* 34 (Cambridge 1981), 11: 21.
24 Samuel Johnson, in *Johnson on Shakespeare*, 7: 62.
25 ibid., 8: 873.
26 Lucy Hughes-Hallet, pp. 132–59.
27 John Dryden, Preface to *All for Love, or the World Well Lost* (1678), in *Essays of John Dryden*, ed. W. P. Ker, vol. 1 (Oxford: Clarendon Press, 1900), pp. 190–1.
28 T. R. Henn, *The Living Image* (London: Methuen, 1972), p. 117.
29 William Hazlitt, *Characters of Shakespeare's Plays* (London: J. S. Dent, 1906), pp. 74, 75, 76.
30 A. C. Bradley, *Oxford Lectures on Poetry* (London: MacMillan, 1909), pp. 300–03.
31 A. C. Swinburne, *Shakespeare* (Oxford, 1909), p. 76. A. C. Swinburne, *A Study of Shakespeare* (1880), p. 191.
32 J. Middleton Murry, *The Problem of Style* (London: Oxford University Press, 1967), pp. 32–6.
33 T. S. Eliot, "Hamlet" (1919), in *Selected Essays*, 1917–32 (New York: Harcourt, Brace, and Company, 1932), pp. 124–5.
34 Rosalie L. Colie, "Antony and Cleopatra: The Significance of Style" in *Shakespeare's Living Art* (Princeton: Princeton University Press, 1974), pp. 198, 202, 207.
35 A. C. Bradley, *Shakespearean Tragedy*, 1904 (London: Penguin, 1991) pp. 35–6.
36 G. Wilson Knight, *The Imperial Theme*, 1931 (London: Methuen, 1965), pp. 289–90.
37 Bradley, *Shakespearean Tragedy*, p. 44 and 44n. In his note Bradley says the following: "I have raised no objection to the idea of fate, because it occurs so often both in conversation and in books about Shakespeare's tragedies that I must suppose it to be natural to many readers. Yet I doubt whether it would be so if Greek tragedy had never been written; and I must in candour confess that to me it does not often occur when I am reading, or when I have just read, a tragedy of Shakespeare."
38 Samuel Johnson, in *Johnson on Shakespeare*, 7: 74.
39 Shakespeare, "The Phoenix and Turtle," ll. 25–8, 39–40. *The Poems*, p. 1891.
40 George Puttenham, *The Arte of English Poesie*, 1589 (reprint Kent: Kent State University Press, 1970), pp. 269.

Chapter 14

1 Shakespeare Association of America, New Orleans, April 2004.
2 Harold Bloom, *Shakespeare: The Invention of the Human* (New York: Riverside, 1998).
3 Jeffrey McQuain and Stanley Malless, *Coined by Shakespeare: Words and Meanings First Penned by the Bard* (Springfield, MA: Merriam-Webster), 1998).
4 Gayatri Chakravorty Spivak, "Translator's Preface" to Jacques Derrida, *Of Grammatology*, trans. Spivak (Baltimore: Johns Hopkins University Press, 1974), p. xv.
5 Spivak, xvi; xvii.

6 Patrick Healy, "Electrician is Indicted in Killing of Millionaire in Hamptons." *New York Times* March 23, 2004, A22.
7 Marjorie Garber, "Who Owns 'Human Nature'?" *Quotation Marks* (New York: Routledge, 2003), 243-267. Reprinted in Marjorie Garber, *A Manifesto for Literary Studies* (Seattle: University of Washington, 2003), 15-43.
8 Barbara Johnson, "Introduction," in Johnson, ed. *Freedom and Interpretation*: The Oxford Amnesty Lectures 1992 (New York: Basic Books, 1993), 3.
9 Jacques Lacan, "The Agency of the Letter in the Unconscious or Reason Since Freud," in *Ecrits: A Selection*, trans. Alan Sheridan (New York: Norton, 1977), p.166.
10 Johnson, "Introduction," p. 6.
11 Lee Patterson, "On the Margin: Postmodernism, Ironic History, and Medieval Studies." *Speculum* Vol. 65, No.1 (Jan.1990), pp.97-98. Terry Eagleton, *Criticism and Ideology* (London, 1976), p.172. David Aers, *Community, Gender, and Individual Identity:English Writing, 1360-1430* (London, 1988). P.17.
12 Here are some recent book titles: *The Invention of Literary Subjectivity* (Michael Zink, trans. D. Sices, Johns Hopkins University Press, 1999); *The Invention of Sodomy in Christian Theology* (Mark Jordan, University of Chicago Press, 1998); *The Invention of Saintliness* (ed. Anneke B. Mulder-Bakker, Routledge, 2002); *The Invention of Racism in Classical Antiquity* (Benjamin Isaac, Princeton University Press, 2004); not to mention *Plato: The Invention of Philosophy* (Bernard Williams, Phoenix 1998) and *Sade, The Invention of the Libertine Body* (Marcel Hénaff, Trans. X. Callahan, University of Minnesota Press, 1999), both on the same model as Bloom's *Shakespeare: The Invention of the Human.* In our own field Gary Taylor's cultural history, acknowledging the variability of historical accounts and literary reputations, was called *Re-Inventing Shakespeare* (1989). And most pertinent of all, there is Hobsbawn and Ranger's *The Invention of Tradition* (Cambridge, 1983).
13 Quoted in Paul Israel, *Edison: A Life of Invention.* (New York: John Wiley & Sons, 1998), p. 75.
14 John Dryden, "Preface to *Annus Mirabilis…*
15 Waldo P. Warren, "Edison on Invention and Inventors," *Century Magazine* 82 (1911), 418.Israel, 29.
16 Otto Jespersen, *Growth and Structure of the English Language* 1906. 10th edition (Chicago: University of Chicago Press, 1982), pp.210-211. Cited in John Willinsky, *The Empire of Words* (Princeton: Princeton University Press, 1994), p.57.
17 *Transactions of the Philological Society* (London: Trübner, 1857, pp. 5-6. Cited in Willinsky, 73.
18 John Willinsky, *The Empire of Words* (Princeton: Princeton University Press, 1994), 90; 72.
19 Ralph Waldo Emerson, "Shakespeare, or the Poet." In *Representative Men* 1850. Reprinted in Joel Porte, ed., *Emerson: Essays and Lectures* (New York: Library of America, 1983), pp. 710, 713.
20 André Gide, *Journal* 1893.

Chapter 15

1 Thus, for example, in response to a Catholic churchman's Op-Ed piece supporting "intelligent design" over what he called "neo-Darwinian dogma," a letter writer to *The New York Times* commented, "the archbishop of Vienna doth protest too much, methinks." Bruce G. Friedrich, letter to the editor, *New York Times*, July 11, 2005, p. A20. Christoph Schonborn, "Finding Design in Nature," *New York Times*, July 7, 2005, p. 23.
2 *Congressional Record*, June 18, 1996 (House), p. H6429.
3 *Congressional Record*, July 17, 1995 (House) pp. H7065–H7066.
4 *Congressional Record*, February 7, 1994. (*People*'s error had been to cite an expert on black English on the etymology of the word "jubilee," which he traced to a Bantu word for a plantation dance, rather than to its Hebrew, Greek, or Latin origins, meaning "ram," "ram's horn," "wild cry," or

shout.")"Talking Black," *People*, February 7, 1994. Interview with Clarence Major, the author of *Juba to Jive: A Dictionary of African-American Slang*.

5 Ronald Knowles, ed., *King Henry VI, Part 2*, Arden edition, Third Series (London: Thomson, 1999), p. 312 (Act 4.4.0.n03).

6 *Congressional Record*, August 18, 1994.

7 *New York Times*, November 25, 2005, p. D1.

8 Stephanie Saul, "To Sleep, Perchance to Eat. Is it the Pill?" *New York Times*, March 14, 2006.

9 My thanks to Peter Stallybrass for a—typically lively and informative—conversation on this point.

10 We might note that he also compiled, with his wife Hannah, a *Complete Concordance to Shakespeare's Dramatic Works and Poems* (1894). In an era without computers, and indeed without typewriters, this task took him, by his own estimate, sixteen thousand hours. Justin Kaplan, "Preface to the Sixteenth Edition," *Bartlett's Familiar Quotations* (Boston: Little, Brown, 1992), p. vii.

11 John Bartlett, "Preface," *The Shakespeare Phrase Book* (Boston: Little, Brown, and Company, 1881).

12 Michael Hancher, "Familiar Quotations," *Harvard Library Bulletin*, n.s.14 (2003[2004]): 13–53. I am indebted to Professor Hancher for calling this important article to my attention.

13 Cited in Hancher, "Familiar Quotations," p. 22.

14 For an extensive and illuminating discussion of "writing tables," see "Hamlet's Tables and the Technologies of Writing in Renaissance England," by Peter Stallybrass, Roger Chartier, J. Franklin Mowery, and Heather Wolfe, *Shakespeare Quarterly* 55: 4 (2004): 379–419. By the time of *Hamlet* (1601) the connection between plays and commonplace books had itself become commonplace. Shakespeare's contemporary, the satirist and playwright John Marston, writes in one of his satires about someone who "Hath made a common-place book out of plays, / And speaks in print," 1598), and in the Induction to Marston's play *The Malcontent* (1604) the actor Will Sly, playing himself, says "I am one that hath seen this play often: I have most of the jests here in my table-book." John Marston, *The Scourge of Villainy*, Book 3, Satire 11, 43–4, in A. H. Bullen, ed., *The Works of John Marston*, vol. 3 (London: John C. Nimmo, 1887), p. 372. Marston, *The Malcontent*, Induction.

15 Alexander Pope, "The Preface of the Editor," in Pope, ed., *The Works of Shakespeare*, vol. 1 (London, 1725, 1728).

16 Dodd himself became the tutor to the son of Lord Chesterfield—the same son to whom Chesterfield wrote his famous letters of advice. But Dodd came, alas, to an unhappy end, despite the indexed wit and wisdom at his fingertips. Deep in debt—he liked to entertain lavishly—he forged Chesterfield's name to a check, and although his patron refused to prosecute, the Lord Mayor of London sent the case to court, and Dodd was found guilty (the jury deliberated for a scant ten minutes) and hanged, in full view of literally "thousands" of sobbing spectators. Howard Engel, *Lord High Executioner: An Unashamed Look at Hangmen, Headsmen, and Their Kind* (Toronto: Key Porter Books, 1996), p. 39.

17 See G. B. Shaw: comments on bardolatry and bardolaters in *Plays for Puritans*, Preface; *Man and Superman*, Epistle Dedicatory; *Saturday Review*, February 11, 1905; *Dark Lady*, Preface; etc.

18 The modern fictional detective who keeps up this tradition of quoting Shakespeare, somewhat to the consternation of his co-workers, is criminalist Gil Grissom of *CSI*. (Grissom's favorite play is *Hamlet*, but he has quoted memorably from *Julius Caesar* and also from the closing lines of *Romeo and Juliet*.) The other members of his unit, none of them big readers, recognize these quotations as "Shakespeare," but only because they are clearly quoted, aphoristically, and because they come from Grissom. On one occasion his sonorous intonation led a colleague to identify a particularly pithy quote as Shakespeare—only to be told that the source was "Grissom."

19 Brian Rotman, *Signifying Nothing: The Semiotics of Zero* (Stanford: Stanford University Press, 1987).

20 150 *Congressional Record* S 11446, November 18, 2004. Senator Robert Byrd, by unofficial but reliable count the most Shakespeare-quoting member of the Senate, remembered, and expli-

cated, a favorite saying of his friend Paul Wellstone, described as "an old Jewish proverb": "You can't dance at two weddings at one time." "When he said, 'You can't dance at two weddings at one time,' he meant that one must not be false. That is the key. One must not be false. He meant that one cannot be all things to all people. He was thinking of the words of Shakespeare, who said: To thine own self be true. Thy [sic] can't now then be false to any man." 148 *Congressional Record* S 10819, November 12, 2002. In this case Byrd skipped the name of the speaker, suggesting that it was "Shakespeare" who said it. Elsewhere, however, he has cited Polonius directly, and with admiration. "Fully aware of the admonition by Polonius that 'those friends thou hast and their adoption tried, grapple them to thy soul with hoops of steel,' it is with pride that I call Bennett Johnston friend." 14 *Congressional Record* S 755, January 11, 1995.

21 E. M. W. Tillyard, *The Elizabethan World Picture* (New York: Macmillan, 1944), p. 101.

22 Ileana Ros-Lehtinen, prepared statement before the House International Relations Committee on "Brazil's Economic Crisis and Its Impact for International Trade," February 25, 1999. Uses of this term are everywhere: it has been adapted by a national retailing association ("All the (Retail) World's a Stage"), used as a headline to trumpet Philadelphia's three hundreth birthday extravaganza for Ben Franklin ("The World's a Stage for Ben," *Philadelphia Inquirer*, September 30, 2005).

23 "Are You Lonesome Tonight?" words and music by Roy Turk and Lou Handman.

24 Jaques is what modern critics of the novel might call an "unreliable narrator." Described in the play as "the melancholy Jaques," who can be counted on to "moralize" a spectacle "into a thousand similes" (2.2.26; 44, 45) for the entertainment of his hearers, Jaques is part cynic, part satirist, part utopian enthusiast, and part mordant, stand-up comic. "Melancholy"—Hamlet's disease—was a fashionable Elizabethan posture, one in fact neatly skewered by Jaques himself later in the play, when he says "I have neither the scholar's melancholy, which is emulation; nor the musician's, which is fantastical; nor the courtier's, which is proud; nor the soldier's, which is ambitious; nor the lawyer's, which is politic; nor the lady's, which is nice; nor the lover's, which is all of these; but it is a melancholy of mine own, compounded of many simples . . ." (4.1.10–16). I'm pretty sure it is no accident that this anatomy of melancholy itself has seven ages, or stages (scholar, musician, courtier, soldier, lawyer, lady, lover). Here is where we really do see Shakespeare the craftsman at work. But Shakespeare the philosopher, or Shakespeare the proverb-maker, is distinctly, and I think deliberately, absent.

25 The artful pathos of his final lines here, "second childishness and mere oblivion, / Sans teeth, sans eyes, sans taste, sans everything," had already been critiqued within the Shakespeare canon by an earlier witty woman called Rosaline: "sans sans, I pray you," said the Rosaline of *Love's Labour's Lost* to her posturing lover, Berowne, who was trying to abjure his own poetic language, but wound up doing so in an arty phrase, "My love to you is true, sans crack or flaw."

26 E. M. W. Tillyard, the author of the book with that title, cited "Shakespeare's version" as the "best known" articulation of this theory of universal order, and thus begins his study with Ulysses' speech, all thirty-three lines, though significantly without citing act, scene, or line number. This is another way of quoting Shakespeare out of context, not as comical as some of the instances we have come upon in modern political discourse, but equally worth noting. For Tillyard, who is writing the history of an idea, this speech is—as indeed it is—a "didactic passage," a place where the playwright allows one of his characters to voice a theory and an ideology. Tillyard completely understands that the rest of Shakespeare's *Troilus and Cressida* is full of "different kinds of chaos" that threaten this view of cosmic order. But he considers Shakespeare, through Ulysses, to be voicing "his version of order." It is not without interest or relevance here that Tillyard's book was first published in 1943, when England was dealing with a highly particular and political threat to its own belief in cosmic order. Tillyard, ibid., p. 102. The threat posed by Nazi Germany is very briefly, though tellingly, glanced at in the book's final sentence, a warning about the way Elizabethan thought sometimes "resembles certain trends of thought in central Europe, the ignoring of which by our scientifically minded intellectuals has helped not a little to bring the world into its present conflicts and distresses."

27 The homily "Concerning Order and Obedience to Rules and Magistrates," and the homily "Against Disobedience and Wilful Rebellion." Similar passages can be found in Hooker's *Ecclesiastical Polity*, in Spenser's *Faerie Queene*, Book 5 (the book on Justice), and as far back as Pythagoras, the Platonists and the Stoics.

28 Ralph Waldo Emerson, "Shakespeare, or The Poet," in *Representative Men*, Modern Library edition, pp. 720–1.

29 "And then, the justice, / In fair round belly, with good capon lin'd, / With eyes severe, and beard of formal cut, / Full of wise saws, and modern instances, / And so he plays his part" (2.7.153–7).

30 Dylan Evans, *An Introductory Dictionary of Lacanian Psychoanalysis* (London: Routledge, 1996), p. 192.

31 Jacques Lacan, "Direction of Treatment and Principles of Its Power," *Ecrits: A Selection* (New York: Routledge, 2001).

Index

invention 274–5, 276
Ireland, Samuel 171–2
Ireland, William Henry 171, 224
Irish wolfhound 182, 183
Isserman, Maurice 325n5

Jabet, George (Warwick) 236
Jackson-Lee, Sheila 282
Jacobi, Derek 115
James, Henry 178–9; *The Aspern Papers* 214;
    "The Birthplace" 12–13
James, William 112
James I: *Basilikon Doron* 88–9, 312n50; Bible
    translation 137; clocks 320–1n28;
    Macbeth 195; mirror 102–3, 104;
    sexuality 105; transgression of boundaries
    105
Jameson, Fredric 137, 196
Jansen portrait 221
Jardine, Lisa 326n31
Jarry, Alfred 144
jealousy 138, 169, 170
Jenkins, Harold 57, 136, 235–6, 237, 238,
    316n21
Jentsch, E. 94
Jerrold, Blanchard 234
Jespersen, Otto 276, 277
Jewishness 216, 219, 220
Jews 192, 193, 195, 210
JFK (Stone) 126–8, 284–5
John Paul I, Pope 164
Johnson, Barbara 16–17, 273
Johnson, Gerard 218
Johnson, Lyndon 127
Johnson, Samuel: on Cleopatra 269; Hazlitt
    on 263; on Pope 229; "Preface to
    Shakespeare" 262, 267–8; speech in
    character 258
Johnston, Catherine 214
joint-stock company 136
Jones, Ernest 179–80
Jones, Tommy Lee 127
Jonson, Ben 5, 114, 219; *Bartholomew Fair*
    145–6; *Poetaster* 145
Joseph, B. L. 26
Jowett, Benjamin 177
Joyce, James:*Ulysses* 4, 46, 71, 167, 170–1,
    195, 323n52
jubilee term 283, 332–3n4
Julian Calendar 206
Julius Caesar: anachronisms 161, 198, 205–6,
    326n25; author-function 21–2; authority

23; Brutus and Cassius 28; court cases
124; courtiers 187–8; ghost 21, 34, 40,
99; honour 281; *JFK* 127; kneeling
315n11; Mark Antony 280; parodied
127
Julius Caesar, film 163, 199
Jung, C. G. 71, 256, 330n5
Juvenal 199–200

Katherine of France (*Henry V*) 141–2
Kaye, Donald 116
Kazan, Elia 115
Keats, John 13, 301
Kennedy, Edward 126
Kermode, Frank 253, 263–4
Kierkegaard, Søren 35
King Lear: anachronisms 207; Cordelia 190,
    191, 298; dogs 189–90; forged letter 24;
    kneeling 133; nostalgia for 110–11;
    Quarto/Folio versions 285–6; repetition
    300
King Lear, television production 115
Kinnock, Neil 122
Kittredge, Professor 9
Kleist, Heinrich von 133, 143–4, 148, 149
Klinkenborg, Verlyn 223
kneeling 131–4, 315n11
knees 131–4
Knight, G. Wilson 267
Komisarjefsky, Theodore 320–1n28
Kott, Jan 211
Kris, Ernst 68
Kristeva, Julia 297
Krüll, Marianne 66, 71
Kubrick, Stanley 149, 319n66
Kundera, Milan:*The Unbearable Lightness of
    Being* 190–1

La Bruyère, Jean de 255–6
Lacan, Jacques: castration complex 36–7;
    disjointing 147; on Freud 35; ghost 34;
    Hamlet 38–9; on Holbein 39; Name-of-
    the-Father 35, 36–7, 41, 65; Oedipus
    297; on Poe 208–9; "The Signification of
    the Phallus" 330n12; signifiers 232;
    splitting 297–8; subject 273; *sujet
    supposé savoir* 63–5; symbolic order 36,
    232; transference 64; "The Unconscious
    and Repetition" 35
The Lady Vanishes 232
Lando, Pope 164
Landor, Walter Savage 200

metonymy 92, 148
Mica, John 282
Michaels, Walter 112
Middleton, Thomas 158
A Midsummer Night's Dream 143, 187, 210,
    299; play-within-play 244, 254–5
Mill, J. S. 253
Miller, J. Hillis 55, 74
Milton, John 296; "On Shakespeare" 41–2;
    Il Penseroso 42
mirrors 102–4
mise en abard 277
mise en abyme 277
mise en scène 277
misplacement 141–2
misquotation 127
Mitchell, S. Weir 24
Mitgang, Herbert 202, 203
Modern Language Notes 182
Moliere 43, 46
Molina, Tirso de 43
Mommsen, Theodore 154
Monette, Paul 186
monsters 101
Montaigne, Michel Eyquem de 200
Montrose, Louis 104–5, 312n57
morality 263, 278–9
More, Thomas 190
Moscow Arts Theater 79
Moses 54, 70–1
mourning 29, 53, 69
Moynihan, Daniel Patrick 283
Mozart, Wolfgang Amadeus 43–5
Much Ado About Nothing 37, 135, 290, 299
Murray, John 287
Murry, J. M. 265, 267

Nabokov, Vladimir 197, 325n4
Name-of-the-Father 35, 36–7, 41, 65
Napoleon (Gance) 20
narrative sketches of character 256
NASA 292
National Archives 285
National Endowment for the Humanities
    116, 122
nativity, casting of 157–8
Nazism 149
necromancy 157
negative capability 13, 15, 301
Neill, Samuel 171
New Bibliography 230
New Historicism 196

New Shakespere Society 241, 243
The New York Times 128–9, 165, 196, 202,
    222–3, 284, 332n1
New Yorker 193–4
Newsam, Bartholomew 320n28
newspaper headlines 284–5
Newsweek 128, 129, 164
Nietzsche, Friedrich 55, 56–7, 58, 195
No Bed for Bacon (Brahms and Simon) 174–5
Nochlin, Linda 201
Noonan, Peggy 124
Norris, J. Parker 218–19
Norton Anthology of Theory and Criticism 300–1
Norton edition 234
noses 138–9
nostalgia 152, 162
Notorious (Hitchcock) 231, 232
numerology examples 156
Nye, Robert 174

Oates, Joyce Carol 108–9
Oedipus complex 29–30, 35, 68–9, 297
Ogburn, Charlton, Jr. 7
Old Corrector 247–8
Olivier, Laurence 78, 114–16, 179
originality/tradition 277
original/reproductions 18–19
Osborne, Francis 105
Oswald, Lee Harvey 126
Othello: bookkeeper 160; cyphers 8; dating
    of 247; Desdemona/Emilia 299; dog
    191; Iago 120, 125, 278; Olivier in 116;
    parodied 127; race 195; reputation 278,
    281; Simpson on 120–1; stone imagery
    44; weapons 61
Other/others 225–6, 297
O'Toole, Peter 115
Oughtred, William 161
out of joint term 136 –140, 144–5, 148
Overbury, Thomas 255, 270
Ovid 138
Owen, Orville Ward 8
Oxford, Earl of 5, 6, 9, 10, 181

Pacioli, Luca 156
paintings, anachronism 198
Paltrow, Gwyneth 226
Parker, Patricia 74
Parker, Sarah Jessica 188
parody of Shakespeare 127–8
Partridge, Eric 138
parts of speech/body parts 26

passion/political stability 263
patchock/peacock 235–6
paternity 28, 37–8, 65, 74
Patterson, Lee 274
Paul, Saint 140, 147
peacock/patchock 235–6
pelican/politician 236–8, 328n24
penis 38, 93–4, 113, 138–9; *see also* phallus
penis-envy 113
People magazine 283
performativity 297
Pericles 28, 101, 138, 277
Perkins Folio 247–9
Perseus 85–6, 87, 103, 106, 107–8
1 Peter 90
Peterson, Scott 279
petrification 100, 105
phallus 41, 97, 113, 114, 118; veiled 34, 35
Philological Society 276
photography 19–20, 229
phrenology 218
Pillow Talk 175
Pinker, Steve 273
Pipher, Mary: *Reviving Ophelia* 187
Plato 177–8, 300–1
Plautus 136
play-within-play 244; *Hamlet* 61–2, 238–46; *A Midsummer Night's Dream* 254–5; *Tempest* 294–5
plot pretext 231
Poe, Edgar Allan 208–9, 245; *Gold Bug* 8; "The Purloined Letter" 228, 232
poetry/childbirth 203–4
political correctness 197, 325n8
politician/pelican 236–8, 328n24
politicization of literature 116–17, 263
Pollitt, Barbara 146
Ponte, Lorenzo de 43
Pope, Alexander 152, 206, 228, 229, 236, 288–9, 326n25; "Epistle to a Lady" 253
Popes 163–4
popular culture/Shakespearean quotations 279–86
portrait-function 216, 223–4, 226–7
portraits *xii*; authentication 215, 220; Chandos 219–20; character x, 215, 217–18, 224; Droeshout 42, 216–17, 218, 219, 220, 221, 226; forgeries 215, 224–5; Grafton 221–3; Jansen 221; Jewishness 220; Richard III 223–4; Sanders 214, 216, 226; Stratford bust 42, 219, 220, 221, 226

possession, repetition compulsion 63
postmodernism 274
post-structuralism 257–8
pregnancy 134, 316n15
presentism 211
Presley, Elvis 292
Preston, Isabella Rushton 287
print culture 157, 228
profiling ix–x, 222
prose portraits 255
prosopopeia 41, 42–4, 47–8
Prosser, Eleanor 73–4
Proust, Marcel 55–6, 307n92
Proverbs 137
Psalms 137
psychoanalysis 178
psychological types 256–7
Public Records Office 167–8
publishing industry 215
Puck 268
punning, visual 156
puppet theater 143–7, 148, 318n53, 318n64
Purcell, Henry 260
Puttenham, George 269

question/disputation 295
quotations 129, 278, 285, 288; *see also* Shakespearean quotations

Rabelais, François 94
race 126, 195
Radcliffe, Ann 199
Raleigh, Walter 105, 173
Ramsay, David 320n28
Ramsey, John 279, 281
Ramsey, JonBenet 279
Ranger, Terence 275
Rawley, Dr 8
Reagan, Ronald 176
Recorde, Robert 161
Reeves, Thomas C. 126
Reitman, Ivan 186
remembering/forgetting 50–1, 60–1
Renaissance geometry 156–7
repetition 55, 61, 62–3, 299–300
repetition compulsion 33–4, 60
Representations 93
Representative Men 125, 209
repression 16, 36, 97, 297
reproductions 18–19
reputation 278, 281
resistance 35, 61, 105

Thackery, William Makepeace 143, 147
Theobald, Lewis 152, 230, 252
Theophrastus 255
Thevet, André 130–1
The Thirty-Nine Steps (Hitchcock) 231, 232
Thomas, Clarence 119–21, 123, 125–6, 129
Thomas, Elizabeth Marshall 185–6
Tieck, Ludwig 234
Tillyard, E. M. W. 25, 291, 334–5n26
Time magazine 115
Time Warner 128
The Times 197, 199–200, 249, 284
Timon of Athens 234
titulus 155
Titus Andronicus 25–6, 114, 198, 298
Titus (Taymor) 207
tourist industry 9–10, 215
Townsend, George Henry 6
Toynbee, J. M. 89
tradition/originality 277
tragedy 16, 62–3
transference 16, 60, 61, 63, 64
transgression of boundaries 80, 81–3, 97, 102–3, 105
transvestism 115–16
Troilus and Cressida: authorship of love 28; Cassandra 27; counterpoint 293; dramatic irony 296–7; elephants 131; joints 137, 139–40, 150; RSC production 207
Truffaut, François 232
Twain, Mark 11, 198
Twelfth Night 19, 24, 115, 166
Two Gentlemen of Verona 143, 187–8, 194
The Two Noble Kinsmen 139, 255
Tyler, Parker 176
Tynan, Kenneth 115, 116

uncanniness: castration complex 33, 92–3; *Hamlet* 49–50; *Macbeth* 77, 79, 80–1, 90–1, 94–5; *The Winter's Tale* 42–4
unconscious 16
universality 208, 257, 262–3
Updike, John 230
US Congress 282–4

vanitas paintings 38–9, 227
Vanity Fair 227
Vasari, Giorgio 106–7
Vere, Edward de 181: *see* Oxford, Earl of

Vest, George Graham 188–9, 190
Viete, François 161
vinculum 155
Vining, E. P. 230
virginity, loss of 134, 315n15

Waller, Fats 136
Wallis, John 166
Walton, William 114–15
Wanamaker, Sam 113–14
Ward, H. Snowden and Catharine Weed 170
Ward, Rev John 168
Warren Commission 126
Warwick, Eden (Jabet) 236
watch dials 161, 320n28
Watson, John T. 288
Watson, Robert 312n54
Webster, John 255
Wegman, William 194
Weld, Philip S. 9
Welles, Orson 78
Wells, Stanley 5
White House 176
Whitehead, Alfred North 307n88
Whitman, Walt 11
Whittier, John Greenleaf 11
widows' rights 168, 169, 170
Wilde, Oscar 224–5, 226
Wilder, Thornton 198–9
Wilhelmina, Queen 176
Willbern, David 311n48
William the sheepdog 191–2
Willinsky, John 276
Will-o'-the-wisp 268
wills 167–8, 172–3
Wilson, John Dover 179, 221–2, 226, 239–40, 326n25
Windle, Mrs C. F. Ashmead 8
The Winter's Tale: American Repertory Theatre 197; counting 160; dramatic irony 296–7; ghost 17–18; Hermione 46, 281; Perdita 297; Prolixenes 162; shoulders 139; stone imagery 44; uncanniness 42–4
Wishbone 186
witches 79, 84, 91–2, 97–9, 311n33
Wivell, Abraham 219
Wolf Man 180
Wolfe, George C. 146
Wolsey, Cardinal 284
Wyatt, Thomas 272

eBooks - at www.eBookstore.tandf.co.uk

A library at your fingertips!

eBooks are electronic versions of print books. You can store them onto your PC/laptop or browse them online.

They have advantages for anyone needing rapid access to a wide variety of published, copyright information.

eBooks can help your research by enabling you to bookmark chapters, annotate and use instant searches to find specific words or phrases. Several eBook files would fit on even a small laptop or PDA.

NEW: Save money by eSubscribing: cheap, online acess to any eBook for as long as you need it.

Annual subscription packages

We now offer special low cost bulk subscriptions to packages of eBooks in certain subject areas. These are available to libraries or to individuals.

For more information please contact webmaster.ebooks@tandf.co.uk

We're continually developing the eBook concept, so keep up to date by visiting the website.

www.eBookstore.tandf.co.uk

DISCARDED
CONCORDIA UNIV. LIBRARY